EDUCATION IN TOKUGAWA JAPAN

EDUCATION IN TOKUGAWA JAPAN

by

R. P. DORE

THE ATHLONE PRESS · LONDON

CENTER FOR JAPANESE STUDIES
THE UNIVERSITY OF MICHIGAN · ANN ARBOR

Published in 1984 in the United Kingdom
by The Athlone Press Ltd, 44 Bedford Row, London WC1R 4LY
and in the United States of America by
the Center for Japanese Studies Publications,
108 Lane Hall, The University of Michigan, Ann Arbor,
MI 48109

© R. P. Dore 1965, 1984

Reprinted by agreement with Routledge and Kegan Paul Ltd.

UK SBN 0–485–11240–X
US SBN 0–939512–15–7

Printed in Great Britain
by Nene Litho, Earls Barton, Northants
Bound by Woolnough Bookbinding,
Wellingborough, Northants

TO MY PARENTS

CONTENTS

ILLUSTRATIONS

TABLES

PREFACE TO NEW EDITION

NEW EDITIONS apparently need new Prefaces. I wish I had the knowledge, or the time to acquire it, to report on subsequent developments in the study of Tokugawa education. My *impression* is that a better acquaintance with the extensive output of Japan's sizeable and productive body of educational historians would not lead me to alter the general picture I present in this book, even if, were I writing today, I would want to change some, and fill out other, details. Nor, I fear, am I aware of having any youthful indiscretions to disavow, of having grown out of any of the opinions, assumptions, prejudices which underlie my treatment of the subject—a sad admission, for one who believes in life-long learning. The best I can do, perhaps, is to spell out a little more clearly what those opinions, assumptions, prejudices were. I often wonder when I have read a book what can have prompted the author to embark on the writing of it. I shall assume that the reader shares the same kind of curiosity.

In the last chapter of a book I wrote in the mid-1970s, *The Diploma Disease*, I was speculating on how viable could be a society in which the intrinsic work satisfactions and sense of importance of those lucky enough to be born intelligent and to have a good education could be seen as compensation for having a *low* salary, rather than as justification for claiming a high one. It seemed natural to me to describe such a society as an extension of Confucian ideals of benevolence and social duty. It only occurred to me afterwards that the ideals of Plato's Guardians were not too dissimilar, and I recall adding a phrase somewhat on the lines: this optimistic Confucian utopia—or what, I suppose, if I had the benefit of a Western rather than a Confucian classical education I would have been inclined to call a Platonic utopia . . .

It is, I think, indeed true that those three years in my early twenties which I spent as a graduate student soaking myself in the writings on education of the Confucian scholars of the Tokugawa period did more to form my ideas as a person and as a sociologist than any other period of my life. In my British grammar school education I suppose it was only the history and English courses which ever did much to refine the views of life and society I derived from a Methodist family upbringing: certainly not the Latin which remained until the very end a matter of mindless mechanical decoding of the texts of Virgil and Caesar. Then came five years, partly in the Army, during which my only required intellectual activity was to master and then to teach the Japanese language. It was the next three years, 1947-50, which I spent in London waiting for a visa to go to Japan, indiscriminantly gathering material for a thesis on Tokugawa education, which really gave me what the French call an intellectual formation—gave me a kind of oriental PPE. They taught me more about the nature of society, about the inter-connection between political choice and personal morality, about notions of right and duty and about the fallability of human institutions than any of my formal education up to that point. It was only later that I began to realise how much it had shaped my perspective on things—when, for instance, I was baffled by how perplexed Western observers seemed to be by Mao's Cultural Revolution. Starting from Confucian premises, it did not seem to me hard to intuit the state of mind of an Old Sage unleashing a campaign of moral regeneration, convinced that the good society can only come from individuals all having good hearts and minds, never from institutions cleverly designed to harness self-interest to the common good. Nor did it seem to me hard to intuit the state of mind of rebellious youth self-righteously convinced that their rebellion was not a selfish assertion of rights but an expression of duty, nor that of their capitalist-roading victims as they made their compromises, and moderated their wish for revenge when the storm was over. Somehow they all seemed to me more familiarly understandable than Calvin or Martin Luther. If I ever get to the Elysian fields, I shall have a hard time deciding whether to try to infiltrate the groups of disciples clustered around Smith and Hume and Russell, or those gathering at the feet of Confucius and Mencius and Kaibara Ekken and Ogyū Sorai. But the Plato-Socrates group, founders of the tradition supposedly at the root of my own culture, would attract me as little as, say, Buddha and his followers, or Mohammed and his.

Not that it was with any such good self-educative intentions that I began research. Having taken a London bachelors degree in Japanese externally while I was still in the Army, and being offered a government studentship on the improbable grounds that my education had been interrupted by the war, it seemed an obvious career ambition (still, as it happens, unfulfilled) to become a Ph.D. For that one needed a thesis topic. I had remembered reading in

Aston's *History of Japanese Literature* how Arai Hakuseki's autobiography describes the rigours of learning as a child to write Chinese characters, and had been struck at the time by the thought that nothing else in my reading had given me the remotest idea of what sort of education went on in Japan before the modern period. Then I had come across a copy of Hakuseki's autobiography while doing a summer job cataloguing Tokugawa books in Cambridge Library and my curiosity was further whetted. And so Tokugawa education seemed a good theme to choose for a thesis topic if I was going to write a thesis. Encouraged by my supervisor, Frank Daniels, I set out with no intention other than to collect all the information I could about schools and schooling in the Tokugawa period and to put it all together in a plausible story. No analytical framework, no hypothesis to test, no theory to prove: just innocent descriptive history, vaguely animated, I suppose, by a belief that education was a Good Thing, and that the story of how Japan gradually came to have more of it would be a Story of Progress.

When I finally got to Japan I was diverted and spent most of my time there—and most of the decade of the 1950s—doing other things: turning myself into a proper sociologist ('proper' meaning only one who could earn his bread and butter in the trade), doing studies of urban neighbourhoods and of post-land reform villages in Japan. It was only at the end of that decade that I came back to Edo Japan and its scholars and pedantic schoolmasters, and only in 1962 that I finally finished the book, after two months writing a first draft in a village in the foothills of the Japan Alps, sitting in a mosquito net tent to keep the house-flies off, and then six months plugging gaps in Kyoto University Library.

At that time Japan was only just becoming a 'success story'. In the 1950s it was still a country about which one was more likely to ask: What went wrong?—what accounts for the dreadful growth of fascist militarism in pre-war Japan?—than: What went right? But slowly that was changing. The awareness of many other contemporary nations gaining independence or in other ways starting out on the process of deliberate 'modernization' as Japan did in 1870, and the consequent growth of 'development studies' seeking to generalize about the pre-conditions for the success of those efforts, steadily altered the way scholars looked at Japan. We were at the beginning of the 'modernization decade' of Japanese studies, full of books and articles explaining the importance of this or that factor in Japan's success. The last chapter of this book on the 'legacy', the benefits modern Japan derived from the growth of educational institutions in the

Tokugawa period, was contributed as a conference paper and published in one of those modernization volumes edited by Marius Jansen.[1]

The explication - of - the - mechanisms - of - Japan's - successful - modernization approach to Japanese history was never popular among the majority of Japanese scholars. Some objected because they were wedded to a particular theoretical view of the course of history as a history of class struggle—which talk of 'modernization' as a *national* ambition, divorced from considerations of the dominant class interest, tended to obscure. More often, perhaps, it was because they felt that the only way to preserve a decent society in contemporary Japan was to keep an all-too-prone-to-be-docile Japanese citizenry vigilantly suspicious of their rulers: to that end it was necessary to keep them ever-mindful of the suffering and repression those rulers' predecessors had visited on their fathers' and grandfathers' generation. It was too risky to let that record get obscured by talk of the 'success' of the modernization policies of the Meiji oligarchs. When one saw the political complexion of much of the 'let us all praise famous men' writing evoked by the 1967 centenary of the Meiji Restoration one could appreciate their point though I do find a little bizarre the subsequent charges of the younger American radical Marxist scholars, children of the Vietnam aftermath, that we writers on the modernization of Japan were concerned to discredit Marxist historiography primarily in order to support the American anti-communist crusade in Asia and to counter the clear attractions of the Chinese model of development with praise for the Japanese capitalist alternative.[2]

Personally, I still see very great merit in trying to generalize about the processes of development (or more narrowly about the processes of 'late', deliberate development) as I shall explain later, but at the time I do not recall being aware of making any politically significant points when I got interested, for example, in the implications of a growing demand for governments by 'men or merit' coming out of the Tokugawa samurai academies, a demand which was clearly related to the growing sophistication of the Confucian scholars, their sense of sharing a common ethos, of constituting, dare I say, a class (the pre-formation, I would be inclined to say today, of the technocratic class who dominate the bureaucracy, media, the corporations and the financial institu-

[1] M.B. Jansen, ed., *Changing Japanese Attitudes Towards Modernisation*, Princeton, Princeton University Press, 1965
[2] See the Introduction to J.W. Dower, ed., *Origins of the Modern Japanese State: Selected Writings of E.H. Norman*, New York, Pantheon Books, 1975.

tions of modern Japan). Nor did I realize that I was taking part in an anti-Marxist crusade when I speculated about the growth of popular education and the extent to which the training in being trained had long-term consequences—speculated how far the effects of intellectual self-discipline on the ability to calculate the future implications of present action, to 'defer gratification' and to weigh alternative futures, may have contributed to the ground-swell of petty incremental innovation in the thousands of family enterprises which, in the early stages at least, contributed as much to Japan's economic growth as the big decisions of the technocrats in charge of big aggregates of resources.

The social evolutionary approach to the study of social change of the nineteenth century Founding Fathers of sociology—the approach which would expect to find continuity between Louis XVI and Napoleon's and Louis-Phillipe's bureaucracies or between Stolypin's reforms and Khrushchev's and not assume that either a bourgeois or a proletarian revolution had to mean that everything, rather then just some things, had changed—was an evolutionary view which had always seemed to me to contain truths which were not destroyed by the 1930s disillusionment with Victorian doctrines of progress, or the structural-functionalist insistence that the path of true scholarship lay in sudy of the static integrity of social systems, or the sentimental anthropologists' wish to convince themselves that 'all cultures are equally valid'. And so it was easy to go on writing about educational history as an evolutionary story, occasionally accelerated by political change (the Meiji government's sudden creation of a new system of primary schools, Castro's each-one-teach-one mass literary campaign, for example), but basically a story of the long haul, a process of cumulation like the process of physical capital accumulation to which (in both capitalist and socialist societies) it was intimately related both as cause and effect.

I see that I wrote a Preface to the Japanese translation of this book in Tanzania in 1970 when I was about to move to the Institute of Development Studies to start working more explicitly on the problems of 'development'—of economic growth and the improvement of social and welfare institutions—in Third World countries. Tanzania was a 'late developer', but a 'late developer' recognizably in the same category as Japan, at least if one uses the criterion of aspirations. The aims of Nyerere's post-independence government—to industrialize, to modernize, to cut a figure in the world—were identical with those of the young samurai oligarchs who took power in 1868 and started the long century of Japan's struggle for equality. And yet what an enormous difference in advantages and handicaps! Tanzania had its World Bank teams and loans, its FAO and WHO assistance schemes, Swedish aid given with little consideration for strategic gain to support one of the few leaders in Africa who clearly cared about the poor and about eliminating exploitation and inequality. But what Tanzania did not have was Tanzanians able to control and domesticate and absorb all the expertise of these foreigners—and then dispense with them—in the way the Japanese could handle all their technical assistants a century ago. They hired them by the score—experts who set up the Mint, the lighthouse system, the first caustic soda works, the first experimental dairy farm, the new system of criminal justice. They hired them, too, with hard-won pounds and dollars earned by their silk and rice and copper exports. And within a few years and sometimes months they were ready to say thank you and goodbye.

The difference was great, and not surprising. Tanzania was only a few decades away from a level of social organization hardly exceeding a few basic bonds of kinship, and a level of technology hardly exceeding hand-tools and a total reliance on human, hardly even animal, energy sources—levels which the Japanese, or their pre-Japanward-migrating ancestors, had surpassed perhaps two milennia ago. And they had used those two milennia—sometimes in short bursts as in the great borrowings from China in the seventh or from Europe in the sixteenth centuries, sometimes in periods of slow, steady, endogenous accumulation of cultural and organizational and technological capital such as, above all, the Tokugawa period—to build up the skills and understanding which made it immeasurably better prepared to cope with the problems of launching itself into the modern world.

Such was the burden of my reflections in that 1970 Preface, but I did not speculate on the reasons *why* Japan in 1860 and Tanzania in 1960 were such very different societies. The early 1970s were days—I suppose these still are days—when nice people did not and do not discuss such matters, largely for fear of seeming to accept the possibility that differences in cultural capital of national groups might derive not just from historical accident, but from differences in their gene pools which were substantial enough to presage differences in ultimate potential. In 1951, a sensitive and humane member of the British intellectual middle-class could speculate as a matter of course what chance the 'native territories of Africa' had of ever becoming prosperous, given that their 'proportion of A and A+ brains' was probably only 2-3 per cent compared with the 10 per cent common in the countries of

N.W. Europe.[1] But ten years later, in deference to the winds of change, most people avoided such talk: the implicit genetic assumptions which he took for granted had become taboo. The equality-of-respect requirement for running a one-nation-one-vote United Nations and the repercussions of the United States' attempts to integrate its blacks into American society caused speculation of that kind to seem offensive. Moreover it seemed not only offensive but pointless. As a matter of intellectual curiosity the enormous difficulty of isolating the element of genetic causation (given the impossibility of devising wholly 'culture-fair' intelligence tests or manipulating total environments even from childbirth, let alone from conception) meant degrees of uncertainty which left ideologues unconvinced and turned many psychologists for their part into embattled crusaders, fighting, as they saw it, a dominant conspiracy to uphold liberal fictions. And intellectual curiosity apart, as a practical matter for those concerned with development patterns, there was no point in speculating about genetic factors about which one could do nothing, when the transfer of physical and intellectual capital and the development of new institutions obviously could do *something*.

I am moved to these reflections by being on the plane to Fiji, a place which revives memories of having noticed fifteen years ago that all the quick-calculating tellers in the banks seemed to be drawn from the tiny Chinese community on the Island. I recall having idly speculated as to the reasons, political or educational or gene-pool-related which might explain the fact, and then having dismissed the matter as speculation which was indeed unprofitably idle. And perhaps it still is, but the growing differences in the 1970s between the 'newly industrializing countries' and the failing-to-industrialize countries, and the limited extent to which those differences can plausibly be explained by differences in natural resources, or in political structures, or in strategic importance to great powers, or in degrees of dependency and exploitation by multi-nationals, brings questions of cultural and intellectual capital to the forefront again, and provokes anxiety about the future of international society. How are we going to construct a world order which assures not only escape from poverty but equality of respect for all nations (as a pre-condition for the more important goal of equality of respect for the *individuals* of all nations) if we are forced to abandon the basic liberal assumptions of thinking about 'development' over the last thirty years—the assumption that all the 'backward' nations can eventu-

[1] M. Roberts, *The Estate of Man*, Faber and Faber, 1951, p.97.

ally manage to 'catch up', and are only, through historical accident, in a temporarily disadvantaged position?

Some people can remain entirely optimistic about this. The
Fijian Island Business (March 1983) which the stewardess offers
reports the arrival in Suva of a Detroit art dealer, Vice-President
of America's 50,000-strong Mensa, come to visit its dozen-strong
local Chapter. No, he tells the reporter, intelligence-meritocracy
does not lead to a 'wider gap between the computerless countries
of the Third World and the whirring tapes and the bleeping
screens of the West.' It brings people together. He 'envisages a
world of high intelligence, via the computer, revolutionizing
food-crops and agricultural technology—one example, to attack
perhaps the Third World's most critical problem: doctors with
the help of the computer will be able to eliminate the possibilities
faster when tracking down diseases, greatly upgrading world
health.

Well, perhaps. It is a reasonable proposition that *no* population
is devoid of people who can be trained to use computer diagnos-
tics, and, even, that none lacks people who could be trained to write
the necessary computer programmes, whatever might be the
difference in the frequency in the occurrence of such abilities
between different population groups. Even if the implications for
'ultimate potential' of the intelligence testers' findings are taken
at face value, the difference in means and dispersal coefficients
are not definitively great and one only has to point to the fact that
Eskimos get the same ratings as Chinese and Japanese in their
tests, well above the white American average, to suggest that the
gap between 'ultimate potential' and present achievement is what
we ought to be concerned about. Speculation about 'ultimate
potential' *is* a waste of time when the possibilities of immediate
improvement remain so obviously vast. Sidney Webb, the father
of British Fabianism, may have been making a racial ('racist')
judgement or he may have been talking in a 'stages of development' framework when he said, after a visit to Korea in 1911, that
he had seen a nation of twelve million 'dirty, degraded, sullen,
lazy and religionless savages who slouch around in dirty white
garments of the most inept kind and who live in filthy mud huts.'[1]
At any rate, whatever he was implying, nobody, looking at
Korean society today, either the northern communist half of it or
the southern capitalist half, could fail to be impressed by the
difference that seventy years of accumulation of physical, social
and cultural capital can make—even though the first half of the
period was spent under a colonial regime.

But that transformation *has* taken seventy years: three generations. It was the short-term over-optimism of the manpower-planners whom the World Bank and UNESCO sent scurrying around the planning offices of the newly independent countries in the late 1950s and 1960s which has led to the malaise and disappointment in such circles today, and the constant search for new gimmicks to retrieve the situation: the plea for more weight to vocational technical training, more teacher aids, a pre-vocational emphasis, the development of 'non-formal alternatives', etc. These new missionary technocrats tended to assume that it was possible to effect a rapid build-up of human capital in the way one can accelerate the build-up of physical capital, than an enrolment of 5 per cent of the age group in tertiary education should have the same meaning (give or take a few differences in that largely unanalysed factor, the 'quality' of education) as between a society which has had primary schools and universities for ten generations, and societies where their history goes back only one or two decades. But of course it is not like that, and the 'quality of education' is not something you can analyse by correlating, as earnest World Bank researchers do, schools' average examination results with the qualifications or average salaries of teachers, or the teacher-pupil ratio, or expenditure per student. (It is symptomatic of the dominance of this quantifying approach that this book is usually cited—I suspect largely by people who have never read it—not for anything it says about the quality of education of Tokugawa Japan, but for one thing and one thing only: the estimated figures—for how tenuous those estimates see the Appendix—for school enrollments at the end of the period.) But, go to Kuwait on the one hand and to Costa Rica or Hungary on the other; expenditure and enrolment figures are poor indices of the levels of intellectual sophistication which *really* count for development.

What the intellectual and educational history of the Tokugawa period should tell us about is the gradualness of the processes of accretion of intellectual capital. Schools (sometimes churches) are the only formal educational institutions that administrators bent on development have to work with. If they do manage to sit children in the classroom for 10,000 of their childhood hours they will be doing well. But (even if children slept regularly ten hours a day) that still leaves some 65,000 waking hours between the ages of two and sixteen which they will spend with family and neighbourhood children. And those hours are immensely

[1] N Mackenzie, ed., *The letters of Sidney and Beatrice Webb*, Cambridge, Cambridge U.P. 1978, Letter to B. Shaw, 29 Oct. 1911.

important—not perhaps for learning the facts of geography and history or even the rules of addition and subtraction—but for learning the more important things—learning to describe and summarize, caring for accuracy and order; to abstract and generalize, proceeding from particulars of seed-corn and gold bangles to the general categories of investment and insurance; to hold future possibilities in mind and compare them with those of the present, assessing the possibilities of jam tomorrow against visible access to jam today; to string a series of 'if x then y' propositions together to relate means to ends, working out how much fertiliser to use to get the best harvest or how worthwhile it would be to accept the constraints of a cooperative; to empathize, to imagine what it would be like to be someone else and how that someone else might react to what you're proposing to do—for learning, in short, to react to the environment with calculation, rules and principles, not just with immediate unrestrained impulse.

These are the truly valuable mental capacities which transform society, transform them economically, socially, even militarily.[1] Their transforming power is multiplied if they are accompanied by certain attitudes—by a belief in the pleasures of using one's head; in the duty of self-improvement; in the fun of solving problems.

Most schools can do something to develop both the capacities and the attitudes. They develop the capacities directly as they teach the use of the native language and develop mathematical skills. They can even, if indirectly, develop these crucial capacities as they teach the facts of history and geography or a foreign language—though (a worry I develop in the only other book I have written on education, *The Diploma Disease*) there is a common tendency in all countries where general educational qualifications are used to select recruits to the society's most desirable jobs (i.e. all contemporary countries) for the teaching of these other subjects like history and geography to become so examination-centred as positively to militate *against* some of these capacities and certainly against the implantation of pro-intellectual

[1] In Hawaii, on the fortieth anniversary of the formation of the 422 US Regimental Combat Team made up of American nisei descendants of men and women who were going to Terakoya in Japan 80 years before, one of its members reminisced for the newspaper about what it was that made it the most decorated American combat team of World War II. 'I think the educational level had a large part to do with the success of the unit in combat. Compared with the average units at the time, our I.Q. was much higher. On the average, we had a very high culture of individuals. We cared for people. That translated into teamwork, concern for your buddies, and that teamwork translating into high morale.' (Honolulu Advertiser, 27 March, 1983

attitudes. (And these tendencies tend to be more marked the more of 'a late developer' a country is.)

Schools do, then, have an important part to play in the 10,000 hours at their disposal but the reinforcement of those capacities and attitudes in application to daily life during the other 65,000 hours is equally crucial, and that is where the processes of accumulation come. The first schooled generation provides a better 65,000 hours for its children, and those children better again for the third generation. And the teachers drawn from the third generation likewise make the learning in the 10,000 hours more effective. It is that steady build-up of intellectual-skills-exemplified-in-daily-life which brought Japan from the asperities and absurdities of Ieyasu's world to the more 'civilized' world of the young samurai who engineered the opening and planned the modernization of Japan, and on to that of the young designers of fashion goods and fifth-generation computers of today. It is that which has made Webb's Korea into the Korea of today. And it is that which has tempered the brutal immediacies of Lenin's and Stalin's Russia and seems to be producing—however little acknowledged that fact in the Reagan age—a society with more regard for reason and due process. I suppose I come back to my initial prejudice that education is a Good Thing. We should not devalue schools, though we should not expect them to do too much too quickly, either.

TABLES

xxii

ACKNOWLEDGMENTS

MY THANKS go first of all to Professor F. J. Daniels with whose encouragement, and under whose guidance, I first became interested in Tokugawa education in 1948 and decided to make it the subject of a Ph.D. thesis; also to Professor Tokiomi Kaigo who broke through the trade barriers to send me my first books on the subject from Japan, and to Professor Ken Ishikawa who not only wrote the works cited so frequently in the footnotes of this book, but also showed me great personal kindness and provided me with many useful introductions to books and to people. Professor Daniels, Dr Maurice Freedman, Professor Ernest Gellner and Mr George Weys have all read the manuscript and given me many excellent suggestions which have helped to remove some of its imperfections. It is lack of the wit to remedy them, not lack of advice, that accounts for those that remain. I am grateful, too, for the kindness I have received at the hands of librarians; to Mr Toshio Iwazaru and his staff at Kyoto University Library, to Mr Kenneth Gardner and his staff at the British Museum, and to Mr Sho Miyamoto of the School of Oriental Studies. For the illustrations I am greatly indebted to Professor Ishikawa, to Mr Yasubumi Morizumi and to Mr Saburo Ninomiya. Several bodies must be thanked for financial assistance. The Treasury Committee for Studentships in Oriental Studies financed my first visit to Japan in 1950 for the purpose of this study, but willingly connived at my abandoning it for other things. The Canada Council, the Rockefeller Foundation and the American Philosophical Society made it possible to retrieve lost opportunities with subsequent visits, and research grants for help with the statistical parts of this study were provided by research committees both at the University of British Columbia and the London School of Economics and Political Science.

R. P. DORE

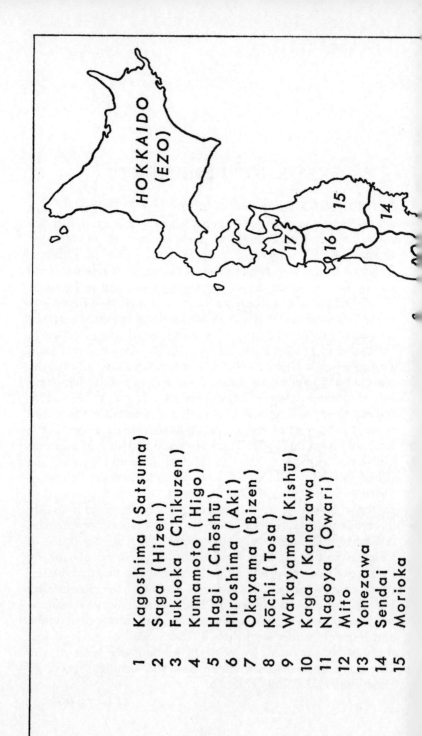

1 Kagoshima (Satsuma)
2 Saga (Hizen)
3 Fukuoka (Chikuzen)
4 Kumamoto (Higo)
5 Hagi (Chōshū)
6 Hiroshima (Aki)
7 Okayama (Bizen)
8 Kōchi (Tosa)
9 Wakayama (Kishū)
10 Kaga (Kanazawa)
11 Nagoya (Owari)
12 Mito
13 Yonezawa
14 Sendai
15 Morioka

HOKKAIDO
(EZO)

15
14
17
16

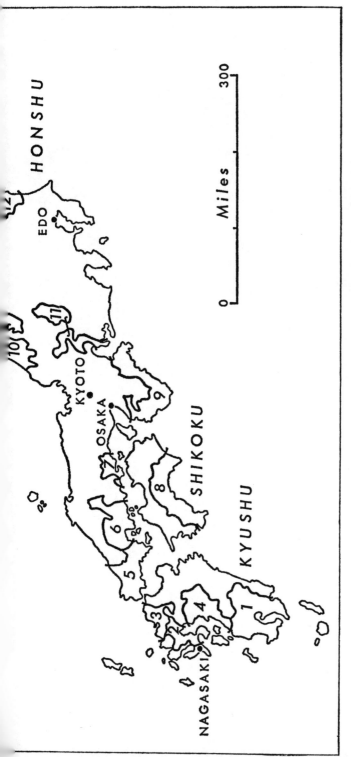

PRINCIPAL TOWNS AND FIEFS: MIDDLE AND LATE TOKUGAWA PERIOD

Chapter I

SCHOLARSHIP AND EDUCATION: A GENERAL SURVEY OF THE PERIOD

For over a hundred years, from the middle of the fifteenth to the end of the sixteenth century, the country was in confusion. There were few who could read. Even in the temples those priests who were of a bold and robust disposition got themselves a lance and set out for the battlefield. So, too, teachers of Confucian learning, doctors, fortune-tellers, calligraphers or painters—all who had the least inclination in that direction learned to ride and use a bow and set off to seek their fortunes in war. Hence the only people concerned with letters were a few weakly priests, a few weakly Confucian scholars, doctors, calligraphers and painters. And the latter, since the layman was always in danger of being impressed into military service, usually buried themselves in temples. Thus reading books became, as it were, a priestly specialty. Children were sent to temples to learn to read and write. If you wanted a cure for an illness, a horoscope read, a picture painted or a document written it was to a temple that you went. All the arts became the monopoly of priests.

SO A WRITER of the seventeenth century[1] describes the low ebb which Japanese cultural life had reached by the beginning of the Tokugawa period. It was not a literary society and hardly even a literate society which emerged when Tokugawa Ieyasu[2] had finished his campaigns and completed the process whereby a nation of warring baronies was pacified and forced to accept the overarching authority of the Tokugawa house. The nearly three hundred fiefs into which the nation was

---

[1] Anon., *Kana monogatari*, extracted in Mozumi, *Kōbunko*, article on *terakoya*.

[2] Names throughout are given in the Japanese order; family name first, given names or pen-names following. Some writers are commonly referred to by their pen-name alone.

I

divided were ruled by men who had gained or kept those fiefs on the battlefield. Their recreations were warriors' recreations; falconry, hunting, feasting and ceremonial pomp and circumstance. Their religion was a mixture of Zen self-discipline and the salvationist consolations of the more popular sects. In administering their territories they relied a great deal on verbal commands; only their more crucial and binding decisions—and the all-important records of land-holdings—were committed to paper. Their codes and edicts were brusquely straightforward and unconcerned with legal subtleties. The people whom they ruled were largely illiterate.

The Japan of 1868, when the first major battles for two and a half centuries culminated in the Meiji Restoration, was a very different society. The warrior's arrogant scorn for the effeminate world of books was hardly anywhere in evidence. Practically every samurai was literate, most had at least a smattering of the basic Chinese classics, some were learned in Chinese literature, philosophy or history, in Dutch medicine, astronomy or metallurgy. They were educated in great secular schools. An American who went to teach at one in 1870 describes his surprise on finding it:

> so large and flourishing. There were in all about 800 students comprised in the English, Chinese, Japanese, medical and military departments. A few had been studying English for two or three years under native teachers who had been in Nagasaki. In the medical department I found a good collection of Dutch books, chiefly medical and scientific, and a fine pair of French dissection models, of both varieties of the human body. In the military school was a library of foreign works on military subjects . . . In one part of the yard young men, book, diagram and trowel in hand, were constructing a miniature earthwork. The school library of English and American works . . . was quite respectable. In the Chinese school I found thousands of boxes, with sliding lids, filled with Chinese and Japanese books.[1]

It was a world in which books abounded. Their production (by printing from carved wooden blocks) gave employment to several thousands of persons in the official school presses and in the free-enterprise publishing houses which sold their wares to the public. Works of scholarship now accounted for only a small

---

[1] W. E. Griffis, *The Mikado's Empire*, 2, p. 431. This was the Fukui School.

part of the total output. There were story books for children, illustrated books, technical books, popular medical books, pornographic books, travel guides, novels, poems, collections of sermons; and they were bought, or borrowed at so much a day from book pedlars, not simply by the samurai, but also, or even chiefly, by members of the other classes. By this time the majority of town-dwellers with a settled occupation, and a good proportion of the farmers of middling status, were literate. Even illiterate parents sent their children in increasing numbers to schools in which many thousands of teachers earned a livelihood by teaching them to read, write and do arithmetic. It was a society which now depended on the written word for its efficient operation. A system of fast postal runners made letter correspondence an important means of communication along the main routes, on which many business operations depended. The overripe bureaucracy consumed vast quantities of paper and ink with its complicated system of ledgers and of file copies and acceptance-signature copies for all official directives.

The transformation which had occurred in these two and a half centuries was an essential precondition for the success of the policy which the leaders of the Meiji Restoration were to adopt —the policy of converting Japan into a militarily powerful industrial state. The nature of this relation between precondition and outcome is a theme to which we shall return in the final chapter. This first chapter will be devoted to a brief survey of the development of scholarship and education during the period. But first, for those readers who are not familiar with the history of Tokugawa Japan, there follows a brief outline of the main characteristics of its social organization.[1]

Tokugawa Society

The main political institutions of Tokugawa society were established in the first four decades of the seventeenth century,

[1] For more detailed accounts of the Tokugawa period, see G. B. Sansom, *Japan: A Short Cultural History;* E. H. Norman, *Japan's Emergence as a Modern State;* J. W. Hall, *Tanuma Okitsugu;* T. C. Smith, *The Agrarian Origins of Modern Japan;* R. Bellah, *Tokugawa Religion;* and E. S. Crawcour, 'Changes in Japanese commerce in the Tokugawa period'. For the Meiji Restoration, see W. G. Beasley, *Select Documents on Japanese Foreign Policy;* M. B. Jansen, *Sakamoto Ryoma and the Meiji Restoration;* and A. Craig, *Choshu in the Meiji Restoration.*

by Tokugawa Ieyasu himself—the man who won supremacy for his family by defeating coalitions of his opponents at two great battles in 1600 and 1614—and during the rule of his two immediate successors, his son Hidetada and his grandson Iemitsu. In assuming control of the country Ieyasu did not eliminate the old Imperial Court in the ancient capital city of Kyoto any more than did the other military rulers who had dominated Japan in the previous four centuries. Instead, like them, he received from the Court the title of *Shōgun*—Generalissimo—a traditional committal of temporal authority, which became the hereditary prerogative of the Tokugawa family.

There was only a blurred distinction between the Tokugawa family itself and the *Bakufu* (literally 'camp government' or 'Shogunate' as it is often called in English), the whole complex of military formations and governmental institutions staffed by the vast body of Tokugawa retainers whose residences were grouped around the Shogun's castle in Edo (the modern Tokyo). The family as an actual descent group (in fact often perpetuated by adoption) and the public institution of government were not fully separated either conceptually or for budgetary purposes. There was nothing to prevent funds which might otherwise be used to buy charcoal for the huts of the military guard being diverted to purchase jewellery for the Shogun's mistress.

The funds of the Bakufu came from its own extensive territories. In all it controlled directly over 15 per cent of the total arable area of the country—or rather of total agricultural production, for land holdings were normally assessed in terms not of area but of 'taxable yield', at so many *koku* of rice (or rice equivalents), one *koku* of rice being roughly the amount that a man would eat in a year. The Bakufu's direct holdings amounted (the figure is for around 1690) to some 4.2 million *koku*. In addition it possessed all the important mines, the major seaports, including particularly Osaka and Nagasaki, and the old Court city of Kyoto. These territories were administered by appointed, rotating officials with a small clerical staff and generally only token military forces.

The main function of these officials was to collect revenue. Each landholding farmer—or rather, farm-family—owed a fixed annual tax to be paid in kind, its amount recorded in the official tax registers and graded to the size and yield of the

4

family's holding. Farmers were in theory bound to their land. Cultivation was an obligation as well as a right, and in most parts of Japan and for most of the period holdings were in theory indivisible and inalienable, though automatically inherited—or rather, to put the matter in Japanese terms, the fact that the headship of a family passed from father to eldest son made no difference to the family's tenure. (In fact, despite the ban on alienation, the mortgaging and sale of land was

THE TOKUGAWA PERIOD: CHRONOLOGICAL BEARINGS

1580s   Hideyoshi's 'sword-hunt' and cadastral survey formalize the separate status of the samurai and lay the basis for the Tokugawa fief and tax system.

1600   Tokugawa Ieyasu achieves acknowledged hegemony at the battle of Sekigahara.

1603   Ieyasu granted the title of Shogun.

1614–15   Battles of Osaka destroy Ieyasu's potential rivals.

1616   Death of Ieyasu.

1630   Hayashi Razan starts his school with Bakufu help in Edo.

1632   Shrine to Confucius built at Hayashi's school.

1635   Daimyo required to reside alternately in Edo henceforth.

1636   Morioka fief establishes what was probably the first fief school.

1637   Matsunaga Sekigo establishes his school in Kyoto.

1638   Shimabara rebellion finally suppressed. Intensification of anti-Christian measures.

1640   Final firm exclusion of all foreigners except Dutch and Chinese. (Japanese forbidden to travel abroad since 1635.)

1670   Yamaga Sokō, Kaibara Ekken, Kumazawa Banzan, Yamazaki Ansai, all active about this time.

c. 1685–1700   The Genroku period. Rapid development of Osaka merchant wealth and of popular drama, literature and colour prints.

1690   The Shogun Tsunayoshi rebuilds Hayashi's school and recognizes separation of Confucian scholarship from Buddhism.

1693   Tsunayoshi begins lecturing the daimyo.

1716–45   Reign of the reforming Shogun, Yoshimune. Ogyū Sorai, Arai Hakuseki, Muro Kyūsō, active during this time.

1755   Kumamoto carries through a 'fief reform' and builds a school as part of it.

1772–87 Regime of Tanuma Okitsugu as Grand Chamberlain and member of Council of Elders. Much corruption in Bakufu.

1774 Translation of Dutch textbook of anatomy.

1787–93 Matsudaira Sadanobu's reforms in the Bakufu.

1790 Rebuilding of Bakufu school and overhaul of its organization. Ban on teaching of heterodox doctrines. Rapid growth of fief schools.

1792 Bakufu holds its first open examinations.

1793 Bakufu establishes a centre for Japanese studies.

c. 1800 First fears of foreign invasion. By now all big fiefs have schools. Edo now the centre of popular culture. Rapid growth in volume of popular literature published.

1811 Bakufu establishes Dutch translation office.

1833 Teacher of Japanese studies appointed in Nagoya school.

1835 More frequent brushes with foreign ships henceforth.

1838 Founding of the Mito fief school on nationalist lines.

1843 Teachers of Dutch medicine appointed in Sakura and Chōshū schools.

1849 First Japanese experiments with smallpox vaccination.

1853 Arrival of Commodore Perry. Bakufu agrees to open some ports to trade.

1856 Bakufu and Chōshū establish schools of Western Studies.

1857–58 Bakufu's reluctant signature of commercial treaties with Western Powers.

1860 Death of Ii Naosuke marks failure of Bakufu's attempts to reassert its authority.

1862 Effective end of the system of alternate daimyo residence in Edo.

1865–66 Bakufu's unsuccessful expedition against Chōshū.

1867 Shogun resigns his office to the Emperor.

1868 Meiji Restoration. New central government established.

sufficiently often condoned for considerable stratification to occur in the villages. By 1870 perhaps a third of the total area was cultivated by tenants, and 'owned' by landlords who might or might not themselves be farmers.)

Farm households were clustered in nucleated villages containing usually between fifteen and forty houses. These villages bore collective responsibility for the payment of the total village tax assessment. The village headman ('evolved' by a mixture of inheritance, election and appointment by the samurai official) represented the village for this purpose, and there was sometimes another level of super-headmen with a general responsibility for, say, ten villages. The samurai intendant who oversaw the collection of the taxes had the power to grant tax reductions in years of demonstrably bad harvests. He was also the judicial authority, though he usually acted only in major matters such as murder, arson or conspiracy, and in disputes between villages (most commonly over irrigation rights and common forest land boundaries). Other matters were left to village headmen and the working of community sanctions.

The revenues thus collected in kind on the Tokugawa territories were transported mainly to Osaka and Edo. There they were in part converted into cash and credits by the rice brokers for the purchase of materials, and in part paid, in three annual instalments, as stipends to retainers and employees of the Bakufu, though by the end of the period few retainers drew much of their rice directly—they preferred to discount their rice tickets with the brokers for cash.

So much for the 15 per cent of the land held directly by the Bakufu. Another 10 per cent was held in small fiefs by the five thousand or so (the figure at the beginning of the nineteenth century) *hatamoto* families—the higher ranks of those Tokugawa retainers who served the Shogun directly. These 'fieflets' ranged in size from a mere 100 *koku* (a single small village, perhaps) to nearly 10,000 *koku*. Only a small number of the biggest of them were directly administered by their owners. The rest were fiefs in name only; in fact, they were incorporated for administrative and taxation purposes into the main Bakufu territories; their owners drew stipends from the Bakufu warehouses in the same way as retainers of lower rank and emoluments, and like them they lived in Edo.

The remaining three-quarters of the arable land, apart from some lesser land-grants made to the Imperial Court and to shrines and temples, was divided among a number of hereditary fiefs (*han*), the smallest of which were assessed at a yield of 10,000 *koku* and the largest over a million. The total number of such fiefs varied during the period between 240 and 280. The feudal lords—or *daimyos*—who held these fiefs did so in theory by grace and favour of the Tokugawa overlord, and in the first century of the period many *daimyos* were in fact disfeoffed or transferred from one fief to another. After about 1680, however,

7

all but the smallest *daimyos* were fairly secure in their tenure and had the same rights to perpetuate the family by adoption as the Tokugawa family itself.

These fiefs were administered in much the same way as the Bakufu territories. The centre of the fief was the castle town where the daimyo had his towering stone castle and his administrative centre, surrounded by the houses of his samurai retainers. Usually only a small number of 'fief elders' (*karō*) among his retainers ever had sub-fiefs, which they administered directly; the vast majority of retainers drew hereditary rice stipends from the daimyo's granary, just as the Tokugawa retainers drew theirs from the Bakufu warehouse. And samurai officials collected the revenues from villages in the fiefs as they did in the Bakufu territories.

There were many nuances in the relation of the daimyos to their overlord, the Tokugawa Shōgun, but they can roughly be put into three categories. Firstly, there were the 'related families' among which the most prominent were the three Tokugawa families which possessed the large fiefs of Wakayama, Owari (Nagoya) and Mito, families founded by sons of Ieyasu from which Shogunal heirs could be chosen for adoption if the main line failed. Secondly, the majority of the daimyos, including nearly all the lesser ones, came into the *fudai* category—the 'loyal' families which had fought with Ieyasu from an early stage in his rise to power. The third category of daimyo, the *tozama*, were those families which either joined him just in time for the decisive battle in 1600 or submitted to him afterwards. This category included some very large fiefs; Satsuma (Kagoshima), Kumamoto, Fukuoka and Saga (Hizen) in Kyūshū; Tosa (Kōchi) in Shikoku; Chōshū (Hagi), Kaga (Kanazawa), Hiroshima and Okayama in the west of the main island, and Sendai in the north-east. (Fiefs are referred to by the names alternatively of the daimyo family, of the castle town, or of the province. Thus, the fief of the Maeda family, occupying the whole province of Kaga and centred on the castle town of Kanazawa is known by all three of these names. In this book the most common name will be used.)

The distinctions between these groups were maintained throughout the period. Only the heads of related and *fudai* houses could be appointed to membership of the Council of

Elders (*Rōjū*) and the Junior Elders (*Wakadoshiyori*), the two policy-making bodies which divided between them the supervision of the various branches of the Bakufu organization. The *tozama* were treated with some suspicion, a suspicion eventually justified by—or rather, perhaps, a suspicion which helped to cause—the coalition of *tozama* fiefs which overthrew the Tokugawa in the Meiji Restoration of 1868. The fiefs of the *fudai* and 'related' daimyos were interspersed at strong points among those of the *tozama* with a policing intention clearly in mind.

Although the daimyos owed no regular fiscal obligation to the Bakufu, they were all, of whatever type, subject to its control in a number of ways. They were bound, in the first place, by a general set of 'Regulations for the Military Houses', issued at the beginning of each Shogun's reign, which defined their military obligations and laid down certain general principles for the government of their fiefs. The marriage and adoptions of daimyo families required Bakufu approval—to prevent threatening alliances. Again, a major motive behind the seclusion policy which limited foreign trade to a few Dutch and Chinese ships a year through the Bakufu port of Nagasaki was to prevent the *daimyos* (especially the *tozama*) from enriching themselves too dangerously. There were other ways in which daimyos who seemed to be in danger of becoming too powerful or who had in some way offended the Bakufu could be cut down to size. They could be instructed to rebuild temples, shrines, palaces or bridges, or otherwise favoured with the opportunity to provide the Shogun with costly gifts. Most important of all as a mechanism of control was the requirement that all daimyos keep their wives and children in Edo and themselves spend half their time in the capital. The diminishing ability of the Bakufu to enforce this regulation, and its eventual reduction of the period of Edo residence to a hundred days in every three years in 1862, was the surest sign of its loss of authority.

There was little direct interference by the Bakufu with the internal administration of the fiefs, either with the regulation of the daimyo's body of retainers, or with the governance of his territories, though clear evidence of maladministration resulting in revolts and petitions to the Shogun might be followed by punitive action. The Bakufu, however, set the pattern of local

9

administration, and important directives addressed to the people of its own territories—concerning, for instance, the suppression of Christianity or the conditions of indentured employment—would be passed on to the daimyos for issue within their own fiefs.

Within the Bakufu the two councils, each containing five or six 'related' or *fudai* daimyos, but especially the senior Council of Elders, held overall control of policy. In practice, however, the locus of decisive power shifted. Occasionally one man would emerge as of unquestionable supremacy. It might be the Shogun himself, the Shogun's Grand Chamberlain, the senior member of the Council of Elders, or a Great Elder—a special office filled only in emergencies. Most of the time policy emerged, if at all, from a gradual process of discussion and compromise in which the Council of Elders played the major part. In the fiefs, too, there was a similar oscillation between conciliar government and temporary dictatorship, often of the 'reforming' nature that will be discussed below.

The system was held together by bonds of loyalty and obligation. They were, however, bonds between families, not between individuals (though one should, perhaps, more strictly say 'house' for the corporate units which made up the Tokugawa system, units which persisted through time, though with a membership which changed through birth and death, through the out-marriage of daughters and the in-marriage of brides for eldest-son successors, and through the adoption out of non-inheriting younger sons or their establishment as the heads of separate 'branch families'. Here the word 'family' will be used as a synonym for 'house' in this sense, leaving the word 'household' for the actual group of kin domiciled together at any one time.) In nearly every case the *raison d'être* of these relationships was a bond of retainership and alliance forged between the ancestors of these families in the wars of the late sixteenth century.

It was a system designed to perpetuate itself unchanged. Its greatest difficulty, therefore, was to cope with change, to cope more specifically with the effects of a growth in production, with those developments usually labelled, and sometimes obscured, as 'the development of a money economy' or 'the rise of the merchant class'.

The samurai, that is to say the warrior class from the Shogun and daimyos down to the lesser hereditary foot-soldiers, which made up between 5 and 6 per cent of the population at the end of the period, were the privileged rentiers of Tokugawa society. They alone had the right to wear two swords and to assume a family surname. Below them, in the ideal picture of the status system as it was described by contemporary writers, came the farmers, the artisans, and finally the merchants, in descending order of social honour. In fact, this four-fold division of estates did not accurately represent reality: the Kyoto aristocracy, doctors and priests did not fit into it, and the boundary lines between farmer, artisan and merchant were not distinctly maintained so that marriage and mobility between them was easy. The really sharp dividing line fell between the samurai and the rest—the *heimin*, or common people. It was on maintenance of the samurai's supremacy that the whole system depended.

In the economically simpler society of the early seventeenth century, when agriculture provided the bulk of the nation's total production, the samurai, whose fiscal system was well designed to tax agriculture, had no difficulty in maintaining that supremacy. Peace, however, brought considerable economic growth; not only an expansion of the cultivated area and increased yields—from which the samurai were able to claim their share—but also of all other kinds of handicraft production: of textiles, lacquer and metal wares, luxury processed foods and dwellings. Competitive conspicuous consumption among the daimyo and their retinues and the Bakufu samurai in Edo provided a constant pressure of demand for these goods. But, since the samurai were much less able to tax the producers in these non-agricultural sectors, their income rose more slowly than their expected standards of living. At the same time, the need of the daimyos to transform rice collected in their provincial fiefs into spending money in Edo meant that an increasing proportion of the rice crop passed through the hands of rice brokers whose commissions (plus interest on the advances for future crops, which helped temporarily to plug the gap between a daimyo's income and his expenditure) further reduced the real income of the samurai class. Political power was used, in property confiscations and debt moratoriums, to redress the economic balance; so, too, by the Bakufu at least, was the power to debase the currency, but the economy soon became too complicated for such measures to be effective, and despite the development of guild regulations which enabled the Bakufu and fief authorities to claim in licensing fees some of the profits of the merchant wholesalers who organized inter-regional trade, a good deal of the wealth of the country passed into the hands of merchants, and the samurai suffered at least a relative decline in their level of living. By the end of the eighteenth century Edo was probably the world's biggest city, and among its large population it was more particularly the *chōnin*, the 'townsmen', the craftsmen and merchants of every trade and speciality, who supported the most vigorously creative arts, of the drama, the novel and colour print.

This discrepancy between the pretensions of the samurai and their economic status was matched by another discrepancy between the high moral ideals of their mission in society, and the aimless routine lives the majority of them were forced to lead. Bravery and loyalty to the death were no longer called for in a world of pompous processions and formal guard duties. Corruption and inefficiency in administration, a general *sauve-qui-peut* abandonment of any higher ideal than to maintain one's own status and emoluments, in short the 'loss of morale' syndrome, became endemic.

It was this situation which the periodic 'reforms' were intended to deal with; the reforms of the Shogun Yoshimune in the 1720s, of Matsudaira Sadanobu between 1787 and 1793, and the more short-lived reform attempts of Mizuno Tadakuni around 1840. Though the administrative and fiscal innovations of these reforms varied, they all shared certain features in common; a clear sense of arresting a moral decline, and the attempt to recall samurai to their ideals and duties, to send them back to their military training for the wars that never came, urging on them sober self-cultivation, stamping out dishonesty and rewarding dedicated efficiency, above all insisting on frugality, for it was largely by reducing expenditure to the level of income that a solution to economic problems was sought. None of these reforms had much more than a temporary effect, though, as we shall see in a later chapter, each reform attempt did jerk Japan a little further along a secular trend towards greater rationality and emphasis on performance in administration. In general, however, the belt, once tightened slowly and imperceptibly, began to slip out again. And as it was in the central Bakufu administration, so, in the fiefs too, there were similar cycles of decline and retrenching reform, sometimes precipitated by the example of the Bakufu, sometimes of independent origin. The only difference was that in some of the *tozama* fiefs the fiscal measures which accompanied these reforms were more successful—by establishing fief trading monopolies and non-agricultural taxes—in augmenting revenues as well as in reducing expenditures.

Such was the inertia which their sacrosanct antiquity gave to the institutions of Tokugawa Japan that the Bakufu might have lasted a good deal longer if the endemic problems it had learned to live with had not been exacerbated by a crisis of foreign relations. The policy of seclusion was one of those institutions to which sacrosanct antiquity had accrued, but in 1853 the appearance of an American fleet demanding trade with menaces made it obvious that from Japan's position of military weakness it was no longer possible to maintain that policy. The Bakufu could not, however, call in question this fundamental policy of the founders of the Tokugawa house without equally calling in question the legitimacy of its overlordship. It had perhaps just enough reserve of power to keep the system ticking over; but when, for the first time in centuries, it was forced into major innovation it found that its stock of authority ran too low to do so effectively. Nationalism, touched off by the intrusion of foreigners, made the Emperor in Kyoto a natural symbol around which the Bakufu's enemies could rally, and the accusation that the Bakufu had failed in its duty of defending the country provided a legitimate excuse for attack. The fifteenth Shogun foresaw the inevitable, and surrendered his charge to the Emperor in 1867. A coalition of his western *tozama* enemies defeated his armies when he tried to save a few privileges from the wreck. The young samurai from these western fiefs (especially Satsuma, Chōshū and Tosa) who were responsible for this coalition were consciously acting not just as partisans of *tozama* fiefs against the Bakufu, but also as malcontented samurai and anxious patriots against a personally frustrating and dangerously inefficient form of society. They formed the nucleus of the new Imperial Government, founded in the

Emperor's absolutist name in 1868, and promptly proceeded to ditch their own daimyo superiors, abolish the fief system and build a centralized state. They also abandoned the xenophobic isolationism which had been the ostensible *raison d'être* of the coalition and set out to use every useful technique and idea the great powers of the West had to offer in order to turn Japan herself into a great power which could rival them in military and economic strength and in world prestige.

Scholarship and Education

This highly elliptical account of the general political and economic background may help to illuminate the educational developments which this book will describe. The rest of this chapter will attempt a brief summary sketch of the main facts, separating as far as possible two themes, on the one hand the growth of scholarship—mainly Chinese scholarship—and on the other the spread of literacy—the ability to read and write Japanese. They are separable because they involved different institutions and different strata of the population, but they are related since both processes required the development of organized means of transmitting knowledge and techniques and attitudes, the emergence of professional teachers and the formulation of educational theories.

The first important step was the liberation of secular scholarship from the temples—the result of a new interest in the Confucian doctrines of the Chinese writers of the Sung period. Their works had in fact been known in Japan for a good many years; they had been read and studied by the monks of the Zen monasteries as early as the thirteenth century, and in later centuries by priests in Satsuma, by some of the Court scholars in Kyoto and by some of the scholars who received the patronage of the Ouchi family in their western fief of Yamaguchi until that family's sudden decline. What was new about the early seventeenth-century generation of scholars was that they rejected the mild eclecticism of their priestly predecessors and declared their adherence to Confucianism as a philosophy and an ethic, incompatible with, and opposed to, Buddhism. Fujiwara Seika (1561–1619) is well known as the leader of this emancipation. A well-connected priest himself, he was distressed by the corruption of a priesthood which was given more to poetry than to philosophy, more to feasting and the accumulation of wealth than to charity. It was partly a puritan reaction which made him see in Confucianism a moral strictness which contemporary Buddhism lacked. One or two others, notably the Tosa scholar Tani Jichū (1598–1649), independently evolved ideas similar to Fujiwara's, but none was as influential and it was his pupils who formed the core of a developing independent Confucian movement.

But if the spiritual emancipation of the Confucianists came early in the period it was some time before they could separate themselves organizationally from the priesthood. At the beginning of the seventeenth century almost the only way a professional scholar could survive was in an endowed temple or in the employment of a feudal lord. And as far as the feudal lords were concerned 'reading books was a specialty of priests'. When, in 1607, Tokugawa Ieyasu appointed as his adviser Fujiwara Seika's pupil, Hayashi Razan (1583–1657) (Fujiwara having declined the post himself), Razan had to shave his head and don priestly clothes.

He was not, however, employed in a priestly function. Like the real priests in Ieyasu's service, his job was to advise on matters of administration, to find historical models in ancient texts and expound them to his master, to help with official correspondence, to draft daimyos' oaths of allegiance, compile genealogies and official histories—and provide Ieyasu with arguments which gave moral justification for those of his past deeds which weighed heavily on the old man's conscience.[1] At the same time he was encouraged to develop Confucian studies. His plans to build a school in Kyōto in 1614 with the Bakufu's assistance were thwarted by the Osaka campaign, but eventually, in 1630, he was helped to build a school in Edo.

It is customary in histories of the period to ascribe the growth of Confucian scholarship at this time to Ieyasu and his immediate successors. The *Tokugawa Jikki*, for instance, says that Ieyasu was brought up in the midst of constant warfare,

---

[1] See Wajima, 'Edo bakufu', pp. 49–50, for an account of Ieyasu's concern with the righteousness of T'ang and Wu who had revolted against their masters—a concern not unconnected with his own usurpation of the Toyotomi succession.

and he naturally had no time to read and study. He took the empire on horseback, but his natural brilliance and his super-human character were such that he early recognized that the empire could not be ruled on horseback. He always had a great respect for the Way of the Sages and knew that it alone could teach how to rule the kingdom and fulfil the highest duties of man. Consequently, from the beginning of his reign he gave great encouragement to learning.[1]

There was, indeed, a tradition of the military class, that successful government required equal attention to *Bun* ('civil studies', 'learning', 'culture', 'intellectual matters', 'the literary arts' are all possible translations in some contexts) and to *Bu*— the military arts. The testament of the fourteenth-century warrior, Imagawa Ryōshun, one of the most popular copy-books for children in the early seventeenth century, begins; 'He who does not know the Way of *Bun* can never ultimately gain victory in the Way of *Bu*', and it may be significant that it was by Imagawa's descendants that the young Ieyasu was brought up. The latter's own Regulations for the Military Houses similarly begins with the exhortation to cultivate equally the way of *Bun* and *Bu*.

To men like Ieyasu the Way of *Bun* meant firstly the study of practical techniques of government. Ieyasu was conscious that he was making history and his intention was to build a governmental system that would last. Just as Yoritomo had employed scholars from the Kyōto court, so he too drew on the knowledge of historical specialists, both Buddhist and Con-fucian. He may even have been consciously following Yoritomo in this. It is significant that one of the books Ieyasu had printed was the *Azuma Kagami*, the history of the Kamakura shogunate.

Secondly, there was a common assumption that the dichotomy between *Bun* and *Bu* was necessarily linked to the dichotomy between *Ji* and *Ran*—peace and war. Concentration on pens and ploughshares would be inimical to the production and use of swords; the encouragement of learning was a way of ensuring the permanence of peace.

Thirdly, *Bun* meant the inculcation of moral principles. Men

---

[1] Hayashi, *Tokugawa Jikki* in Kuroita, *Kokushi Taikei*, 38, p. 339. The Jikki is here quoting the *Itasaka Bokusai-ki*, an early seventeenth-century work. See also Yamaguchi, 'Ieyasu to Jugaku' in Fukushima, *Kinsei Nihon no jugaku*, p. 4.

like Ieyasu were not bookish men, but they held firmly to a tradition of self-discipline, the practice and the process of acquiring which had given them a respect—sometimes a rather distant respect—for moral 'teachings', and a readiness to patronize those who preached what they believed themselves to practise. And again, they saw a direct connection between morality and the maintenance of peace. The system of government which Ieyasu established was one which depended on personal loyalties, and given the casual way in which personal bonds had been broken in the preceding centuries (not least by Ieyasu himself) he saw it as needing the reinforcement of an enhanced sense of moral obligation. It was in this respect that the moral emphasis of the Sung Confucianists suited his purposes. A writer at the end of the Tokugawa period who quotes Ieyasu on the deplorable way in which sons had been killing fathers and subjects their lords, claims that it was Ieyasu's encouragement of learning as a corrective which explained why the Tokugawa regime had outlasted any previous period of military rule.[1]

The orthodox view which sees the development of Confucian studies as due to official patronage has a good deal of truth. Ieyasu's subsidies for the printing of books,[2] his provision of funds for libraries, his employment of Hayashi, and Iemitsu's grant for the foundation of Hayashi's school, certainly gave a great impetus to Confucian studies in the early seventeenth century. So, too, did the patronage of other feudal lords who followed the Tokugawa example. There seems, indeed, to have been a seller's market for such talents if we are to believe the story that Yamaga Sokō (1622–85) was offered a post at a salary of two hundred koku when he was still only eleven years old—and that by Japanese reckoning, so that he may only have been in his tenth year.[3]

Official patronage was, however, not the only factor. There was much in the growth of scholarship that was entirely spontaneous as the nation's reserves of intellectual curiosity were given free play in a world of peace, and, for the samurai at

[1] Saitō, Shidō yōron (1837) in Inoue and Arima, eds., Bushidō Sōsho, 2, p. 423.
[2] Kawase, Kokatsujiban no kenkyū, pp. 152, 326, 354. Okano, Shuppan bunka-shi, pp. 10–12.
[3] Nakayama, Yamaga Sokō, p. 4.

least, of leisure. Yamaga Sokō in Edo in the 1630s, seeking some supplement to the instruction he received at the Hayashi school, was able to find teachers of military strategy, of Shinto doctrine, and of Japanese literature. In many other fields men's minds began actively to work again. The rediscovery of mathematics led to rapid and original developments culminating towards the end of the century in the invention of the calculus by the Bakufu retainer Seki Kōwa (1642?–1708).[1] The arrival of Chinese translations of Jesuit works gave a new impetus to the study of astronomy. Systematic inquiry into agriculture— through the study both of Chinese writings and of indigenous Japanese practices—was greatly advanced by Miyazaki Yasusada (1623–97) whose great compendium, the *Nōgyō Zensho*, was published at the turn of the century.

It was more especially in Kyōto that the revival of non-official Confucian scholarship gained impetus. The old Kyōto court families which traditionally had a monopoly of Confucian learning (as late as 1603 one of them complained bitterly that Hayashi had given public lectures on the classics without Imperial permission)[2] were by now intellectually moribund. How much so is illustrated by the story of the man who registered himself as a pupil of one of these teachers on the promise that he would be taught the basic Confucian classics, the Four Books. When they had somehow completed the first three, the shortest and easiest, his teacher excused himself from launching into Mencius on the grounds that he had lent the book to someone else.[3] But still Kyōto was traditionally the centre of learning and the place where books were available. It was here that Ieyasu had established a short-lived school and library in 1601, here that Hayashi first proposed to build his school a decade later, and here that another pupil of Fujiwara Seika, Matsunaga Sekigo (1592–1657), actually established his. Again Matsunaga received some official help in this—this time from Itakura, the Governor of Kyōto—and he was also for a short period in the service of the daimyo of Kaga, but it is as a private Kyōto teacher that he is famed. He is said in the course of his life to

[1] An exposition of Seki's methods may be found in L. Hogben, *Mathematics for the Million*.

[2] *NKSS*, p. 533, and Hayashi, *Tokugawa Jikki* in Kuroita, ed., *Kokushi Taikei*, 38, p. 341.

[3] Yokoyama, *Kinsei Kyōikushi*, p. 8.

have had some five thousand pupils, though many of them, perhaps, were visitors who came for only a short period of respectful consultation. His even more famous successor, Kinoshita Jun'an (1621–98), also for two short periods in his life served successively the Maeda family of Kaga and the Bakufu, but for the most part he, too, was a professional teacher and writer, supported by the gifts of his pupils. So also was his contemporary, Itō Jinsai (1627–1705), many of whose pupils (they were supposed to have numbered three thousand) were like himself (the son of a timber merchant) of non-samurai origin. Not far from Kyōto, in Omi province, lived another influential teacher, Nakae Tōju (1608–48), a former member of the retinue of a Shikoku daimyo. Having been converted to the Sung doctrines when he was the only samurai to brave the scorn of his fellows and take lessons from a Zen priest who came to lecture in his fief, Nakae had given up his retainer's status for the life of a private scholar, moralist and teacher.

The movement developed its own impetus as the standard of living rose. Inquiry was free and the expression of opinion nearly so[1]—except for a ban on all study of Christianity—and although the doctrines of the Sung Confucianists were dominant, being taught by Hayashi in Edo and by Kinoshita in Kyōto, they had by no means a monopoly of the field. Both Yamaga Sokō and Itō Jinsai rejected the Sung commentaries and propounded their own differing interpretations of the basic Confucian canon. Nakae Tōju became in later years a convert of the Ming scholar, Wang Yang-ming. Yamazaki Ansai (1618–82) modified his rigid support of Sung moralism with liberal admixtures of Shintō mysticism. Some of these scholars, too, were less morally inclined and more interested in scholarship as an intellectual exercise and in the aesthetic pursuits of writing Chinese prose and poetry, something in which Kinoshita Jun'an in particular is said to have excelled.

[1] Yamaga Sokō was, indeed, banished from Edo for ten years, and the fact that his scorn of the Sung scholars offended Yamazaki Ansai's pupil, the Shogun's uncle Hoshina Masayuki, is said to have been one reason. It seems, however, that the fear that he might lead a revolt of *rōnin* (unemployed samurai) was an equally important factor (Nakayama, *Yamaga Sokō*, pp. 63–5). Kumazawa Banzan also suffered house arrest, but this appears to have been more for his temerity in presenting a policy memorandum to the Bakufu than for his philosophical opinions (Masamune, ed., *Banzan Zenshū*, 1, p. 18).

The schools of these teachers were still somewhat unorganized affairs where a limited number of disciples gathered to receive personal guidance from the teacher, though already by the 1670s the Hayashi school in Edo had instituted a regular system of specialized classes, each with a defined curriculum and with a strict method of ranking the thirty or so full-time students according to their accomplishments.[1] Already, too, in the first half of the century, as many as five fiefs had established fief schools, a first step towards the beginning of organized tuition on a new non-personal basis.

By the last two decades of the century Japan had already vastly changed. Saikaku writes with scorn of a certain samurai who had an income of two hundred *koku* but could not read or write—'a retainer sadly behind the times; there is nothing more shameful than being illiterate'.[2] Saikaku himself was a professional writer and literacy was sufficiently widespread in the cities of Osaka, Kyōto and Edo to provide a ready market for his and his contemporaries' illustrated novels and collections of verse. The level of living had risen considerably by this time and the division of labour was much advanced. (It was even possible to make a living in Osaka as a professional delouser of domestic pets).[3] There are estimated to have been over six hundred publishers and booksellers in Japan by 1710. Still the majority of them did commissioned work for temples and other private patrons, and Buddhist works still made up over half of the titles produced,[4] but a good proportion published on a commercial basis for the general market and their wares covered a wide range: popular literature, an increasing number of editions of the Confucian classics provided with detailed notes and intended for the self-taught student, and also translations into contemporary Japanese of popular Chinese literature—the vulgar counterpart of the philosophical Chinese studies of the scholars. There must by this time have been many who earned their living as professional teachers of reading and writing. The administration, too, was being increasingly

[1] Ogyū Sorai, *Seidan* (*NKT*, 9), p. 191.
[2] Ibara Saikaku, *Nagori no tomo*, in *Chimpon zenshū* (Hakubunkan, ed., *Teikoku Bunko*, 31), p. 131, quoted in Kaigo, *Nihon kyōikushi*, p. 140.
[3] Ibara Saikaku, *Oridome* (Tsukamoto, ed., *Saikaku bunshū*, 2), p. 182, quoted in Yokoyama, *Kinsei kyōikushi*, p. 166.
[4] Uesato, *Edo shoseki-shō-shi*, pp. 45–51.

routinized. By about 1660 the script for official documents had been effectively standardized to the *o-ie-ryū* style, and the registers he had to keep and the documents he had to prepare required that every village headman be adept in its use.

The last decade of the century was also a time when Confucian scholarship, especially that of the Sung school, received an additional impetus from a Shogun who did not merely see it as a useful adjunct of government, but fell in love with it as well. Tsunayoshi, the fifth of the Shoguns, was a devout follower both of the teachings of the Sung Confucianists and of Buddhism. He constantly commissioned scholars to lecture (or perhaps more accurately to preach) to him; what is more, he gave such lectures himself, as Gibbon remarked of a similar weakness on the part of Marcus Aurelius, 'in a more public manner than was perhaps consistent with the modesty of a sage or the dignity of' a Shogun. From 1693 onwards the daimyos and lesser officials were frequently invited to the palace to hear Tsunayoshi expound the message of the *Greater Learning*, the *Golden Mean* or even of more recondite works such as the *Book of Changes*.[1] When he visited the residences of his more powerful daimyos he likewise expected a lecture to be part of his entertainment and the opportunities for scholastic employment were that much increased.

Tsunayoshi also showed his taste for Confucian learning in more practical ways. In 1690 he ordered that the Hayashi family should be established in a new and much enlarged school, well endowed by the Bakufu and granted semi-official status as the school of the Bakufu. A new site was chosen explicitly to dissociate the school from the temple area of Ueno where the old buildings had been,[2] and the next year marked the final symbolic emancipation of the Confucian scholar from identification with the Buddhist priesthood. The head of the Hayashi family was given the hereditary title of *Daigaku no Kami*— Rector of the University—and allowed for the first time to 'let

---

[1] See Ono, *Taihei nempyō*, ff. 41, 43. Tsunayoshi first started lecturing to the palace staff in 1690. It took him three years to work up enough confidence to summon a larger audience but between 1693 and 1700 he is said to have given 240 lectures (Yokoyama, *Kinsei kyōikushi*, p. 115). Gibbon's view of this kind of activity was shared by Ogyū Sorai (*Seidan*, *NKT*, 9, p. 191) and by the later scholar of the Sung school, Shibano Ritsuzan (Yokoyama, *op. cit.*, p. 117).

[2] Hayashi., *Tokugawa jikki* in Kuroita, ed., *Kokushi taikei*, 43, p. 79.

his hair grow'.[1] In this Tsunayoshi was following a precedent set by his relative, the daimyo of Mito[2] (one of the few who took Confucianism so seriously as to insist on a Confucian burial) but the Bakufu's recognition of Confucian scholarship as a distinct and worthy profession was none the less important. Buddhist priests henceforth lost their function as political advisers. Before long every fief had its *jusha*—its Confucian scholar—and although most of these *jusha* ranked low in the hierarchy of their fief and few held positions of direct administrative power, some of the more outstanding personalities among them often exerted considerable influence, as tutors of young lords or as their advisers later in life.

And increasingly fief-supported schools were established in which they exercised their other important function as teachers of the samurai young. Some fourteen new schools were founded in the twenty years after Tsunayoshi began his lectures, and a good many of them were staffed by graduates of the Hayashi school. A later writer describes with some poetic exaggeration the school's flourishing state at the end of the century:

> The most talented of the youth of Japan vied for the honour of being taught by [Hayashi Nobuatsu] and swarmed at his door. Shod in their stoutest sandals, their books on their back and a pack on their shoulder, they would arrive panting and tottering, the salt sweat pouring from their faces, and apply to become his disciples. They were to be numbered in thousands. Of these thousands some, benefiting from the reflected splendour of Nobuatsu, attained high positions. Others were offered high salaries to become the teachers of feudal lords of high or low degree. Those who did not get official posts became fortune tellers or doctors, some became tramps and sank into obscurity.[3]

By the time of Yoshimune's reign as Shogun, from 1716 to 1745, the world of scholarship was a large and well-developed one. Hayashi Razan is supposed to have read all the books there

---

[1] *Kokushi taikei*, 43, p. 95. The order hardly came in time for Hayashi to have a respectable head of hair for the lavish ceremony of transferring the image of Confucius to the new school which took place a month later.

[2] Kasai, *Hankō*, p. 177. Oddly, this was only two months after strained relations had prompted the Bakufu to force Mitsukuni's retirement from the headship of his fief. (Hayashi., *Tokugawa jikki* in Kuroita, ed., *Kokushi taikei*, 43, p. 88.)

[3] Inoue Randai, quoted in Hara, *Sentetsu sōdan* (in *Yūhōdō, Kambun sōsho*), p. 36.

were. A century later the deepened acquaintance of scholars with Chinese writings and their own voluminous productions would have made such a claim impossible. And as the branches of learning and the approaches to them proliferated, so the lines of division between them hardened. Tsunayoshi's primarily moralistic interest in Confucianism had fortified the position of the followers of the Sung scholars and had made the sermonizing lecture the type form of public scholarly activity. Ogyū Sorai (1666–1728), one of the truly original minds of the period, was the most outspoken critic of these developments. He not only—like Itō Jinsai—rejected the Sung interpretations of the classics and presumed to make his own; he went further and rejected the whole assumption that the purpose of studying the classics was the moral cultivation of the individual. It was rather, he asserted, to learn the principles the Sages had discovered and the social techniques they had invented for governing men and keeping them in good order, or alternatively to learn to appreciate and to write good Chinese prose and poetry.[1] He did not conceal his scorn for the orthodox school,[2] and his bitterness was returned in equal measure by such rivals for the Shogun's favour as Muro Kyūsō (1658–1734) who longed for a Sage Emperor who would ban pernicious doctrines with an arrogant pretence to originality and burn all immoral books.[3]

The rivalry between the various schools, and especially that between the adherents of the Sung Confucianist school and the followers of Sorai—both those who inherited his practical political concerns and those who adopted his aesthetic literary approach—continued throughout the century. By now the most lively centre of scholarly activity was Edo rather than Kyōto (just as the centre of creative activity in the *chōnin* arts was moving from Osaka to Edo). It was still largely a world of private academies where a single teacher instructed his personal disciples. It received little official encouragement in the middle years of the century but students were not lacking. In contrast to former times, '*bun* is now down below', a contemporary writer remarked, 'there is no intellectual accomplishment at the top, but there are large numbers of scholars

---

[1] See, for the political aspect, McEwan, *Ogyū Sorai*, esp. pp. 7–8.
[2] E.g. *Taiheisaku* (Kishigami, ed., *Nihon Bunko*), p. 10, *Seidan* (*NKT*, 9), p. 191.
[3] Hara, *Sentetsu sodan* (Yūhōdō, *Kambun sōsho*), p. 303.

among the people'.[1] Some of these scholars became relatively prosperous from their pupils' fees. One is supposed to have had an income of 150 *ryo* a year, equivalent to that of a samurai of medium rank and 'much more than any unemployed samurai could usually aspire to'.[2] Learning, in fact, was becoming fashionable—so much so that some serious-minded scholars were led to complain that it had degenerated into a mere collector's hobby. There were far too many so-called scholars who prided themselves on their collections of books as if they were collections of tea-bowls, and lacked any knowledge or appreciation of their contents.[3]

Such fashionable dilettantism, in part the result of Sorai's influence and in part a reflection of what is generally described as a growing 'hedonistic degeneracy' of samurai morale at the time, was likewise a reflection both of a real decline in creative scholarship[4] and of the lack of official concern with the public functions of scholarship and scholars. Official posts were still available for those who were skilled in the Chinese classics, and in the provinces there was a slow growth in the number of fiefs which established schools (about half a dozen per decade between 1710 and 1770.) But the Bakufu itself showed little interest beyond a few half-hearted attempts to get samurai to go to public lectures at the beginning of the century. The Hayashi school, victim of the hereditary system, declined in incompetent hands. The Shogun's official *jusha* were said to be the frequent object of jeers from the palace pages, and were asked offensive and sacrilegious questions about, for instance, the comeliness of Confucius's wife. There was even, according to the same collection of anecdotes illustrating the low ebb of Confucian learning in the 1770s, an economy plan which involved pulling down the shrine to Confucius attached to the Hayashi school.[5]

---

[1] Yuasa, *Bunkai zakki* (*NZZ*, 2), p. 611.

[2] *Ibid.*, p. 623. The scholar was Hattori Nankaku.

[3] Ota, *Gosō mampitsu* (*NZZ*, 17), p. 64. Quoted in Yokoyama, *Kinsei kyōikushi*, p. 448.

[4] Maruyama, for instance, sees no development of creative value in the Confucian field after the death of Sorai (*Seiji shisōshi*, p. 147).

[5] Matsuura, *Kasshi yawa* (Kokusho kankōkai, *Sōsho*), 1, p. 56, quoted in Yokoyama, *Kinsei kyōikushi*, p. 309. The Shogun's principal private secretary, when charged with the task of transmitting the suggestion to the Shogun is supposed to have asked Omae, the chief of the Shogunal secretariat: ' "What is it a shrine to?

The situation changed radically in the last two decades of the century, a fact well attested by the sudden establishment of no fewer than fifty-five fief schools in these twenty years. Suddenly a new moral urgency was injected into the development of scholarship. There were several reasons: a succession of natural calamities in the 1770s, the universal tendency of the daimyos' rising standards of expenditure to outrun their income, and the consequences, in peasant revolts and poor samurai morale, of their attempts to meet the situation by increased tax exactions and cuts in samurai stipends. These circumstances prompted many intelligent men in the fiefs to think seriously of ways of reordering their world. It was natural in the intellectual climate of the day that they should consider the cure to lie in men's hearts and minds. If the samurai could regain their moral standards, retrieve their sense of duty, of loyalty and of filial piety, there might be some chance that they would obey the orders to economize and avoid luxury which were the only solutions most fief rulers could think of for their financial difficulties. 'Generations of our ancestors have constantly urged the necessity for each of our retainers to cultivate earnestly the literary and the military arts (*bun* and *bu*) and other skills, and all are aware of the importance of diligent and unfailing devotion to these matters. However, in these recent years of increasing financial difficulty, while it is natural that unavoidable circumstances should have interfered with such study, it has come to our attention that there are some who are especially lacking in diligence and loose in their behaviour.' So ran the preamble of an order issued by the Tokuyama daimyo in 1785, explaining his reasons for building a school for his samurai retainers.[1]

This trend in the fiefs was greatly accelerated when, with Matsudaira Sadanobu's accession to power in 1787, it became

---

[1] *NKSS*, 1, p. 777.

A Buddhist or a Shinto god?" Omae replied that he believed it was a shrine to Confucius. "And who's Confucius?" "I understand that he is the gentleman who comes in a book called the *Analects*," replied Omae. "Ah, now I understand," nodded the secretary, "so that's why someone was saying that, according to Hayashi the Rector, if we did away with the shrine and the news got abroad it would reflect badly on our reputation in China. Perhaps we had better leave it for the moment." '

the keynote of Bakufu policy. Like Yoshimune in his earlier attempts at reform he stressed the importance of *bun* and *bu* for the restoration of samurai morale, but unlike Yoshimune, whose personal predilections disposed him to emphasize *bu*, Sadanobu was in earnest in his attempts to stimulate scholarship. He carried out a thoroughgoing reform of the Hayashi school, making it now fully a Bakufu establishment, reinforcing its staff with outside scholars, increasing its endowment, broadening its curriculum and instituting a system of regular examinations. He is equally famous for his order, addressed to the head of the Hayashi school in 1790, instructing him to keep to the doctrines of the Sung Confucianists and to banish from the school 'the heterodox doctrines of those who make a cult of novelty, the fashion for which is a danger to public morals'.

This was the famous 'ban on heresy' which marked an important turning point in the development of Confucian scholarship in Tokugawa Japan. Sadanobu's motives are understandable, given the atmosphere in which, and the ends for which, he was working.[1] In part the ban was the result of pressure from scholars who were close to him. The followers of the Sung school had fallen on evil days, particularly in the easygoing atmosphere of the Tanuma regime when their heavy moralizing hardly suited the temper of the times. Some of them were engaged in hand-to-hand disputes with scholars of different persuasions—disputes which were also struggles for power. Rai Shunsui (1746–1816) who is supposed to have had great influence on Sadanobu, had himself to defeat a strong Sorai faction in his Hiroshima fief.[2] The motives of these scholars are clear enough. Muro Kyūsō's prayer for a wise ruler who would burn the books was answered at last—if in a somewhat milder form.

But what were the motives of Sadanobu himself? According to one writer, primarily a desire for unity.[3] The Confucian teachings could not have general prestige if there was to be constant dispute about their meaning. Hence uniformity must be imposed. And if so, it was better to make it the uniformity

---

[1] They have been well analysed in Morohashi, 'Kansei igaku no kin', in Fukushima, *Kinsei Nihon no jugaku*, and Wajima, 'Kansei igaku no kin no kaishaku'.

[2] Morohashi, *op cit.*, p. 172.

[3] *Ibid.*, p. 174.

urged by his advisers—the Sung teachings which had always been the doctrine of the Hayashi school. The same writer quotes Sadanobu himself, speaking with the true politician's impatience of the intellectual. 'Who shall support scholarship if this superfluity of scholars—one could count them by the dozen and ship them by the cartload—continue to argue and abuse one another with their various theories, like the bubbling of boiling water or the twisting of strands of thread.' (Alternative Chinese metaphors to describe such a situation as, for instance, the blooming of a hundred flowers did not occur to him.) And again, 'the study of Sung Confucianism should be continued. Its orthodoxy has stood the test of time; it has commanded the respect of the majority of good men and a good many men have respected it; one can well say that one is least liable to err if one puts one's trust in the Sung teachings'.[1]

There was probably, however, something more positive in Sadanobu's motives, or rather something more positively negative. The doctrines he was trying to suppress (or rather to drive out of the Bakufu school, though the ultimate effect was practically that of total suppression) did not merely make for an undesirable diversity. They also made a positive virtue of diversity—of originality and free criticism.

The opponents of the Sung doctrines who were the object of the ban—loosely termed the 'school of ancient learning' (koga-kuha) since they shared the claim that they based their doctrines on a direct reading of the classical texts—were men either avowedly within, or at least largely influenced by, the Sorai tradition. Many of them had inherited the cantankerous and somewhat arrogant disposition of their original mentor, but without a fraction of his scholarship or originality. Both the dilettante literary and the politico-philosophical wings of the later Sorai school came in for attack. The standard charges are well summed up by a member of the Sung school writing some twenty years after the ban. He denies their claim honestly to interpret the ancient texts and the ancient Sages; their real concern is with the intrigues of power and with practical utility. They twist the teachings of the Sages into a heterodoxy which tries to fascinate by its novelty. 'They revile former scholars. Their pupils, without any self-cultivation, talk grandly

[1] Matsudaira Sadanobu, *Taikan zakki* (*NZZ*, 14), p. 177.

about affairs of state. This appeals to the vigour of the young and has a spirited and rousing effect on them, but its poison makes them despise the world about them and slander their betters. Either they fall into dissolute ways and gorge themselves on food and drink,[1] or else they criticize the government, scorn their superiors and exercise a totally bad influence on public morality.'[2]

The faults of the *kogakuha* in the eyes of the Sung scholars were all of a piece. They refused to accept authority. A benevolently paternal ruler like Matsudaira Sadanobu had every reason to take exception to them. His order to Hayashi used the same word as the author just quoted to describe the doctrines to be outlawed—*shinki*, that which tries to fascinate by its novelty. It was the element of originality and non-acceptance of the existing order which offended and which—again to quote the order to Hayashi—'endangered public morality'. The doctrines of the Sung school were eminently better adapted to the purpose of a reformer of feudal morals.

The ban was not by any means accompanied by police repression. Open letters of protest against it were addressed to Sadanobu and to his advisers with impunity.[3] The ultimate effect was far-reaching, however. The kind of favour that led to employment in the Bakufu came only to the orthodox. The order which Hayashi addressed to his students as a sign of his acceptance of Sadanobu's instructions is clear. 'The Seidō is a place for the training of talent and there are immediate official uses to which such talents will be put.' Hence there is room within the Sung Confucian training for a variety of specialities. But they must all be within the framework of the Sung interpretation.[4]

In practice the heterodox scholars soon found their disciples falling away. Kameda Hōsai (1752–1826) is supposed (doubt-

---

[1] The association of political radicalism with dissolute living may not be simply the usual polemical attribution of all undesirable qualities to one's enemies. Radical movements in recent Japanese history have often contained the *gōketsu*—the self-conscious hero who makes a cult of drinking hard and whoring hard as well as fighting hard. The *shishi* of the Restoration and the young officer conspirators of the March 1931 incident are examples.

[2] Karashima, *Gakusei wakumon (NKSS*, 8), p. 8.

[3] Morohashi, *op. cit.*, pp. 175–6. Wajima, *op. cit.*, p. 56.

[4] This is the version given by Karashima (*Gakusei wakumon*, p. 9). Morohashi gives a different version (*op. cit.* p. 160).

less an exaggeration) to have had a thousand students among the Bakufu retainers at the time of the ban, but gradually they slipped away until finally he had to close his school.[1] Letters of orthodox and heterodox scholars alike describe, the ones jubilantly, the others sadly, wholesale defections of pupils.[2] In the fief schools, too, uniformity was gradually achieved partly by replacing staff, partly—and with far worse effects on the integrity and the morale of the scholastic profession—by judicious conversions.[3] By Ishikawa Ken's count, of the scholars employed by daimyos in the period 1710 to 1790, nearly 40 per cent of those whose affiliations are known were declared followers of one of the *kogakuha* schools. In the period after 1830 this proportion fell to 13 per cent.[4]

In the field of traditional scholarship the first half of the nineteenth century was not a period of new departures, except, possibly, for the development of a militant nationalistic school of Sung Confucianism in the Mito fief. True, new knowledge of Ch'ing textual scholarship[5] did cast new doubts on the accepted Sung interpretations of the classics, but by now the Sung doctrines were so firmly embedded in the established order that there was no recurrence of the doctrinal disputes of the previous century.

Koga Dōan (1788–1837) the Bakufu scholar and son of one of the principal authors of the ban on heterodoxy, recognized the justice of the new Ch'ing criticism but is supposed to have stilled his doubts with the reflection that, 'my father was a filial son of Chu Hsi (the founder of the Sung school). I will be his loyal retainer'.[6] In any case the best minds of the day now found in the challenge of Western learning and the political problems of meeting the encroachments of Western military power a more stimulating field of intellectual application than doctrinal disputes over the interpretation of the classics.

In the first part of the seventeenth century the recommenda-

---

[1] Morohashi, *op. cit.*, p. 166.
[2] *Ibid.*, pp. 166, 175.
[3] See Wajima, *op. cit.*, p. 58.
[4] Ishikawa, *Gakkō no hattatsu*, pp. 266–7.
[5] One of the most important critical compilations, the *Huang Ch'ing ching-chieh* is said to have arrived at Nagasaki within seven years of its publication in China (Kume, *Kaikoroku*, I, p. 123).
[6] *Ibid.*, I, p. 123.

tions of his adviser, Arai Hakuseki, and the Shogun Yoshimune's own interest in astronomy had led him to relax the ban —originally imposed as a measure against Christianity—on the import and study of European books. 'Dutch learning', which until that time had been confined to oral interpreting and directly imitative surgery, began gradually to take deeper roots. By the end of the eighteenth century anatomy and astronomy had been revolutionized. The first Japanese-Dutch dictionary had been published, and already there were students of Newtonian physics, of Western botany, geology, art, mathematics and surveying methods. Such studies were not entirely freed from the fearful suspicions of being un-Japanese, disloyal, and tainted with Christian subversion, and in 1839 the jealousy of Confucian scholars succeeded, at a time of mounting fear of foreign attack, in reviving suspicions to the point where a number of prominent 'Dutch scholars' were jailed. The recovery was quick, however, and towards the end of the period these studies attracted a growing number of adherents, especially in the Western fiefs.

So, too, did the so-called National Learning, the study of Japanese history and Japanese literature, often associated with a revived interest in the Shintō religious tradition. In part it was a by-product of Sung Confucianism; Fujiwara Seika's anti-Buddhism disposed him favourably towards Shintō ideas and such seventeenth-century scholars as Yamazaki Ansai and Yamaga Sokō were keen students of Shintō. In part it was a reaction against the tendency of Confucian scholars of all persuasions to adulate the traditions of China and scorn those of their own country. The critical study of Japanese literature and the early chronicles which began at the end of the seventeenth century was put on a firm basis by the perceptive and careful scholarship of Motoori Norinaga (1730–1801). By the time of his death it was an accepted branch of study, incorporated into the curriculum of a number of fief schools. As it grew thereafter, the movement took a more specifically religious and political turn, and its potent influence in bringing about the political changes of the 1860s is well known.

If Confucian scholarship stagnated in the first half of the nineteenth century, educationally it was a period of growth rather than of mere consolidation for the Confucian schools. Enforced uniformity had its advantages. It became easier to formulate standard curricula independent of the personal bent of particular teachers. The fief schools took on a new, more organized form, and as they expanded in size and in number— there were well over two hundred by the time of the Restoration —their curricula became not only more systematic but also more varied. Particularly with the incorporation of elements of Dutch learning into the curriculum of some of these schools there was a growing tendency to consider the kind of education they gave as a necessary prerequisite for official employment, and even to modify the rigours of the hereditary ranking system in order to place acquired skills where they could be most efficiently used.

Already before the end of the eighteenth century some fiefs had also begun to show a concern for the education of their commoner subjects—again as a reflection of revived official interest in the moral uses of Confucianism. Only rarely did this go beyond the employment of touring lecturers to instruct villagers in the importance of filial piety and obedience, but occasionally it led to the establishment of schools where commoners, too, could learn the elements of Chinese. Such training a good many of them managed to acquire without official help. By the turn of the century the richer merchants and village headmen were often as learned as the average samurai, and at a lower level the spread of Japanese literacy continued.

The feudal rulers did not always approve of the way this literacy was used and issued frequent edicts banning books which, by reason of their pornography, their frivolity or their lack of respect to the ruling house, were detrimental to public morals. By now the fiction trade was highly organized. Authors were receiving regular payments for their work and there was a recognized division of the market between the more substantial and literary novels, written in an erudite and heavily Sinicized style, and the more popular illustrated books written largely in a phonetic script for the masses. The former, which might cost about as much as the rice a man would eat in a month for a five-volume work, rarely ran into editions of more than a thousand, but the latter, shorter, less lavishly printed and therefore much cheaper—a slim comic-strip book might sell for the price of a single meal—often ran to editions of seven or eight thousand.[1] Each copy, however, might have multiple readers, thanks to the activities of lending-library pedlars who took up a large share of these editions and lent them to their clients at so much a day. In 1809 there were reputedly 656 of these pedlars registered in Edo.[2]

This increasing spread of literacy was largely the work of the many thousands of teachers who ran the reading and writing schools for commoners. How many such schools there were it is difficult to estimate, and their numbers probably fluctuated with fluctuations in the economy, but throughout the first half of the nineteenth century there was a secular trend of expansion. When, in 1868, the new government took over and began its programme of forced-pace modernization, its decrees ordering the establishment of a universal system of elementary schooling already had substantial foundations on which to build.

---

[1] Yokoyama, *Kinsei kyōikushi*, pp. 731–2.
[2] Nakamura, 'Yomihon no dokusha', p. 623.

Chapter II

THE AIMS OF SAMURAI EDUCATION IN THE TOKUGAWA PERIOD

IN MODERN SOCIETIES with universal elementary education so long established that compulsory attendance is no longer considered an infringement of individual liberty, it rarely occurs to anyone but lecturers in the philosophy of education to ask what the school system is intended to do. The situation was different in Tokugawa Japan. Schools were still rare and their organization was constantly evolving. The youth who conceived a 'desire for learning' and travelled half-way across the country in search of a teacher was no mere myth of the moral story books, and official or parental encouragement of education was still rather a matter of choice than of convention. In consequence, discussion of its proper form and ultimate purpose was frequent and earnest.

One difficulty in describing these discussions is that of terminology. The word education tends to mean for us 'what goes on in schools', more elaborately 'deliberately influencing the development of a child's abilities, knowledge or attitudes under some formal and regular arrangement', and is distinct in this sense from 'upbringing' with its emphasis on parental moulding of character, or 'study' with its emphasis on purely intellectual accomplishments. From the end of the eighteenth century onwards the Japanese word *kyōiku* begins to be used with increasing frequency in much the same sense[1]—as it still is in modern Japan. A great variety of other words are used in Tokugawa discussions of education, however. *Kyōka, kyōkun, kyōdō, kyōyu,* and sometimes *kyōkai* all mean something like moral instruction or guidance—of adults as well as of children—though *kyōka* is more specifically used to refer to the moral

[1] Ishikawa, 'Edo-jidai makki no kyōka undō' and *Shakai kyōikushi*, pp. 72-80.

33

guidance of the people by their rulers, and *kyōkun* for compilations of written precepts. *Gakumon* (or sometimes *gaku, gakushū*) approximates more to 'study', but its meaning varies. To illiterate peasants it meant the ability to read, while in the title of Nawa Rodō's *Gakumon genryū* (1794) it meant philosophical speculation. To most people, perhaps, it meant acquiring some acquaintance with the Chinese classics. Since this was, in effect, the major activity of most schools it was chiefly the proper nature of gakumon which most writers discussed. They would not, perhaps, have denied if challenged that children might need some other form of organized instruction, but it is mainly 'learning' in the narrower sense with which they were concerned.

The wide range of possible emphases which educational systems might adopt can be roughly schematized as follows:

Emphasis may be laid on moulding or influencing the development of:
A. Moral attitudes.
B. Intellectual capacity, techniques, attitudes or knowledge.
C. Artistic or physical attitudes or skills.

With the aim of equipping a child with:
(*a*) Qualities of vocational utility for his later life.
(*b*) Qualities which will make him most useful for society.
(*c*) Qualities which are held to be of direct non-material value to him. Making him approximate to an ideal of manhood, making him 'more acceptable in the sight of God', allowing him to 'live more fully', 'enriching his experience', etc.

Moral Education

The overwhelming emphasis of Tokugawa writers on education is on field A for aims (*b*) and (*c*), a natural consequence of the Confucian tradition they inherited, of the kind of society they lived in and of the role which their patrons expected them to play in it. Most of them define the gakumon with which they are chiefly concerned as a system of ethical training through study of the Confucian classics. 'Study', declared one of the Sung scholars, 'is the path whereby men become *seijin*'[1]. Sages,

[1] Chu Hsi and Lu Ts'ou-Ch'ien, *Chin-ssu lu* (Yūhōdō, *Kambun sōsho* edn.), p. 30.

that is, such as Yao and Shun, the hero paragons of antiquity, or Confucius, the interpreter of their work. He is supposed to have astounded his examiners with this statement, and a good many Tokugawa scholars also had doubts about the over-confident assumption that the ordinary sensual man could become a Sage, but they would agree that the closer the approach the better and that this was the major purpose of study.

Kaibara Ekken (1630–1714) is responsible for one of the most systematic accounts of the rationale of this approach. Study of the classics, he claims, is a universal duty, and in his *Yamato zokukun* he explains why.[1] Although he takes over the general ideas of the Sung philosophers he drops the sophisticated complexity of their dualistic doctrines. His central concept is *Tenchi*[2] (literally, 'heaven and earth') which stands, it seems, for a personal, rational and humanly sentient being which is the source and origin, the 'great father and mother' of the universe. Man, one of the progeny of *Tenchi*, is especially favoured in that he is born with a heart (or mind, the word *kokoro* refers to a centre both of cognition and emotion) which is the heart of *Tenchi*; man is made, spiritually at least, in *Tenchi's* own image. He is especially enlightened because he receives from *Tenchi* a nature fully equipped with the five virtues—human kindness, a sense of justice, knowledge of correct social conduct, wisdom and trustworthiness.

All this entitles man to be called the 'most spiritual of all creation'.[3] *Tenchi*, which loves all creatures (as demonstrated by the fact that it brings them into existence), especially loves man,

---

[1] In Tsukamoto, ed., *Ekken Jikkun*, I, pp. 67 ff.

[2] Or sometimes just *ten*, the two words are for him practically synonymous. A similar idea of *ten* had existed in China since the beginning of the Chou period. Tsuda Sōkichi ('Jōdai Shina . . .') distinguishes three senses in which it is used; for the physical firmament, for a presiding deity, anthropopathic, though not, as he emphasizes, anthropomorphic, and for a rational abstraction, a 'natural law', physical and ethical. Feng Yu-lan (*Chinese Philosophy*, p. 31) analyses this last concept into a 'fate' controlling human affairs, 'nature'—the law governing the seasons, etc., and an ethical principle. (See also J. Spae, *Itō Jinsai*, p. 111.) Ekken's *ten* seems to be all these at once, but more particularly the presiding deity. His use of *tenchi* as a synonym for *ten* does, however, seem to be fairly uncommon. *Tendō* which, originally meaning the 'way' ordained by *ten*, later became equivalent to *ten* alone and eventually a common word for the sun, is used by Ekken in its original sense.)

[3] *Bambutsu no rei*. The phrase comes from the *Shu ching*. See Legge's translation, V, Bk. I, i, 3.

and a man who, when he might have been any one of ten thousand other things, is selected to be a man is thereby under a great obligation to *Tenchi* which can only be discharged by serving *Tenchi* all his life. This is therefore the duty—the 'way'—of man.

Such service consists chiefly in keeping intact the five virtues with which *Tenchi* has endowed us, in particular by displaying to all that virtue of human kindness which *Tenchi* has shown to us, thus 'aiding the benevolence (or human kindness) of *Tenchi*'. In daily life these virtues manifest themselves chiefly as correct attitudes in the five human relationships; that is, love on the one hand and filial piety on the other in relations between parents and children; just dealing on the one hand and loyalty on the other in relations between master and servant; a proper distinction between their respective spheres and mutual respect in relations between husband and wife; due respect of the younger brother for the elder and affection of the elder for the younger; and mutual trust between friends.[1] Keeping these virtues intact is not, however, as easy as it might seem. They are constantly menaced by the natural appetites (*yoku*) and by the material nature (*kishitsu*), the source of emotions such as envy. (For which, however, *Tenchi* appears not to be responsible, a difficulty Ekken has got himself into by dropping the dichotomy of *li* and *ch'i* which is at the core of Sung dualism.) The retention of the five virtues is thus a matter of free will, of deliberate choice.

We are not, however, without guides in this matter of maintaining the purity of our inborn dispositions. We may seek our models in the *Seijin*,[2] the Sages of ancient Chinese antiquity, who developed these virtues to the supreme degree. As a guide to later ages they left the Four Books and the Five Classics, and in order to keep men up to the mark they later sent the 'wise men', such as the brothers Ch'eng and Chu Hsi, the founders of the Sung school.[3] Thus gakumon—

---

[1] This systematization of the five human relations—*gorin*—derives from Mencius (Legge's translation, III, 1, 4, 8).

[2] Ekken seems to include in this term Yao and Shun, Wen Wang, Wu Wang, the Duke of Chou, Confucius and Mencius.

[3] Ch'eng Hao (1032–85), Ch'eng I (1033–1106) and Chu Hsi (1130–1200), collectively referred to in Japanese as Teishu. In this category of *kenjin*—later exponents of Confucianism not sufficiently original or remote in time to qualify as *seijin*—some would also include Mencius.

learning to read the works of the *Seijin* and their interpreters—is a religious duty, an essential precondition for the virtuous life which is enjoined on us by our debt to *Tenchi*. Its fulfilment is measured not by the acquisition of knowledge but by the virtue of the student's conduct.

A very similar conception of the nature of man and of education is to be found in the work of Ekken's contemporary, Nakae Tōju (1609–48).[1] In later life Tōju largely followed the ideas of Wang Yang-ming (1475–1529), from whom he takes his terminology. His key term is *meitoku*.[2] This, he says, is equivalent to the five virtues of Ekken, and is, in addition, a principle diffused throughout the universe. Without attempting any elaborate proof of the matter he declares it axiomatic that it is every man's duty to 'make clear' his *meitoku*—and this is what gakumon consists of. When his *meitoku* is clear a person automatically practises the true virtues, especially filial piety, which is for him the core of the virtuous life. The Sages were men who were born with their *meitoku* already clear and are thus a useful model for the less fortunate. In ancient China they themselves provided the model by their own actions, but for later generations they have left their writings, and thus the reading of the sacred books is the beginning of gakumon, its true fulfilment being, of course, virtuous conduct.

The majority of Tokugawa writers on the subject shared (with, indeed, Aristotle and Dr Arnold and many other Western writers) this view that the chief end of study is virtue, not usefulness, whether they called the process 'making clear one's *meitoku*', 'rectifying the heart',[3] 'returning to one's original nature',[4] 'returning to beginnings',[5] or 'acting out conscience'.[6] It was an attitude which cut across the conventional divisions of Tokugawa scholars into their respective philosophical schools. Thus, for instance, the view of Itō Jinsai (1627–1705),

---

[1] See especially his *Okina mondō* and *Tōju sensei seigon* in Tsukamoto, ed., *Tōju bunshū*.

[2] Sometimes, alternatively, *shitoku yōdō*. See, e.g. *Okina mondō*, p. 3.

[3] *Seishin*, from the Greater Learning. See Legge's translation, ch. 3.

[4] *Honsei ni kaeru*, e.g. in Kaibara Ekken's *Yamato zokukun*, p. 78.

[5] *Fukusho*, a phrase used first, oddly enough, by Chuang Tzu (Yūhōdō, *Kambun sōsho* edn.), p. 318.

[6] *Chi-ryōchi*, the key term of Wang Yang-ming, used, for instance, by Kumazawa Banzan in the oath of the Okayama fief school (*NKSS*, 2, p. 582).

the founder of a branch of the 'ancient learning' school is summed up by a biographer as follows:[1]

At the basis of Jinsai's educational work lay two fundamental ideas. First, education should perfect not only the mind but above all the will; in other words, it is more important to be a good man than a learned man. Second: education can only be achieved through the study and practice of the Way of the Ancients, especially Confucius. This way is their works, above all the *Analects*.

So, too, Yamaga Soko (1622–85), a temperamental contrast with Jinsai, but of a similar philosophical bent:[2]

Gaku consists simply in studying the teachings of ancient times; in extending one's knowledge of them to the utmost, and moreover applying them to daily life.

Even a pupil of Ogyū Sorai, Miura Baien (1723–89), gives a similar definition, though with a final twist, the significance of which will be considered later.[3]

Gaku means learning. A bird learning to fly, a cat playing with a ball, are each learning their own 'way' in life. *Gaku* is learning the particular 'way' of man. It is precisely the 'way' by which one becomes a full human being, and the 'way' of ruling men which the Four Books and the Six Classics teach.

And so, too, even the National Learning (*Kokugaku*) movement, for all its history of reaction against the Sinophily of the Confucian scholars, reveals much the same basic attitudes though now the 'way of man' becomes 'the ancient way of our own country' as portrayed somewhat hazily in the early Shinto mythology. Motoori Norinaga (1730–1801) was writing at the beginning of the movement and his advice to prospective students is obviously designed for the already educated adult convert, rather than as an educational programme for children. He speaks of this religious aspect of study of the 'ancient way of our country' as only the chief of the five branches of 'national learning' and he is loath to call it obligatory since each branch of study plays its own particular part. If, however, a prospective

---

[1] Spae, *Itō Jinsai*, p. 164.
[2] *Seikyō yōryoku* (Tsukamoto, ed., *Yamaga Sokō bunshu*), p. 3.
[3] *Baien sōsho* (Tsukamoto, ed., *Meika zuihitsu zenshū*, vol. 2), p. 227.

student was unable to make up his mind which to choose he would advise him to take up this fundamental moral study for three reasons. Because, when one has been born a man, it is a pity not to study the 'way' of man; because it is fundamental to all the other historical and literary studies; and because, for one born in the particular country which, of all the countries in the world, was especially favoured with the divine revelation of the 'way' of man, it would be a waste of a Heaven-sent opportunity not to study it.[1]

Half a century later Motoori's successor, Hirata Atsutane (1776–1843), in whom the prophet dominated the scholar, is much more explicit:[2]

> As men, we must know the 'way' of man. To know the 'way' of man we must first know our parents and our ancestors and understand our country's polity. To understand our country's polity we must first know the circumstances of its foundation. It is here that the laws governing the relations between master and servant, the order of precedence in human relations, the whole of the 'way' by which men are ruled takes its origin. And to know the circumstances of its foundation we must read the sacred books. That is to say the *Kojiki*, the *Nihongi* and all the other ancient books of our country. To read these books and to understand the 'way' is called the 'study of the old way'.

Finally, one may find similar ideas in the writings of the leaders of the Shingaku movement. As promoters of a kind of moral rearmament for adults of the lower classes, they were, of course, only peripherally concerned with the encouragement of systematic study, but when they do discuss gakumon it is quite naturally with the accents of the Confucian scholars from whom they drew their original inspiration. Thus, Shibata Kyūō (1783–1839) takes, as a text for a lecture, Mencius's phrase from the parable of the Bull Mountain concerning the good soul which has gone astray. 'And this being so,' he goes on, 'the Seijin feeling sorry about it, gave us indications of what the 'way' of man is, and it is the process of learning these indications which is called gakumon.'[3]

This universal assertion that study is an absolute duty of man

---

[1] *Uiyama-bumi* (*Zenshu*, 1927, vol. 9), pp. 479–82.
[2] *Kodō taii*, p. 377.
[3] *Kyuō dōwa* (Tsukamoto, ed., *Shingaku dōwa shū*), p. 17.

provides a clear-cut answer to both the what and the why of study. Occasionally, however, supplementary 'whys' are offered. One is through the appeal to individual self-respect. Matsudaira Sadanobu (1758–1829), less a scholar than a promoter of scholarship in others, adds to his conventional definition of gakumon ('learning to be a human being ... so that we can achieve that spiritual status which corresponds to our position in nature') an additional argument. Those who do not study, he suggests, are little better than the birds and the beasts. Anyone born to look like a bird or a beast would take pains to improve his appearance; so should anyone who is born with a mind (or heart) which resembles a bestial mind.[1] 'People will laugh at you', says Kaibara Ekken more explicitly, though talking in this instance of the particular defect of being unable to write a good letter rather than of gakumon in general.[2] More positively, 'study will improve your character and habits of speech and people will look up to you', says Oe Gempo (1728–94), the author of a rather pedestrian compendium of useful hints for beginners.[3]

At a somewhat more popular level a few writers promise that the virtuous conduct which results from gakumon has its own direct rewards. Some Shingaku writers, with their usual eclecticism, take over the Buddhist doctrines of *inga*—cause and effect—to promise their merchant audiences that their devotion will be rewarded. The blurb of a book of moral sermons published in 1836 describes it as one which 'shows interestingly and with humour a short cut whereby even those who have slipped into evil ways will become filial to their parents and loyal to their masters and achieve harmony in the home. And hence, 'their family business will naturally flourish, they will gain comfort of both body and soul, and their line will extend to eternity'.[4] Even some Confucian scholars proper were not above using this kind of argument on occasion.[5]

---

[1] *Taikan zakki* (*NZZ*, 14), p. 342.

[2] *Bumbukun* (Tsukamoto, ed., *Ekken jikkun*, 2), p. 302. The same sentiment is expressed about learning in general in the testament of the daimyo, Doi Toshikatsu (1573–1644). See *NKSSS*, 3, p. 105.

[3] *Ma-ni-awase haya-gakumon* (Hakubunkan, ed., *Nihon bunko*, 4), p. 9.

[4] Kinoshita, *Kokoro no yukue*.

[5] See, e.g. Kaibara Ekken, *Kakun* (Tsukamoto, ed., *Ekken jikkun*, 1), p. 7, and Hosoi Heishu quoted on p. 239.

A further 'why' argument is to emphasize the importance of the ethical training provided by gakumon for the good of society as a whole. If all men are virtuous then society will be harmonious and stable. (As we shall see later, some writers completed the circle and pointed out the value of a stable society to the individual, though usually à propos of expounding the blessings of the beneficent rule of the Tokugawa. See p. 235.) The text most frequently quoted in this regard is from the Greater Learning.

> Things being investigated, knowledge became complete. Their knowledge being complete, their thoughts were sincere. Their thoughts being sincere, their hearts were rectified. Their hearts being rectified, their persons were cultivated. Their persons being cultivated, their families were regulated. Their families being regulated, their states were rightly governed. Their states being rightly governed, the whole kingdom was made tranquil and happy.[1]

'They' are the rulers of feudal states in the Chou period, but the passage is frequently quoted in support of the argument that when all individuals in a society do have rectified hearts and cultivated persons there is harmony in the state.[2] Hence, study becomes a social duty, not simply a matter which rests between a man and Tenchi, or a man and his own conscience or sense of self-respect.

Vocational Education

It is in this sense that—for the samurai class at least—moral education is also vocational education. Most of these discussions are about 'man', and some writers do indeed specify that the duty of study is truly universal and that their prescriptions apply equally to all ranks of society—with consequences for official attitudes towards the education of the subordinate classes which will be considered in a later chapter. But a good many of them mean by 'man' male members of the samurai class. The sumarai's vocation was government and—to interpret the passage just quoted in its original sense—good government was largely a matter of correct moral dispositions on the

---

[1] Legge's translation, ch. 5.
[2] See, e.g. Kumazawa Banzan (1619–91), *Shūgi washo*, p. 246.

part of governors. Hence, moral training was the fundamental element of the samurai's vocational education, an assumption well reflected in some of the favourite names given to fief schools, such as Meirinkan or Meirindō (School or Hall for Clarifying Ethics) in at least sixteen fiefs, Kōdōkan (Hall for Diffusing the Way) in at least six, or Chidōkan (Hall for Practising the Way) in at least five.[1]

One writer stands out firmly against this view, and that is Ogyū Sorai. He scorns the emphasis of the Sung school on the rectification of the individual heart or the clarification of innate virtue, and attributes its moralistic bias to the corrupting influence of Buddhism. The real purpose of study is to acquire an intellectual knowledge of the techniques of government which were invented by the Sages and practised in ancient China. When he says this, however, he is discussing the purposes of scholarship, not a programme of education for the average samurai. He admits that it takes a lifetime of professional scholarship, of gradually deepening acquaintance with the culture and institutions of China, before one can get to the point where, like himself, 'one knows the Way of the Sages like the back of one's hand' and can compare the institutions of ancient China, of later Chinese dynasties, of ancient Japan and of contemporary Japan, with sufficient insight to predict the future course of development of existing institutions and discover their defects. This is impossible for the man of affairs and the best he can do is to rely on the advice of professional scholars. He can, however, get some distance himself, and given the purpose as defined the reading of history should play the major part in his study. Some reading of morally improving works may be appropriate for the lower classes in order to inculcate in them a proper sense of loyal obedience, filial piety, honesty and respect. But, as he repeats several times, the pretensions of the Sung school to make this the whole of learning are preposterous and pernicious.[2]

These two versions of the vocational relevance of gakumon for the samurai class are not, however, mutually exclusive and despite Sorai a good many writers would prefer to have it both

---

[1] See the analysis of fief school names in Kasai, *Hankō*, p. 28. These names are all, of course, taken from famous passages in the classics.

[2] *Taiheisaku* (Hakubunkan, *Nihon bunko*, 2), pp. 3–7, 31–2, 43–4.

42

ways. Hence, the version of Sorai's pupil, Miura Baien, already quoted—'the "way" by which one becomes a full human being *and* the "way" of ruling men'. By the beginning of the nineteenth century this had become the general view. The first clause of the statement of principles read monthly to the students of the Hikone fief school from its foundation in 1799 says, succinctly:

> The essentials of book learning (bun) are, cultivating as a basis the 'way' of filial piety, respect for elders, loyalty and trust, to clarify the principles whereby nations are governed and the people made content, and so to strive to be useful in the public service.[1]

The absorption of this element of Sorai's ideas into the general stream of educational thought marks a change in the general conception of the role of the samurai, a change brought by the continuance of peace and the increasing complexity of civil administration. In the seventeenth century the role of the samurai was simple enough. All he needed, says Ekken, was firstly his moral training and secondly military skills. (And he incidentally provides an additional 'why' argument—a samurai who fails to equip himself with these is taking his samurai stipend without paying for it and is therefore a shameless thief. In other words, study is not merely an absolute human or a general social duty, but also a particularistic duty towards one's superior.)[2] Kumazawa Banzan has an equally simple version of the samurai's function. It is to 'love men', more specifically, having rectified one's heart and cultivated one's person by study, 'as regards superiors to await the coming of a wise lord. As regards inferiors to admonish the faults of the common people. To achieve proficiency in the military arts, to prevent crime and to protect the country against invasion.'[3]

---

[1] *NKSS*, 1, p. 389.

[2] *Kakun* (Tsukamoto, ed., *Ekken jikkun*, 1), pp. 10–11. Saito Setsudō (1797–1865) talking not specifically of study but of the duty for 'intellectual labour' in government on the part of the samurai, has a rather different, and for his time unusual, argument to emphasize the samurai's duty. He records that once, while taking a walk with some of his pupils, they saw a group of farmers industriously working well into the dusk to take in the harvest. He pointed out to them that it took ten or twenty households of farmers working day and night to support a single samurai. A samurai who did not fulfil his part of the division of labour deserved—and could expect—'divine punishment' (*Shidō yōron* in Inoue, ed., *Bushido sōsho*, 2, p. 420.)

[3] *Shūgi washo*, p. 495.

They were writing at a time when fief administration was still very much a rough-and-ready affair, when administrative skills consisted largely of a little basic fiscal arithmetic, intuitive judgment of persons, and the qualities of leadership needed to give authority to decisions. Half a century later Ogyū Sorai was complaining that the distinction between the civil and military branches of the administration was not clearly enough established.[1] Already the problems of administration seemed to him complex enough to warrant specialization, and they were to become more complex as the economy expanded, particularly for the Bakufu which, as well as directly controlling a large area of the country, provided a model for the other fiefs, exercised general control over them and held responsibility for managing the currency. From the middle of the seventeenth century a new word appears in fief edicts announcing the establishment of schools or redefining educational policy. The word is *jinzai*[2]—human talent—often linked with the phrase just quoted from the Hikone document—'to be useful in the public service'.[3]

The stress on *jinzai* was a result of the growing need for efficient administration. Its especial emphasis in the Bakufu under the regime of Matsudaira Sadanobu at the end of the century was also intended as a reassertion of the importance of ability for official appointments and of the intention to reverse the practice which prevailed under the preceding Tanuma regime of selling offices to those who offered the highest bribe.

[1] McEwan, *Ogyū Sorai*, p. 84.

[2] One of the first occurrences of the word is in the Kumamoto fief where the establishment of a school in 1755 was part of one of the earliest 'fief reforms' (*NKSS*, 3, p. 196). Hayashi Shihei speaks of the need for producing *jinzai* in his memorial to the daimyo of Sendai in 1781 (*Jōsho* in *NKS*, 15, p. 8). The word also occurs in the regulations of the Bakufu school after the reform of 1793 (*NKSS*, 7, p. 31), of the Hagi school in the 1790s (*NKSS*, 2, p. 665), in a memorial concerning the Yonezawa school at about the same time (*NKSS*, 5, p. 470), and in the nineteenth century in documents of the Mito fief (*NKSS*, 5, p. 470), the Sendai fief (*NKSS*, 5, p. 642), the Hamamatsu fief (*NKSS*, 5, p. 457) and the Tokushima fief (*NKSS*, 5, p. 596). Doubtless many other examples could be found. Sorai had used the word earlier (*Taiheisaku*, in *NKS*, 3, pp. 551, 562) and Shōji Kōgi, stressing the need to promote *jinzai*, quotes an eighth century Japanese Imperial edict which uses the term (*Keizai mondō hiroku* in *NKS*, 22, p. 53).

[3] Literally, 'to be of useful service to the *kuni*', the word which at this time meant 'fief', but could also mean 'nation', an ambiguity which helped to smooth the transition from parochialism to nationalism at the ending of feudalism in the Meiji Restoration.

As will be shown in a later chapter, the demand for *jinzai* was eventually to eat away at the foundations of the hereditary ranking system, but in the first instance it did not necessarily imply an end to the practice of limiting each grade of official appointments to a fixed range of hereditary ranks. It meant simply that among the available candidates in each of these ranks the most able should be chosen.

The production of such able men was the function of the schools. Here, indeed, was a test of the Confucianist's claim that the study of the classics was the essential key to the art of government. They did not generally, it seems, succeed in making their claim good. A Kumamoto scholar writes, probably about 1790:

> The purpose of educating the children of retainers in the fief school is to develop human talent to be useful in the public service ... It is now already more than thirty years since the school was established, but I have never yet heard of any particularly talented person being produced by the school and proving of service to the fief. I have not heard that the school has trained large numbers of people skilled in the arts of political economy and well acquainted with the institutions of our country. There must by now be several hundreds or thousands of graduates who can compose Chinese verse and prose, who have read the classics and are well versed in the history of both China and Japan. But none is able to discuss matters of practical politics, knows the arts of government or is capable of useful work in present-day administration.[1]

Hiraga Gennai put the matter a little more forcefully some thirty years earlier in his parody of the style of a well-known Edo story-teller:

> The so-called teachers of the present day write treatises on government and morals which remind one of someone trying to learn to swim in a dry field. And thus, poor fools, they seek to astonish the masses! In their anxiety to preach the Way of the Sages they forget the Sages' teaching that only those in a position to govern can expound the principles of government. They are like wrestlers who go into the ring without a loin-cloth ... These frog-in-the-well scholars are earnest admirers of things

[1] Nakayama Shōrei, a memorial quoted in *NKSS*, 5, p. 612. The memorial is undated, but the Kumamoto school was established in 1775.

45

Chinese and call Japan—their native land—the country of the Eastern Barbarians ... But for all their farting drivel about the 'Way' and the arts of peace and the arts of war, if they had their rice salaries measured out in ancient Chinese bushels, they might not be so admiring of their Sages.[1]

Partly because of their moralism, partly because they were usually of low rank and hence remote from the higher reaches of administration in the fiefs, but more particularly because of their assumption that wisdom had been exhausted in ancient China, the Confucian scholars were not usually a success as trainers of *jinzai*. The same complaints were still being made in the middle of the nineteenth century.[2] Sorai, at least, while asserting that the Sages had discovered for all time the principles of just government, also speaks somewhat inconsistently as if he is developing an inductive science of the comparative sociology of government, with ancient China as only one instance from which data are drawn. But reverence for antiquity was too strong for this line of approach to be developed. For the average Confucian scholar the study of the classics was a preparation for government because it directly provided 'lessons' for the management of affairs. A few practical men did have doubts about this assumption. 'Even in the days of Yao and Shun and the three ancient dynasties I doubt if China compared with present-day Japan', Matsudaira Sadanobu once wrote. The power, loyalty and harmony of the great feudal lords with just and liberal government in their provinces must be unsurpassed in any country in the world. The only thing Japan lacks is that she has not been properly written up.[3] But this kind of heresy made little impression on the world of the Confucian scholars.

[1] *Fūryū Shidōken-den* (1764) (Kamimura, ed. *Shisō zenshū*, 5), pp. 374–5, 373, also quoted in Yokoyama, *Kinsei kyōikushi*, p. 346. Actually, he was wrong about the bushels. The Chinese were bigger. But it is unlikely that contemporary scholars would have bothered to acquire such trivial arithmetical knowledge.

[2] See, for instance, a Kagoshima fief order of 1856 which complains that a good many of the so-called scholars of the day are remote from contemporary affairs and ill-acquainted with the principles of government. They consider themselves 'outside the system'—like priests (*NKSS*, 3, p. 284). Also Saitō Setsudō in a letter quoted in Yokoyama, *Kinsei kyōikushi*, p. 823. His type case, illustrating remoteness from practical affairs, is of the young man who studied for thirteen years, but not until he went home at the end of his studies did he discover that one needs a heavy stone to make *takuan* pickles.

[3] *Taikan zakki* (*NZZ*, 14), p. 302.

Their assertions that the classics provided a complete education read rather like the claims of the last defenders of the exclusive merits of a classical education against the encroachment of modern studies in the older British universities. The only difference is that there were few advocates of fundamental curriculum reform in Japan. The Kumamoto author of the complaint quoted above did indeed propose that a compendium of useful information should be compiled for the use of students, including the genealogy of the fief lord and his related families, the geography of the fief, its population of people and livestock, its production of foodstuffs and other products, the division of functions and the channels of authority in the fief administration, protocol at the Shogun's court and in Edo and Kyoto, the proper forms of official correspondence, and so on. There should also be similar practical examinations in current affairs.

Suggestions such as these did, as we shall see in a later chapter, eventually make some impression on Confucian educators, but their efforts at reform were half-hearted and they came too late. They were overtaken by the invasion into the educational world of the new 'Dutch learning' which, with its emphasis on technology, did provide something substantial enough to satisfy those who wished to train themselves to be 'useful in the public service'.

Even the more morally inclined Confucian scholars did, of course, give some consideration to the vocational skills required by the samurai, beyond his basic moral training. Their discussions of the subject are made somewhat difficult to interpret, however, by the fact that they acted on the principle they preached, namely that what was good for ancient China was the best for contemporary Japan. So, scholastic disquisitions on the proper functions of schools generally begin with a description of the schools supposed to have existed in ancient China,[1] and their recommendations for the practical curriculum consist largely in describing the nature of the ancient Chinese curriculum. They did make their own original suggestions, but they had to be presented as interpretations of the meaning of traditional Confucian terms.

The most common phrase summarizing the requirements of

---

[1] To give a few random examples, Nakayama Shōrei in *NKSS*, 5, pp. 607–8; Aizawa Yasushi in *NKSS*, 5, p. 459; Nishijima Junzō in *NKSS*, 5, pp. 602–3.

the samurai is the 'six arts': rites and etiquette, music, writing, arithmetic, archery and chariot-driving.[1] All were severely practical accomplishments for the Chou dynasty official. He had to know how to behave at court ceremonies and in all the strictly regulated affairs of official life. Music was necessary at these ceremonies and, since each note of the scale had an affinity with a particular grade of the social hierarchy, harmonious music was a way of producing social harmony by sympathetic induction.[2] He had to write, he had to survey land and provision troops, he had to be prepared to lead his men in war.

These, say the Confucian scholars, are the practical contents of the arts of peace (*bun*) and the arts of war (*bu*), the traditional and more specifically Japanese definition of the requirements of the complete samurai. The first two belong to *bun*, the last two to *bu*, while writing and arithmetic are necessary for both. Rites and etiquette, in the form of the practices of the Ogasawara school[3] were indisputably accepted as a part of education, though formally provided for in only a few fief schools. Music rather lost its practical significance when 'rites' were thus limited to social behaviour, though Banzan still maintained that it was valuable for producing rain in time of drought[4] and a Kyūshū scholar, writing later in the period, recommends music—provided it is of the right kind, i.e. classical *gagaku* music rather than contemporary *samisen* music—for its moral effect. ('An ignorant farmer about to start a fight would calm down at the sound of *gagaku* music and goodness would grow in his heart, but the sound of *samisen* is enough to put lewd thoughts into the mind of a saintly priest with years of Zen meditation behind him.')[5] Others interpret 'music' to mean the writing of prose and poetry.[6]

[1] The *rikugei*, from the *Chou Li*, ch. 3. The terms are, in Japanese, *rei, gaku, sho, su, sha, gyo.*

[2] See, e.g. the *Li chi*. Couvreur's translation, *Li Ki*, vol. 2, p. 48.

[3] A school of etiquette, originally concerned solely with formalized archery competitions, but later covering all aspects of social life, which was accepted as authoritative throughout the Tokugawa period. The Ogasawara family derived its authority by direct esoteric transmission from a son of the Emperor Montoku (reigned 851–8).

[4] *Shūgi washo*, p. 252.

[5] Shōji Kōgi, *Keizai mondō hiroku* (*NKS*, 22), p. 74.

[6] E.g. Nishijima Junzō, *Gakkan ryakusetsu* (*NKSS*, 5) p. 606.

Similarly, 'writing', which Ekken interprets as calligraphy[1], is taken by Yamaga Sokō to mean all training involving reading, i.e. gakumon in general, including especially the study of instructive history.[2] 'Arithmetic', it is generally agreed, is to be limited to the severely practical—money exchanges, percentages, surveying, trench-digging and so forth. (There was, however, some doubt, particularly at the beginning of the period, whether a samurai should so demean himself as to know of such things,[3] and that something of the same scorn for petty calculation still persisted into the nineteenth century is clear enough, not least in one or two fief edicts admonishing samurai against such pride.)[4] The last two, archery and chariot-driving, are specific enough, though chariot-driving, not being altogether a common preoccupation of the samurai, the term kyūba is often substituted —meaning literally archery and horse-riding, but commonly extended to include all the military skills; swordsmanship, the use of the lance, weapon drill, and also the study of military strategy. Ekken is careful to point out that the relative proportions of weapon training and strategy should vary with the samurai's rank.[5]

It is stressed, however, that these skills are the least fundamental part of education. The usual simile is the root and the branch. The root, of course, is the moral training in the virtues of loyalty, filial piety, justice, courage, benevolence and so on, which ensure that the skills are properly employed.[6]

The Fuller Life

Nitobe Inazō, giving his version of the 'national character' story concerning the international competition for an essay on

[1] *Bumbukun* (Tsukamoto, ed., *Ekken jikkun*, 2), p. 287.

[2] *Shidō* (Tsukamoto, ed., *Yamago Sokō bunshu*), p. 116.

[3] See, e.g. *NKSSS*, 3, p. 25, a quotation from the *Shōhei Yawa* (Anon., 1796). A mid-eighteenth-century writer remarks on the softening of these puritan scruples. Whereas formerly none but a samurai unfortunate enough to be employed in fiscal administration would be able to count, now it is common enough to see a samurai take his abacus when he goes shopping in order to check the shopkeeper's calculations.

[4] E.g. at Saga in 1809 (*NKSS*, 3, p. 540) and at Sasayama (1789?) (*NKSS*, p. 333).

[5] *Bumbukun* (Tsukamoto, ed., *Ekken jikkun*, 2), pp. 358–9.

[6] See, e.g. Kaibara Ekken, *Bumbukun* (Tsukamoto, ed., *Ekken jikkun*, 2) p. 357; Kumazawa Banzan, *Shūgi washo* p. 35; Aizawa Yasushi in *NKSS*, 5, p. 459.

the elephant, once remarked that the Japanese entry would probably be entitled 'The duties and domestication of the elephant'. The view that pleasure was a major purpose of life was certainly not lacking in Tokugawa Japan, but it was a principle more often practised than preached, and its exponents had little to do with the business of education. Life, for writers on education, was real and earnest; its main purpose, the fulfilment of duty. The educational preparation for life should be equally earnest.

> It is ludicrous the way some people who think having a child is delightful try to make the child's gakumon delightful too. Vulgar learning is fun, but learning the 'way' is no fun at all. It is a means of reforming one's natural propensities. It is like a painful cauter which you use because you must. Think of learning as just hard work. In the words of Chu Hsi, 'When I was seventeen or eighteen, I struggled with my reading'. 'Struggled' means hard work.

So runs a report of a lecture by Satō Naokata[1] and in case the struggle was not hard enough such ascetic practices as deliberately getting up in the middle of cold winter nights to study in unheated rooms were developed to heighten the student's sense of the serious purposes in which he was engaged. 'Compared with other forms of training study is dull and it is not surprising that, as his lordship has recently been apprised, some pupils are indolent in their studies', begins a directive to the youth of the Fukuoka fief which goes on to urge that such indolence should cease.[2]

Intellectual pleasure was not the object of learning, nor was it, except in rare instances, consciously used as a bait. This is perhaps odd, for it would be hard to defend the thesis that the Japanese people have traditionally shown a lack of intellectual curiosity. The early travellers who set out in flimsy, ill-navigated boats and with less than a 50 per cent chance of survival to find out what they could about Chinese civilization, the pioneers of Dutch learning in the eighteenth century, the persistent questioning and the notebooks of the envoys to Rome in the 1580s or in America in 1860, the Shogun Yoshimune with his clocks and his armillary spheres and his bucket outside the

---

[1] Quoted in Yokoyama, *Kinsei kyōikushi*, p. 138.
[2] *NKSS*, 3, p. 4.

bath-house for measuring rainfall, the Regent Matsudaira Sadanobu describing with glee how he attached a bamboo pole to a float and sat in his garden for hours to settle the question whether there were tides in wells,[1] the volumes of *zuihitsu* written in the Tokugawa period and largely devoted to guesses at the origin of Japanese customs or the etymology of words—any amount of evidence could be adduced to show that there have been a good number of intellectually curious Japanese. But there were no Japanese Lockes to urge that curiosity was 'the great instrument nature has provided to remove the ignorance' that children are born with and that its stimulation was an important pedagogical device. There was not even a Japanese word which corresponds to the English 'curiosity', nor is there one, in fact, today.[2]

One can find rare exceptions. One is a benevolent old teacher who quite explicitly urges the importance of making learning pleasurable to young children. He advocates giving them picture books—the illustrated children's encyclopaedia, the *Kimmō Zui* for example, or an illustrated version of the story of the twenty-four paragons of filial piety. When the child's interest is aroused by the pictures he will begin to ask questions, and this is the chance for instruction. Later, when he sees other people reading, he will want to read too, and this is the opportunity to hold his attention and teach him a little at a time. The author claims that he has had considerable success in this way with his own boy of six whom 'in our old age, with all the doting fondness of a cow licking her new calf, we have always let have his own way in everything'. He adds apologetically that he knows this is not the proper way recommended by former wise authorities, but he has found that it works.[3]

Yuasa Jōzan, too, recommends picture books for young children for similar reasons[4] ('The important thing is to arrange things so that children get to like study') and the abundance of

---

[1] *Taikan zakki* (*NZZ*, 14), p. 214.

[2] The modern word *kōkishin* has vaguely derogatory overtones, meaning something like 'love of curiosa'. *Chishiki-yoku*, also a modern word, means an 'appetite for knowledge' but suggests the absorption of instruction as well as independent inquiry.

[3] Emura Hokkai, *Jugyō-hen* (Hakubunkan, *Nihon bunko*, 3), p. 24, quoted in Ototake, *Shomin kyōikushi*, 1, pp. 328–30.

[4] *Bunkai zakki* (*NZZ*, 4), p. 617.

illustrated books for children suggests that this was, indeed, a widespread view. The reading and writing schools were certainly not torture-chambers for the young.

But all this applies to young children and to the teaching of basic Japanese literacy which was beneath the attention of most writers on education. The acquisition of such practical skills was a morally neutral activity. Hence it was a field in which Japanese parents could give free rein to that fondness for, and tendency to indulge, their children which has impressed Western visitors from the sixteenth century onwards.[1] But the learning of Chinese, as the gateway to the teachings of the Sages, was a more solemn matter. In this, little attempt was made to tap the resources of the child's spontaneity with the possible exception of his desire for achievement, for 'getting through', a given task. The one exception I have yet discovered is a scholar of the Nakatsu fief who urges that excessive concentration on the moral purposes of study becomes tedious and produces a distaste for study of all kinds. A little laxity is necessary in everything and children should be able to look on the school as a place 'to enjoy themselves'. Even he, however, does not elaborate on the kind of enjoyment or suggest that the child's desire to find out for himself should be stimulated.[2]

The neglect of curiosity and the pleasure of independent discovery is not, after all, surprising. Tokugawa Confucianism was not a progressive branch of study, constantly pushing at the frontiers of new knowledge. All that was worth inventing had been invented by the Sage Emperors; all that was worth knowing had been known by Confucius. The task of later generations was simply to absorb this body of knowledge passively and with humility. We have seen that the chief sin of the scholars against

[1] See, for instance, P. Crasset, *The History of the Church in Japan*, p. 15; 'In the education of youth they use altogether sweetness for fear of cowing their spirits and never either threaten or chastise them, be they never so untoward, but seeing the Holy Ghost commands parents to correct and chastise their children to make them governable, we cannot much admire this piece of conduct.' Or Arnoldus Montanus, *Atlas Japannensis*, p. 314; 'The Japanners breed up their children not only mildly, but very prudently, for if they should cry whole nights they endeavour to silence them by fairness, without the least snapping or using bad language to them'. Most Tokugawa writers on the upbringing of children urge gentleness, though without any suggestion that most parents are not gentle. See, e.g. Teshima Toan, *Waga tsue* as quoted in Ototake, *Shomin kyōikushi*, 1, p. 513, and Komachi Gyokusen, *Jishūhen* (*NKS*, 19), p. 434, quoted in Ototake, *op. cit.*, pp. 518–19.

[2] Nishijima Junzō, *Gakkan ryakusetsu* (*NKSS*, 5), p. 606.

whom the 1790 ban on heterodoxy was directed was their pro-
pounding of novel doctrines; their presumptuous insistence on
intruding their own personal opinions in spheres where personal
opinions should have no place. 'In study groups', runs one of
the rules of the Yodo fief school, 'examine the principles of the
true teachings of the Sung scholars with a humble unprejudiced
mind. You should not put forward your own preconceived
opinions or engage in argument.'[1] The sin of pride, warns
Ekken, is one of the worst that can beset a scholar. [2]

The effect of such attitudes in stifling independent inquiry
is illustrated by the well-known story of the first major break-
through in the study of Dutch medicine. For years there had
been anatomy lectures at the execution grounds, but it was not
until a Dutch textbook became available that anyone thought
of actually examining the organs which were cut out and held
up for inspection to see if they did correspond with the illustrations in the Chinese texts hitherto accepted as authoritative.[3]

The parallel with the mental climate of medieval Europe is
a close one. (It would be even more exact if Moses had been an
ancient Greek and Christ a Roman, thus combining the
religious, philosophical and proto-scientific traditions in a
single authoritative corpus.) Europe was converted into a for-
ward-looking society by the visible and material success of
physical science which elevated curiosity, as the mainspring of
scientific advance, to the status of a socially desirable virtue.

But Japan had to wait longer for such a development. For
the Tokugawa scholar, pious reverence was the only proper
approach to gakumon. 'Whenever Tsunayoshi (the Shogun)
took up a book or put it down,' said Yanagisawa Yoshiyasu in
praise of his late master's love of scholarship, 'he invariably
raised it above his head and bowed in a gesture of respect.'[4]
The rituals at the Confucian shrines which were attached to
most schools served to reinforce this attitude. So, too, did the
insistence on respect for teachers which was much more
rigorous in Japan than in the Confucian homeland, China.[5]

[1] NKSS, 1, p. 86.
[2] Yamato zokukun (Tsukamoto, ed. Ekken jikkun, 1,), p. 86.
[3] See Yokoyama, Kinsei kyōikushi, p. 505. The story is told in Sugita Gempaku's
Rangaku kotohajime (1813).
[4] Quoted from the Tokugawa jūgodaiki in Ototake, Shomin kyōikushi, 1, p. 638.
[5] Yoshikawa, Nihon no shinjō, 1960, pp. 148–50.

The disciplinary advantages are obvious, and perhaps Tokugawa teachers were not entirely unconscious of the pleasure of receiving flattering respect. But in theory, at least, the teacher was respected only as the embodiment of the authority of traditional wisdom. Dazai Jun (1680–1747) is supposed to have admonished a daimyo's son who failed to make the usual reverential bows when he came to receive instruction in these words:[1]

> Far be it from a mere commoner to appear to lay down the law to a nobleman. However, what I am propounding to you is the teaching of the ancient Sages. Anyone with any pretensions to be their follower must, be he king or duke, observe true forms and attitudes. In you I find extreme rudeness. It is not that you neglect the proper forms to me personally, but that you thereby lose all right to be considered one who professes the teachings of the ancients. And one who does not profess their teachings I have no desire to talk to.

If it was the general view that learning was hard work and no fun at all, there were nevertheless those who recognized that once scholarship was acquired intellectual activity could be, in itself, a great source of pleasure. Thus Ekken, who for all his moralism had a great capacity for delight even if it was, usually, of a rather solemn kind: 'There is no pleasure in the world to be compared with reading. One has a sense of personal colloquy with the Sages, and it is the only pleasure which does not depend on other people.'[2]

There was, indeed, in the corpus of Chinese literature which the Confucian scholars inherited a whole tradition of prose and poetry written explicitly for the purpose of aesthetic enjoyment. Music, too, one of the six approved arts, was also known to be not without its pleasure and many people enjoyed reading history. There are considerable differences between Tokugawa writers concerning the correct attitudes to be taken to these activities.

A few take the rigid view that they are an obstacle to the proper devotion of one's scholastic talents to moral improvement, and as such to be rigorously eschewed. 'All books which

---

[1] Hara, *Sentetsu sōdan* (Yūhōdō, *Kambun sōsho*), p. 381.
[2] *Bumbukun* (Tsukamoto, *Ekken jikkun*, 2), p. 339, and *Rakukun* (*ibid.*, 1), p. 307.

do not have reference to the serious business of life, however clever they are, have no value', quotes Itō Jinsai with emphatic approval.[1] So, too, Yamaga Sokō quotes one of the Ch'eng brothers to the effect that while the reading of history is a useful method of acquiring vicariously necessary experience of life it should never be looked on as a mere hobby. As soon as it becomes enjoyable its purpose is perverted since it destroys the desire for self-improvement.[2] He also had an additional reason of his own for objecting to the reading and writing of Chinese prose and poetry—it leads people to forget their Japaneseness and fall in love with China. Another seventeenth-century scholar, Yamazaki Ansai, whose fiercely aggressive moralism was legendary in Tokugawa Japan[3] was one of the most rigorous exponents of this point of view.

Others, while agreeing in principle, are more inclined to make tolerant concessions to human weakness; if people can really find nothing better to do to amuse themselves, intellectual games are to be preferred to positive wickedness. 'For those who do not know how to do good, even playing *go* is better than thinking evil thoughts' was Kumazawa Banzan's verdict on a man who had sweated for hours to find a rhyme for a Chinese poem. It was a pity, however, that this particular man, who had talent, should waste it in this way.[4] *A propos* of the game of *go* itself and of similar amusements, Miura Baien (1723–89) has much the same opinion. They may be permitted to assuage the fatigue of a journey, or when the only alternative would be to 'sit with your hands in your lap gossiping about other people'.[5]

Writers who positively recommend recreational pursuits do so for a variety of reasons. For some, there are certain social graces which a man must acquire. Thus Banzan, for all his scorn of the writer of Chinese poetry, recommends that everyone

[1] *Dōjimon* (Inoue, *Rinri ihen*, 5) p. 517. He is quoting She Shui-hsin.
[2] *Bukyō shōgaku* (Tsukamoto, ed. *Yamaga Sokō bunshu*), p. 41.
[3] It is said that so intimidating was Yamazaki's lecturing style that his bachelor students found the mere mental evocation of his image an adequate substitute for Baden Powell's cold bath. All embers of sexual desire would be immediately extinguished and cold shivers run up and down the spine (Hara, *Sentetsu sōdan* (Yūhōdō, *Kambun sōsho*), p. 126).
[4] *Shūgi washo*, pp. 328–9.
[5] *Baien sōsho* (Tsukamoto, ed., *Meika zuihitsu zenshū*, 2), p. 227.

should learn to write *waka*, the thirty-one-syllable Japanese poems, 'because it is a custom of our country'.[1] Ekken agrees; if you do not study *waka*, 'you will have no sense of the elegant and will be looked down on by your fellow-men'.[2] (His low regard for the pleasure of individual creation was such, however, that he goes on to urge that it is better to 'learn off some fine old poems with which you can console or amuse yourself on appropriate occasions than to rack your brains trying to compose a miserable poem of your own'.)

Then again, there are some who see intrinsic value in these things, even though it is a rather solemn kind of uplift that is sought; not mere enjoyment. Culture has to be pursued seriously, in the manner of the ladies' literary luncheon club in 'midcult' America, rather than in any spirit of frivolity or self-indulgence. Banzan unbends most on the subject of music. 'Music exercises control over the spirit. A spirit which is calm will be liberal and inclined to the good.'[3] Similarly, Amemori Hōshū (1621–1708) says of Chinese poetry that 'when written by men of genius it is richly pulsating with the spirit of nature. As one reads one's mind is refreshed, one's heart delighted'.[4] So with the tea ceremony, painting, admiring landscapes and reading history which are to be cultivated, according to Asaka Konsai (1791–1860), 'to nourish the spirit, to banish banal affairs and to have room in one's heart to respond to all the things of creation'. This is the real meaning of 'elegance' (*fūryū*) which the contemporary world wrongly takes to mean expensive luxury, and its spiritual benefits are 'an aid to good government'.[5]

A third argument for the defence is used in the special case of Chinese prose and poetry. It was, after all, in Chinese. Familiarity with the Chinese language was a necessary prerequisite for studying the classics. Hence prose and poetry could be recommended as a means of acquiring that familiarity. It is from this point of view that Sorai condemns the Sung scholars' attitude of scorn for *belles lettres* (he implies that it is partly a

---

[1] *Shūgi washo*, pp. 35–6.

[2] *Bumbukun* (Tsukamoto, ed., *Ekken jikkun*, 2), p. 293.

[3] *Shūgi washo*, p. 402. For a similar opinion much later in the period see Hoashi Banri, *Nyūgaku shinron* (Inoue, ed., *Rinri ihen*, 16), p. 264.

[4] Quoted by Maekawa, 'Tokugawa jidai no kambungaku', p. 842.

[5] *Konsai kanwa* (*NZZ*, 15), p. 360.

rationalization of their own inability to write decent Chinese) and urges the Shogun Yoshimune to start poetry parties at his court. 'If you cannot manipulate words you cannot write Chinese poetry and this manipulation of words is necessary for reading the classics and histories.' He points out that for this reason in eighth-century Japan the Doctor of Letters took precedence at the Court over the Doctor of Classics.[1] Sorai, however, though he uses this means-to-an-end argument with Yoshimune, was far from being an enemy of the pleasures of the mind (or of the flesh for that matter),[2] and as the preface to his *Yakubun sentei* (1715) makes clear he had a high regard for literary skill as an end in itself.

By the end of the eighteenth century these more tolerant views had become general. The Sorai argument was used on one occasion by Shibano Ritsuzan, one of the strongest proponents of the ban on heterodox opinions which sought to restore the supremacy of the moralistic Sung school.[3] Shibano Ritsuzan (1736–1807) himself, although an admirer of Yamazaki Ansai, had considerable literary talents and was not ashamed to display them. His contemporaries no longer shared one of the main motives of the seventeenth-century scholars who had scorned literary pursuits, namely the desire to dissociate themselves from the Zen monks for whom they were a major preoccupation. In addition, the standard of proficiency in writing Chinese is said to have been generally much higher than at the beginning of the period. Incompetence no longer added an extra fillip to zealous moral condemnation. Indeed, it was in Chinese verse, rather than in the more restrictive forms of Japanese poetry, that the most sensitive minds of the day sought literary expression.

Again, however, the expression of these more tolerant views regarding the value of prose and poetry is usually qualified by the reminder that they must always take second place. As the rules of the Omura school put it: 'First nourish your virtue with the classics, then nourish your intellect with history and the

---

[1] *Seidan* (*NKT*, 9), p. 191.

[2] He was said, unlike other contemporary teachers, to be tolerant of his students drinking and paying occasional visits to *geisha*; it had, he held, an educational effect (Kan Sazan, *Sazan fude no susabi* (*NZZ*, 17), p. 360).

[3] Shionoya On, 'Rai Sanyō no shihitsu', p. 552.

writings of non-Confucian philosophers, then nourish your sentiments with prose and poetry.'[1] Those scholars who failed to observe such priorities were guilty of 'confusing the root and the branch'.

> There are people like the *rōnin* scholars who make a profitable thing out of this kind of *gakumon* and use it to fill their bellies ... They talk much about the Way of the Sages and the Rites and Music of the Three Dynasties, but their personal behaviour is deplorable ... They hold what they call poetry parties, hire a room in a tea-house for their meeting, get their poetry composition over with quickly and concentrate on the main business of wine and women. They do not copy the Sages; in the manner of the Chinese profligate eccentrics they talk scornfully of convention, and honest upright people they despise as small-minded.[2]

There were indeed scholars, particularly in the eighteenth century, who stood out against the tide of moral earnestness and chose as their heroes the T'ang poets rather than the Sung philosophers. Hattori Nankaku was one of these (and it may have been he whom the writer just quoted had in mind since he was renowned for the affluence which his popularity as a teacher brought him). Whether his poetry parties took the form described or not, it seems clear that his was a conscious stand for the priority of aesthetic values. He is reported once to have told a friend that he was not the kind to take responsibility for the character training of his pupils 'like a Buddha engaged in the salvation of mankind'. Being of a retiring disposition himself he leaves his pupils' characters as he finds them.[3] This was a common attitude of the Sorai school's literary wing, of which Hattori was a leading figure, and it was this (see the preceding chapter) which with the attendant charge of dissolute conduct formed one of the chief counts against the scholars at whom Matsudaira Sadanobu's ban on heterodoxy was directed. The decline of the Sorai school after the ban helped to exorcise this hedonistic disease from the body scholastic.

---

[1] *NKSS*, 3, p. 184.
[2] Ise Sadatake, *Yōgaku mondō* (Hakubunkan, *Nihon bunko*, 4), p. 5.
[3] Yuasa Jōzan, *Bunkai zakki* (*NZZ*, 2), p. 563.

Pitfalls for the Unwary

The dominant view of samurai education in the Tokugawa period may be roughly summarized as follows: the means of education were provided by Chinese writings, especially the Confucian classics; its purpose was primarily to develop moral character, both as an absolute human duty and also in order the better to fulfil the samurai's function in society; a secondary purpose was to gain from the classics that knowledge of men and affairs and of the principles of government which was also necessary for the proper performance of the samurai's duties. Certain other technical vocational skills were necessary which could not be gained from classical Chinese study. Also, classical Chinese study itself brought certain legitimate fringe benefits in the form of life-enhancing aesthetic pleasures.

It was not a particularly indulgent kind of educational theory, and the progress of the scholar pilgrim was beset with hazards. There was, first of all, a valley of doubt. Was his journey really necessary? If the purpose of learning was moral, and if the principles of morality required could be imparted in a few easy lessons, why bother with the difficult and tedious task of learning Chinese?

The Sages themselves spoke on this point with a lack of unanimity,[1] and so did their Japanese followers. Nakae Tōju quite specifically accepted the legitimacy of the doubt. Salvation is not only for the literate. Everyone has an intuitive knowledge of right and wrong which serves as a mirror to help us make clear our *meitoku*. One need only appreciate the general gist of the message contained in the classics, not necessarily the texts. This the common populace can well get from a few teachers who have read, and can expound, the classics. Like the medieval Catholic Church, in fact, he held that this was actually preferable to universal study, for in the hands of 'ignorant scholars' literary study can degenerate into mere playing with words and so lose sight of its true purpose.[2]

His pupil, Kumazawa Banzan, is inclined to demur. Such methods, he says, may produce a good man, or even a good samurai. But 'there is a lot contained in the words of the

---

[1] See the *Analects*, Bk. 1, ch. 7, and Bk. 17, ch. 8, 3.
[2] *Okina mondō* (Tsukamoto, ed., *Nakae Tōju bunshū*), p. 40.

59

Sages ... and it is not to be found in the literal meanings of their words. We naturally, by reading the classics, try to penetrate to the inner meaning of the Sages'.[1] Over a century later Matsudaira Sadanobu says much the same thing.[2] By his time, however, the question was no longer of any great importance for the samurai. It was becoming increasingly accepted that samurai *did* get an education without much questioning of the reason why. And in any case, the 'principles of government' objective provided an additional supporting justification which was by then generally accepted. The question did, however, arise *apropos* of the lower orders, as we shall see in a later chapter.

The passage quoted from Tōju already indicates a second hazard—the bog of bookishness, mistaking the means for the end. The tendency of educational systems to gravitate towards what Barker calls the 'clerkly approach' (as opposed to the 'knightly approach')[3] is probably universal. Teachers, living in the world of books and abstract knowledge, are prone to place a high value on these things as ends in themselves. As intellectual specialists they tend to mould their pupils in their own image. Moreover, books are easy tools, and proficiency in their use is more easily measured than other kinds of virtue. So there was a tendency for teachers to become *zokuju*—ignorant scholars who 'cram into their heads and pour from their mouths the mere words of the classics' without getting at their proper spirit.[4] Their pupils tend to be infected by this 'ear and mouth learning' (as opposed to 'learning of the heart') and, as Amemori Hōshū pointed out, the usual method of teaching beginners' Chinese, with its appeal solely to the child's desire for achievement, for 'getting through' material, rather than to his interest in the content, tends to reinforce this infection.[5] Gakumon, in another scholar's formulation, is always in danger of becoming a *gei*—a mere skill.[6]

Close by the bog of bookishness were the various byways of pleasure. We have already considered the strongest of these

---

[1] *Shūgi washo*, pp. 70–1.

[2] *Taikan zakki* (*NZZ*, 14), pp. 341–2.

[3] Ernest Barker, *National Character*, p. 210.

[4] *Okina mondō* (Tsukamoto, ed., *Nakae Tōju bunshū*), p. 40.

[5] *Kisso sawa* (*NZZ*, 9), p. 196, quoted in Ototake, *Shomin kyōikushi*, 1, p. 287.

[6] Shionoya Kōzō, Notes for teachers at the Hamamatsu school, *NKSS*, 5, p. 457.

temptations—the attraction of the aesthetic pleasures of reading and writing literary prose and poetry. A second led straight into the bog of bookishness itself—excessive concentration on *kinko*, textual criticism as an intellectual game. A third was the temptation of *hakushiki*—the jackdaw-like passion for accumulating esoteric information and using it to dazzle one's friends. Indeed, intellectual pride was a trap which commonly awaited those who strayed into these byways. A series of admonitions to students at the Matsumoto school issued in 1846 already uses the word *shoseifū* which was to become common in the Meiji period to describe the arrogance of the young student with his head in the intellectual clouds who 'thinks himself different from the mundane world and looks down on other people'.[1]

And if he was not to take pride in his intellectual accomplishments, the student should equally beware of parading his virtue; there was the precipice of prating moralism.

> There are some scholars who say they are concerned with 'learning of the heart' whose whole doctrine is one of 'reverence'. Like priests keeping their vows, awake or asleep, at home or abroad, their talk is all of reverence. Their shoulders crouched in a permanent attitude of reverence they look on the world and their fellow-men with a fixed expression of reproving distaste. The slightest thing will set them talking of 'examining principles' and launch them into a disquisition on the Great Ultimate, Ying and Yang, or the Five Elements.
>
> Put your son in the hands of such a narrow-minded teacher and ... his mind will shrink instead of growing freely and naturally; he will become ill-tempered and imagine himself the sole repository of virtue in a wicked world. He will begin to want to withdraw to a mountain hermitage, will dislike the society of his fellow-men, and he will be disliked by them. He will develop a thoroughly bad disposition.

So warned Ise Sadatake in 1781.[2] Ogyū Sorai had brought much the same charge against the whole school of Japanese followers of the Sung Confucianists half a century earlier, and remarked that many people are afraid to give their sons gakumon since it produces men of bad character.[3] Matsuzaki

---

[1] *NKSS*, 1, p. 516.

[2] *Yōgaku mondō*, quoted in Ototake, *Shomin kyōikushi*, 1, p. 358.

[3] *Taiheisaku* (Hakubunkan, *Nihon bunko*, 2), p. 10.

Kankai (1725–75), though himself a scholar, is said to have thought this inevitable and drawn the logical consequences— a samurai should devote his chief energies to his military training rather than to gakumon since it is a matter of common observation that scholars generally turn out to be either overweening pedants—if they are narrow-minded by nature—or, if they have talent, dissolute playboys, but in any case of a distinctly less attractive character than those who have specialized in military matters.[1]

Finally, there was the abyss of ambition, the temptation to engage in study for unworthy ulterior motives. Admonitions against this usually employ the word *meiri*—fame and profit— to describe the tempting but unworthy objectives. Learning was, after all, a respected accomplishment and some of the more outstanding scholars did acquire something like national fame.[2] But the student who took pride in displaying his accomplishments and studied *in order* to gain prestige was already corrupted. Confucius had said, 'in the olden days people used to study [to improve] themselves, nowadays people study [to impress] other people', and this is a text frequently quoted in disapproval of the preoccupation with fame.[3] Study for profit meant being distracted by vocational ambition, either to become a free-lance teacher with a good income from fees like Hattori Nankaku, to gain employment as a professional scholar or, for the ordinary samurai to use one's scholastic accomplishments as a lever for getting jobs in the administrative hierarchy. 'Getting on' was not a laudable ambition in Tokugawa society and the hereditary system severely limited the possibilities of advancement in any case. But it did not, as we shall see in a later chapter, entirely eliminate them. There was room for competitive ambitious striving, and with the increased emphasis in the nineteenth century on the function of the schools to produce 'talent' the acquisition of gakumon was increasingly recognized as a means

[1] According to Yuasa Jōzan, *Bunkai zakki* (*NZZ*, 2), p. 539.

[2] See, for instance, Hirose Tansō's *Jurinhyō* in which he describes how, as a boy of ten in a small Kyūshū town, he heard stories of the great contemporary scholars of Kyōto and Edo (Katō, ed., *Tansō Zenshū*, 2, p. 8).

[3] *Analects*, (Legge's translation), Bk. 14, ch. 25. See Kaibara Ekken, *Yamato zokukun* (Tsukamoto, ed., *Ekken jikkun*, 1), p. 87, the oath of the Okayama school (*NKSS*, 2, p. 593) and a memorandum of the teachers of the Yonezawa school (*NKSS*, 1, p. 737.) The warning against study for fame and profit is also an important theme of Chu Hsi's rules for scholars, the *Po-lu-tung Shu-yüan chieh-shih.*

of demonstrating ability and improving one's chances in the competition. But the temptation to take such an instrumental view of education was one that had to be avoided according to the more morally inclined scholars.[1] Ogyū Sorai, on the other hand, who saw the secret of government as the devising of institutions which would allow the pursuit of individual self-interest to serve desirable social ends, had no hesitation in recommending that the bait of good jobs for the scholastically accomplished should be used as an explicit means of encouraging the *hatamoto* to study.[2] Later in the century an admirer of Sorai, a daimyo member of the Bakufu's Council of Elders, Honda Tadakazu (1739–1812), is even more forthright. The ambition to gain promotion was not simply a useful incentive; it was desirable in itself.

> The general tendency to look on ambition as mere undesirable self-seeking is doubtless one of the ill-consequences of the spread of Sung Confucianism. While one certainly would not want to see a samurai doing wrong, or using flattery or bribes to enrich himself, to seek to raise one's status and pursue the path of righteousness in a higher position is a manly ambition and a proper expression of filial piety.[3]

Honda was a statesman, not a professional scholar, and it was easier for him to be straightforward and unqualified. The scholars themselves were in something of a dilemma. While sharing in theory the belief that study should not be pursued for base instrumental motives, they nevertheless are anxious to see the value of learning for administrators recognized. Thus, a Tokushima scholar, when recommending that more account should be taken of educational accomplishments in making appointments, adds uneasily that the use of personal advantage as a bait is, of course, something 'which does not appeal to the superior man. On the other hand there is nothing wrong in giving encouragement to scholarship, and it was a practice of the Sages to promote and make use of those who had acquired it'.[4] Likewise Nakai Chikuzan (1730–1804) urged that self-

[1] See, e.g. Kumazawa Banzan, *Shūgi washo* (Tsukamoto, ed., *Yuhōdō bunko*), pp. 401–2, Matsudaira Sadanobu, *Taikan zakki* (*NZZ*, 14), p. 177, and a 1790 edict to the samurai of the Aizu fief quoted in Ogawa, *Aizu-han kyōiku-kō*, p. 17.
[2] *Seidan* (*NKT*, 9), p. 189.
[3] *Kyōsei-ron* (Inoue, ed., *Bushidō sōsho*, 2), pp. 249–50.
[4] Shūdō Yasuzaemon, *Kengisho* (*NKSS*, 5), p. 596.

interest is the only incentive which can be relied on to ignite the desire for learning in the ignorant. Once its work as a catalyst is done the fires of scholarship burn of their own accord, and he quotes a Sung writer who began his studies for base motives of worldly ambition but eventually became a scholar of distinction.[1]

Ambition was not the last of the pitfalls for the unwary. There were also the dangers of Sinophily—assuming that all that is Chinese is good and everything Japanese to be scorned—and of 'civilian effeminacy'—excessive concentration on literary studies to the detriment of military virtues.[2] These latter warnings usually come from samurai outside the scholarly profession, but their views were none the less important for it was they who established schools and often retained direction of them. Perhaps the best short summary of what constituted a desirable education in the eyes of this body of sympathetic but non-professional samurai opinion is to be found in the following passage by Hayashi Shihei, written about 1786:

> With the eight virtues as your basis [his list is filial piety, respect for elders, loyalty, trust, courage, justice, straightforwardness and a sense of honour], cultivate a boldness of spirit without losing self-discipline; acquire wisdom and wide learning without despising other people. Do not become weak and feeble; do not lose your dignity. Do not sink stagnantly into mere logic-chopping, nor allow yourself to be carried away by prose and poetry. Do not lose your courage; do not become introverted. Do not become an admirer of China who sees no good in Japan. Do not fall in love with novelty or with pleasures of the eye. Practise your military skills with devotion and at the same time learn something of astronomy and geography, of the tea ceremony and of the Nō drama.[3]

The Education of Women

It is unfortunate that the education of the female half of the samurai class has to be treated in a short appendix to this

[1] *Sōbō kigen* (*NKS*, 16), p. 324.
[2] 'Bunjaku'. See, e.g. instructions to students at the Sakura school (*NKSS*, 1, p. 254).
[3] *Fukei-kun* (Dōbunkan, *Nihon kyōiku bunko, Kunkai-hen*, 1) p. 685, quoted in Ototake, *Shomin kyōikushi*, 1, 384–402.

chapter, but this at least reflects the small amount of space devoted to the subject in Tokugawa educational writings. The problem of feminine education was thought to be relatively simple. For the samurai woman, too, moral education was of the first importance. The *Onna Daigaku*[1] summed up well enough the kind of moral qualities which were required—pre-eminently self-abnegating obedience to her parents, to her husband, and in widowhood to her son. There is also occasional insistence[2] that these yielding qualities should be spiced with reserves of aggressiveness which would make her capable of defending her honour and her husband with the ferocious courage of some of the heroes of the *Lieh nu ch'uan*, a book which was indeed often used as a copy-book for girls.[3] This is more especially the case in the seventeenth century. In Ieyasu's time it was still common for women to attend hunts on horseback, but with the continuance of peace exclusive emphasis on domestic virtues became more common.[4]

It was not thought necessary for women to engage in an arduous training in classical Chinese in order to acquire these virtues. Some would grant that they should read at least the Four Books and the *Hsiao-hsüeh*,[5] while others spoke of even the Four Books as unnecessary for women.[6] One scholar who does urge some kind of gakumon of this kind for women explains that it is necessary because women have the chief responsibility for bringing up children, and in addition 'men of medium intelligence or less are often led astray by the folly of their wives'.[7] Ota Kinjō held much the same view of the role of women. As he once put it facetiously, the world is kept in order by the three hō (*sambō*, the three treasures); Buddhism (*buppō*), rifles (*teppō*) and wives (*nyōbō*).[8]

In any case, however, women should not make any outward

---

[1] A translation of this famous moral treatise for women is to be found in B. H. Chamberlain, *Things Japanese*, (1st ed., 1890), p. 367.

[2] E.g. Yamaga Sokō, *Shidō* (Tsukamoto, ed., *Yamaga Sokō bunshū*), p. 42.

[3] A Han dynasty work revised by Wang Hui in the Sung period. There were also numerous similar compilations of potted biographies of Japanese heroines.

[4] Nishida Naojirō, *Nihon bunka-shi josetsu*, p. 531.

[5] Matsudaira Sadanobu, *Naniwa-e* (Hakubunkan, *Nihon kyōiku bunko, jokun-hen*), p. 728.

[6] E.g. Ibara Saikaku, *Buke giri monogatari*, quoted in *NKSSS*, 3, p. 133.

[7] Shūdō Yasuzaemon, *Kengisho* (*NKSS*, 5), p. 595.

[8] *Gosō Mampitsu* (*NZZ*, 17), p. 30.

display of what learning they have; 'they should keep it a profound secret, especially from the men who generally look with a jealous and malignant eye on a woman of great parts or a cultivated understanding'. Dr Gregory's advice[1] would have been echoed by his eighteenth-century Japanese contemporaries. Matsudaira Sadanobu cites a number of Chinese examples to prove that 'when women are learned and clever in their speech it is a sign that civil disturbance is not far off'.[2]

Women could, however, acquire some literary skills without losing, and in fact in the process enhancing, their femininity—they should concentrate on the study of the *Japanese* classics. The Heian tradition of separate cultures for men and women, each with its own literary language and its own style, was still a live one. Women should concentrate on *wafū no narai*—Japanese-style education in the poetry and novels of the Heian period as opposed to the masculine rigours of a Chinese education. This would give them a knowledge of *ninjō*, of the workings of the human heart; it would encourage in them an appreciation of the beauties of nature, refine their feelings, sharpen their intuitions and give them the skill in literary expression in Japanese necessary for social intercourse.

There was a difficulty, however. Yamaga Sokō insists that they should steer clear of the *Tale of Genji* and the *Tales of Ise* as lewd and frivolous books which can only corrupt.[3] Banzan had no such scruples, nor had the author of a book for women published in the Genroku period who recommends *Genji* as 'the acme of elegant diction and graceful manners'.[4] Matsudaira Sadanobu in his usual sadly gentle way regrets that the immorality of such books makes it impossible to take them as models of conduct (which is what all educational books should be), but it would be going against custom to ban them and if read in the right frame of mind there is much elegance to be gained from them.[5] This was, perhaps, the general view.[6]

[1] *A Father's Legacy to his Daughters*, 1774, quoted in J. W. Adamson, *A Short History*, p. 229.

[2] *Naniwa-e*, p. 722.

[3] *Bukyō shōgaku* (Tsukamoto, ed., *Yamaga Sokōbunshū*), p. 43.

[4] The *Honchō jotei kagami*, quoted in S. Okuma, *Fifty Years of New Japan*, 2, p. 200.

[5] *Naniwa-e*, p. 728.

[6] It was shared, for instance, by Nonaka Anritei, the scholarly spinster daughter of Nonaka Kenzan (*Oboroyo no tsuki*, quoted in Yokoyama, *Kinsei kyōikushi*, pp. 254–5) and Shimokōbe Shūsui, *Onna kuku no koe* (1787).

The education of samurai women was carried on in the home. It was a lower-class custom to send girls out to school with boys and no fiefs provided schools for women. It was in the home, too, that women acquired the practical household skills of home management, sewing and weaving—necessary, said Ikeda Mitsumasa, the seventeenth-century daimyo, for even daimyo daughters since even if they did not have to make clothes themselves the ability to do so was an essential element of femininity.[1]

These qualities were all vocational qualities, for a woman's profession was her womanliness and her vocation was marriage. Successful vocational training was even more important for women than for men, for women were subject to dismissal. The books of moral exhortation for women sometimes make the sanction explicit; if you grow up to be a selfish girl; if you do not learn to obey; if you do not take care of your appearance; if you cannot cook or sew—*sarareru*, you will be divorced.[2] The samurai, by contrast, had to be very incompetent indeed to be deprived of his hereditary stipend.

---

[1] Quoted in *NKSSS*, 3, pp. 123–4.
[2] See, e.g. Shimokōbe, *Onna kuku no koe.*

Chapter III

THE FIEF SCHOOLS

AT THE BEGINNING of the Tokugawa period such samurai as received any formal book education did so at home from their parents or from tutors, in temples, or in the homes of samurai who had special talents for it and undertook to teach the children of their fellows. By the end of the period perhaps the majority of the children of samurai above foot-soldier rank were receiving formal education in one of the more than two hundred schools which had been established by fief authorities.

The idea of educating children in a special building with specialized teachers following a regular course of tuition was not, of course, a new one in Japan. There had been schools established by the Imperial Court and by aristocratic families in the Heian period, and one old foundation, the Ashikaga Gakkō, was still in existence in 1600, although it was by then little more than a small seminary for priests.[1] There may also have been short-lived schools established by the Kobayakawa family in Chikuzen[2] and by the Chōsokabe family in Tosa[3] about the turn of the century, but no details of them have survived.

The Tokugawa schools, however, were new in kind and unprecedented in the scale of their diffusion. The motives which prompted the daimyos and their advisers to found them are implicit in what has been said concerning contemporary assumptions of the aims and functions of education, and often

---

[1] The origin of the Ashikaga Gakkō is obscure, but it was certainly founded in the Kamakura period and seems to have reached a peak of activity under the patronage of Uesugi Norizane (1410–66).

[2] *NKSS*, 3, p. 21.

[3] See Takahashi, *Nihon kyōikushi*, 1934, p. 189.

explicit in the edicts of fief authorities. Bun—the literary arts—
were means of keeping men in good order. Study would
improve the morals of the samurai. As Kaibara Ekken wrote
in a letter to an elder of the Kuroda fief urging him to establish
a school, it would make them not only more conscious of their
duties to their lord and more loyally co-operative in economy
drives (thus helping to keep the fief solvent) but also more
earnest in practising their military skills.[1] And from the end of
the eighteenth century onwards there was added the emerging
idea that scholastically trained samurai would make better
administrators. Hosoi Heishū (1728–1801) chooses a somewhat
original metaphor to make his point in a memorial to the
daimyo of Yonezawa, but his meaning is clear enough. The
daimyo is the rice and water; the common people are the fire;
the samurai are the cooking-pot. However excellent the rice
and however fierce the fire, a cracked pot will spoil the cooking.
The daimyo should make sure he has a good pot, forged in the
bellows of a good school.[2] He does not specify who was to eat
the cooked daimyo.

In the early part of the period it was the exceptional daimyo
who took these arguments seriously enough to spend money on
building schools—men such as Ikeda Mitsumasa and Hotta
Masayoshi who had some scholastic talent themselves and a
genuine personal interest in, and reverence for, Confucian
teachings. The example of the Shogun Tsunayoshi made such
men less exceptional, but still the majority were sceptical.
Muro Kyūsō (1657–1735) records a conversation he had with
a later Shogun, Yoshimune, when the latter asked him for
ideas concerning the best way of improving economic conditions.
He brushed aside Muro's suggestions for reform of the currency
saying that he wanted a more fundamental solution. Someone
had suggested that the moral effect of building a school would,
in the long run, work wonders. What did Muro think? Muro,
suspecting ambitious empire-building on the part of the official
Bakufu scholar, Hayashi, was not encouraging. First things
must come first. 'When the people are properly clothed and
fed then and only then can they think of morals.' Yoshimune

---

[1] Letter to Kuroda Ikkan, 1690, Tsukamoto, ed., *Ekken jikkun*, 2, pp. 507–17.
[2] *Omeikan isō* (Inoue, ed., *Nihon rinri ihen*, 9), p. 64, quoted in Ototake, *Shomin kyōikushi*, 1, p. 428.

replied that this was his opinion, too, and he was glad to have it confirmed.[1]

Such scepticism was rarer at the end of the eighteenth century. Between 1780 and 1810 new schools were being founded at the rate of two or three a year, and thereafter the growth was steady as is shown by the figures of Table 1. It is not easy to discover where the initiative for the founding of schools came from, given the tendency of the written records to ascribe everything to the virtue and wisdom of benevolent daimyos, but there are at least some cases where things were set in train by enterprising individuals who petitioned their fief authorities, and sometimes the building of a school was part of a general attempt by new-broom chief ministers to reform the administration of insolvent fiefs.[2]

Once schools became common the force of fashion aided their spread. The example of the Kumamoto school in 1755 is said to have prompted the founding of many others,[3] and the example set by the Bakufu in establishing the Shōheikō as a fully Bakufu-endowed and Bakufu-operated school was almost certainly a partial cause of the spurt in school building in the 1790s. Scholars urging their daimyo to build schools often point to such examples: the desirability of keeping up with the Matsudairas was an argument a daimyo[4] could understand. By the mid-nineteenth century a school was almost something which every daimyo had to have, though there were still some, as the Saga merchant Shōji Kōgi complained, who preferred to put their money into temple endowments, foolishly unaware that the hypothetical advantages of Buddahood in a future life

[1] *Kenzan hisaku* (*NKS*, 2) p. 522, also quoted in Ototake, *Shomin kyōikushi*, 1, pp. 655–6, and Tokutomi, *Yoshimune jidai*, pp. 377–9.

[2] The Kumamoto school is an example of both. According to one version a group of young samurai were accustomed to spending their summer afternoons in group reading at the house of a teacher, followed by desultory gossip lying naked on the veranda until sunset provided an excuse for a *sake* party. In one such session they worked out plans for the financing of a school by a special levy on the samurai and sent off their suggestion to the daimyo's staff in Edo. Its arrival coincided with independent plans for a school which a new chief minister had been tentatively toying with as part of a wholesale fief reform, and within a year or two the school was built (*NKSS*, 3, p. 201, and Uno and Ototake, *Hangaku shidan*, pp. 31–2).

[3] See the article *hangakkō* in Keizai Zasshisha, *Nihon shakai jii*, 3rd edn., 1907.

[4] See, e.g. the letter of Kaibara Ekken to Kuroda already quoted and Hayashi Shihei's memorial of 1781 to the daimyo of Sendai (*Jōsho*, *NKS*, 15, p. 8).

TABLE I. (A) ANNUAL NUMBER OF FIEFS NEWLY ESTABLISHING SCHOOLS; (B) AS A PERCENTAGE OF HITHERTO SCHOOL-LESS FIEFS

	(A)	(B)		(A)	(B)		(A)	(B)
1620–29	2	0.07	1710–19	5	0.19	1800–09	15	0.90
1630–39	2	0.07	1720–29	6	0.24	1810–19	13	0.86
1640–49	2	0.07	1730–39	1	0.04	1820–29	16	1.16
1650–59	0	0.00	1740–49	4	0.16	1830–39	13	1.07
1660–69	1	0.04	1750–59	10	0.42	1840–49	14	1.28
1670–79	1	0.04	1760–69	4	0.17	1850–59	12	1.26
1680–89	0	0.00	1770–79	12	0.53	1860–67	8	1.22
1690–99	7	0.26	1780–89	21	0.97	1868–70	35	15.77
1700–09	1	0.04	1790–99	28	1.45			

Notes

These are very approximate figures since:

1. They are calculated by decade, not by individual years. Thus, ninety-five fiefs had no school in 1850. Twelve established them during the decade. 12.6 per cent divided by the number of years gives the figure 1.26.
2. The date of foundation of some schools is not precisely known and is indicated only by the year period. Where such year periods overlap decades, foundations are allocated by guess-work.
3. The calculations assume that the number of fiefs throughout the period was the same as at the Restoration, though this was certainly not the case.
4. They are based on the dates of school foundations and the lists of fiefs given in Heibonsha, *Daihyakka-jiten*, which may not be altogether accurate.

TABLE 2. FIEF SIZE AND DATE OF SCHOOL FOUNDATION
Percentage of daimyos

With a koku *assessment of*	*Who had founded schools by*		
	1703	*1814*	*1865*
500,000+	(2/7) 29%	(7/7) 100%	(7/7) 100%
200,000–500,000	(4/16) 25%	(12/15) 80%	(15/15) 100%
50,000–200,000	(8/80) 10%	(49/78) 63%	(66/76) 87%
20,000–50,000	(5/75) 7%	(46/78) 59%	(67/81) 83%
Less than 20,000	(1/58) 2%	(19/84) 23%	(47/97) 48%
All daimyo	(20/236) 9%	(133/262) 51%	(202/276) 73%

Sources: Heibonsha, *Sekai rekishi daijiten*, 22, pp. 296–316 (list of daimyo), Kasai, *Hankō*, pp. 274–91 (list of school foundations).

were not to be compared with the desirability of having a fief properly managed by educated officials in this one.[1]

It is hard to say what further factors determined whether a daimyo and his advisers followed the fashion or not, beyond their own personal character and predilections. It does appear, however, that the insecurity of the smaller *fudai* daimyo who were liable to be moved from fief to fief was a strong deterrent to investment in an expensive school[2] and Table 2 makes it clear as a general principle that the bigger fiefs with larger total resources[3] founded schools more readily than smaller ones. If the dates of school foundations are plotted on a map, there is no clear evidence of the spread of the fashion by geographical propinquity—hardly surprising, however, since the chief contacts of the daimyo and his advisers were not in the country with neighbours but in Edo with equals in rank.[4]

The formal founding of a fief school is not, however, a full measure of the spread of samurai education. There were often private schools available both before and after the fief school was established, and indeed a good many of the fief schools themselves remained, for many years after their foundation, little more than small private schools given assistance and a building by the fief.

For in the early part of the Tokugawa period education was entirely a matter of personal contract between an individual teacher and his pupil. If one wished to study more than one subject one found more than one teacher. Those who were especially serious about the matter, and particularly those who had the intention of becoming professional scholars themselves, might board with the teacher—just as an apprentice would board with a master craftsman.

Many of the fief schools were in origin simply private schools of this kind given assistance and finally adopted by the fief (the assistance not necessarily being confined to a single school—in

---

[1] *Keizai mondō hiroku* (*NKS*, 22), p. 58.

[2] Yokoyama, *Kinsei kyōikushi*, p. 754.

[3] It may also be, as Ernest Gellner has pointed out to me, that the larger fiefs had a greater likelihood of containing the critical men of initiative and love of learning —if one assumes that those qualities were randomly distributed in the population.

[4] Though there must have been some examples of local contagion. The Hasuike school, for example, is said to have been modelled on the nearby Kumamoto school (*NKSS*, 3, p. 179).

the early stages at least).[1] Frequently these seedling schools were run by the *jusha*, the Confucian scholars employed as advisers to the daimyo. The Hayashi school in Edo is a typical example. When it was first built (with a Bakufu subsidy) in 1630 it was a private school of the Hayashi family. After it was rebuilt on a more splendid scale in the 1690s it became a Bakufu establishment as far as the fabric was concerned and gave officially sponsored lectures for Bakufu retainers, but the taking of regular pupils was still a private matter for the Hayashi family. A century later it was taken over more completely by the Bakufu, which thenceforth directly appointed its teachers and controlled the curriculum.

Not all schools developed in this way from the fief's own resources. A scholar of some distinction might be invited by a daimyo to take service in his fief, given a large house and an income to allow him to take pupils. Sometimes the primary purpose of such invitations was to provide periodic lectures on the classics for the adult samurai of the fief. In such cases a lecture hall was often the first school building proper to be built, the regular instruction of full-time pupils being rather a secondary occupation which the teacher carried on in his private home. Sometimes, again, since one of the important functions of the Confucian scholars in the employment of daimyos was to act as tutors to their heirs, they were stationed at the fief residence in Edo (where daimyos had to keep their families) rather than in the fief itself. Consequently, schools were often started at the Edo residences for the children of the samurai stationed there, as well as in the fief itself, and in some cases the Edo school came first.

Personal discipleship, rather than institutional membership, remained the dominant principle of organization of perhaps the majority of fief schools at the end of the period. The pupil was a pupil of a particular teacher, rather than of the school, though he might pass from the hands of one teacher to another

---

[1] The Fukuoka fief, for example, at first provided buildings for two schools each run by one of the two Confucian scholars (of violently differing scholastic persuasion) employed by the daimyo (*NKSS*, 3, p. 8). The Nihonmatsu fief at one time gave its support to seven different teachers before founding the school which itself was little more at first than a building which the various teachers could use in turn (*NKSS*, 1, pp. 688–90). Ishikawa gives more examples, usually of sharing arrangements within the same building (*Gakkō-shi no kenkyū*, pp. 435–42).

as he progressed. The teacher prescribed his course of study and if he were ill his pupil would have to wait until he recovered. If fees were paid they were paid directly by pupil to teacher. But a good many schools, and most of those in the larger fiefs, had been transformed by a process of gradual rationalization. A clear distinction came to be recognized between the apprentice training of a small group of would-be professionals or dedicated amateurs on the one hand, and the provision of comprehensive instruction for large numbers of children on the other. In order to accomplish the latter task there had to be an increasing standardization of a curriculum prescribed for the school as a whole rather than by individual teachers, and a division of the school into grades through which pupils advanced in accordance with their age and ability.

The Yonezawa fief school is one of which considerable details have survived, and being fairly typical of the larger and better organized schools it will serve well enough as an example.[1] It was in a fief of medium-to-large size (150,000 *koku*) whose ruling family, the Uesugi, was traditionally noted more for its military prowess than for its love of learning. Unlike the edicts of the Tokugawa with their insistence on the importance of 'both the way of Bun and the way of Bu', the rules for the guidance of samurai issued by the early Uesugi daimyos urge them to develop their fighting skills without even a polite nod in the direction of Bun, the civil arts. It is not until 1679 that a grudging addendum to this exhortation suggests that 'what time they have to spare' should be devoted to book learning and the more ceremonial and less useful military arts such as archery.[2] A few years later, however, under the influence of Tsunayoshi's example, the fief gave its support to a private school run by its Confucian scholar. It declined as most such private schools did —sons did not always inherit the talents of their fathers—but it was ostensibly at least[3] as a revival and enlargement of this private school that the Kōjokan was built in 1776. (In a traditionally oriented society, where antiquity sanctions all, expensive ventures invite less criticism if they can claim not to

---

[1] See *NKSS*, 1, pp. 729–826. The following description is based on these documents unless otherwise stated.
[2] Uno and Ototake, *Hangaku shidan*, p. 416.
[3] Saitō, *Nijūrokuhan*, p. 648.

be entirely new.) Like most other schools it had its ups and downs; there were times when its teachers were highly respected, its pupils numerous and financial help from the fief generous. There were other times when it had to struggle with only meagre success against hostile neglect.

In the late 1820s the school was recovering from one of these periods of neglect, in part the result of an economy drive prompted by crop failures and a crippling temple-building project imposed on the fief by the Bakufu. A new head professor had been appointed—a pupil of Koga Seiri, one of the scholars brought into the Bakufu school to revitalize it and firmly establish the supremacy of the Sung Confucianist doctrines during the reforms of the 1790s. The system of instruction then worked out lasted with few changes until the Restoration.

The school, burned down and rebuilt several times in the course of its history, was a congeries of single-storey thatched buildings occupying an enclosure of about four acres. The main lecture hall and attached building covered about a third of an acre; in addition there were a Confucian shrine, a library, a smaller medical school, teachers' houses, offices and dormitories.

The latter housed the *shosei*, some twenty young samurai between the ages of twenty and thirty who had shown an aptitude and a zeal for learning. They were drawn exclusively from the four upper ranks of samurai; the two lowest ranks and the *ashigaru* foot-soldiers were not eligible. Their appointment as shosei was for a three-year term, which, however, could be extended by one or two years. They were boarded at fief expense, being teachers as well as students. After graduation some went for further study in Edo; most eventually became either regular teachers at the school or officials of the fief administration.

Theirs was a strict regimen—at least if the rules by which they were guided were at all conscientiously followed. Their day began at dawn when the monitor for the day rose to tour the dormitories with a pair of clappers, calling each of his fellows by name until he received an answer. After they had washed themselves and cleaned the dormitories all the shosei would repair to the lecture hall for their morning's first task— the instruction of the younger day-students, mostly between the ages of six and fourteen, in the reading of the basic Chinese classics, the Four Books. Each of the shosei had his own students —the personal relation between teacher and pupil was important here, too—and a popular teacher might have many times the number of a less popular colleague. Each in his own corner of the large lecture hall would take his students individually, or in groups of two or three, in the order in which they arrived at the school, going over the page or half-page that made up that morning's lesson, giving them an interval to master it and then having them back again for a final check. If he was not feeling well a shosei could get permission to receive older students in the dormitories but not (a precaution, perhaps, against seduction?) younger students.

The monitor for the day would not teach his students. His duties, conducted under the supervision of the two senior shosei who held the positions of Lecturer Supervisor (*Tokō*) and Registrar (*Tenseki*) were onerous. He had to stay in the office, direct the cleaning activities of the porter and the servant, and keep the log-book in which were recorded details of the weather, the phases of the moon, notes of all visitors, letters or messages coming to the school, and records of eclipses, earthquakes or other unusual happenings. He had to be particularly careful about etiquette, wearing formal broad-shouldered *kamishimo* on the various festival days and being careful, when he saw visitors off the premises, to make his parting bow at a distance inside the outer gate appropriate to the visitor's rank. It was his duty to warn the more senior lecturers of the time lectures were to begin, summon the students with his clappers and then inform the lecturer when the class was assembled and ready to receive him. During lectures he had occasionally to leave the hall and make a tour of the dormitories. He had to see that the dormitory rules were obeyed—no *sake*-drinking (except for small medicinal doses before retiring in privileged cases), no heating apparatus, no congregation of more than three people in one room, and so on. At night it was his duty to order lights-out about an hour before midnight, to tour the dormitories to make sure that his call was obeyed, and then to tour them again at midnight when he finally locked up for the night.

After an hour or so teaching the younger pupils, the clappers would sound again to summon the shosei to their breakfast.

Such summonses, the rules said, were to be obeyed immediately, but with no unseemly rush; there was to be no rude and noisy opening of doors and partitions. The quality of their meals varied according to the financial health of the fief. As a rough indication it appears that around 1800 the cost of the shosei's meals was distributed approximately in the proportions: ten parts for rice, ten parts for *miso* bean-paste, and three parts for vegetables.

After breakfast the shosei would return to the lecture hall, this time for their own study. They would be joined by another group of boarders, the *kijukusei*, who sometimes numbered as few as five, sometimes as many as thirty. These, unlike the specially selected shosei, had no duties to perform, and they were boarded at their own expense, though at some periods particularly promising students among them were given free board. Any samurai of the upper four ranks who applied could be admitted as a kijukusei if he had sufficiently progressed in his studies as a day-boy. One or two of the senior teachers would supervise these morning sessions. There were usually three or four of these, one or two Professors (*Teigaku*) and one or two Assistant Professors (*Jokyō*). They were generally from families which made a hereditary profession of scholarship or were appointed from the ranks of lower samurai. On appointment their hereditary stipends were supplemented to give them an income of 125 and 100 *koku* respectively, though one of the Professors was usually *de facto* Director with a salary made up to 200 *koku*. Particularly outstanding Professors were given the full title of Director (*Sōken* or *Tokugaku*) with an income of 250 *koku* or more. These posts were not usually filled, however. The Assistant Professors lived in the school compound, the Professors were later allowed to live outside.

In the hall the shosei and kijukusei would take their seats strictly in order of age seniority, regardless of rank. Each brought the book he was currently studying—for the most part Chinese histories and the more difficult classics. At this stage students relied chiefly on the resources of the school library (unlike the younger students who were expected to acquire their own copies of the more elementary texts). At the time of the Restoration the library is said to have contained about 700 Chinese 'works' (including nearly two hundred collections of

77

separate works) but how many duplicate copies this included is not indicated. In these morning sessions the shosei busied themselves with private study, usually reading aloud to themselves as they went along, though during periods of mourning for members of the daimyo's family, and for the afternoon preceding and the actual day of death-anniversary rituals at the daimyo's palace, silent reading was obligatory. As they read the teachers would summon them in turn for private guidance and questioning on what they read.

On most days this continued until lunch-time, but on the three and eight days (i.e. the 3rd, 8th, 13th, 18th, etc., of each month) the latter half of the morning would be taken up with 'group reading'. The students became a class rather than a group of individuals. Three would be chosen by lot to read two or three passages of a prepared text—usually one of the more difficult writers such as Hsün Tzu or Chuang Tzu, or the T'ang collection of Chinese political maxims, the *Chen-kuan cheng-yao*.

In group reading the purpose was simply to construe the text by accurately 'reading it off' in the peculiarly barbarous dialect of Japanese which was designed for this purpose. There were also 'group discussions', however, held at the same time on the four and nine days, and these were concerned with the meanings and the 'lessons' of the texts. Again three students were chosen by lot and expected to expound the significance of passages, usually drawn, for this purpose, from the *Analects* or from *Mencius*.

Meanwhile, a larger group of day-boys had arrived at another lecture hall soon after breakfast. At some periods there were several hundreds of them. These, as distinct from the pre-breakfast younger pupils, were known as the 'self-readers' (*jidokusei*), and were usually over fifteen by Japanese reckoning (that is to say at least in their thirteenth year, since the Japanese counted in ages all calendar years, through the whole or part of which one had lived, so that someone born on the last day of the year would be fifteen the day after his—Western-style—thirteenth birthday. On the average the Japanese reckoning adds one and a half years to one's age.) These were students who had completed the basic reading of the Four Books and were allowed to read by themselves under supervision in much the same way as the shosei, though at a more elementary level. Three of the senior shosei with the title of Reading Assistant (*jodoku*) had charge of these pupils, one of them supervising the morning session each day. They were assisted by other teachers engaged *ad hoc* from outside the school and by five Upper-Seat Students (*jōsekisei*) chosen from the most able of the jidokusei themselves. The latter were paid no salary, but they were rewarded for their efforts at the end of the year by a meal, with *sake*, sent down from the daimyo's kitchen. (The modern counterpart of this traditional and rather inexpensive way of rewarding inferiors was the practice, common until 1945, of distributing Imperial *sake* and Imperial cigarettes to troops before and after battles.)

For a short period after their arrival the jidokusei were allowed freely to ask questions of their teachers. From about mid-morning they settled in their seats for the formal session, being called to their teacher individually or in small groups, and otherwise reading by themselves until lunch-time. After another hour or so of free study and free questioning their school day was over, though most of them then set out for the booth of a teacher of swordsmanship, the lance, archery or horsemanship in the near-by military school. Six times a month they, too, had sessions of 'group reading' or 'group discussion' in place of the morning's free-reading session. For this purpose they were divided at first into two, later into three, grades, those aged by Japanese reckoning fifteen to seventeen, those aged eighteen to twenty and those aged twenty-one or more, the upper limit usually being twenty-four or twenty-five. These age limits were not rigidly fixed, however, and bright students could reach the upper grades at an earlier age. The problems of discipline in the free-reading sessions must sometimes have been considerable since there were frequent admonitions against gossiping and moving about the room.

On the two and seven days the morning sessions were preceded, immediately after breakfast, by formal lectures given by one of the Professors or Assistant Professors. These were attended by all the students, both day-boys and boarders, and sometimes by older samurai as well, though their attendance was usually limited to the more ceremonial lectures held twice a year after the spring and autumn ceremonies at the Confucian shrine.

79

Students were expected to bring a text—usually one of the Four Books—in order to follow the lecturer's exposition.

Three times a month, on the ten days, a lecturer in etiquette came to the school and held a practice session in the latter half of the morning—again for all students, both boarders and day-boys—demonstrating table manners, ways of giving and receiving presents, and ceremonial bows and formulae for all occasions.

Another regular event was the afternoon poetry session held on the eight days, three times a month. These were primarily for the boarding students, though senior day students could also take part if they wished. The teacher—one or more of the Professors or Assistants—set a topic and judged the grammar and style of each student's effort. This was followed by a slightly more lavish evening meal than usual, with a small allowance of *sake* when the fief budget could afford it.

This regular monthly time-table was interrupted by a number of festivals and holidays; there were no classes during the last ten or the first fifteen days of each year, during the five days before each spring and autumn ceremony at the school's Confucian shrine, during the Bon celebrations in mid-summer and for a period before the annual examinations. There were also one-day holidays for various annual festivals and for such occasions as the arrival and departure of the daimyo on his yearly trips to Edo. In the summer, depending on the weather, midday and afternoon classes might be cancelled for a period of two or three months. The shosei were allowed six twenty-four-hour holidays each month; they could choose their day, but new regulations in 1866 forbade the taking of holidays on the days when group discussions or poetry sessions were held. They could also get leave for a variety of other reasons which the regulations minutely prescribed—three days for getting married, three days if one's father was to set out for distant parts on official business (one day only if he was going on private business), appropriate periods for the mourning of relatives, and so on.

Most of the disciplinary offences which were listed as deserving punishment for the shosei concerned such taking of leave and failure to complete the necessary formalities. The punishment consisted of confinement to dormitories; the gravity of the offence being measured by the number of meals which had to be taken alone, deprived of the society of one's fellows. Thus, returning late from leave, or reporting one's intention of taking leave only to the Lecture Supervisor and not to the day's monitor—or vice versa—were one-meal offences; taking mourning leave for a second-cousin on the pretext that he was a first-cousin was a three-meal offence. On release from confinement the shosei had to put on semi-formal dress and make an apologetic call on the senior Professor and the Lecture Supervisor. What offences the day-boys were prone to is not recorded, but they could be punished by suspension for a number of days, and in the last resort by expulsion.

The examinations were formal affairs. For the day-boys they were held in November, and the shosei gave up their own studies for two months beforehand to help them in their preparation. First came the 'internal' examination—in effect an eliminating contest. Each student was summoned before the examiners and given a passage from the books he had studied either simply to read, or to expound, according to the stage he had reached. Examination etiquette was precise. Students of the two upper ranks of samurai were allowed to remove their short sword after they had moved to their place before the examiners in the centre of the room. Those of the next two ranks had to remove it at the entrance before they moved to the centre of the room. The next rank, as well as removing their sword at the entrance, had to kneel not more than one mat's length within the room, and the next rank half a mat, while such luckless footsoldiers as were emboldened to enter such exalted company had to leave their sword in a waiting-room and proceed no further than the threshold of the room itself. Students (of the upper four ranks only) who proved the most able in these trial runs were selected to appear at the more formal examinations, held, either in the school or at the castle, in the presence of the daimyo or his chief minister and a retinue of other officials. These followed the same pattern. It seems that all who were selected to appear on these grand occasions received a first prize of approximately a gallon of *sake*. According to one record for the year 1807 there were sixty-seven such students. There were two other grades of prizes for students designated 'filial, respectful and diligent in their studies'; a full meal from the diamyo's kitchen (given to eighty-three students in 1807) and a partial meal (given to 104). It is not clear whether there were students who got no prize. In later years, however, the number of prizes was drastically reduced to a dozen first prizes and about thirty full or partial meals; this, less in order to stimulate competition than as a measure of economy.

The shosei were examined in the second month of the year and were allowed to give up their teaching duties for a month beforehand. They, too, were given a similar oral examination in the presence of the daimyo or his chief minister. They, however, had no trial run and received no prizes. They were professionals.

Even more formal than the examinations were the spring and autumn Confucian ceremonies, held around the equinoxes in quite strict imitation of Chinese practices. These, too, were usually attended by the daimyo and a large retinue and centred on the school's shrine housing images of Confucius and a number of his direct disciples. The ceremonies were lengthy, the more so since each participant—and there were many involved in the long procession bearing offerings to the shrine— had to perform with slow dignity a carefully regulated routine which included marks of respect not only to the shrine but also to the daimyo and any other superiors present. The ceremonies included, besides the offerings (of grains, fruit, nuts, fish and swords), the reading of the daimyo's invocation to Confucius by the head of the school, the ceremonial drinking by the daimyo of *sake* taken from the altar, and two lectures on passages from the *Analects* by the senior Professor, one from the shrine itself and another in the lecture hall after the daimyo had been given time for a change of clothes. After the daimyo's departure each of the students made his own individual obeisance at the shrine. Their reward was a free lunch with what was left over of the *sake*.

The students paid no fee, though they were expected to make presents to their teachers on entering the school, and twice annually, at the end and at the beginning of each year. The initial present—called *sokushū* after Confucius's 'bundle of dried meat' ('Even down to the man who brings his bundle of dried meat, I have never refused instruction to anyone')—was usually a gift of fans presented as a token of entering discipleship, to the senior Professor by the shosei, and to their particular shosei teachers by the day-pupils. The year-end and new year presents—usually dried fish or rolls of cloth or of paper—were presented collectively by the boarding students and cost each student the value of approximately five days' rice. The other students gave similar token gifts to their own particular teachers.

The senior of the Professors had charge of the instruction given at the school, but he by no means had administrative autonomy. The school was for administrative purposes under the command of a number of senior samurai officials, all superior in rank to the Professors. One Minister, one Councillor, one Junior Elder, and one official each from the Treasurer's department and the General Affairs section of the fief bureaucracy were appointed to oversee the school. Appointments of teachers came through this chain of command, as did more detailed regulations, such as orders to the effect that shosei were not to receive leave to attend memorial services for cousins. The school had no budget distinct from the general fief budget. All food, firewood, candles and paper were supplied in kind by the fief office which also saw to the repair of buildings and, on application, provided labourers for such tasks as the weeding of the compound. Two low-ranking samurai with an office in the school acted as quartermasters to keep account of all these transactions and to make applications for supplies.

These rules and regulations of the Yonezawa school cannot convey a full impression of the general atmosphere which prevailed. They do, however, indicate one important constituent of that atmosphere—the heavy weight of ceremonial and of formal bureaucratic regulations. Designed though it was to heighten the student's sense of the seriousness of the business of learning, it was hardly conducive to spontaneity or intellectual adventurousness, the more so since, from the beginning of the nineteenth century onwards, all texts used were those of the Sung Confucianist school and no discussion of varying interpretations was expected or even permitted. The teachers themselves, after all, were retailers of packaged knowledge, not participants in a developing branch of inquiry, and one could hardly expect them to convey a sense of intellectual excitement. The result was a petty formalism against which only a few bold spirits reacted. One was a shosei who is supposed one morning to have packed his bags, written his resignation, and posted on the wall of the dormitory a manifesto in which he denounced the masters and demanded their dismissal. They were, he said, more concerned with enforcing obedience to footling regulations than with education.[1] Another Yonezawa samurai who distinguished himself as a *rōnin* at the time of the Restoration (he chose to fight for the losing side, however) cut short his career as a day-student, withdrew to a temple in disgust and educated himself with books deviously borrowed from the school library.[2] By 1866 it was the general opinion that morale in the school was low and the Professors were required to make recommendations for a reform. Their diagnosis was chiefly that the students were lazy, content to get the general meaning of what they read without proper attention to detail, over-concerned with poetry and literature (which still left some room for individual creation) and generally lacking in a serious attitude to their work. The only cure they could suggest was a reduction in the number of holidays, official exhortations to diligence, more visitations by the daimyo or his ministers (they had become less frequent) and more sympathetic consideration by the fief authorities of the school's financial requests.

Variations: Attendance, Organization, Examinations

The organization of the Yonezawa school was fairly typical, though there were local variations in many respects. At Yonezawa attendance was a voluntary matter but in some fiefs towards the end of the period it became compulsory for certain classes of samurai—with sad results for learning as one critic pointed out. (Real scholars, he said, have always come from non-samurai ranks for the simple reason that non-samurai students are students for the love of it while samurai study from a reluctant sense of duty.)[3]

Where compulsion was applied it always weighed more heavily on the upper ranks and on eldest rather than younger sons, and it was very rare, indeed, for it to reach down into the ranks of the *ashigaru* foot-soldiers. (In some fiefs they were

[1] Saitō, *Nijūrokuhan*, p. 668.
[2] *Ibid.*, p. 669.
[3] Shōji Kōgi, *Keizai mondō hiroku*, p. 85.

not admitted at all;[1] even if they were it was rare for them to take advantage of the permission. As the report on the Yonezawa school says, 'they were too busy'.) At Mito, for instance, a scale of minimum attendance was laid down ranging from fifteen days a month for heads of households and eldest sons of the highest rank, to eight days a month for younger sons of the lowest rank of full samurai.[2] The theory was that those of higher ranks were destined to have heavier responsibilities and hence had greater need of education.

In most fiefs, as at Yonezawa, Chinese studies provided the core of the curriculum, but the process of grade division and standardization of the work of each grade was carried further in some. Often it went hand in hand with a system of examinations. It was the Bakufu which set the trend in this regard, and in the case of the Bakufu the examinations were standardized first and set the framework for later attempts to reorganize the teaching.[3] The Bakufu first held examinations for all who cared to volunteer in 1792[4] and they later became formalized into a double-banked system. The annual oral examinations were for those aged less than fifteen (by Japanese reckoning) and tested their ability simply to read the Four Books and the Five Classics, the standard number of books to be mastered by each age being specified. The written examinations, on the other hand, were held every three years (in clear imitation of the Chinese state examination system), and required exposition of the textual meanings of a greater range of texts, grouped for the purpose into four sections: a beginners' section, a classics section, a history section and a prose composition section, the last three being parallel specializations rather than stages of progression.

In its original conception the system of examinations was intended to encourage study among the samurai in general,

---

[1] E.g. in Chōshū (*NKSS*, 2, p. 658), Fukuoka (*NKSS*, 3, p. 46), Hikone (*NKSS*, 1, p. 373) and in Aizu after 1820 (Ogawa, *Aizu-han kyōiku-ko*, p. 44). In the Kashima fief the eldest sons only of the very top rank of *ashigaru* were ordered to attend (*NKSS*, 3, p. 186).

[2] *NKSS*, 1, p. 351. The Fukui fief had exactly the same scale of attendance (*NKSS*, 2, p. 11) and there were similar regulations at, among other fiefs, Tsu (*NKSS*, 1, p. 68).

[3] As is pointed out by Ishikawa, *Gakkō no hattatsu*, pp. 221–7.

[4] For the edicts announcing these examinations, see Takayanagi and Ishii, *Tempō shūsei*, pp. 415–16.

by awarding recognition and prizes to those who excelled. Any Bakufu retainer could apply. Eventually, however, it set standards for the organization of the Bakufu school. By the 1850s the lower school alone (for those under (Japanese) fifteen) was divided into seven grades corresponding to the examination grades, and the upper school was divided into a large number of groups which students entered according to the particular text they happened to be studying.[1] At the Hikone school there was a regular system of fourteen progressive grades.[2] Altogether, according to Ishikawa's count, by the time of the Restoration at least eighty-four schools had a basic division between the upper and lower schools and half of these had a more elaborate division into a larger number of separate classes.[3]

Generally, promotion from one grade to the next depended on age, but in some cases it is quite clear that also achievement counted. At the Aizu school there were clear regulations governing the standards required for passing from one of the four grades in the lower school to the next. The books which had to be mastered in each grade were specified, as was the number of mistakes which marked the dividing line between pass and failure. Students who were ready to advance at less than the standard age were re-examined in the presence of higher officials and rewarded with books as well as promotion.[4] In a few fiefs which did in this way prescribe grade standards and stick conscientiously to them there was special provision for the slower student. At Mito, for instance, an examination was required for entry into the upper school at about the age of (Japanese) fifteen. Those who failed to pass were required to go to school more frequently and their teacher had to present attendance records to the school office. (In Mito this lower school teaching was carried on in the homes of licensed teachers supervised by the school.) If they still had not qualified by the age of twenty they were moved into a special class where they read histories and suitably warlike novels written in Japanese.[5]

[1] NKSS, 7, pp. 101–2.
[2] NKSS, 1, p. 377.
[3] Gakkō no hattatsu, pp. 242–4.
[4] NKSS, 1, pp. 682–3. The Tsuchiura fief had a similar system (NKSS, 1, p. 359).
[5] NKSS, 1, pp. 350–3. The Hikone and Aizu fiefs had a similar 'remove' class (NKSS, 1, p. 377; Kasai, Hankō, p. 202).

However, a certain indulgence was shown to the duller students. In Kumamoto, too, an examination was held at the age of fifteen to test ability to enter the upper school, but students who reached the age of (Japanese) eighteen without qualifying were moved up regardless—unless they expressed a wish to remain longer in the lower school and work their passage.[1]

The increasingly common assumption that every samurai had to have a basic Chinese education (even where attendance was not compulsory it was generally expected that children would go to private schools or study at home) and the development of internal tests both from the necessity of rationalizing teaching methods and in order to titillate the student's sense of achievement, led naturally to the idea of graduating qualifications. No formal graduating certificates seem to have been used for Chinese studies (which is odd given the long-standing tradition of issuing 'proficiency certificates' and 'full licences' for excellence in the military skills), but a number of fiefs did lay down minimum standards of proficiency and impose sanctions on those who failed to meet them—disbarment from official appointments (as at Mito);[2] this plus a tax of two *ryō* of gold for every 100 *koku* of salary (at Aizu);[3] refusal of permission to succeed to a family headship (at the three Kyūshū fiefs of Fukuoka, Kashima and Kumamoto),[4] or if succession was permitted the reduction of hereditary stipends (at Saga, Tosa, Sakura and Toyohashi).[5] Usually these were temporary and curable disabilities, but Tatebayashi introduced a rule in 1856 that such reductions in stipend would be permanent if a family failed to produce a suitably qualified head for three successive generations.[6]

In some fiefs different standards of proficiency in Chinese studies were required of different ranks (the higher the rank the higher the standard) and usually there were parallel standards of skill required for swordsmanship and the use of the lance, though sometimes these were alternatives. Thus, at Sakura, one

[1] *NKSS*, 3, p. 211. At Tsuchiura the age for automatic promotion was seventeen *NKSS*, 1, p. 359).
[2] *NKSS*, 1, p. 354.
[3] Ogawa, *Aizu-han kyōiku-kō*, pp. xx, 37, 108. The system was introduced in 1788.
[4] *NKSS*, 3, pp. 11, 188, 210.
[5] *NKSS*, 3, p. 123; 2, pp. 906–7; 1, p. 253; 1, p. 143.
[6] *NKSS*, 1, p. 587.

could be put back on full salary again if one reached a certain standard in any one of the following: Chinese studies, military strategy, swordsmanship, the lance, etiquette or arithmetic.[1] In one or two cases the standards of achievement required were made explicit: a student was expected, for instance, to be able to read a specified number of books. (This was so at Aizu, Kashima and Sakura.) But generally the standards are vaguer, being defined as 'diligence' or 'suitable progress', combined often with good behaviour. The Kumamoto fief accepted the teacher's assessment that the student had or had not reached in Chinese studies a level which approximated to a full licence in swordsmanship,[2] while in Kōchi attendance for a certain minimum number of days a year over a number of years was enough.[3]

In most fiefs these rules were introduced in the last two or three decades of the period, though in Aizu they apparently date from 1788 and in Fukui, where they were introduced in 1856, they were spoken of as a revival of an order of the early eighteenth century which 'on compassionate grounds' the daimyo had allowed to lapse.[4]

Indeed, attempts such as this to give concrete administrative form to the ideal of the samurai as an educated man were bound to meet with difficulties in a particularistic society such as Tokugawa Japan and it is not surprising that 'compassion' was called for. The relation between pupil and teacher was supposed to be a close one in which the teacher played the role of guide and benevolent protector. It would be asking a great deal of such a teacher to assess his pupil as unworthy of succeeding to the headship of his family unless the latter's deficiency sprang from culpable recalcitrance rather than lack of ability— the more so since Tokugawa Japan was not a society which generally took a tough-minded, devil-take-the-hindmost attitude towards natural deficiences. (If it had, which of the grand families would have survived to the end of the period?) This is probably why the ideal was applied somewhat half-heartedly

---

[1] *NKSS*, 1, p. 253. There were similar alternatives at Fukue (*NKSS*, 3, p. 189) and at Aizu (Ogawa, *Aizu-han . . .*, p. 37).

[2] *NKSS*, 3, p. 210.

[3] *NKSS*, 2, pp. 906–7.

[4] *NKSS*, 2, p. 31.

and the standards usually left vague and discretionary, or even defined explicitly in terms of diligence and regular attendance. Where they *were* precisely defined in terms of achievement, in Aizu at least (where in general a rather more ruthless atmosphere prevailed than in most fiefs), superior samurai officials attended the tests of proficiency and so relieved the teacher of the burden of decision. We shall return to the role of competition in Chapter VI.

The difficulties and heart-burnings inevitable in such a system may also explain why at least three fiefs abandoned it. The Saga fief ordered reductions in stipends for those who failed to reach certain standards in 1850;[1] the Kōchi fief for those who failed to attend school regularly enough in 1845.[2] They both abandoned the system in 1859 on the grounds that it led merely to formal 'going through the motions'.[3] The Tatebayashi fief gave no reasons, but it, too, having instituted such a system (with the necessary qualifications clearly defined) in 1856, first modified it in 1860 and then abandoned it altogether two years later.[4] It is possible in all these cases, of course, that the changes result from shifts of power within the fief bureaucracies, not simply from the revision of policy in the light of experience.

Quite apart from individual tests used for qualifying purposes or for grade promotions, most fiefs also held the same kind of formal ceremonial examinations as at Yonezawa, opportunities for the fief authorities to demonstrate their benevolent concern for the school. Prize-giving was common, usually in the form of food, clothes or money, though a number of schools gave books[5]—usually as prizes for the particularly proficient; the average sensual student being given something he was more likely to appreciate.

Usually the value of the prizes depended on rank as well as performance. Thus, the Bakufu had two scales of prizes; one

---

[1] According to the documents in the *NKSS* (3, p. 123). Kume Kunitake speaks of the system having been started in 1827 though he does not provide supporting evidence (*Kaikoroku*, 1, p. 98).

[2] *NKSS*, 2, pp. 906–7.

[3] *NKSS*, 3, p. 124; 2, pp. 902–3.

[4] *NKSS*, 1, pp. 587–94.

[5] E.g. at Aizu (*NKSS*, 1, pp. 682–3), at Tsuchiura (1, p. 359), at Mito (1, p. 354), at Kaga (2, pp. 187–8), at Kuwana (1, p. 91) and at Iwamura (1, p. 478).

for students of families with the privilege of direct access to the Shogun, and a less lavish scale for those of lesser rank. Their efficacy as an encouragement to learning, however, was not proportionate to their economic value. It was the honour which mattered and it seems to have mattered very much indeed. Ota Nampo, for instance, a lower samurai of considerable talents, sought to redeem his youthful indiscretions as a novelist and writer of comic verse and volunteered for the second Bakufu examinations in 1794. He distinguished himself and was rewarded with ten pieces of silver. He seems to have been immensely impressed. Sophisticated adult though he was, he stowed them away in a luncheon box he had been given some years previously as a member of the Shogun's guard on a journey to Nikkō—a relic of the only other occasion he had received personal recognition from high authority—and preserved them for his descendants.[1]

The categories receiving prizes were generally quite broad—the purpose of these affairs was more often to encourage the average student than invidiously to single out exceptional excellence. It never seems to have been the practice to place students in numerical order; often there were two categories—the very good and the rest—or sometimes three—the very good, the good and the rest. Some schools had as many as nine grades of achievement in which students could be placed. At one of these, at Wakayama, the top three grades received prizes, the next three received commendations for their achievement, and the bottom three were commended for their efforts in taking the examinations.[2] In some schools regular attendance was enough to get a prize. Thus, at Kōchi, a complicated schedule of prizes was related to the number of days' attendance at the school or at military training establishments. One could reach the top prize—a personal gift from the daimyo—in twelve years by dint of attending two hundred days a year at the school and two hundred days for military training, or alternatively one hundred and three hundred days respectively. At a lesser rate of attendance it might take twenty-four years.[3]

[1] Tamabayashi, *Shokusanjin no kenkyū*, p. 521.
[2] *NKSS*, 2, p. 828.
[3] *NKSS*, 2, pp. 906–7.

Ceremonies

The spring and autumn ceremonies were also a regular part of the annual programme at most schools. According to Kasai's count, at least fifty-nine schools had a Confucian shrine in the school compound—very often the most lavishly appointed building of all—and at least 113 schools performed equinoctial ceremonies, either once or twice a year, whether they had a shrine or not. At another seventy schools similar ceremonies were performed at other times than the equinoxes—either at the beginning or end of the school year or at the winter solstice.[1] These *sekiten* ceremonies, as they were called,[2] were, of course, of Chinese origin, but their practice in Japan was not a Tokugawa innovation. The T'ang version of these rites was performed at the Japanese Imperial Court at least as early as 702 and they continued to be held regularly until the fifteenth century. When they were once again revived in the Tokugawa period Ming practices were followed at first under the influence of the Chinese scholar, Chu Shun-shui (1599–1682), who became an honoured refugee guest of the Mito daimyo. From the end of the eighteenth century, however, there was a general reversion to the more colourful T'ang style as it was recorded in the *Engishiki*, the Japanese compendium of ceremonies compiled in the Heian period.

Tokugawa daimyo often attached considerable importance to these rites. In not a few cases the building of a Confucian shrine actually preceded the building of a school[3]—Ieyasu's son, the daimyo of Owari, for instance, built Hayashi a shrine in Edo before the Bakufu built him proper premises for a school. Iemitsu himself attended a ceremony there (on his way back from a service at a Buddhist temple)[4] and from Tsunayoshi's time attendance at the ceremonies held in the new

---

[1] Kasai, *Hankō*, pp. 99, 110–11.

[2] The word is an abbreviation of *sekisai tempei*—the dedication of vegetable offerings and decoration with the ritual streamers (which were the substitutes for earlier animal sacrifices). The words *sekisai* or *sekisai no ten* are also used, though *sekisai* is properly a very abbreviated form of the ceremony. In China these rites were performed on many occasions during the year in Chou times, but by the Sui dynasty were generally confined to the equinoxes.

[3] E.g. at Sakura (*NKSS*, 1, p. 225). There is somewhere, apparently, classical authority for the view that this is the proper order of priority. The text is quoted by Nakayama Shōrei (*Gakusei-kō*, in *NKSS*, 5, p. 613).

[4] J. W. Hall, 'The Confucian Scholar', p. 289.

and more magnificent shrine which Tsunayoshi had built became a regular part of the shogunal calendar—though one which was often delegated to deputies.

Some among the daimyo—such as Ikeda Mitsumasa of Okayama—showed much more than a formal interest in these ceremonies; they were genuinely enthusiastic. One can only guess at their motives. The ceremonies were, of course, a natural expression of that attitude of pious reverence which was the keynote of Japanese Confucianism. Although the majority of Japanese Confucianists followed the Sung school, they were not altogether impressed by its philosophical attempts to provide a rational underpinning for the Confucian ethic and preferred to invest these doctrines with the absoluteness of a divine revelation whose revealers, the Sages, were proper objects of worship. Confucianism was the nearest thing Tokugawa Japan had to a 'religion' as the term is understood in Protestant northern Europe, combining an emphasis on ethical doctrine with an atmosphere of solemnity, awe and decorum. As Hall has pointed out, however, it never came near monopolizing the realm of the sacred for the Tokugawa military class; Buddhist and Shinto ceremonies still carried more weight in the average daimyo's ritual calendar.[1] But there was a division of function; each type of ritual had its own sphere of competence within the realm of the sacred. The daimyo's Buddhist rites (and Buddhist-influenced Shinto rites such as were held at the Tokugawa mausoleum at Nikkō) took care of his own personal fear of death and his hope of salvation, and expressed his awareness of, and sense of responsibility for maintaining, his family traditions; Shinto rites evoked his national consciousness, and his pride in his military traditions, improved his luck and acknowledged his dependence on the hazardous natural world; Confucian rites expressed his concern for (and helped perhaps to regulate) the social order; they affirmed his adherence to moral values which marked the difference between the virtuous and the wicked and kept men in good order.

Such a categorization, of course, was not made explicitly or deliberately, and some daimyo doubtless adopted Confucian ceremonies in much the same way as they had been adopted at

---

[1] J. W. Hall, 'The Confucian Scholar', p. 289.

the Imperial Court a thousand years earlier, as an impressive piece of pomp and circumstance which lent added dignity to a ruler's position, and as yet one more approved and tested piece of magic which helped to get the forces of the numinous on one's side—the more gods one appealed to, the greater the spread of one's risks.[1] There was certainly good Chinese authority for believing that Confucian rites helped to make the crops grow[2] and prevent natural calamities—something that was traditionally in the province of Shinto. But it was only in rare instances—such as Ikeda Mitsumasa's adoption of Confucian burial services—that Confucian rites invaded the sphere of Buddhism.

The rites had, of course, a more specific purpose when—as was almost always the case by the nineteenth century—they were held in schools. They served to impress on students the sanctity of the studies in which they were engaged. As one scholar put it, when urging his daimyo to build a shrine, the *sekiten* ceremony 'inculcates respect for the Way and teaches reverence for former teachers'.[3] By extension, too, it fortified respect for present teachers, an effect of considerable disciplinary advantage for which those teachers whose personal qualities made them least deserving of respect had most reason to be grateful.

In some fiefs the *sekiten* ceremony was associated with another ceremony in honour of the aged. This *yōrō no ten* traditionally followed the *sekiten* ceremony in China.[4] As the ceremony is described for the Akita fief[5] it was not much less formal than the *sekiten* ceremony, but it included a fairly liberal feast for the honoured elders of the fief—including both sexes and commoners as well as samurai, though they were feasted in different rooms. (At Omura, at least, the minimum honourable age varied according to rank. Upper samurai were feasted when they reached seventy; lower samurai had to wait until they

---

[1] A Hakata merchant who attempted to build a Confucian shrine in the Genroku period did so because prayers to Confucius had cured him of an illness (*NKSS*, 3, p. 21).

[2] Local farmers near the 'country school' of the Okayama fief at Shizutani believed, according to a local guide, that the particular quality of the creak made as the doors of the Confucian shrine swung open during the ceremony had a good deal to do with the quality of that year's rice crop.

[3] Nakayama Shōrei of Kumamoto (*Gakusei-kō*, *NKSS*, 5, p. 613).

[4] See Couvreur, *Li Ki*, 1, p. 469, and for the forms the ceremony is supposed to have taken under different dynasties, 1, pp. 316–17, 648–52.

[5] *NKSS*, 6, pp. 71–3.

were eighty.)[1] At Akita the assembled elders also had read to them a little homily pointing out that the purpose of the ceremony was to provide a model for the proper respectful treatment of the aged. They were given copies to take home so that the admonition should reach the right quarters. Students of the school had the task of serving at the feast, and this, and the implicit lesson in filial piety, was the point of having the ceremony at the school. At least six fief schools held such ceremonies regularly;[2] more may have held them irregularly. Matsudaira Sadanobu describes one he gave at his school in 1795. He invited his aged guests to exchange poems with him, and it seems altogether to have been a somewhat more genial affair than at Akita.[3]

There was always a certain uneasiness about Japanese Confucianism, a suspicion made explicit by such men as Yamaga Sokō, Yamazaki Ansai and later the whole Kokugaku movement, that perhaps this acceptance of things Chinese was not entirely patriotic. Though dormant, a national consciousness was there, nourished by memory of the Mongol invasions, of the Christian menace, perhaps by a sense of guilt about Hideyoshi's invasion of Korea,[4] and certainly, towards the end of the period, by a growing awareness of the pressures of the Western world. It found mild ceremonial expression at some schools in the addition of Japanese saints to the pantheon of Sages and wise men honoured in the school shrines. Thus, at Okayama, the portrait of the founder of the school, Ikeda Mitsumasa, was hung in the school shrine twenty-four years after his death.[5] In the Tsu fief Kibi no Mabi and Sugawara Michizane were included,[6] and one or other of these was found also in a number of other school shrines.[7]

[1] *NKSS*, 3, p. 185.

[2] Kasai, *Hankō*, p. 111.

[3] *Taikan zakki*, p. 195. He called his ceremony a *shōshikai*.

[4] Matsudaira Sadanobu, in a list of 'things to be regretted' in the manner of Sei Shōnagon's *Pillow Book*, includes 'that Toyotomi Hideyoshi invaded Korea' (*Taikan zakki*, p. 292). It is possible, however, that it was the expedition's failure rather than its aggressive intent which was the subject of regret.

[5] Okayama-ken Kyōiku-iinkai, *Kyōikushi*, 1, p. 91.

[6] *NKSS*, 1, p. 85. An additional reason at Tsu was that both had been governors of Ise province in which the fief was situated. There is said to have been a good deal of opposition when the proposal to add them to the shrine was first mooted (Uno and Ototake, *Hangaku-shi-dan*, p. 8).

[7] Kasai, *Hankō*, p. 108.

These, however, were honoured as Japanese *Confucian* saints. They had played a large part in bringing Confucian learning to Japan; Kibi no Mabi was supposed to have been responsible for the introduction of the *sekiten* ceremony itself and Sugawara Michizane was a renowned calligrapher and scholar, known to generations of school children as the Shinto god Tenjin-sama, a patron saint of learning worth praying to before examinations. The mere addition of such Japanese Confucianists to the pantheon was therefore, from the nationalist point of view, only a half-measure and it was condemned as such by Fujita Tōko (1806–55) who adds that it is the more deplorable in that Kibi no Mabi is justly suspected of disloyalty to the throne.[1] In Fujita's fief, Mito, a more radical departure was made. A Shinto shrine was built in the school compound and by its location given precedence over the Confucian shrine.

Bun and Bu, the civil and the military arts, the two wheels of the chariot, the two wings of the eagle, were equal constituents of the Way of the Tokugawa samurai, and if it had to be admitted that Bun came from China, Bu at least was an entirely indigenous product. The gods from whom the warriors of the sixteenth century sought protection were Shinto gods (even though their shrines might actually be managed by Buddhist priests), and still in the Tokugawa period it was by Shinto gods that daimyo swore their oath of fealty to the Shogun and pupils of swordsmanship to their teacher.[2] In building a shrine in the school compound the Mito fief was giving symbolic expression to the doctrine of the equal importance of Bun and Bu, and to the particular Mito Confucian doctrines which tried to integrate the Confucian and the Shinto traditions. As the matter is phrased in the famous Mito school charter—a sacred text of some of the less attractive forms of modern Japanese nationalism—'We hold to the Way of the Land of the Gods and base ourselves on the Way of the Western Land (i.e. China). Loyalty and Filial Piety are one. Bun and Bu are indivisible. Study and practical affairs are not to be separated.'[3] Take Mikazuchi no kami, the Shinto god honoured in the Mito shrine was a particularly suitable choice for the purpose, apart

[1] *Hitachi-obi*, p. 491, quoted in Kasai, *Hankō*, p. 108.
[2] See the example given in Kasai, *Hankō*, p. 143.
[3] *NKSS*, 5, p. 636.

from the fact that his original main shrine was in the Mito district. He had been, according to the legends, a paragon of loyalty and military valour, and had become a favourite war-god of the Japanese warrior. Fujita explains that it might have seemed more appropriate and to have made a better parallel with the worship of Confucius, to dedicate a Shinto shrine to an Imperial ancestor, but Nariaki, the Mito daimyo, thought it more suitable that loyal servants of the Emperor should honour, and take as their model, a god renowned as a loyal *servant* of one of the Emperor's divine ancestors.[1]

A number of other fiefs honoured Take Mikazuchi no kami, or similarly warlike figures of legend such as Yamato Takeru no mikoto or Takenouchi no Sukune, sometimes in a special shrine built near the military training sheds,[2] sometimes worshipped with Confucius himself.[3] A few fiefs, stressing more the Japan-as-well-as-China rather than the Bu-as-well-as-Bun aspect, honoured Shinto deities not particularly known for military prowess,[4] and the Kuwana fief recognized its proximity to Ise by having no images of Confucius. Its rituals centred instead on a tablet from the Ise shrine, set in an alcove of the main lecture room.[5]

Military Training

At Yonezawa the military training establishments were separate from the school, but in a number of fiefs they were all brought into the school compound, each teacher being given his own separate training shed, usually ranged around the edge of the compound with archery butts, riding grounds and often swimming pools near by. Thus the Tsu fief had four jūjutsu sheds, three for gunnery, one for archery, three for riding, one for strategy, three for the lance, three for swordsmanship and one for the halberd. Since military arts were exclusively taught on an individual teacher-pupil basis there was no strong reason for concentrating them in a single establishment, especially

---

[1] *Hitachi-obi*, pp. 490–1.
[2] E.g. at Numazu (*NKSS*, 1, p. 206).
[3] E.g. at Kanō (*NKSS*, 1, p. 478).
[4] E.g. at Morioka (*NKSS*, 1, p. 705) which enshrined Onamuchi no kami, another name for the Izumo deity, Okuni-nushi no kami.
[5] *NKSS*, 1, p. 90.

since there was still a great deal of esoteric mystery attached to such training and teachers were reluctant to have their secrets exposed to any but disciples bound to them by an oath of loyalty. However, the advantages of easy control, the desire to emphasize the equal importance of *Bun* and *Bu*, and the convenience of students who, after the age of (Japanese) fifteen, were usually expected to spend their mornings in book-work and their afternoons practising military skills, led an increasing number of schools to concentrate everything in one establishment. The Okayama school was a rare exception in combining both Chinese studies and military training from its foundation in the seventeenth century. There were still only about fifteen such schools by the beginning of the nineteenth century but by the time of the Restoration their number had grown to around sixty,[1] and in a number of other fiefs—as at Yonezawa—separate concentrated military establishments had been built close to the school.

Ages

The common age for entry into these schools was, by Japanese reckoning, eight to ten, though the Hikone fief was exceptional in expecting students to start—apparently from scratch as far as Chinese studies were concerned—at the age of fifteen. It was also exceptional in taking account of full ages calculated in the Western manner. Children had to apply for entrance at the age of (Japanese) fifteen, but attendance was not compulsory if they had not yet reached the age of full fourteen years.[2] In most schools the Japanese age of fifteen, usually the time for the *gempuku* ceremony which symbolized with a suitable ritual and a change of name the boy's entry into manhood,[3] marked a change in the child's educational life—from mere parrot-like reading of the classics to an attempt actually to understand

[1] Kasai, *Hankō*, p. 142.
[2] *NKSS*, 1, pp. 379–80.
[3] The age for this ceremony seems to have varied greatly in earlier times. Two of the early Tokugawa Shogun went through it at the age of five, but in the Tokugawa period fifteen seems to have been the general age—still too early according to Ogyū Sorai, who thought that early *gempuku* only encouraged a superficial precocity and produced children who were supposed to be men but were only capable of being complaisant to their superiors. *Taiheisaku* (*Nihon bunko*, 2), p. 42.

them. It was also the age at which training in the military skills was generally expected to begin.

If entry into the school made a sharp change in a child's life, leaving it was a much more gradual affair. The work of the upper schools was mostly, as at Yonezawa, a matter of individual study or group discussions which one could miss without necessarily having to 'catch up' before the next occasion. The shosei students at Yonezawa were quite at liberty to miss classes on the days on which they took their permitted holidays. So leaving the school was often less a matter of a sudden break than of a gradual falling off in attendance. Where attendance of the young was made compulsory an upper age limit was often specified, but this did not mean that attendance at the school necessarily ceased at that limit. At Hikone the regulation was phrased in the form 'after the age of thirty attendance shall be voluntary' (except for students who had shown themselves lacking in diligence who were not to be released from compulsory duty until later).[1] At Mito the upper age was forty; though men who had reached a certain stage in their studies could exceptionally be released from the duty of compulsory attendance (at so many days a month according to rank) before that age.[2] At Omizo, a student once on the books of the school stayed there all his life since 'the cultivation of the Way of Bun and Bu is the lifelong duty of the samurai'.[3] Where upper age limits for compulsory attendance were specified they usually fell between twenty and thirty, though a few fiefs, such as Tsu, somewhat exceptionally set the upper limit at fifteen.[4] (All these ages are by Japanese reckoning.)

Boarders

At least 170 schools had some kind of boarding establishment like the one at Yonezawa by the 1870s.[5] They were not always built for the same purpose, however. The convenience of students who lived at some distance from the school was a very minor consideration, though they are mentioned as one class of

---

[1] *NKSS*, 1, p. 380.
[2] *NKSS*, 1, p. 354.
[3] *NKSS*, 1, p. 442.
[4] *NKSS*, 1, p. 79. The Ogaki fief was another (*NKSS*, 1, p. 465).
[5] According to Kasai's count (*Hankō*, p. 210).

boarder at, for instance, Saga.[1] Except in those few fiefs with extensive sub-infeudation or where there were still a number of *gōshi*—country samurai scattered through the fief, relatively few samurai lived with their families at any great distance from the school; for the most part they lived in the castle town where the school was situated. The point of having pupils boarded at the school was rather to keep them under closer and more disciplined supervision and so give them a chance for more intensive study.

A few fiefs considered this necessary for all samurai. At Ogi, for instance, all eldest sons had to board at the school between the (Japanese) ages of fifteen and twenty-four, and their meals were provided at fief expense. Younger sons could board if they wished—at half price. Altogether the school had 100 boarders and eighty day-students. More commonly, again on the principle that the upper samurai had more need of education, boarding was compulsory only for the upper ranks. This was so at Saga (where the students apparently objected when the scheme was instituted and had to be reminded of the gravity of their duties),[2] and also at Kashima where the upper four ranks had to board for three years and eldest sons of the next rank for two.[3] Saga provided all except rice for those with an income of less than 40 *koku*; Kashima half the total cost of meals regardless of rank and income, with a little more for those who showed themselves exceptionally diligent. At Mito, instead of a concentrated period of intensive study as boarders, all eldest sons of families with an income of more than 300 *koku* had to board at the school in groups of ten for two weeks a year between the (Japanese) ages of eighteen and twenty-four.[4] This was said to be so that they should learn, among other things, 'to eat plain food, taste hardships, and become acquainted with the conditions of the lower classes'.[5]

In most fiefs, however, the function of the boarding establishment was somewhat different; to give special training to a relatively small number—usually between fifteen and forty—of particularly apt pupils. They were very often boarded wholly or

---

[1] *NKSS*, 3, p. 135.
[2] *NKSS*, 3, pp. 121–2.
[3] *NKSS*, 3, p. 186.
[4] *NKSS*, 1, p. 351.
[5] Kasai, *Hankō*, p. 212.

partially at the fief's expense and frequently it was a part of their duty, as at Yonezawa, to teach younger students. (The so-called Lancaster system, which is hailed as a great innovation in British elementary education, seems to have been taken for granted in Japanese schools from the beginning.) Sometimes the regulations speak of the fief authorities 'ordering' such able students to become boarders, sometimes the phrasing specifies 'those who show aptitude and apply for permission' (and since all samurai were under military command, 'ordering', too, might include the granting of a request).

These students were destined to be the educated *élite* of the fief. Some of them would become professionals—either teachers in the fief school itself or men employed in an administrative post which required particular erudition. For this reason, and because many of these professional posts were of relatively low rank, the opportunity to enter dormitories of this kind was not, usually, limited to the upper ranks. Thus, at the Bakufu school, although admission was easier for upper samurai, a special point was made of admitting lower samurai (those who did not have the right of audience with the Shogun) if they 'were especially keen and seemed likely to be able to turn their gakumon to good use in the Bakufu service'.[1] In the Chōshū fief, one order of 1739 suggests that the fifteen pupils boarded at fief expense are to be mostly younger sons or *rōnin*—those, that is to say, who did not have an established hereditary place in the fief hierarchy and would therefore need to establish themselves by acquiring a professional skill.[2]

The Bakufu dormitories attached to the Shōheikō were exceptional in that they did exist largely for the convenience of out-of-town students. They are described in detail by Kume Kunitake who, as a young student from Saga, entered them in 1862.[3]

His first move, on arrival in Edo, was to get himself accepted as a personal pupil of Koga, one of the Shōheikō teachers. After this he soon got entrance to the dormitories since 'ever since the events of the 'fifties the serious desire to take up Chinese studies had become a rare phenomenon', and the dormitories were

[1] *NKSS*, 7, p. 161.
[2] *NKSS*, 2, p. 662.
[3] *Kaikoroku*, 1, pp. 523–8.

only 70 per cent full. Normally one would have had to wait one's turn, but he, as a personal pupil of Koga and as a Saga retainer, would in any case have had a high place on the waiting list. Each student had a two-mat space in an eight- or six-mat room, and normally students progressed by seniority from a dark 'back-mat' status to the position of 'front-mat' boy who could usually read by daylight on his mat even in winter. 'The dormitory had been built about fifty years earlier and, after generations of untidy students had been through it, it was a mess. The shelves were thick with dust, there were clutters of soya-sauce bottles and *sake* bottles and lamp-oil bottles' and— very different from the dormitory in his home fief in Saga— the students were careless in their dress, even when they went into the presence of their teachers. Meals (two a day) were of the simplest and paid for monthly according to the number taken, one of the students acting each month as caterer. Eating and cooking in the dormitories were forbidden, but happened. A dormitory feast was known as a '*Li chi* study group', after an apocryphal occasion when Koga Seiri had discovered some students in the act but out of the goodness of his heart had accepted their claim that they were studying the *Li chi* and complimented them on their midnight industry.

The meals worked out at seven-sixteenths of a *ryō* per person per month which, says Kume, was very hard on the poor students, many of whom were subsisting on an allowance of half a *ryō* a month. Farewell parties at a near-by restaurant whenever anyone left the dormitory cost another one-sixteenth *ryō*—sometimes earned by taking work as a copyist. They were gay affairs. Indeed, memoirs such as those of Kume serve to correct the impression, gained from reading school regulations and the exhortations of teachers, that Tokugawa education was entirely dampened by a wet blanket of moral seriousness. The favourite Chinese poems of Kume and his friends which stuck in his memory in later years were all about the tragic deaths of famous courtesans.

Discipline

The disciplinary problems of these schools seem to have been little different from those of schools anywhere else, though they were intensified, perhaps, by the fact that so much of the school day was spent in private study rather than in class teaching and by the special atmosphere of solemnity required for the study of what were, after all, sacred texts. 'The school is different from other places and it is even more important to preserve a proper decorum and be on your best behaviour', begin the disciplinary rules of the Tottori school.[1] The admonitions which occur most frequently are against quarrelling, talking during classes, running in corridors, banging doors and partitions, scrambling for clogs when leaving, talking or laughing in a loud voice, leaving one's seat without permission, illegally delaying one's return from the lavatory, abusive speech, late arrival, illegal absence, the offering of false excuses and, in one case, lewd talk of women.[2] The punishments employed were also much the same as educators devise anywhere; detention after school and the imposition of cleaning chores are the most common. Physical punishment was rare, though it was practised in at least three schools. The Isezaki school used the moxa cautery, commonly used in Sino-Japanese medicine. The little cone of powder burned on the skin, as well as inflicting pain, was also supposed to have a direct therapeutic effect in quelling rebellious spirits.[3] At Fukue a cane was used and the report on the school gives conscientious details to the effect that it was of bamboo, four to five feet in length, and used on the flesh of the elbows (very probably a misprint for the buttocks).[4] At Izushi caning was only for younger students, with a fixed scale of strokes related to the gravity of the offence; older students had to pay money fines.

Temporary suspension from the school was also a common punishment for older children, sometimes accompanied by confinement to the home. In fact, in the case of the adult pupil there was no clear distinction drawn between offences against the school rules and offences against the military discipline to which he was subject as a samurai; fines and house detention were simply applications of general military discipline. One fief had a reformatory in the school compound which housed all

[1] *NKSS*, 2, p. 446.
[2] The Hirado school (*NKSS*, 3, p. 173).
[3] *NKSS*, 1, p. 626.
[4] *NKSS*, 3, p. 191.

samurai who had disgraced themselves, whether regular pupils or not. There they were at first confined without baths or salt for anything up to three months. Thereafter their regime was relaxed somewhat; they could bathe and their food improved, but they were subject to a rigorous diet of reading and military training and firmly locked in their dormitories every night for anything up to two years.[1]

Suspension from the school was chiefly a matter of symbolic disgrace, and for younger pupils, too, shame was a sanction frequently appealed to. Pupils were summoned before superiors to be scolded, or held up to the disapproval of their peers by being isolated in separate seats, having their names posted on boards or, as at Kumamoto, having their name plaque 'turned over'. (The names of all the students were written on wooden tablets, black on red on one side and white on black on the other. They were hung on a board, normally with the red and black side turned up, except for defaulting pupils whose names stood out glaringly in black and white.[2]) In a number of schools bad-conduct registers were kept, and sometimes, also, good-conduct books for recording particularly praiseworthy behaviour. Tokugawa writers on education commonly insist that praise is a better educational weapon than punishment,[3] and Squeersism seems not to have been common. There was usually a general accounting at the end of the year and in Okayama, at least, reports were sent to parents indicating how many points the child had earned for good behaviour, for academic proficiency and for regular attendance and how many had to be subtracted for disciplinary offences.[4] It seems to have been rare for punishment to be used as a spur to learning, though the Kumamoto and Hirado schools at least did mark in the black book pupils' repeated failure to learn what they had been taught,[5] presumably on the assumption that abnormal slowness was voluntary and, as John Wesley held, 'every voluntary blockhead is a knave'.

---

[1] *NKSS*, 2, p. 361. (The Miyazu fief.) The reformatory was called a *tsutsushimi-dokoro*.

[2] *NKSS*, 3, p. 207.

[3] See, e.g. Nishijima Junzō, *Gakkan Ryakki* (*NKSS*, 5), p. 606.

[4] See the example given in Okayama-ken Kyōiku-iinkai, *Okayama-ken kyōikushi*, 1, p. 80.

[5] *NKSS*, 3, pp. 170, 207.

The Sages, while commending the wise use of rewards and punishments had also insisted, as Ogyū Sorai was never tired of pointing out, on the importance of institutional arrangements for keeping men naturally and painlessly in good order. Their Japanese followers sought in numerous ways to apply this principle in their schools. One points out the importance of insisting on correct dress and a spotlessly clean, and if possible architecturally imposing, lecture room as a means of inducing a sense of proper decorum in the pupil.[1] Many schools devised elaborate rules for determining seating positions and orderly methods for filing out of lecture rooms to the sandal lobby and the sword lobby. One problem arose from the fact that times were rather vaguely defined and pupils were expected to appear well before the appointed hour at which lectures were supposed to begin.

The system at the Tsu school was probably not uncommon in its reliance on a samurai disciplinary officer as distinct from the teacher and on its use of the written word to carry greater authority than mere verbal commands. Pupils were expected to arrive at five hours (which varied between six and seven-thirty according to the season). Each was provided with a wooden tablet inscribed with his name which he handed to the attendance officer on entering the room. He then went to his seat and busied himself with his work. The attendance officer stacked the tablets in strict order of arrival. About an hour later the teacher entered the class-room, and the attendance officer then began to call each child in the order indicated by his stacked pile of tablets to go to the teacher for his day's allotment of personal instruction. Meanwhile, as soon as the teacher entered the room, the disciplinary officer—another lesser samurai whose job it was to police all these goings on—set up in the room a large tablet on which was written 'Late'. Pupils who arrived after this had to present themselves to him, make their apologies and receive his reprimand. After another hour the disciplinary officer set up another tablet, this time inscribed 'Silence'. For the last hour of the session pupils were expected to work quietly, learning what they had been taught. If they wished to leave the room they had two choices in the form of wooden tablets marked respectively 'Tea' and 'Water'. If they

[1] Nakayama Shōrei, *Gakusei-kō* (*NKSS*, 5), p. 620.

wished to go to drink tea in the tea-room they set their tea
tablet upright on their desk and awaited the disciplinary
officer's nod. If they needed more water to make ink they set up
the other. Either, presumably, could serve as a euphemism for
the privy. Finally, at the end of the period, the attendance
officer read off the names from his pile of tablets, again in the
order of arrival, and the pupils left one at a time, taking their
name tablets as they went.[1]

One writer of a memorial to the daimyo of Hikone suggests
that another useful trick—in this case urged specifically as a
measure to cure habits of rough and lewd speech among the
students—would be to have a plain-clothes detective, a *kage-
metsuke*, who would be secretly appointed from among the un-
suspecting students and given the job of reporting offenders.[2]
Whether his advice was taken or not is not recorded, but some
schools did use another totalitarian device—or highly demo-
cratic device depending on one's point of view—to help solve
disciplinary problems. This was a system of pupil self-govern-
ment, the best-known example of which was that developed at
Aizu.

Pupils of the Aizu school were formed into 'ten-men groups'
(only approximately ten) of children whose homes were close
together. An older boy was selected as leader, and the group—
in effect a kind of licensed gang—was governed by his authority
under a code of honour which enjoined hostility towards
members of other gangs and willingness to avenge any insults
inflicted on fellow-members. Offenders against the code were
either ostracized (a fact of which the leader would formally
apprise the outcast's parents) or beaten—in some instances to
death. Every morning one member of the group had the task of
gathering the others from their homes. Once assembled they
marched together to the school under the command of their
leader. On arrival there was a prescribed ritual for passing up
their swords to the leader, who put them on the rack, and,
when they reached their places, for the exchange of formal
greetings between leader and followers. The leader kept the
attendance registers for the group, and during tuition periods
it was his permission that had to be obtained to leave the room.

[1] *NKSS*, 1, p. 78.
[2] *NKSS*, 5, p. 526.

He it was, also, who reprimanded his followers for any offences against the school regulations. After school he marched them home again and they spent the rest of the day in play together, though the leader was expected to hold occasional formal sessions at which he lectured the younger members on the importance of 'revering parents, respecting elder brothers, showing affection for younger brothers, revering teachers as if they were fathers and ... never mixing with members of other groups'.[1] It seems that similar groups were formed among the younger students at the Bakufu school and at Tatebayashi, though it is not clear whether they took quite the same totalitarian form as at Aizu.[2]

School Finance

None of these schools seems to have been financed out of students' fees; such payments as students made were, as at Yonezawa, formal personal gifts to individual teachers, or, for some boarding students, payment for their food. Getting himself educated was a part of the normal duty of the samurai to prepare himself for service to his lord, hence it was natural that his lord should provide the facilities. It was not something to be undertaken for personal benefit for which the beneficiary or his parents could properly be expected to pay.

Teachers' salaries were not an important part of school expenses since most teachers had a hereditary stipend, though by the end of the period salaries-for-the-job had become common and the majority of teaching appointments carried either a small flat-rate automatic salary, or a standard salary—hereditary stipends being made up to the standard amount if the incumbent's hereditary stipend was below it. In a good many fiefs, as at Yonezawa, these and other expenses were merged into the general finances of the fief, but in a number of cases the school had a separate account and a fixed source of income.

This might take the form of an annual grant in rice or money, or, according to the system prevailing in the fief, the apportionment of a certain number of villages as the school's property

[1] Ishikawa Ken, *Jidōkan*, pp. 244–85.
[2] *NKSS*, 7, p. 101; 1, p. 601.

(This *gakuden* system was based on Chinese practice.) In one or two cases where the building of a school was part of a general fief reform, the school was apportioned virgin land to be newly reclaimed. The Sendai fief tried to kill three birds with one stone in this way—to secure finances for the school, to improve the fief's resources in general, and to find some employment for younger sons of samurai who were to direct the reclamation and receive some of the tax income from the land when it was productive.[1] In the Sakura fief it would appear that tax rights in the land apportioned to the school (in 1849) were sold off to a merchant; at least the land (with a yield of 1700 *koku*) was capitalized at 4250 *ryō* of gold and the school received a 10 per cent annual interest from this fund.[2] A number of other fiefs made straight capital grants in money to fund the school's finances, the capital being either loaned on the Osaka market[3] or in penny packages to samurai in the fief.[4] Other methods were used by some fiefs; in Tottori a fairly substantial part of the proceeds of the fief wax monopoly was given to the school and at least two fiefs imposed a school tax on its samurai, the tax being graded according to income, but in neither case progressively or even proportionately.[5] In Hikone, for instance, a fief elder with 10,000 *koku* had to pay only six times as much as a samurai with fifty.

In nearly every case which can be checked the grants to schools showed a steady increase, particularly in the last twenty or thirty years of the period. The Saga school, for instance, received 150 *koku* in rice in 1781, but the amount had risen to 1000 by 1850.[6] The Chōshū fief school started with a modest 200 *koku* in 1719, but by 1849 this income had been supplemented by money grants worth about double that amount and these grants were then quadrupled the following year.[7] Such

[1] Kasai, *Hankō*, p. 152. It is possible that the younger sons were expected to farm the land themselves.

[2] *NKSS*, 1, p. 332.

[3] E.g. at Chōshū (*NKSS*, 2, p. 671).

[4] E.g. at Kaga (*NKSS*, 2, p. 204). One or two anxious directives suggest that the fief had trouble in collecting the interest from some of its samurai.

[5] See, for Fukui, *NKSS*, 2, p. 27, and for Hikone, *NKSS*, 1, p. 420. Hayashi Shihei once suggested that a small flat-rate tax should be levied on everyone in the fief, samurai and commoners alike (*Jōsho* (*NKS* 12), p. 10).

[6] *NKSS*, 3, p. 143.

[7] *NKSS*, 2, p. 751.

grants for the running expenses of schools were not, however, so very large in the general context of fief finances. The Kaga school, for instance, was given a flat-rate grant of 20 *kan* of silver annually from 1805 (about the same total as for the Chōshū fief before the expansion of 1850). But this was a small fraction of the total resources of the fief. A fief budget for 1791 shows that it had a 'free' income (i.e. after payment of all hereditary stipends of samurai, though not of foot-soldiers) of about 7000 *kan* of silver, and of this over 550 *kan* was spent on the single item of the daimyo's return journey to Edo and back.[1] The burden on some of the smaller fiefs may have been considerably greater, however, and the initial cost of buildings was something which might well discourage the daimyos of fiefs on the verge of insolvency.

There survives an itemized budget for the Chōshū fief school for the year 1797 which is worth recording (pp. 109–10) for the details it incidentally provides of the life of the school and the way it was administered. It will be seen that ceremonial expenses weighed fairly heavily on the budget.

Books and Libraries

The 'annual book-airing' mentioned in the budget was a measure of protection against the ravages of book-worms. Many schools had well-equipped libraries (though it is unlikely that they were often stocked according to Hayashi Shihei's broad-minded prescriptions to include 'recent novels, popular books, and battle tales').[2] Their rules carefully discriminated between books to be read only in the library, those to be borrowed for use in the school compound and those which could be taken home. Borrowed books had to be signed for and there were regular stock-takings, though not, apparently, any filing system. The Librarian, presumably, was expected to know his books.[3]

A good many schools—nearly fifty by Kasai's count[4]—also had printing presses of their own—a good many of them, perhaps, having been prompted to start them by the Bakufu's active example, or more particularly by a Bakufu edict to

[1] *NKSS*, 2, p. 205, and Heibonsha, *Sekai rekishi daijiten*, 22, p. 405.
[2] *Jōsho* (*NKS*, 12) p. 10.
[3] See the Saga library rules, *NKSS*, 3, pp. 131–3.
[4] *Hankō*, p. 125.

daimyos in 1842 urging that it was an example worthy of emulation.[1] There is no record that any of these presses succeeded in fulfilling Ogyū Sorai's ambitious plan to raise sufficient profits from the sale of books to finance a whole school.[2] Rather, a more common objective was to provide cheap sub-

CHŌSHŪ SCHOOL BUDGET: 1797[3]

	Koku
Rice Income	
Tax from school land (assessed yield 500 *koku*)	200.000
Budgeted Rice Expenditure	
Full meals of 15 boarding students, 1 administrative director, 1 assistant director, 1 accountant, 1 head janitor, 6 janitors. Half meals for 1 calligraphy teacher. Total: 25½ persons at 1.752 *koku* per person	44.262
Flour rice for the *sekiten* ceremonies	5.600
Occasional meals for music sessions, riding exhibitions, for helpers at the annual book-airing and for copyists occasionally employed in the library	7.925
Evening meals for the 30 subsidized students	7.394
Salaries: 5 teachers of Chinese and 15 of military skills at 3 *koku* p.a. 1 teacher of calligraphy, 1 of mathematics and 2 tutors at 1.8 *koku* p.a. 2 librarians and 1 clerk at 1.5 *koku* p.a. 2 shrine attendants at 1 *koku* p.a. All less 40 per cent salary cut	44.220
Honorarium: 1 bale of rice for each of 3 teaching assistants	1.314
Rats and other wastage	3.500

Total	114.219[4]
Balance of rice	85.781

Money Income	*Momme of silver*
Proceeds from sale of 85.781 *koku* of rice	5,045.94
Receipts from interest on invested funds	11,323.02
Total	16,368.96

[1] Yokoyama, *Kinsei kyōikushi*, p. 764.
[2] *Seidan* (*NKT*, 9), p. 189.
[3] *NKSS*, 2, 671–2.
[4] The accountant was not very good at arithmetic. Presumably the rats ensured that he was never found out.

Budgeted Money Expenditure

Repairs to school buildings	1,088.70
Offerings for *sekiten* ceremonies, paper, ink, brushes, tea, candles, whale oil, crockery, cleaning cloths, tobacco pipes, cooking pots, rain-capes for janitors	1,647.26
Equipment for military training	1,593.40
For library: repairs to books and equipment for annual book-airing	554.56
Annual salary for book-binder-copyist	300.00
Expenses for spring and autumn *sekiten* and January school-opening ceremony	2,021.38
Vegetables for meals of boarders and occasional meals	2,556.00
Salts, bean paste, soya sauce and other condiments	911.60
Re-covering *tatami* mats for lecture rooms	666.60
Expenses for daimyo's visits to the school, for musical functions, riding exhibitions, medical school ceremony and prizes to students	728.05
Honorarium to six janitors	300.00
Firewood and charcoal for baths and heating	2,157.87
Set aside for food expenses for following intercalary month	282.00
Surplus	1,561.54
Total	16,368.96

sidized publications of basic classics for the use of students—for it was not a function of the libraries to provide multiple copies of basic texts. Their other function was to publish special works which were not easily available: either rarer Chinese works specially valued by one of the teachers at the school, new translations of western books—particularly common in the last decades of the period—local histories or genealogies, pamphlets of moral instruction for students, the samurai or the general populace of the fief, or vanity publications of the works of scholars at the school. Still at the end of the period, however, manuscript copies were a major means for the propagation of rarer works.

Even with subsidized publications books were not really cheap. A set of the Four Books, for instance, cost 924 *mon* of copper from the Kagoshima school press in 1857—the equivalent of about an eighth of a *koku* of rice.[1] Shōji Kōgi, in his

[1] *NKSS*, 3, p. 282.

memorandum on school organization, might well question whether attendance should be made compulsory, given the strain which the expense of books, ink and paper would impose on the budget of samurai with an income of 5 or 7 koku[1] per annum. The Kagoshima school made provision for those 'in straitened circumstances who cannot buy the books they need' by offering second-hand copies on loan, a month at a time, for a small fee, and the order which announced this offered to buy such second-hand copies from anyone who had them to sell.[2]

Scholarships

It seems to have been rare, however, for fiefs to provide direct subsidies to poorer students—something which Shōji went on to suggest in the memorandum just quoted. The Kagoshima fief did exempt from a general fief tax all families whose head was still at school,[3] but most student subsidies seem to have been given for the same purpose as dormitories were often established—to encourage and develop the abilities of particularly bright pupils. This was the purpose of the item 'Evening meals for the 30 subsidized students' which appeared in the Chōshū budget, and Kagoshima was another fief which gave a 4 koku per annum grant to fifteen selected students.[4] Alternatively grants were given in particular to younger sons.[5]

Subsidies were also provided, in increasing amounts by the end of the period, to allow promising students to travel for study to other parts of Japan. The practice began, in a small way, in the mid-seventeenth century, mostly in northern and in Kyūshū fiefs, but became general in the nineteenth century especially in western Japan and Kyūshū.[6] By the middle of the 1860s such a small fief as Hasuike was financing between fifteen

---

[1] *Keizai mondo hiroku* (*NKS*, 22), p. 100.

[2] *NKSS*, 3, p. 282.

[3] *NKSS*, 3, p. 275.

[4] *Ibid.*

[5] At Matsuo (*NKSS*, 1, p. 234), at Kashima (*NKSS*, 3, p. 185), and if they showed particular promise and had served for some time as assistant lecturers, at Hiroshima (*NKSS*, 2, p. 653). For the special circumstances of younger sons, see *infra*, p. 192.

[6] Watanabe, 'Yūgaku-seido'.

and twenty travelling students at a time and Kumamoto gave its school a special tract of newly reclaimed land, the proceeds from which were wholly devoted to such scholarships.[1] By no means all travelling students were subsidized by their fief, however; probably the majority went at their own expense, though usually with the fief authorities' permission and encouragement.

At the receiving end such schools as the Bakufu's Shōheikō and the Mito school had special boarding establishments for students from other fiefs,[2] though a good many of these travelling students went not to a fief school but to private teachers in Edo, Osaka or Nagasaki. The truth seems to be that at the end of the period the most stimulating teachers were to be found outside the fief schools; in particular in the 1840s and 1850s it was from private teachers rather than in established schools that one could get a training in the new 'Dutch learning'. It was a growing desire on the part of fief authorities to acquire the new and patently useful expertise of these teachers—as well as the fact that they attracted some of the liveliest minds among the young samurai—which explains the popularity of 'Nagasaki scholarships' or grants to study at the flourishing Dutch schools of Ogata Kōan (1810–63) in Osaka (the school vividly described by Fukuzawa Yukichi in his autobiography) or of Tsuboi Shindō (1795–1848) and Itō Gemboku (1800–71) in Edo.[3]

The fiefs had other motives, too. A directive of the Kagoshima fief issued in 1856 urges that as many students as possible should travel and study 'abroad' for much the same reasons as lay behind the Grand Tour of English aristocratic youth. It was, said the directive, particularly important for the children of high-ranking samurai. They were destined for high positions in which they would have to make up their minds on weighty matters which required a wide experience of the world. Moreover, they tended to be spoiled in their own fief, receiving the respect and adulation of their inferiors and even of their teachers at the fief school. It would be good for them to travel; to gain information about the state of the country, to experience hardships, to find teachers who would treat them on their

---

[1] Watanabe, 'Yūgaku-seido'.
[2] *NKSS*, 7, p. 212; 1, p. 357.
[3] Watanabe, 'Yūgaku-seido', p. 7.

merits, and to see the world from the position of a nobody in particular.[1]

From the point of view of the students themselves, too, formal study was only one—and often a minor—purpose of these study trips. Kume Kunitake, a Saga student sent to Edo in the 1860s, describes the life of his fellows in the Shōheikō dormitory. These were, of course, stirring times, when almost every young samurai's mind was seething with political excitement.

> At every opportunity for leave, bright students who really desired to improve themselves would get themselves introductions and go to visit famous men, to interview them and discuss the state of the world. The chief object of travelling scholarships was not so much the formal course of study as to call on great scholars and thinkers, not so much to read books as to improve one's learning by contact with the famous.[2]

One important effect of this wide interchange of students between fiefs was, of course, to help in the creation of a nation-wide intellectual community, to establish the contacts and the channels of communications which aided the emergence of an articulate national consciousness and helped to ensure that the political upheaval, when it came, should lead to the creation of a centralized national state.

Staff

The pattern of administrative control of these schools was generally similar to that at Yonezawa. Almost invariably the school was put under the general direction of a senior samurai who was not a professional scholar—and sometimes not even sympathetic to scholarship. He might well be one of the highest administrative officers in the fief. His function was to lend official dignity to ceremonial occasions, to emphasize by his interest the importance of the school (a mere professional scholar might have difficulty in gaining the respect or even the attendance of samurai, particularly in the early part of the period), and to ensure that the school was kept on a 'solid' foundation, not too far removed from the world and its proper

---

[1] *NKSS*, 3, p. 285.
[2] *Kaikoroku*, 1, p. 528.

mission in serving the fief. He was expected, in fact, to fulfil much the same functions as retired generals who become the presidents and chancellors of modern universities. The appointment of such senior officials seems to have been welcomed by the scholars who served under them; there are at least two instances in which they urged fief authorities to make such appointments to lend weight to the school.[1]

Under the general direction of this senior samurai president —or, as at Yonezawa, of a chain of such senior samurai officials —came those who actually performed the work of the school. In the organization of most schools three separate functions were distinguished. There was usually an academic director who was a professional scholar. Sometimes he had control over the teaching of military skills, too, but this was often a separate, parallel office. Secondly, there was a bursar, a samurai, often superior in rank to the administrative director. Thirdly, there was a disciplinary director, again a samurai and again often superior in rank to the academic director. The actual teaching of the school, and the subordinate teachers, were under the control of the academic director. The bursar, or rather his subordinate officers, looked after the school's financial accounts and buildings. The disciplinary director was usually one of the disciplinary officers of the fief, the military police of the fief's army of samurai or a 'censor', as the term *metsuke* is usually translated, specially delegated to discipline those of the samurai who happened to be students of the school. His subordinate officers also kept the attendance records, thus emphasizing the fact that attendance at the school was also a part of the samurai's military obligations.[2]

Many schools were somewhat overloaded with administrative officers. At the Tsu school, for instance (the class-room discipline of which was described earlier), there were twenty-six administrative officers and fifty-eight teachers to look after between 200 and 250 students.[3] The Hikone school, with approximately twice that number of pupils, had eighty-nine

---

[1] Shūdō Yasuzaemon, *Kengi-sho* (*NKSS*, 5), p. 596, and Hirose Tansō, *Ugen* (*NKS*, 32), pp. 121–2.

[2] Detailed descriptions of staff organization are given in the *NKSS* for Tottori (2, pp. 447–56), for Tsu (1, pp. 82–3) and for Sakura (1, pp. 266–76. See also Shinomaru, *Sakura hangakushi*).

[3] *NKSS*, 1, p. 84.

administrative and guard officers to forty-seven civil and sixty-nine military teachers.[1] The Maebashi school had, for about 300 pupils, twenty-nine administrative and guard officers and forty-three teachers.[2] The proliferation of bureaucratic formalities was one reason for this high proportion of administrators. Another was the need to find suitable employment, if only of an honorific nature, for a large number of samurai who otherwise lacked any particular purpose in life.

TABLE 3. SALARIES OF TOKUGAWA SCHOLARS

Scholar's date of birth	Number reported to have received salaries of		Total number of scholars
	100–300 koku	More than 300 koku	
Before 1675	14 (12%)	14 (12%)	120 (100%)
1676–1750	17 (7%)	20 (8%)	249 (100%)
1751–1800	14 (7%)	7 (4%)	196 (100%)
1801–1850	7 (4%)	4 (2%)	171 (100%)
Not known	3 (2%)	2 (1%)	224 (100%)
TOTAL	55 (6%)	47 (5%)	960 (100%)

The academic director, along with perhaps one or two of the senior teachers in the large schools, often held the separate appointment of *jusha* (Confucian scholar), *jidoku* (attendant reader) or *jikō* (attendant lecturer), in which capacity he rendered direct advisory service to the daimyo. In Mito (where it was held that 'study and practical affairs are indivisible') senior scholars were appointed concurrently to executive posts in the general administrative hierarchy.[3]

This, however, was an exceptional case; in general, the rank of these professional scholars was a low one. The academic

[1] *NKSS*, 1, p. 419.
[2] *NKSS*, 1, p. 577.
[3] Fujita Tōko explains that the daimyo, Nariaki, was in this instance consciously drawing the logical conclusion from the tradition established by his ancestor Mitsukuni, who in the seventeenth century had been the first daimyo to allow his Confucian scholars to divest themselves of priestly clothes, had given them ordinary samurai rank, and had refused to establish a separate post of *jusha*—'If *jusha* means a man who studies the Way, then I am a *jusha* too' (*Hitachi-obi*, p. 484).

director normally received at the most 300 *koku*, which usually put him in the middle rank of samurai; other teachers came into the ranks of what were generally considered lower samurai —those without the privilege of direct audience with the daimyo. Table 3 tabulates all the references to salaries found in the short biographies of a sample of Tokugawa scholars who were known at some time to have taken feudal service and achieved that sufficient modicum of distinction as scholars which justified their inclusion in one or other of the two major reference works from which the biographies are drawn.[1] It seems a reasonable inference from the table that the market price of scholarship was falling during the period, a reflection, probably, of the fact that the supply grew even faster than the demand.[2]

The teachers of the military arts were usually of a similar lowly status. Both the scholars and the military teachers were often considered to be in a separate category of 'professional families'. Thus, in fiefs which insisted on all samurai having full training in 'both Bun and Bu', they alone were often exempted and permitted to specialize in the family skill alone.[3] They were, in other words, 'clerks and tradesmen' rather than all-round gentlemen. An adviser of Matsudaira Sadanobu expressed the distinction very clearly in a memorandum written in the 1790s. His opinion had been canvassed on the desirability of reducing the hereditary stipends of incompetent doctors and of samurai guilty of misconduct. He was all in favour of reducing doctors' salaries, but not those of delinquent samurai; it was enough to exile them to Kōfu as heretofore. His reason was that doctors' salaries were in the nature of wages for services rendered—they were paid for their skill, and no skill should mean

[1] Ogawa, *Kangakusha shūran*, and Seki and Seki, *Kinsei kangakusha taisei*.

[2] It may also be that in so far as volume of publication was one of the editors' criteria of selection the sample for the later periods (when publication was easier) includes a higher proportion of men of mediocre talent, though this is not likely to have been a very important distorting factor. Again, there is no obvious reason why the biographers should have been less likely to mention a highly paid appointment in the case of those who lived later in the period.

The growth in the supply of scholars does not necessarily invalidate what is said about the specialist's lowly status. There were still a good many men of even lower status for whom such a position might seem desirable advancement, especially younger sons.

Changes in the purchasing power of rice in terms of other commodities were not significant enough to affect these arguments.

[3] E.g. at Saga (*NKSS*, 3, p. 123).

no salary. Samurai stipends, on the other hand, were awarded to their family in recognition of the deeds of loyalty and heroism performed by their ancestors on the battlefield, and these acts of loyalty no subsequent fall from grace by later generations could efface.[1]

This separate—and inferior—status of the specialist position was not altogether satisfying to those who led it. A Chōshū fief order of 1718, which deplores the general decline in the civil and military arts in the fief, attributes it to the fact that those families which were originally employed for their family profession or had since been designated as such were reluctant to practise their skill as teachers and even to train their children since 'they consider themselves, and are considered by others, to be one rank below ordinary samurai, and so are concerned solely to escape their professional position, while ordinary samurai are anxious not to be confused with professionals and so are reluctant to develop their skills to perfection.[2] To correct the situation it ordered that professional families were henceforth to be included in the samurai military formations and given ordinary guard duties in order to improve their status. It does not appear, however, that this was a usual practice.

Separateness did not always imply inferiority in everything, however. Though they rarely had power or wealth, scholars of some attainments and strength of character were often treated with a special deference despite their low official status. Thus Arai Hakuga (1725–92) was invited to Kaga with a stipend of 300 *koku* and the position of *jidoku* and director of the school. But the report on the school records that he was, as a 'scholarly guest', accorded a respect far exceeding his rank as a 'retainer'. He was allowed, on account of a physical infirmity, to ride in a palanquin right to the door of the daimyo's palace, and he was privileged to wear special clothes of a kind normally worn only by Kyoto court nobles.[3] During lectures, particularly serious-

---

[1] Moriyama Takamori, *Ama no takumo*, pp. 59–61.

[2] *NKSS*, 2, p. 659. The Aizu fief, too, had trouble with professional families who wished to change their status. A couple of edicts of 1772 take a very stern line in insisting that they are to stick to their last (Ogawa, *Aizu-han*, p. 16).

[3] *NKSS*, 2, pp. 164–5. Similarly, Kamei Nammei records that in Kumamoto at the time of Hori Hiratazaemon's reforms in the mid-seventeenth century, a certain 'farmer' (presumably of the village headman class; Kumamoto had a number of scholarly village families some of whose offspring distinguished themselves in the

minded daimyos might show their devotion to the Way and their respect for the lecturer's scholarship by taking an inferior seat in the room, below the lecturer.

Scholars might well have preferred this respect to be expressed in a more material form. The Tokushima scholar, Shūdō, pleads for high salaries for teachers at the fief school,[1] and his plea is echoed, though mostly a propos of the teachers of military skills, by the leader of the Chōshū reform faction in 1840.[2] Shūdō goes on to urge that teaching appointments should not be hereditary if the quality of the teaching is to be maintained. A good salary would enable teachers to provide for their children to some extent, and if they turned out to be incompetent they could be appointed as lower samurai rather than as teachers.

This was, indeed, supposed to be the practice at Kumamoto in the mid-eighteenth century,[3] but it was difficult to carry it through with rigorous consistency in a system where the allocation of rank, status, and within limits, function, was wholly based on the hereditary principle. In most fiefs the senior scholarly positions which carried the title of jusha or jidoku were hereditary, and with deplorable results to learning, as Kamei Nammei, who reports the Kumamoto practice, pointed out at length.

Learning is a matter of natural ability; some are good at it, others are not. It is difficult to imagine a more irrational system than making the position of jusha a 'family skill'. It is equally

[1] Kengisho (NKSS, 5), p. 596.
[2] NKSS, 5, p. 591. It is not quite certain, however, that Murata Seifū is actually the author of this document. He points out that doctors, artists and Nō actors often enjoy higher status than teachers, but his requests are modest enough; teachers should receive at least 100 koku.
[3] Kamei Nammei, Higo Monogatari (NKS, 15), p. 495.

Meiji period) was given a low samurai status for his scholarly accomplishments. Despite his low status, Hori insisted that he be given direct access to him. When, on one occasion, he diffidently broached a certain matter through one of the secretaries he got a direct reply in Hori's own hand. Hori is supposed later to have remarked to friends: 'You know, it is a funny thing with scholars. The other day I wrote a letter to Igata (the ex-farmer). When I looked over what I had written, somehow it didn't satisfy me; it seemed to lack a tone of proper politeness. I tried again and still it was no good. I must have rewritten it three times before I sent it. I hardly ever rewrite letters in the ordinary course of business, and Igata, after all, is a man of low salary only just appointed to samurai status. One is just overborne by the authority of learning, I suppose' (Higo Monogatari (NKS, 15), p. 494).

irrational, of course, to make horsemanship, military strategy or swordsmanship a family skill, but these being times of peace such arts which prepare for war are never tested out and one never knows whether their practitioners are good at them or not. The skills of the *jusha*, however, are supposed to be of immediate use and their deficiencies are consequently glaringly obvious. The trouble is that feudal lords make the profession of *jusha* a family skill and imagine that anyone who can read a few books and give some sort of a lecture is a *jusha* and as such (although they secretly regard them as somewhat peculiar creatures) to be treated with a certain amount of deference. And the *jusha*, for their part, are satisfied with this; they lose a proper sense of self-respect and feel no shame involved in being treated like a Nō dancer or a teacher of the tea ceremony, a permanently depressed class of mean-spirited people inferior to ordinary samurai—and their contentment with such a status serves as if to advertise to the world at large the irrelevance of learning to practical affairs.[1]

Matters were not always as bad as this, however, particularly towards the end of the period. Mediocrity might pass, but glaring personal deficiencies were recognized. In fact, although these appointments were in principle hereditary, the turn-over in the families holding them was considerable, as is clear from the small number of scholars who are recorded as the sons of scholars in Table 4. It is also clear from Table 5 that scholars of some talent could move with relative ease from the service of one daimyo to that of another. Altogether, the 1215 scholars of things Chinese who were included in the sample on which these tables are based, belong to 913 families. (For the sense in which 'family' is used here, see p. 10). Of these, 768 produced only one scholar of sufficient note to figure in the reference books,[2] 112 lasted for two generations, twenty-one for three, nine for four, one each for five and six, and one, the Hayashi family which headed the Bakufu school, for nine.

The Hayashi family, however, was only perpetuated by judicious adoption. After several generations of mediocre Hayashi sons, Matsudaira Sadonobu, as part of his measure to

---

[1] Kamei Nammei, *Higo Monogatari* (*NKS*, 15), p. 495.
[2] The qualifications implied by this phrase should be noted. A number of these families may have held appointments longer without any other of their members distinguishing themselves in any way.

revitalize the Bakufu school, arranged for the adoption of Hayashi Jussai (1768–1841) who succeeded to the headship of the family and the position of *Daigaku no kami* in 1793. In this somewhat exceptional case the adoptee was of high birth—a daimyo's son, in fact—but the headship of the Hayashi family was the plum of scholarly appointments carrying a salary of 1200 *koku*.

TABLE 4. SOCIAL ORIGINS OF CONFUCIAN SCHOLARS

Father's profession	Scholar's date of birth						
	–1700		*1700–75*		*1775–1850*		*Not known*	
Confucian scholar	33	(14)	51	(13)	53	(16)	21	(8)
A. Employed by a fief	21	(9)	30	(8)	38	(12)	2	(4)
B. Not so employed	8	(3)	7	(2)	7	(2)	2	(1)
C. Whether A or B uncertain	4	(2)	14	(4)	8	(2)	7	(3)
Doctor	26	(11)	20	(5)	19	(6)	9	(3)
Samurai	30	(13)	63	(16)	65	(20)	15	(5)
Others	25	(11)	40	(10)	17	(5)	12	(4)
Not reported	119	(51)	210	(55)	169	(52)	218	(79)
	233	(100)	384	(100)	323	(100)	275	(100)

Sources: As for Table 3. I am indebted to Mr N. Maekawa for his help in preparing these tables.

Before this Matsudaira had already imported into the school three able scholars from other fiefs to compensate for the decline in the Hayashi family. This was, in fact, a very common solution to the problem of hereditary decline—to leave the incompetent successor with his father's appointment in the hope that things would improve in the next generation while bringing in someone from outside to a newly created parallel appointment.

Secular Decline

The hereditary system, the weight of ceremonial and minute bureaucratic regulation, the non-progressive nature of Chinese studies inviting the worst forms of pedagogic formalism, all helped to make the problem of 'decline'—of the general lowering of morale such as beset the Yonezawa school—a common

TABLE 5. CAREERS OF CONFUCIAN SCHOLARS

Career	Scholar's date of birth				Total
	−1700	1700–75	1775–1800	Not known	
A. Never took feudal service	49 (21)	105 (27)	60 (19)	51 (19)	265 (22)
B. Men who, formerly retainers of some lord, left his service for an independent life	27 (12)	38 (10)	27 (8)	6 (2)	98 (8)
C. Men who moved from their native fief and service of their original lord to service of another lord	17 (7)	13 (3)	22 (7)	7 (3)	59 (5)
D. Men who served as *jusha* the lord as whose retainer they were born	16 (7)	46 (12)	49 (15)	11 (4)	122 (10)
E. Men who entered the service of a feudal lord having never previously been his, or any other lord's retainer	95 (41)	112 (29)	107 (33)	56 (20)	370 (30)
F. Men who belong either to category D or E; data incomplete	16 (7)	37 (10)	43 (3)	33 (12)	129 (11)
Career not recorded	13 (6)	33 (9)	15 (5)	111 (40)	172 (14)
Totals	233 (100)	384 (100)	323 (100)	275 (100)	1215 (100)

Sources: As for Table 3.

121

one in the fief schools, as, indeed, it was a general phenomenon of the samurai class and its governmental administration as a whole. Periodic 'reforms' were needed, even if they only amounted to a symbolic tightening of the belt and straightening of the shoulders. Financial difficulties sometimes contributed to the decline. A series of directives from the Chōshū fief authorities in the middle of the eighteenth century attributes the admittedly low state of the school to the effect of a fief economy drive. The school itself had been considered too important for its budget to be cut, but it had suffered in two ways. Firstly, there had been a decline in moral standards; with incomes reduced and in danger of further reductions, samurai tended to fawn on their superiors and concern themselves with ways of enriching themselves, while their sons spent all their time in hunting and other pleasures. (Did they eat the wild duck they hunted, or is this really a *non sequitur*?) Secondly, samurai were deterred from going to school by being unable to wear the clothes or bring the servants which were considered appropriate to their rank, a consideration which the edict discounts as trivial, urging that ragged clothes were, in times of economy, a sign of honest obedience to fief directives.[1]

Such exhortations, however, were not easily accepted in the rank-conscious and etiquette-ridden world of the Tokugawa samurai. In any case they probably did not go to the root of the problem. One cannot doubt the evidence of the great expansion in educational facilities and endowments towards the end of the period. Equally, there is no doubt that the samurai class as a whole was provided with a basic Confucian training. But not many of them got intellectual stimulation.

Nor, perhaps, was intellectual stimulation called for; stimulated intellects could be dangerous to stable feudal society and we have seen how critical independence of mind was consciously discouraged. But by the middle of the nineteenth century, the society was no longer stable. External and internal pressures required the ability to think afresh, to make radical innovations rather than to follow tradition. And it is no accident that a good number of the men who managed to provide the answers and who, by responding to the growing crisis won themselves the leadership of Meiji Japan, received the most important

[1] *NKSS*, 2, pp. 665, 669.

part of their education not in the fief school but at the hands of private teachers; teachers whose liveliness or eccentricity kept them outside of the orthodox educational establishments.[1]

[1] A random sample of the entries in the two major biographical encyclopaedias, covering 613 men who were born before 1850, died after 1880 (and achieved sufficient note to be included in one of these encyclopaedias) was examined for details of their subjects' education. Attendance at a Bakufu school or fief school was mentioned in only sixty-eight entries, whereas 230 entries mentioned study under a particular teacher. This is not a clear measure of the contribution of public and private education to the training of the Meiji *élite*, since it is clear, on further examination, that a good number (possibly between a quarter and a half) of the particular teachers mentioned were, in fact, fief-school teachers. (Biographers are more likely to record the personal connection rather than the institutional affiliation because this was, after all, for advanced pupils considered more important.) This still means, however, that a very high proportion of those who distinguished themselves in the Meiji period studied with private teachers. I am grateful to Miss Sumako Tanabe and Mr Minoru Tanabe for their help with the survey from which this information is drawn.

Chapter IV

THE TRADITIONAL CURRICULUM

WRITING (OR CALLIGRAPHY, RATHER), Chinese studies, a little arithmetic, some training in formal etiquette and practice of the military arts were the basic constituents of the education the samurai received. They were integrated by common attitudes of reverence for knowledge and for the teacher, and by a common insistence on the need for a serious-minded approach to learning which was intended to develop the character as well as to impart skills. But there was little attempt to integrate their content into graded diets appropriate to particular ages. Teachers were usually specialists in one branch or the other, and, except for a general preference for starting writing early and for leaving the military skills until adolescence, these various subjects could be tackled severally in almost any order.

One of the oddest results of this was the divorce between the teaching of writing (Japanese) and the teaching of reading (Chinese). The reading of Japanese was not something that was specifically taught or practised; it was developed as a by-product of practice in writing. (The difference between Japanese and English practices in this respect is a consequence of—or at least something made possible by—the different nature of the scripts. One is still learning to write new characters at an advanced stage of literacy in Japan.) The education of a good proportion of the non-samurai stopped at this acquisition of a basic Japanese literacy without any incursion into the Chinese classics. But the separation of the two pursuits was such that it was also possible to learn to read Chinese without learning to write Japanese. It was rare, and it was usually considered deplorable, but it happened.[1]

[1] See Yamamoto, *Dōji-tsū*, p. 20. One unorthodox scholar preferred this order of priorities—Reading not later than (Japanese) seven, writing not before eleven,

This is not, after all, so surprising since although the Japanese language which children learned to write and the Chinese they learned to read both employed the same script, a large number of the characters and uses of characters found in the Chinese classics did not occur in contemporary Japanese, and, moreover, the styles of script were customarily different. Japanese was always written, and printed, in the cursive script, while Chinese was always printed—and usually written—in the original square characters from which the cursive script derived—and the derivation was not always obvious unless it was pointed out.

This division symbolized the dual nature of Japanese intellectual culture in the Tokugawa period. The vernacular had gained considerable ground since the Heian period when it was a 'woman's language' which men, except for a few determined aesthetes, naturally scorned. There was now an established, manly, and already somewhat archaic form of epistolary Japanese, much influenced by Chinese in vocabulary and use of the script, and serving for all letters and official communications. Styles closer to contemporary vernacular speech were used even by Confucian scholars in their casual writing of diaries and occasional essays. Still, if he could, a scholar wrote his philosophy in Chinese and tried his hand at Chinese poetry and prose essays, but the ability to write Chinese easily was fairly rare, and the ability to write it well was even rarer.

But if Japanese had become the normal means of expression, it was not the accepted medium of education. One could *write* Japanese, but wisdom could only be obtained by *reading* Chinese. Hoashi Banri's suggestion[1] that the Chinese classics should all be translated into contemporary Japanese for educational purposes seems never to have been acted on. It would probably have seemed slightly shocking to his contemporaries, in much the same way as colloquial translations of the Bible make a good many Christians feel uncomfortable. Books written in Japanese in any case were considered inferior. The dull students at Mito who could not manage to read Chinese were set to reading Japanese books. The Osaka City Magistrate, in

[1] *Tōsempu-ron* (*NKS*, 26), p. 395.

was his motto—but he suggested that children should be taught from the beginning to read Japanese books as well as Chinese before they start to practise writing. (Suzuki Akira, *Hanareya-gakukun*, p. 397.)

presenting to teachers in Osaka a moral treatise written in Japanese, does so half apologetically, pointing out that despite general prejudices there is often a great deal of information to be gained from such books. Moreover, the yielding cursiveness of the script in which Japanese was normally written still carried some of the old associations of effeminacy in contrast with the masculine squareness of the characters used for Chinese, and this, by helping to perpetuate the idea that the reading of Japanese books was a most suitable means of education for women, reinforced the idea that their content must necessarily, therefore, be inferior.

For these reasons the writing of Japanese and the reading of Chinese were normally separate activities, and the former, as an inferior pursuit like arithmetic, was not always accorded the dignity of being included in the curriculum of the fief schools. In a good many fiefs children received this phase of their education from private teachers.

It consisted almost entirely of the assiduous copying of models under the supervision of the teacher. Sometimes the teacher wrote out the models himself, sometimes printed copy books were used. Each student sat practising at his desk and awaited his turn to go to the teacher to have his efforts corrected. Sometimes the teacher would sit behind him and guide his hand, though the experienced could write upside-down and guide the pupil's brush as they sat facing him. Practice of the cursive characters used for general phonetic purposes would come first. These were usually followed by lists of basic ideographs, or collections of phrases most commonly used in letters, or sometimes connected passages.

Learning to write was not, however, simply a matter of acquiring a skill; it was also practice of the Art of Calligraphy. As such it had to be approached in a properly serious frame of mind, with due attention to correct posture and careful 'concentration of the spirit'. There was also much emphasis on constant repetition; partly, one suspects, because repetition was tedious and tedium is an excellent means of self-discipline, but ostensibly, at least, because it was the only way to perfection.[1] It was considered axiomatic that everyone should strive to develop a good script. It was a rare and unorthodox scholar

[1] See e.g. the section 'tenarai' in Kusata Sankeishi (??), *Otoko Chōhōki*.

126

indeed who wrote that 'characters are a practical device', intelligibility is all and 'a bad hand is nothing to be ashamed of'.[1]

A good many teachers of calligraphy confined themselves entirely to the cursive script, but some went on, in the later stages, to teach the square script too, and there were a few who thought that the square script should come first.[2] A very small number of printed copy books also indicated the square forms from which the cursive characters to be copied were derived.[3] Thus, occasionally, writing practice directly connected with, and provided some preparation for, training in the reading of Chinese.

Chinese Studies

The child's introduction to Chinese studies usually between the ages of eight and ten by Japanese reckoning, was at first largely a matter of parrot-like repetition called *sodoku* (or sometimes *su-yomi*), 'plain reading'. The favourite first books were the *Classic of Filial Piety* and the *Greater Learning*, the first chiefly because of its moral appropriateness, the second because it was thought to be the easiest—it was certainly the shortest— of the Four Books.

Although the text was Chinese the student did not learn to read it in Chinese. Over the centuries the Japanese had devised an ingenious if tortuous system of notation for Chinese texts which indicated the way in which, by changing the order of words and adding Japanese particles and verbal inflections, they could be 'read off' in Japanese. The Japanese which resulted was a weird and strange tongue, rather distantly removed from ordinary conversational Japanese. Eventually the child would learn to understand this new tongue. In the early stages it was enough for him to master the technique of 'reading off' the text.[4]

---

[1] Tamiya Nakayoshi, *Tōyōshi* (*NZZ*, 1), pp. 199–200.

[2] Ototake, *Shomin kyōikushi*, 2, pp. 338–9.

[3] An example is Anon., (*Santai ryōten*) *Taizen shōsoku ōrai*. It also indicates alternative readings for the characters in *katakana*, one of the phonetic scripts.

[4] The result of such a 'reading off' would sound about as far removed from ordinary Japanese as the following translation of a piece of Mencius is from contemporary English:

The King in delight spake, 'In the Book of Odes it saith, "another feeleth

The child would sit with such a doctored text in front of him and the teacher would read off a short passage slowly, indicating with a pointer the order in which the characters were to be taken. When the child was able to repeat the passage by himself the teacher might give him some general idea of the sense. For the rest of the morning he was set to read the passage over and over again until he had completely mastered it. The next day would begin with revision, followed by a new passage and more practice.

Again, this was a serious business. 'When reading,' run the rules of one school, 'always sit squarely upright, maintain an expression of gravity and concentrate all your attention on what you are reading. Never glance around or fiddle with your fingers.'[1] Kaibara Ekken adds that the student should first wash his hands and dust the table. Books should never be thrown, stepped over (much less on), bent double or used as a pillow. Nor should scraps of paper on which are written the names of the Sages or quotations from their works ever be put to improper uses.[2] Constant repetition, too, was thought to have a moral effect. Children, says one writer, constantly wish to rush ahead. They are concerned to 'get through' large quantities. But this leads to a hasty, uncontrolled and superficial disposition. They become the kind of people who cannot read a letter without jumping ahead of themselves and having to go back and read parts over again.[3]

To ensure thoroughness the amount each day should be strictly limited—to one phrase of four or five characters a day according to most prescriptions and at the most half a page[4]

[1] The Fukuoka school (*NKSS*, 3, p. 13).
[2] *Wazoku dōjikun* (Tsukamoto, *Ekken jikkun*, 1), p. 368.
[3] Komachi Gyokusen, *Jishūhen* (*NKS*, 19), pp. 482–3. Quoted in Ototake, *Shomin kyōikushi*, 1, p. 532.
[4] See, e.g. Kumazawa Banzan, *Daigaku wakumon* (*Banzan zenshū*, 3), p. 273; Nishijima Junzō, *Gakkan ryakusetsu* (*NKSS*, 5), p. 605; Shōji Kōgi, *Keizai mondō hiroku* (*NKS*, 22), p. 86.

---

unwitting. I gauge his heart". Thus saith it. Thy words are an example thereof. I have thus acted, but in reflection seeking, failed to find the reason in my heart. Thou hast spoken it. Thou art close to my heart. The impingement of this feeling on the Kingly Way lies where?

He spake: 'There is one who speaketh to you, King. He saith, "My strength sufficeth with it to raise one hundred bars of metal, but it sufficeth not with it to raise one feather." etc. '

even later on. Likewise, for a good many teachers, rote memorization was the desirable ultimate of thoroughness.[1] This is real learning which stays with one for the rest of one's life, says one of its advocates. 'It would be hard to find nowadays a samurai who had not read the Four Books and the Five Classics but'—because they have failed to memorize them—'as soon as they have "done" them and leave school the majority forget all about them'.[2]

The same intransigent disciplinarian insists that this kind of instruction should continue to be the child's sole educational fare until the Japanese age of fifteen, except that he would be given general lectures—not related in detail to the passages he was reading—on the general purport and the moral lessons of the texts.[3] In a number of schools his prescriptions were followed and a student would go through the whole of the Four Books and the Five Classics in this mechanical way before he would be allowed to begin any intelligent consideration of their contents. In others, sodoku of the Four Books was considered an adequate basis. Thereafter, while he continued with the sodoku of other works, the student would go through the Four Books again, reading commentaries and studying in detail the meaning of the text.

At any rate, sodoku was not concerned with such elucidation, though the Chinese phrase 'if one reads a passage a hundred times the meaning becomes clear of itself' was supposed to indicate that diligence provided its own eventual reward. A more realistic assessment by a teacher who seems entirely satisfied with current methods was that a child might get a 'vague understanding of about a tenth of what he read'.[4] In order to maximize this ratio he suggests that where there is a choice between giving a character an indigenous Japanese reading, or reading it with a Sino-Japanese loan-word, the former should be preferred as being more likely to be familiar to the child.[5]

---

[1] At the Fukuoka school, for instance, where the rules also urged quiet measured repetition, unspoiled by any hasty desire to 'get through'.

[2] Shōji Kōgi, Keizai mondō hiroku, p. 80.

[3] Ibid., p. 87.

[4] Yamamoto Shōitsu, Dōjitsū, p. 5.

[5] If Latin had been an ideographic language and the script had been taken over to write English, the character for the Latin word discutio might have been taken

The general theory was that sodoku was a hard disciplinary process of *preparation* for true reading of the classics. The classics were, after all, of profound philosophical content, and it would be unreasonable to expect unformed minds to understand them. A few writers, however, take a more liberal attitude to the child's abilities and needs. Thus Kaibara Ekken suggests that 'while the child is still learning to read he should already be told—here and there—the meaning of the text'.[1] Ogyū Sorai, who considered the whole business of sodoku a second-best approach in any case, says much the same thing, though he adds that the whole purpose of such explanations should be to retain the child's interest by picking out passages of easy construction which he can understand; never to provide an opportunity for pontifical moral lectures.[2] At the Hirado school especially bright children who asked for it were given explanations of what they were reading—as a special dispensation.[3]

There seem to have been only a few teachers, however, who advocated the regular analytical approach of always explaining the meaning of each individual character in a sentence and the grammatical principles on which they were strung together. One who does speaks of it as an idea he has got from another writer which struck him as startling, but sensible.[4] He also, as a corollary, deplores the practice of rote memorization. It derives, he says, from China where students had to sit for examinations

[1] *Wazoku dōjikun* (Tsukamoto, *Ekken jikkun*, 1), p. 373.
[2] Preface to *Yakubun sentei* (*Yakusen-shohen*, 1715, f. 7).
[3] *NKSS*, 3, p. 170.
[4] Emura Hokkai, *Jugyō-hen* (*Nihon bunko*, 3), p. 23. (Quoted in Ototake, *Shomin kyōikushi*, 1, p. 333.) He is quoting Amemori Hōshū.

over to write the Anglo-Saxon word which is now the English *talk*. At the same time it would continue to represent an English version of the Latin *discutio*, a Latin-English loan-word *discussion*. If Latin texts were construed in a special kind of English in the way in which Chinese texts were construed in a special kind of Japanese, this particular character could be read either as *talk* or as *discussion*. Yamamoto's point was that *talk* should be preferred as being more likely to be familiar to the child. He qualifies this, however, by saying that the Japanese words should be avoided if they sound vulgar or unpleasant to the ear. There were other extraneous considerations, too. Ota Nampo was puzzled to know why Hayashi Razan had insisted that two characters which would normally be read *kuni-hito* should be read *kunitami*. He eventually discovered that a long-since-dead Japanese Emperor had once had the name Kunihito and hence the word was taboo (Ota Nampo, *Ichiwa ichigon* (*Nihon zuihitsu taisei*, 2), p. 980).

which require regurgitation of whole passages of the classics, but it is a bad practice which gets in the way of proper understanding.

One obstacle in the way of analytical teaching was the fact that there was little systematic formulation of the principles of Chinese grammar and syntax. There were a few attempts at such grammars, but they consisted less of generalized analysis than of a series of examples of sentence constructions and they seem to have been used more as guides for composition than as a means of mastering the language.[1]

If few carried analytical teaching to the point of syntactical analysis, it was, however, a little more common to teach children the readings of individual characters out of context. Various texts were used for this including the Chinese *Thousand Character Classic* and an excellent Japanese illustrated encyclopaedia.[2] There were also one or two Japanese attempts to provide rhythmical memorizable verses containing mnemonics for remembering the shape of individual characters.[3]

For the most part, however, sodoku was a matter of straightforward recitation of texts. A reading knowledge of Chinese was acquired, if at all, by the direct method rather than by analysis. After he had had enough examples it was hoped that the child would come to know by instinct that such and such a character when it came at the beginning of a sentence would be read *izukunzo* and in other contexts *yasushi*, that a certain complex of characters required a passive verb and another a hypothetical ending.

Theoretically, perhaps, it was good *gestalt* psychology, even if not a very enthralling educational experience. Occasionally it worked. Moriyama Takamori describes in his autobiography how in his mid-eighteenth-century childhood he was taken through the usual sodoku course by his mother. He had finished all the usual books by the Japanese age of ten, 'but with no understanding at all. I simply learned to read them uncomprehendingly as a priest reads the sutras'. He was much more impressed and influenced by the bedtime stories his

[1] Examples were Ogyū Sorai's *Yakubun sentei* and Itō Tōgai's *Kimmō yōji-kaku*. They seem to have had few imitators.
[2] Respectively the *Senjimon* and the *Kimmō zui*. The latter, as its title indicates, was expressly intended for children.
[3] E.g. Minamoto Takashi, *Jirin-chōka*.

mother told him—Japanese fairy tales, stories of the Minamoto, the Taira and their battles in the heroic age of the twelfth century, and also of the Chinese Sages. These gave him a taste for '*kana* books' (books written in simple Japanese)—battle tales, histories, the texts of puppet plays and the like. For a time he read avidly everything he could get hold of. Then, a couple of years later, he began to learn archery and riding and for a time he was interested in nothing else.

> The Four Books and the Five Classics which I had read when I was young I had completely forgotten after four or five years. But later, at the age of sixteen, I got the books out in an idle moment and found that I could read them easily. I was astonished. Even books which I had not earlier learned I found I could read quite easily and in general terms get their sense. I borrowed a few unannotated Chinese books without diacritical marks and found that—though of course I didn't have a scholar's understanding of them—by dint of thinking hard I could work out what they meant.[1]

Moriyama, however, was a somewhat exceptional person (as, without undue modesty, he is at pains to point out in his autobiography) and there is little doubt that for the average and below-average samurai student sodoku did not result in practice either in the ability to read Chinese texts which had not been 'learnt' or in the hoped-for osmotic absorption of the meaning of the texts which had. Not many of the samurai went back to their books at the age of sixteen in a receptive mood; most of them remained, as the proverbial expression had it 'an *Analects*-reader but not an *Analects*-knower'. They rested on their achievement of having completed a difficult and distasteful task. Perhaps Hattori Nankaku was exaggerating when he said of sodoku that 'it has no effect on the student whatever except to make him thoroughly miserable',[2] but it is unlikely to have given him much zest for further study. Tsurumine Shigenobu was another who survived early deterrents well enough to develop a taste for writing and leave a description of his early education:

> When I got to the age of [Japanese] eight or nine and started writing and sodoku I hated it. My father taught me reading

---

[1] *Ama no takumo*, pp. 3–4.
[2] According to Yuasa Jōzan, *Bunkai zakki* (*NZZ*, 2), p. 591.

himself and at the mere sound of his summons, 'Bring your *Greater Learning*', I would scuttle off to hide in the storehouse or spend the whole day in the guard's quarters. When I was forced into it I would sometimes get the idea that if I memorized the passage quickly it would be over that much sooner and tried as hard as I could. Then my father would say, 'Yes, you've learned it very well. Let's go on to another bit'. At which I would burst into tears of frustration at the thought of my wasted efforts, and my father would dismiss me saying that I was a hopeless child.

In his case, however, his soul was saved by a startling discovery two or three years later. He had asked his father who Chu Hsi was whose name appeared on the edition of the *Analects* they were using. Next he inquired about the Dōshun who had done the annotations. He was told that he was Hayashi Razan, the ancestor of the present Rector of the Bakufu school—'Do you mean that Japanese can put their names to books, too?' His astonishment, he says, was soon converted into the ambition to become a scholar himself and thereafter he never looked back.[1]

One saving grace was that the system of individual tuition allowed each student's pace to be fitted to his abilities. Teachers did, apparently, sometimes teach five or six pupils together and get them to read in chorus, but this was not common. About twenty pupils per teacher, each to be taught individually, seems to have been considered the ideal ratio.[2] So, while most schools planned for sodoku of the basic classics to be the major part, if not the whole, of the Chinese curriculum until the age of fifteen, a bright child might graduate to higher things by the age of eleven or twelve. Yamaga Sokō describes his own J. S. Mill-like childhood in breathtakingly modest terms. (And remember that for the Western equivalents one has to take one or two years off these ages.) 'From the age of six my father arranged for me to learn to read. I was very inexpert, but by the age of eight I had more or less finished reading the Four

---

[1] *Kaisai manroku* (Kokusho kankōkai, *Hyakka zuihitsu*, 3), p. 12. Also extracted in *NKSSS*, 4, p. 314. The anecdote is an interesting illustration of the alienness of Chinese studies as they were commonly taught, and as such lends force to the argument that the Japanese were more easily able than the Chinese to exchange the Confucian for the Western world-view in that Confucianism was still for them only a 'suit of borrowed clothes'.

[2] Shōji Kōgi, *Keizai mondō hiroku* (*NKS*, 22), p. 86.

Books, the Five Classics, the seven military classics and various anthologies of prose and poetry.'[1]

One heretical school of thought objected to the sodoku system and to the whole practice of 'reading off' Chinese texts in bastard Japanese. Chinese, it was held, was a foreign language and should be treated as such. In order to put oneself on a par with contemporary Chinese students of the classics, one should first learn to speak and write the contemporary Chinese language.

The study of Chinese as a modern language—the 'Nagasaki study' as it was called because it started from contacts with Chinese traders and its earliest exponents were the official interpreters—developed in the seventeenth century,[2] but it was Ogyū Sorai who first advocated that it should be a means of approaching the classics. Sorai was chiefly concerned with the inaccurate comprehension which resulted from tying to individual Chinese words a conventional translation which may have been the nearest approximation to the sense of the Chinese a thousand years ago (when Chinese characters were first used to write Japanese) but often was so no longer. Trying to get at the sense of a Chinese passage by reading it off in Japanese by the usual 'upside-down method' (changing the order of words to conform to Japanese syntax) was 'like trying to scratch an itching toe through your boot'. 'The flow of words, the general spirit of the two languages, the respective rules for conjunction and separation, are fundamentally different.'[3] Translations, where necessary, should be real translations in ordinary colloquial Japanese. The beginner should first learn modern colloquial Chinese to get the feel of the language, then start classical Chinese from simple sentences, gradually progressing to more difficult books.

---

[1] *Haisho zampitsu* (Tsukamoto, *Yamaga Sokō bunshū*), p. 459.

[2] Okajima Kanzan (1674–1728) and Amemori Hōshū (1668–1755) were chiefly responsible for popularizing the study. Okajima had been an interpreter at Nagasaki, and Amemori as adviser to the daimyo of Tsushima was in frequent contact with Chinese and Koreans. Interest in modern China seems to have been common enough by the end of the seventeenth century for the author of a compendium of useful knowledge for men to give, sandwiched between a list of 208 varieties of sweetmeats and a breviary of correct etiquette, a few rules (rather hopelessly inaccurate rules) for guessing the modern Chinese pronunciation of a character from its *on*—the pronunciation of the corresponding Chinese loan-word in Japanese Kusata Sankeishi (??), *Otoko chōhōki*, 1963). Sorai had been a pupil of Okajima.

[3] *Yakubun sentei*, preface.

The full Sorai doctrine had few adherents, and even he admitted that it was an ideal difficult to attain. His arguments against the traditional method of 'upside-down reading' had more weight than his claim that Japanese students should start on a par with Chinese students by learning contemporary Chinese, and they could be met by a less radical solution—reading the Chinese text straight through in the original Chinese order, using only Chinese loan-words with their Japanese pronunciation. This was the way in which priests read Buddhist scriptures, though the object of priestly reading was usually incantation rather than understanding. As a method of teaching the Confucian classics it was not usually practised, though it was the rule at the Kumamoto school when it was first founded by a pupil of Sorai in 1755.[1] By the nineteenth century the idea was still just enough alive for a conventionally minded teacher to mention that there were some who favoured it and who would, in this way, give readings even to all the 'meaningless' particles which come at the end of Chinese sentences (particles, that is, for which no conventional Japanese equivalent existed and which were, therefore, traditionally ignored). This, he declares, may be the road to proficiency in Chinese for the one student in a thousand of exceptional brilliance. He, for his part, is concerned with the other 999.[2]

A compromise which went part of the way towards meeting Sorai's objections to the mechanical equation of the Chinese words of the original texts with the Japanese words which the characters were conventionally used to write was to avoid such words as far as possible when construing the text and keep to the Japanicized pronunciation of the Chinese words—a device which helped to preserve a sense of the foreignness of the text and to ensure that words would be treated on their Chinese merits.[3] This was the practice of some editors of printed annotated versions of the classics such as Hayashi Razan at the beginning of the period and Satō Issai (1772–1859) later on. The most popular annotated texts, however, the so-called Gotō-ten edited by Gotō Shizan (1721–82) used Japanese words as far as possible. Even if they did obscure the precise meanings of the

---

[1] *NKSS*, 3, p. 206.
[2] Yamamoto, *Dōjitsū*, p. 4.
[3] I.e. in terms of the note on p. 130, always using *discussion* rather than *talk*.

Chinese original, they did presumably, as the advocates of this procedure held,[1] by using as far as possible words familiar to the Japanese student, make his painless incidental absorption of the sense a little easier.

Further Chinese Studies

The Chinese language was the royal road, and the only road, to all knowledge at the beginning of the period. The classics, the most instructive history, the most refined literature, the most authoritative works on military strategy were all written in Chinese. So, too, were books on medicine, astronomy, mathematics and law. Even knowledge of the beginnings of Western science came from the Chinese translations or the original writings of the Jesuits in China.

Medicine, mathematics, astronomy and usually military strategy were from the first treated as separate subjects, but the Confucian classics, prose literature and poetry, the philosophical writings of non-Confucianists, history and the study of political and legal institutions were at first largely undifferentiated. A teacher might give his advanced students a varied diet ranging over all these fields, though the Confucian classics were likely to provide the core. By the nineteenth century, however, a number of schools had separated these studies into different courses which were functionally, rather than formally, defined —so that, for instance, at the Bakufu school and at the Chōshū school history included Japanese as well as Chinese history, and political institutions dealt with Japan as well as with China.[2] (Though since the emphasis was on the earlier periods of Japanese history the texts used were still usually written in Chinese—the *Rikkokushi*, for instance, or the *Ryō no gige*.)

Still, however, even if there was such a clear-cut classification, it did not follow that the student had to confine himself to one course or the other. Usually he could spread himself over several courses simultaneously, and the teachers themselves did not necessarily specialize. In any case the study of the Confucian classics was compulsory. Having completed his basic course of sodoku the student would begin to study the meanings of

[1] See p. 129.
[2] *NKSS*, 7, p. 101; 2, p. 743.

the text, usually starting with one of the Four Books, or with the work which summarized the moral teachings of the Sung Confucianists, the *Hsiao-hsüeh*. He might have for this purpose a detailed commentary with notes in Japanese explaining difficult words and allusions, and sometimes paraphrasing whole passages and offering summaries of the general argument. Large numbers of these commentaries were produced during the Tokugawa period.[1] Although some listed different interpretations of doubtful passages, those in use at the end of the period generally confined themselves to giving the Chu Hsi version unadulterated. There were also, for advanced students, Japanese reprints of Chu Hsi's own Chinese commentaries.

If no commentary was available the student usually had, at least, a 'doctored' text with the notations indicating how the text was to be 'read off' in Japanese. If he had a second-hand copy it would probably be spattered with additional annotations in the form of red lines marking off proper names—one line to the right of a character indicating a place name, a line through the middle a personal name, two through the middle for the title of a book and so on—the conventional rules were conveniently summarized in an easily memorized jingle,[2] and were of considerable value for a language without capital letters.

There were also dictionaries, sometimes arranged in some order that would allow one to find a character by its shape, but more frequently on the traditional Chinese vocabulary system which requires that one should have some idea of the *meaning* of a character before one can find it. There were also dictionary concordances for particular works. One such, for two common Chinese history texts, advertised itself as being arranged in radical order (using the shape of the characters) to facilitate reference. But the advertisement went on: 'beginners who wish

[1] The large collection of Chinese classics published in 1910, the *Kanseki kokujikai zensho* series, consists entirely of reprints of such works. The first commentaries were made by Zen priests in the fourteenth century, but it was not until the Tokugawa period that they were produced in large numbers and printed for wide distribution.

[2] See, e.g. Yamamoto Shōitsu, *Dōjitsū*, p. 3. Such devices had to be used discriminatingly, however. A *kokugakusha* student of Japanese history describes his shocked horror at finding a secondhand copy of the *Nihongi* with red lines sacrilegiously drawn through the name of the Sun Goddess, Amaterasu no Omikami, just as if he were an ordinary person (Ono Takanao, *Kasan kanwa* (*NZZ*, 13), p. 486).

to study the *Tso chuan* and the *Kuo yü* will derive great benefit from first memorizing this dictionary before they begin to read'.[1] Even the more rigidly disciplinarian of teachers seem not to have encouraged the memorization of dictionaries, however.

Either at home or in a crowded class-room the pupil would be left to read by himself (always aloud, one teacher urges, in order to avoid the temptation to gloss over characters to which he could not give the correct reading),[2] sticking in little pieces of red paper to mark passages he could not understand. Ten pages a day was the recommended stint at one school.[3] Daily, or every two or three days, students would have an individual or group session with their teacher at which he would elucidate their difficulties and question them to make sure that they had properly understood the rest.

Muro Kyūsō was probably speaking for most Tokugawa teachers when he insisted on the importance of close, detailed understanding even if it did mean the slow covering of a limited amount of ground.[4] A few took a more libertarian view. 'Read the parts which you find interesting, leaving what you cannot understand', recommended Matsudaira Sadanobu. 'If you do not find one book interesting try another. As time goes on in this fashion you will find that you can read parts you could not read before, and understand what formerly seemed obscure.'[5] He, however, is talking of works other than the Confucian classics. The latter, he urges, do require serious concentrated effort, and proper attention to every detail.

Some teachers relied more on 'lectures' than on private reading. The word *kōshaku* or *kōgi* seems, however, to have covered a fairly wide range of activities. In some schools[6] they were the chief means of instruction, the teacher giving verbally

---

[1] Advertisement for the *Taisei sakoku jibiki* at the back of the British Museum copy of Minamoto Takashi, *Jirin chōka* (1769).

[2] Emura Hokkai, *Jugyō-hen* (*Nihon bunko*, 3), p. 43.

[3] The Hirado school (*NKSS*, 3, p. 170).

[4] *Sundai zatsuwa* (*NZZ*, 3), p. 354. And for similar sentiments, see Yuasa Jōzan, *Jōzan-rō-hitsu* (*NZZ*, 5), pp. 721–2, and Amemori Hōshū, *Kissō sawa* (*NZZ*, 9), pp. 150, 177.

[5] *Taikan zakki* (*NZZ*, 14), p. 248. Much the same recommendation is made by Ogyū Sorai (*Yakubun sentei*, preface), Motoori Norinaga (*Uiyama-bumi* (*Zenshū*, 9) pp. 481–2) and by Hirose Tansō in an iconoclastic moment, in his *Yakuge wakumon* (*Tansō zenshu*, 2), p. 20. Nine years later, however, in his *Ugen* (1840), he is much more conventional.

[6] Fukuyama was an example (*NKSS*, 2, pp. 638–9).

the kind of information provided by written commentaries. More often they were supplementary to private reading, held three or six times a month, and concerned with the general purport of the texts rather than with detailed exposition. In many schools they were even less frequent ceremonial affairs at which a carefully prepared lecture was delivered to a large audience of adult samurai as well as full-time students. The latter type of lecture usually dealt only with the Confucian canon, especially the Four Books or Chu Hsi's educational manifesto, the *Po-lu-tung shu-yüan chieh-shih*.

Yamazaki Ansai was one of the first to adopt the *kōshaku* as a regular form of teaching, but it was the Shogun Tsunayoshi's passion for listening to—and giving—lectures which popularized the practice at the end of the seventeenth century. Even the more ceremonial lectures which were held at the Shogun's court varied from detailed textual exposition to sermon-like exhortation spiced with anecdotes—a style for which Satō Naokata later achieved considerable fame.[1] The Shogun Yoshimune, apparently, was not quite sure what to expect when he once invited Muro Kyūsō to lecture to him and tried to insure himself against a possible display of pedantry by pointing out that he was no great scholar and would be obliged if Muro would forget about the textual details and concentrate on the general meaning—a fact which the latter, missing the point, records as an example of His Highness's great and becoming modesty.[2]

Some scholars were very much opposed to the lecturing habit. Ogyū Sorai records that one of the Hayashis rounded sharply on a fellow-scholar who tried to play the candid friend and suggest that he should cultivate a better lecturing style. He had retorted that fancy lecturing was something which had no place in the tradition of solid scholarship of the Hayashi school. By Sorai's time, however, even the Hayashi family had fallen victim to the prevailing fashion.

Ever since His Highness Tsunayoshi concentrated so much on *kōshaku*, the Bakufu's Confucian scholars have studied nothing else. They have got the idea that their sole business in life is

---

[1] Yokoyama, *Kinsei kyōikushi*, pp. 133, 135-7.
[2] *Kenzan (reitaku) hisaku (NKS, 2)*, p. 485.

giving *kōshaku* with the result that they are all ignorant and useless in practical matters.[1]

In another context Sorai admits that the popular kind of kōshaku for the moral instruction of statesmen and officials might have a place, but he is unrelenting in his scorn of the kōshaku as a method of training scholars:

> The meaning of individual words, the sense of the phrase, the purport of the chapter, the construction of the book, the ostensible meaning, the implied meaning, the varying interpretations of the commentators, even down to historical snippets and anecdotes and the etymology of characters; everything, in fact, which has any connection with the text is lumped together, laid out in order like goods in a shop, strung out like pearls on a necklace ... The lecturer cultivates a well-modulated voice to charm the ears of his listeners. The worst of them mix in a few funny stories to wake up sleepers in the audience, and some mercenary ones stop not far short of suggesting an increase in their fees. It is a practice which degrades the teacher's character and corrupts the student's intellect.

It is bad for students because it allows for no possibility of grading material to suit individual abilities. It trains them only in formal pedantry, destroys their ability for independent inquiry and makes them into passive automatons.

> They sit at the teacher's feet and take down every word of his lecture. Word for word, from beginning to end, not a syllable out of place. The worst of them will even mark a pause where the teacher stopped to clear his throat. They study his intonation and imitate his gestures.[2]

---

[1] *Seidan* (*NKT*, 9), p. 191.

[2] *Yakubun sentei*, preface. Sorai was not alone in his condemnation of kōshaku. Hayashi Shihei also dismissed as 'useless', 'the usual form of education—the teacher going to the school only in the daytime to give kōshaku on a page or two of the Four Books'. Far better, he held, to collect a fine library, let students read for themselves, and have teachers on hand to answer questions (*Jōsho* (*NKS*, 12), p. 10). In a different tradition Motoori, too, while not rejecting the kōshaku, is equally stern about the evils of excessive note-taking. The student who is too assiduous a note-taker is likely to miss the point and end up with nothing in his head and an unintelligible jumble in his notebook. Lectures are valuable only if the student prepares his text thoroughly beforehand, and if he goes over the passage which had been expounded immediately afterwards in order to fix it in his mind (*Tama-katsuma*, extracted in *NKSSS*, 4, pp. 224–5).

The kind of exposition-for-students type of kōshaku which Sorai was attacking was probably not very common in the latter half of the period, but the general lecture type of kōshaku continued to be popular. Most schools held them periodically and they were usually open to the public—to the samurai public and in some fiefs to the non-samurai public as well. Lecturers who had a powerful and attractive style often drew great crowds—Hosoi Heishū's triumphal visit to Yonezawa at the end of the eighteenth century is an example.[1] But the ordinary run-of-the-mill lecturer seems to have been less inspiring, and samurai had to be frequently reminded that it was their duty to attend.[2] When Hosoi Heishū began his lectures in the newly built hall at Nagoya his audience overflowed into the courtyards, but he prudently restrained the enthusiastic fief officials from building a yet bigger hall with the warning that the samurai's ardour would soon cool. And, he records, he was proved right.[3] One reason, probably, for the failure to hold audiences, was the fact that scholars did not discriminate between different types and purposes of kōshaku. Even in their general lectures they tended towards the textual pendantry of the class-room. A directive of the Chōshū school in 1843 is concerned to revive the general lectures and urges that lecturers should 'expound the principles of loyalty and filial piety, benevolence and justice, simply and in ordinary language that the average person can easily understand, so that large audiences will attend of high rank and of low'.[4]

Since these lectures were normally set-piece affairs, there was no opportunity for questioning the lecturer, though in one fief school the teacher regularly appointed six questioners whose job it was to think up a question during the lecture and come forward in turn to pose it at the end. No one else was allowed to ask questions.[5]

One device which did, however, allow for more active participation by the students was the 'repeat lecture' (henkō). After hearing a lecture and taking notes, the next day, or several days later, students were expected to regurgitate what

[1] NKSS, 1, p. 734.
[2] See p. 239.
[3] NKSS, 1, p. 749.
[4] NKSS, 2, p. 679.
[5] NKSS, 3, p. 170. The Hirado fief.

they had learned by giving the same lecture—or a part of it—themselves. This procedure was followed at the Aizu school as part of the system of instruction in military strategy, though it seems not to have been common. At Aizu a special dispensation was allowed to officials over fifty who found difficulty in expressing themselves in front of others. They could invite the teacher to their homes to listen to their 'repeat lecture' if they were of sufficiently high rank.[1]

More important than lectures as a means of training students were the group readings and group discussions, which in some schools started as soon as the student began his individual reading and in some were reserved for more advanced students only. Again there seems to have been some variation in the nature of these *kaidoku* and *rinkō* sessions as they were respectively called, though they nearly always stuck closely to a text and began with the simple reading (for *kaidoku*) or with the exposition (for *rinkō*) of prepared passages by students appointed beforehand or chosen on the spot—sometimes, as at Yonezawa, formally by lot. The nature of the discussions at the *rinkō* sessions varied from a simple concern with elucidating the meaning of the text to broader examination of the content, discussion of the practical application of moral principles, historical or literary criticism, the tracing of historical parallels and so on. Some teachers kept a tight hand on the proceedings, but at one school it was deliberate policy to let discussion run freely among the students until, when a consensus seemed to be emerging, the teacher stepped in to make such corrections as seemed necessary.[2] One scholar thought that these discussions did not usually range widely or freely enough. He suggested that a large veranda should be built on to the school library and the sessions held there so that works of reference could be consulted whenever necessary.[3]

One of the early Fukuoka schools, started at the end of the eighteenth century by Kamei Nammei, a follower of Ogyū Sorai, was probably exceptional in introducing a competitive element into the proceedings. First each student was required in turn to expound a different passage from the book they were

---

[1] Ogawa, *Aizu-han kyōiku-kō*, p. 29.
[2] *NKSS*, 3, p. 180. The Hasuike school.
[3] Shūdō Yasuzaemon, *Kengisho* (*NKSS*, 5), p. 597.

reading, and the teacher gave each plus or minus marks in the register. One pupil was then appointed 'questioner' and his questions on the text had to be answered by each student in turn. The questioner then gave his evaluation of the answers he got, and discussion was free if any of the others objected to his evaluations. When discussion had subsided the teacher again took over, resolved disputed points and added anything that had been missed. Meanwhile he had been unobtrusively awarding plus and minus marks for each pupil's performance during the discussion and at the end they were all totted up. Seating at the next session was determined by the number of marks received and the top student took over the honoured role of questioner.[1]

Individual reading and group discussion were thus the major methods for all branches of Chinese studies. The favourite texts for Confucian studies proper were, of course, the Four Books and the Five Classics, and the major ethical and philosophical works of the Sung scholars; the *Classic of Filial Piety*, the *Hsiao-hsüeh* and the *Chin-ssu-lu*. For literary studies a greater variety of texts was used, though the two favourites (both used, according to Ishikawa's count, in at least fifty schools)[2] were the *Wên-chuan* anthology of prose and poetry and the beginner's book of verse, the *Meng-ch'iu*. More advanced students would read the T'ang anthologies and the works of individual writers—mostly T'ang and Sung writers, though after Sorai the Ming poets became fashionable and so later did some of the Ch'ing writers. Literary studies were also varied by occasional poetry meetings or, less often, prose meetings to which students either brought compositions on themes previously set, or composed on the spot. They had, of course, to observe the rhyming rules of Chinese verse forms, even though they were quite meaningless when the poem was 'read off' in Japanese, and there were numerous rhyming dictionaries for this rather tortuous purpose, the only possible point of which was to avoid being considered illiterate should any Chinese chance to see their compositions.

For military strategy—at least in its more erudite forms—there was the Sung compilation of the Seven Books; for

[1] *NKSS*, 3, p. 16.
[2] *Gakkō no hattatsu*, p. 248.

institutional studies the T'ang and Ming codes and the T'ang collection of political maxims, the *Chen-kuan cheng-yao*, while for history there was again a wide variety. The *Tso chuan* and the *Shih chi*, which dealt with the earlier periods of Chinese history, were used in more than a hundred schools, and the *Han shu*, the *Kuo-yü*, the *Shih-pa-shih-lüeh*, and the *Tzu-chih t'ung-chien* (usually Chu Hsi's version, the *T'ung-chien kang-mu*), together with Rai Sanyō's history of Japan, the *Nihon gaishi*, were used in more than fifty.[1]

The dividing line between Confucian study proper and history was no sharp one. One of the Five Classics was the Book of History (the *Shu ching*); another was the *Ch'un-ch'iu*, Confucius's own interpretation, purportedly, of the history of the state of Lu; the *Tso-chuan*, again, was a commentary on the latter. Moreover, the purpose of reading history was primarily to seek moral instruction. The Chōshū school rules say, by way of definition of the nature of the history course, 'students should concentrate on appreciating virtue and condemning wickedness, and study the factors which make for peace or disorder, for loss or advantage, for goodness or badness of human character'.[2] Students had, however, to be careful not to intrude too far their own personal opinions on these matters if they conflicted with the conventional ones. Matsudaira Sadanobu provides a model for the correct approach in his discussion of T'ang and Wu, the founders of the Yin and Chou dynasties respectively. They were held traditionally to be Sages, and yet they had achieved their positions only by revolt against their lords. The Japanese emphasis on the importance of absolute personal loyalty led many to wonder whether they really deserved that appellation and the 'T'ang and Wu problem' was one which bothered Japanese writers. Matsudaira's resolution of the problem is simple. 'Since a whole line of scholars from Mencius on have conceded their right to be described as Sages, how can I dispute the matter? ... In all such discussions it is necessary to recognize one's own limitations, the more so in matters which concern a foreign land and happened a long time ago.' He admits that he is rather worried about the teaching of Japanese history since there are no

---

[1] Ishikawa Ken, *Gakkō no hattatsu*, p. 248.
[2] *NKSS*, 2, p. 743.

accepted authorities for the judgments that have to be made. 'What is one to say, for instance, about the struggle between the Northern and Southern Courts? Should one describe it without touching on the question of legitimacy? I would like to be instructed on this point.'[1] Already, as we shall see in the next chapter, Japan was beginning to breed people with the *hubris* to offer such instruction.

At these advanced levels, examinations were usually written, and followed closely the Chinese practice. They most commonly took the form of exposition in Japanese of the sense of a short text formally divided, at least if a specimen answer given for the Kaga school is an accurate guide, into four parts—the general meaning, comment on individual words, the significance of the passage, and 'further discussion' including the citation of texts of similar or related purport.[2] In the Bakufu school this was the form used for examinations in the classics, but for historical texts there were additionally specific questions on the content of the quoted passages to be answered.[3] Some schools had more advanced forms of examinations called *sakumon* which, like one form of the Chinese examinations after which they were named, required an essay, written in Chinese, on a set theme. At the Wakayama school, at least, Chinese methods were also used to ensure that there should be no suspicion of favouritism. All examination answers were transcribed by clerks in a sealed room before being judged anonymously by the teachers.[4]

The Sciences

Study methods for medicine were traditionally not substantially different from those just described. The reading of Chinese text-books formed almost the whole of the curriculum, and the business was made somewhat more difficult in at least one fief school by the fact that it was a 'tradition' in reading medical books to give the characters a slightly different pronunciation from that normal when reading the Chinese classics.[5] And in the

[1] *Taikan zakki* (*NZZ*, 14), pp. 301, 298.

[2] *NKSS*, 2, p. 194.

[3] Ishikawa, *Gakkō no hattatsu*, p. 220.

[4] *NKSS*, 2, p. 828. This device was introduced in China early in the Sung dynasty. See Miyazaki, *Kakyo*, p. 31.

[5] *NKSS*, 2, p. 835. The Wakayama school. 'The *'go-on'*, not the usual *'kan-on'*, was required.

formal atmosphere of these medical schools such distinctions were important.

There might, however, be a certain amount of practical instruction also by means of anatomical models and clinical demonstrations. The Bakufu school had an attached hospital for this purpose (which fed as well as treated patients at no charge).[1] Other schools had herbal gardens attached to supplement the instruction in herbal medicine which was usually based on the exhaustive Ming botanical compendium, the *Pên-ts'ao kang-mu*. Students in Edo could also attend occasional dissections at the execution grounds, though they did not get close enough to observe the deficiencies of the accepted Chinese accounts of the internal structure of the human body until Dutch texts arrived and began to arouse their suspicions.

Examinations also took the same form of exposition of passages from the medical classics, though at Morioka, at least, these were supplemented by the posing of a certain number of practical questions which tested the ability to organize accumulated knowledge.[2]

Astronomy, too, was traditionally largely a matter of the study of Chinese texts, supplemented by practical observation of the heavens. Mathematics alone depended less on the reading of texts and more on straight teaching of techniques, though even for mathematics the curriculum at three schools is described in terms of the 'nine chapters'—the divisions of an ancient Chinese mathematical work[3]—and some of the more advanced mathematical works, such as those of Seki, were written in Chinese. There were, however, quite a large number of mathematics primers available by the nineteenth century which were written entirely in Japanese, and it was presumably these which were chiefly used in the fief schools. They fall into two broad types: firstly, there were books of practical arithmetic and plane geometry giving rules (often with exhaustive diagrammatic illustrations) for multiplication and division on the abacus and empirical formulas for interest rates, ex-

---

[1] *NKSS*, 7, p. 643.

[2] *NKSS*, 1, p. 704.

[3] The *Chiu-chang suan-shu*. See *NKSS*, 1, p. 704 (Morioka); 1, p. 719 (Hirosaki); 2, p. 646 (Fukuyama). The division of these nine chapters was not according to the mathematical techniques involved but by field of application—taxes, quantities, distances, etc.

changes, estimates of distance, area, volume and so on.[1] Secondly, there were more systematic works which were less concerned with practical problems and progressed from arithmetic rules through cube roots and conic sections to problems involving calculus such as the area of ellipses.[2] In a good many schools the arithmetic taught seems to have been exclusively of the first kind,[3] but in others the second more theoretical discipline was followed, providing an intellectual exercise which had well surpassed the range of application in the technology of the times.[4] Whether intellectual exercise was the main object or not is uncertain. There seems also to have been some kind of Pythagorean belief in the mystical properties of numbers. Thus, the rules of the Tsuwano school, having urged the practical value of a knowledge of mathematics add, 'however, you should not be solely concerned with profitable utility, but endeavour in your training to plumb the principles of numbers',[5] and the prospectus for the Kumamoto school speaks of mathematics in these terms: 'the mysteries of the fluctuations of Ying and Yang, of the movements of the heavens and of astrology, the secrets of the calendar, the details of surveying, of logistics and proportions, the essence of the Way lies in them all'.[6]

As a rare and somewhat esoteric skill, mathematics was developed and taught in the framework of a number of 'schools' —ryū—each with its own methods, terminology and notation and its own 'mysteries' which were not printed in their books but reserved for oral communication to advanced pupils. In this it resembled the teaching of the military arts, of dancing, acting, sword-making and most other practical techniques. In fact, Chinese studies were almost unique in the relative looseness of 'school' affiliations and the absence of any licensing system or of esoteric mysteries. For all the particularism of the

---

[1] The father of these works, itself reprinted many times in the Tokugawa period, was Yoshida Mitsuyoshi's *Jinkōki* (1627).

[2] Examples in the British Museum are: Isomura Yoshinori, *Zōho sampō kangisho* (reprint 1830); Kaneko Masayoshi, *Tōsei kaisanki* (1843); Chiba Tanehide, *Sampō shinsho* (1830).

[3] This seems to have been the case at Izumi (*NKSS*, 1, p. 646) and at Sono (*NKSS*, 1, p. 664.)

[4] E.g. at Tatebayashi (*NKSS*, 1, p. 600) and at Fukuyama (*NKSS*, 2, p. 646).

[5] *NKSS*, 2, p. 503.

[6] *NKSS*, 3, p. 206.

practical ethics taught, and for all the (peculiarly Japanese) emphasis on the bond between teacher and pupil, there was a strong strain of universalism in the Confucian tradition. Learning was for everyone so that, for instance, it was bad manners on the part of a Confucian scholar to refuse to lend a book to another scholar—as Hayashi Razan was supposed once to have hoarded a Chinese work which was the source of his inspiration and refused to lend it to Fujiwara Seika.[1] It was something thereafter always remembered to his discredit.

Military Training

The military side of the school curriculum also had its bookish element. There were some seven major schools of *heigaku*—military studies—and a number of minor ones, each with their own texts and oral traditions. These texts, written by the founders of the various schools, were sometimes in Chinese, sometimes in Japanese, sometimes lengthy expositions, sometimes little more than notes on which to pin oral explanations.[2] They mixed practical advice on the development of troops, the building of fortifications, moving camp, mobilizing supplies, military gamesmanship and the like, with a great deal of moral advice on the importance of using force only in just wars, or of character-training as the sole means to military success, and not a little mystical discussion of the nature of military luck. They quoted liberally from Sun Tzu and the other Chinese military classics, and it was these Chinese originals which the serious student often went on to read. The teachers of *heigaku*, however, were somewhat outside the ambience of Confucianism proper— they belonged to the military rather than the civil half of the schools—and they were much less Sinophile than the teachers of literature or history. Indeed, there were some, as a member of the Bakufu Council of Elders complained at the end of the eighteenth century, who claimed that the Japanese military tradition derived in direct line of descent from the deified hero, Yamato Takeru no Mikoto, and discouraged their students from reading the alien Chinese military works. And what was

[1] Yokoyama, *Kinsei kyōikushi*, pp. 14–15.

[2] Compare the lengthy Chinese *Hei-yōroku* (Saeki, *Bushidō zensho*, 4) written by Naganuma Muneyoshi (1634–90), the founder of the influential Naganuma school, with the briefer note-like Japanese of *Shikan-yōhō* (Saeki, *Bushidō zensho*, 2) by Hōjō Ujinaga (1609–70).

148

even more outrageous, from his point of view, they held that even a knowledge of the basic Confucian canon was unnecessary.[1]

These studies, however, were only for the upper samurai. For the vast majority military studies meant acquiring certain physical skills. It was in this field that the proliferation of schools reached its height. A work published in 1843 lists and describes the following number of different *ryū* in existence at that time, the relative numbers in each branch providing, incidentally, a rough measure of their relative importance.[2]

Swordsmanship		61
„	(*iai*—quick drawing from a sitting position)	5
Lancemanship		29
Musketry		19
Jūdō		20
Archery		14
Horsemanship		9
Use of the halberd		2

Other arts which were taught in some fiefs include swimming and water-horsemanship, the capture of criminals alive, drumming and the blowing of the shell-horn—both the latter being used as a means of giving battle-signals.

Most fiefs had several teachers of each skill, all belonging to different *ryū*, each of whom taught his own pupils at his house or went himself to the houses of high-ranking families to instruct their children. When, in the nineteenth century, the teaching of military skills was increasingly concentrated in the fief schools, each teacher was given a separate booth, or alternatively had the use of a booth on alternate days. The strong personal bond between teacher and pupil was the only organizing principle of the tuition process. It was established by an oath sealed in blood, which usually ran something like this example from one of the archery schools:[3]

1. I deem it a great honour to have imparted to me the secrets of the XX-*ryū*.

[1] Honda Tadakazu, *Kyōsei-ron* (Inoue, *Bushidō sōsho*, 2), p. 253.

[2] Hanejima Terukiyo, *Bujutsu ryūso-roku* (Hayakawa, *Bujutsu sōsho*). Even this list is incomplete. The *Geki-ken sōsho* (by Minamoto Tokushū, also reprinted in Hayakawa, *Bujutsu sōsho*), another work also written in 1843 and concerned with swordsmanship alone, lists some eighty different *ryū*.

[3] *NKSS*, 1, p. 10.

2. I shall concentrate on my training day and night without remission. If, unfortunately, I have no time to practise, I shall give up the bow.

3. I understand that as I progress in my training you will gradually unfold to me the secrets of your art, and that you will regulate my progress not according to the length of my discipleship but according to the skill and accomplishment I display. Realizing this I shall never harbour any resentments against my teacher.

4. The verbal instructions and the written tradition which you give me I will never reveal even to my parents or brothers, much less to anyone else. If it should happen that after receiving the written tradition my house should die out, it shall be immediately burned or returned. It goes without saying that I shall not take pupils of my own until you give me a licence to do so.

5. I shall never indulge in criticism of other schools of archery.

Should I ever offend against any one of these rules, may I receive the divine punishment of Hachiman-bosatsu, Bunten, Taishaku, the Four Tennō, all the Great and Lesser Gods of Japan, the Two Gongen of Izu and Hakone, Temman Tenjin and the Ancestors of my Clan.

In sign whereof I lay my oath and set my seal.

As the reference to the extinction of the pupil's line suggests, it was common for samurai families to adhere from generation to generation to the same *ryū*. In the Chōshū fief adoption—which sometimes meant that the adoptee had to change to his foster family's *ryū*—was the only permitted reason for abandoning a contract of discipleship once it had been made. Those who failed to get along with their teacher and tried to change *ryū* on the grounds that his style didn't quite suit their particular temperament were severely condemned.[1]

What particular arts a samurai learned depended in part on his rank. Horsemanship was for those middle-to-upper ranks of samurai who were supposed to be mounted in battle. (They were expected as a part of their feudal obligations to maintain a stable in any case, though many of them could not afford to do so and had to rent horses for practice.) Rifle practice, on the other hand, was largely for the *ashigaru* foot-soldiers. It was considered a somewhat inferior skill which a gentleman should

[1] *NKSS*, 2, p. 690.

have no part in, and as a consequence was often excluded from the fief schools altogether. Archery was again largely an elegant hobby of the upper classes, having already lost any practical military value by the time the last wars were fought at the beginning of the seventeenth century, though in some fiefs supposedly practical bowmanship was still required of the lowest-ranking foot-soldiers. The two chief weapons of the samurai, however, thought to be both honourable and of practical value, were the sword and the lance, and samurai of all ranks were expected to know how to use them. Altogether the greater the variety of skills a samurai possessed the better, though it was not really expected that he could achieve the highest level of competence in many. Usually he was permitted to specialize and those fiefs which laid down minimum standards of accomplishment as a condition for succession to a family headship generally counted a licence in one branch as enough.

Even the supposedly practical military arts, however, became less so as the peaceful years passed by. The practical uses of the sword were obvious enough in 1600, and the training given to students was rigorous and clearly oriented to its murderous objectives. Life was held cheap and the proponents of one school of swordsmanship were willing enough to challenge the adherents of other schools from motives of sheer self-assertive rivalry, and risk their lives in single combat with real swords. It was a part of the deliberate pacification policy of the Tokugawa rulers to discourage this kind of aggressiveness, and the pledge not to criticize other schools in the oath quoted earlier is evidence of attempts to discourage such a spirit of rivalry. In most fiefs combat between pupils of different schools—even with harmless mock weapons—was strictly forbidden. Given the samurai's pride it could only too easily have led to feuding and general unpleasantness. Even within *ryū*, combat was less and less practised, and swordsmanship and the use of the lance became increasingly a matter of formal gymnastics and disciplined choreography—nothing more than a game for children, as Fujita Tōko said.[1] The object of the training was no longer efficient manslaughter—until the nineteenth century samurai did not envisage the realistic

[1] *Hitachi-obi*, p. 493.

possibility of actually having to use their weapons in earnest—but to secure a certificate of proficiency, first the *menkyo* and then finally the *mokuroku*, the licence which certified that the teacher had taught his pupil all he knew.

It was a peacable kind of approach suited to the peaceful world of the middle century of the Tokugawa period. The samurai had reached a nice compromise between the militancy of their ostensible ethic and the pacific nature of their society. The formalism of the education they received helped to produce men capable of maintaining the niceties of rank and status on which the stability of the social order depended, and the ethic which was imparted was equally designed to reinforce by the sanctions of conscience the existing structure of authority. But it was not an education which intrinsically stimulated and held individual interest, nor did it appear to contemporary samurai as a useful and desirable means to the attainment of personal or group goals. It was quite plainly dull and in addition almost meaningless. It is small wonder that the pages of the Ministry of Education's large compilation of Tokugawa educational documents[1] are filled with fief edicts deploring the samurai's lack of diligence in the study of the civil and military arts and urging them to greater efforts.

In the 1870s, education was a different matter; students were learning something new, something their fathers did not know; they had clear objectives held out before them—their own personal advancement and the strengthening of their nation. The contrast between education in 1770 and education in 1870 is enormous, and the changes of the Meiji Restoration were largely responsible. But these changes were not as sudden as they might seem. The Meiji Restoration was the bursting of the dam, but there had been minor breaches earlier. The situation which produced the cultural and educational changes of the 1870s—the growing contact with Western culture and the awakening of a national consciousness in the face of a foreign military threat—was one which developed gradually. And, as we shall see in the next two chapters, the kind of response to it which the new regime adopted was already foreshadowed in gradual innovations in the fief schools during the last half-century of the old regime.

[1] *NKSS, Nihon kyōikushi shiryō.*

Chapter V

INNOVATIONS

A FAVOURITE ITEM in the historian's conventional list of the ideological sources of the Meiji Restoration is the *Kokugaku* movement—the study and exaltation of Japan's literary, political and religious traditions. It is usually considered, and with good reason, to have developed in the eighteenth and nineteenth centuries as a protest against the adulation of things Chinese which characterized a good many Confucianists and particularly those of the Sorai school. The Confucianists were not all Sinophiles, however. Some of the earlier scholars such as Fujiwara Seika and Hayashi Razan had been sympathetic towards Shinto which they thought closer to Confucian traditions than the Buddhism from which they sought to free themselves. Yamaga Sokō was an ardent nationalist, and Yamazaki Ansai as much a Shintoist as Confucianist and a founder of a school of Shinto doctrine of his own.

It was a revival of this kind of syncretic tolerance, rather than capitulation to the missionary zeal of the Kokugaku movement bent on extirpating Confucian heresy, which led to the gradual introduction of Japanese studies into the curriculum of fief schools from the end of the eighteenth century onwards (though it is certainly true that without the Kokugaku movement proper this might not have happened). In one case, at least, the line of descent is clear. Yamazaki Ansai's influence in the Aizu fief in the mid-seventeenth century was responsible for the grant of official patronage there to students of his particular brand of Shinto theology. It was this which was eventually, over a century later in 1792, incorporated along with the study of ancient Japanese literature into the fief school curriculum.[1]

[1] Ogawa, *Aizu-han kyōiku-hō*, p. 127.

In most cases, however, it was primarily from historical rather than religious concerns that Japanese studies became established in the schools. They achieved a symbiotic relationship with Chinese studies for the reason that Sorai had recommended them earlier, namely in order that, by studying the origins of Japanese institutions, one would better know how to apply the principles of the Chinese Sages in the contemporary world. A lengthy disquisition on the proper nature of learning issued in the name of the fief authorities in Izushi in 1792 makes the point. Everything in the Confucian classics can provide a model for later times:

> However, China and our country differ in climate and in geography. Times have changed since the days of the Sages; each country has its customs, each house its own code of laws.

Hence it is necessary to reinterpret the teachings of the Sages in the light of the present.[1] It is not altogether clear whether the commendation of Japanese studies which comes in a supplementary order is entirely an earnest of the intention to use such studies to supplement this deficiency. There is a slightly different twist, a suggestion of the element of national pride at the root of the Kokugaku movement in the definition of Japanese studies (in this case, *Wagaku*) as 'preserving the country's traditions and the laws of the house'. But the whole tenour of the discussion is to point out the subordinate nature of these studies to the proper Confucian end of learning—'to cultivate the person, regulate the house and rule the kingdom'. Thus, the study and practice of Japanese poetry is recommended because, if approached in the proper spirit, it can contribute to this end by cultivating the sensibilities and hence imparting useful knowledge of human nature and human feelings.[2]

Even poetry is spoken of as an adjunct to historical studies in the plan of organization for the Hirado fief school issued in 1783—the first, as far as the information is available, to state an explicit intention of including Japanese studies in the curriculum (though whether it actually did or not is uncertain). The argument here is similar to such as might have been used by Motoori, the founder of the Kokugaku movement, except

---

[1] *NKSS*, 2, p. 370.
[2] *NKSS*, 2, p. 372.

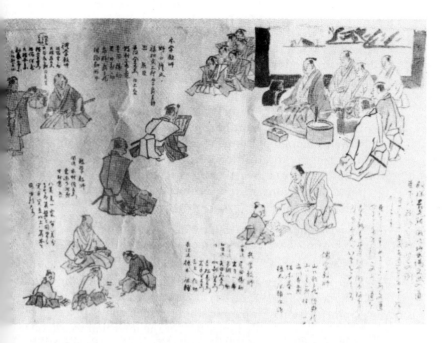

1. Impressions of the Tsuwano fief school drawn from memory in 1915 by a former pupil. An unannounced visit of inspection by the daimyo who sits in front of the screen, top right, his long sword on the rest behind him, a charcoal brazier to his left and a tobacco tray in front of him. (His aides who surround him have had to leave their long swords in an ante-room, like all the other teachers and pupils.) A pupil (centre) is being put through his paces for the daimyo's benefit, expounding a passage from the classics to his fellows, the teacher sitting, anxiously or proudly, behind him. Top left shows a lesson in etiquette, bottom left in mathematics—for which sticks were used as a method of notation. In the bottom right a young pupil receives a sodoku lesson, the teacher using his pointer to indicate the order in which the Chinese characters have to be 'read off' in Japanese.

2. A Meiji brush drawing showing a Confucian scholar lecturing to the daimyo (sitting in the raised alcove with a page boy) and to miscellaneous samurai and pupils. In this obviously civilian-minded fief all present have removed their short swords for the occasion and some of the audience, like the daimyo, have brought along a text to follow the exposition.

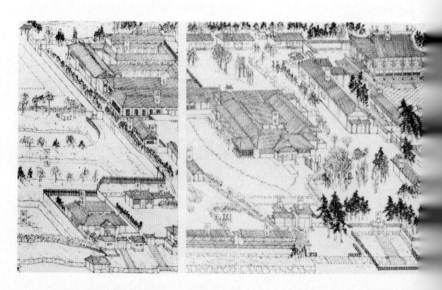

4. The Bakufu school, the Shōheikō, after it had been rebuilt in

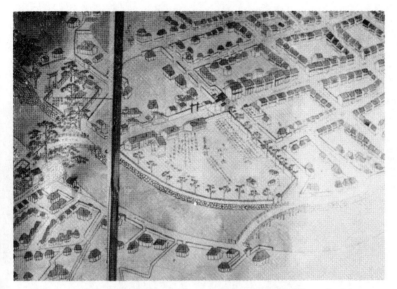

3. The modest fief school at Tsuwano, a small fief in what is now Shimane prefecture. It occupies the compound shown in the centre.

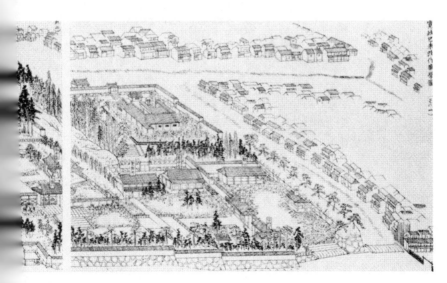

e compound is dominated by the shrine to Confucius in the centre.

5. A room at the Bakufu school used for group reading and group discussions. There are at least two separate groups working as groups to the left (one of them seems just to have sent for a work of reference to the library) and the group on the right appear to be having individual guidance in turn from their teacher. A 1915 copy of an earlier drawing, now in Tokyo University.

that the prime object is less to heighten national consciousness than to analyse the factors making for 'peace or disorder'.

In ancient times the descendants of Heaven came down to earth and set up the Imperial principle. The Emperor Jimmu succeeded to their rule and established the national institutions. There followed periods of peace and periods of disorder. How can we plumb their mysteries? We must start with the *Three Histories*. But to observe and study the ways and customs of the time is the basis for knowing its spirit, and for this we must study the Manyōshū collection of ancient poetry. These are distant times. After the passage of centuries customs change and with them language changes too. Hence the ancient books are difficult to understand, and for this reason we shall appoint a number of specialists in Kokugaku.[1]

It was, again, largely with an eye to historical studies that Hanawa Hokiichi (1746–1821) was given funds by the Bakufu to establish a special school of Japanese studies—the Wagaku Kōdansho—in 1793. Hanawa is said to have been urged to make the petition which resulted in this act of patronage by a highly placed admirer who pointed out that while there were many students of poetry and of Shinto, there were few who could interpret the ancient histories and codes of laws.[2] There is no suggestion that the Bakufu considered a training in Japanese studies a necessary part of a complete education. Hanawa's establishment was not incorporated in the main Bakufu school, and its purpose was rather to train a few specialists in order to keep alive the tradition and at the same time to collect and edit Japanese historical texts. The latter in fact was the chief of Hanawa's functions; a considerable library was collected and scribes were sent to Kyoto to copy everything they could lay hands on. The result, published with the Bakufu's assistance, was the great compendium, the *Gunsho ruijū*, a product of Hanawa's scholarship and the Bakufu's recognition of its duty, as the guardian of the nation, to preserve the national traditions.

In a good many schools Japanese history was brought into the curriculum in the nineteenth century, not in a separate

[1] *NKSS*, 3, p. 168.
[2] *NKSS*, 7, p. 606.

department of Japanese studies, but as part of the historical branch of Chinese studies. The *Nihongi* and the other of the Six Histories, the chronicles covering the period from legendary times to the ninth century, together with the *Ryō no Gige*, the commentary on the eighth century legal codes, were favourite texts, and since they were, after all, written in Chinese, there was no difficulty in admitting them to a Chinese programme of study. By the end of the period Rai Sanyō's *Unofficial History of Japan* (first printed in 1836) had become the most popular text for Japanese history, almost as widely used in the schools as the major Chinese history texts.[1] It, too, owed its acceptance not only to the fact that it appealed to an awakening interest in the Japanese tradition, but also to the fact that it was respectably written in Chinese—and employed good Confucian concepts.[2]

Its significance was much greater than this, however. It provided a model of do-it-yourself Confucianism which encouraged a more independent and critical attitude on the part of the student and a less dulled acceptance of authority. The reader may recall Matsudaira Sadanobu's anxiety, expressed a decade or so before Rai Sanyō had written, about the proper interpretation of Japanese history for which no accepted authority existed. 'What is one to teach, for instance, about the struggle between the Northern and Southern courts? Should one describe it without touching on the question of legitimacy? I would like to be instructed on this point.'[3]

The startling thing about the mid-nineteenth century was that Japan suddenly became full of young samurai who would have been only too delighted to instruct him on this point. The reading of history had always in theory taught how to apply moral principles not only to the evaluation of past events, but also to current problems. As soon as Japan was faced by a crisis situation which required political decision it turned out that the theory had in fact worked in practice. Despite the efforts of generations of cautious Tokugawa educators who thought like Matsudaira Sadanobu and sought to discourage unduly hubristic independence of mind, there was no shortage of men

[1] See p. 144.
[2] Yokoyama, *Kinsei kyōikushi*, p. 739.
[3] See p. 145.

who believed that they had acquired sufficient knowledge of the principles to justify them in vociferous advocacy of policies they believed to be right. Rai Sanyō probably had as much to do with this as anyone. A man of strong passions and intense moral conviction his *Nihon gaishi* showed how one could apply ethical principles to Japanese history. There was no careful skirting round the tricky questions for him. He swept through the centuries distributing praise and blame in no uncertain terms according to his own Confucian criteria; of loyalty, of devotion to the 'public' as opposed to 'private' interests, and of conformity, or otherwise with the 'trend of the times'.[1] It was not that he developed a consistent philosophy of history, or himself pointed out how the criteria by which he judged events in the remoter past could be used for contemporary forecast and action. It was his demonstration that the thing could be done at all which was important. Just as Tsurumine Shigenobu's life was changed by the discovery that Japanese, too, could become the authors of books, so Rai Sanyō must for the first time have opened the eyes of many samurai to the notion that Japanese, too, could make their own applications of principle to history and contemporary politics.

The Kokugaku movement proper, meanwhile, developed outside the world of officially sponsored education, in the nineteenth century with an increasingly strident politico-religious tone. Eventually its nationalism began to seep into the fief schools. Japanese studies began to be granted independence as an integrated field covering Japan's literary and religious as well as political and institutional traditions. The Nagoya fief appointed a teacher of Wagaku in 1833,[2] the Saga fief in 1840,[3] the Tsuwano fief in 1849,[4] and the definition of the purpose of such study at the latter school indicates the kind of compromise which was achieved—accepting the Kokugaku movement's insistence on developing a proper national pride, but rejecting its Sinophobia and sticking tenaciously to Confucian principles of the purpose of learning.

---

[1] See Carmen Blacker, 'Japanese historical writing in the Tokugawa period', pp. 261–2, and Maruyama Masao, 'Chūsei to hangyaku', pp. 393–7.

[2] *NKSS*, 1, p. 135.

[3] *NKSS*, 3, p. 158.

[4] *NKSS*, 2, p. 502.

Kokugaku is the study of the ancient texts of our country, basing itself on the traditions of the Age of the Gods and the native virtue of sincerity. Study ancient matters and ancient writings in a true spirit of loyalty and filial piety, and with no reckless scorn for the classics of Buddhism and Confucianism. Range widely over the chronicles, the histories, prose and poetry, and above all approach these studies with the firm resolve to make them of practical value as an aid in 'ruling the country and giving the people peace'.

Whether a growth in national consciousness resulting from the threat of foreign invasion directly stimulated these developments in the 'thirties and 'forties is not clear, but it is certain that the critical reality of the threat demonstrated by Perry's arrival greatly stimulated the incorporation of Japanese studies in the curriculum. A Wakayama fief order of 1854, significantly issued just one month before a similar order encouraging 'Dutch studies', announces the employment of the grandson of Motoori, and urges Wakayama retainers stationed in Edo diligently to study Kokugaku because

> of recent years foreign ships have frequently visited our shores and it appears that nowadays the various foreign nations are open to each other and each country is well acquainted with matters which are none of its concern involving the internal affairs of other lands.[1] Hence, if anything should happen, it would not do to be ignorant of the history and traditions of our own Imperial land.[2]

Two years later the daimyo of Satsuma comes closer to the Kokugaku position in damning those so-called Confucian scholars who 'think of our Imperial land as a country of "barbarians" and know nothing of the Six Histories or the ancient Japanese codes, much less the Japanese classics', but he still does so in Confucian terms, condemning them as neglecting the true meaning of the Three Principles and the Five Virtues and acting incompatibly with the Way of Confucius, as well as blasphemously offending against the divine wisdom of the goddess Amaterasu.[3]

---

[1] This is presumably the sense of a rather obscure passage.
[2] Horiuchi Shin, *Nanki Tokugawa-shi*, 17, pp. 119, 124.
[3] *NKSS*, 3, p. 284.

It is not clear how much importance was attached to Japanese studies in the schools where they were adopted, but in the one case where it is possible to judge with some accuracy—at the Fukuoka school—its subsidiary position is clear from the fact that by the time of the Restoration, of the twenty-nine appointments to the top four ranks of teachers, only four—of the two lower ranks—were specialists in Japanese studies.[1] Even at Mito where it was the avowed intention when the school was established in 1838 to give equal prominence to both Shinto and Confucianism, to Japanese and to Chinese studies, and where symbolic expression was given to this intention by building a Shinto shrine alongside the Confucian temple,[2] it seems that in actual fact the teaching at the school was predominantly Chinese.[3]

Only the Chōshū school went further and attempted to give Japanese studies pride of place, but this was in 1864, when the fief was already at war with the Tokugawa and firmly committed to the policy of ousting the barbarians and restoring the Emperor. The order announcing the rearrangement of the curriculum into two parts, Fundamental (i.e. Japanese) studies and Chinese studies, makes the intention abundantly clear in terms which were to echo through the history of the following century.

> Our national polity differs from the foreign (meaning, presumably, Chinese) tradition of revolution, and our adherence to the Imperial line, unchanging for ages eternal, has nothing in common with foreign practices of submitting to self-made rulers. Hence to revere the Emperor and oust the barbarian is the fundamental and everlasting duty of subjects of the Emperor. To appreciate this is to understand the national polity, and to establish the basis of our national structure. It is something of which every single one of the fief's retainers must be thoroughly aware.[4]

Even in Chōshū, however, there was no intention of abandoning Confucian studies altogether. The Confucian tradition was too strong, and the Japanese philosophical tradition too thin.

[1] NKSS, 3, p. 19.
[2] See p. 95.
[3] NKSS, 1, pp. 351-2.
[4] NKSS, 2, p. 725.

It was the Mito synthesis which proved most attractive and was eventually to set the pattern for the mixture of Shinto theology and Confucian ethics which formed the official ideology of Meiji Japan.

Western Learning: Medicine

Learning in the Tokugawa period came in national packets. There was Chinese learning—fully equipped with a philosophy, an ethic, a view of history, medicine and other sciences; there was Japanese learning with its much less varied complement of elements; and, a newcomer in the nineteenth century, there was 'Dutch learning' (later 'Western learning'), which gradually unfolded into something comprehensive enough to become a possible rival even of Chinese learning. It was at first, however, only the scientific—and to a lesser extent the artistic—elements of Western culture which appealed to the Japanese, and still at the end of the period it was only for the sake of these elements that Western studies were tolerated in the fief schools.[1]

The successful translation of a Dutch anatomy text-book in 1771 is generally taken to mark the beginning of serious 'Dutch learning'. By the turn of the century interest in the West was no longer merely a matter of superficial exoticism and a love of Western gadgetry such as men like Matsudaira Sadanobu scorned,[2] but a serious pursuit of scientific knowledge acknowledged to be superior to that traditionally available from Chinese texts. Medicine continued to be the major concern, but soon there were translations of Western treatises on physics, chemistry, astronomy, mathematics, geography, metallurgy, navigation, ballistics and military tactics—the last four receiving increasing attention as the need for military defence against possible foreign invasion came to seem increasingly urgent.

The early development of these studies owed little or nothing to official patronage and everything to the energy of individual *rōnin* or low-ranking samurai motivated by intellectual curiosity, by a humanitarian desire to improve medical

---

[1] For the early beginnings of 'Dutch learning' in Japan, see C. R. Boxer, *Jan Compagnie in Japan*, and G. B. Sansom, *The Western World and Japan*.

[2] See his comments on an 'electricity machine' and flying balloons in *Taikan zakki* (*NZZ*, 14), pp. 169–70.

knowledge, by a patriotic concern for the military danger which faced the nation, by a simple enthusiasm for the exotic world beyond the seas, or, according to one cynical observer,[1] by the desire to make a name for themselves quickly in a branch of study which required the mastery of only twenty-six letters rather than many thousands of difficult Chinese characters. It was not until the 1850s and 1860s that they managed to penetrate into the world of the official fief schools; they did so by virtue of the belated recognition of their immediate practical value either for medicine or for military defence.

The developments at the Chōshū fief school seem fairly typical and since they are described in relative detail they will serve as an example. A medical school was first opened in Hagi in 1840 by a doctor of some note who had been trained exclusively in Chinese medicine, but was sympathetically curious about Dutch practices. He showed this sympathy in 1843 by appointing a 'Dutch scholar' to lecture in the medical school.[2] It is evident, however, that the latter did not confine his work to medicine. The following year funds were granted to allow him an assistant because he had been ill and so fallen behind in his work of translating Dutch treatises on saltpetre and copper.[3] (Both, presumably, were for gunnery purposes.) In 1849 the medical school was rebuilt and incorporated as part of the enlarged fief school. By this time the son of the original Dutch scholar had been appointed as a second assistant, and his father was given an increase in rank and salary.

At the same time, not, perhaps, a direct result of the introduction of Dutch studies, but symptomatic of the gradually burgeoning spirit of rationalization in the pursuit of efficiency, a general system of control over all fief doctors was established. In each *gun* district of the fief a Correspondent of the medical school was appointed to pass on directives from the school to other doctors and to act as a model of doctorly conduct. All pedlars of quack medicines and practitioners of dubious patent cures coming from outside the fief were to be reported immediately to the local authorities and examined at the school. Any recognized as skilled doctors would be allowed to stay and take

---

[1] Kume Kunitake, *Kaikoroku*, 1, p. 78.
[2] *NKSS*, 2, p. 679.
[3] *NKSS*, 2, p. 680.

pupils; others would be sent packing. All outbreaks of epidemic diseases were to be reported by the Correspondents through the local samurai offices with full details of symptoms. All local doctors, or would-be doctors, who left the fief for study elsewhere should report their departure to the Correspondent of their district and should appear for interview at the medical school on their return—presumably to report any interesting new cures they had come across. All doctors who wished to practise had to register at the medical school first.[1] It seems that there were also further measures suggested by the head of the medical school which were not put into practice. They included the licensing of all new patent drugs, a prohibition on the administration of drugs by druggists except under doctors' orders, the institution of spot checks on the quality of drugs sold, and the establishment of a free clinic for the poor to be held six times a month at the school.[2]

Although Dutch medicine had managed to penetrate into the official fief school, it was some time before it overcame traditional prejudices. In 1857 it was still necessary to issue an order urging on doctors the value of Dutch medicine and insisting that they should study it in addition to established Chinese practices.[3] A year before this the medical school had been enlarged and a new Seiyō-gakusho—a Centre for Western Learning—had been separately established, though in the same wing as the medical school since it was impossible to divide the library of foreign books.

The purpose of the new centre was primarily the study of Western military techniques and from this point there develops something of a conflict between the medical and the military branches over the allocation of scarce resources of knowledge. A request from the centre in the year of its foundation plaintively urges that it is not being fairly treated, either symbolically or materially. Even if it does have to share the same wing as the medical school, at least it should have its own separate entrance. Only one of the 'Dutch scholars' has been appointed to lecture on military texts, and he is still burdened with unnecessary guard duties. Could he not be released from these, and could

---

[1] *NKSS*, 2, pp. 686, 691.
[2] *NKSS*, 5, pp. 583–6.
[3] *NKKS*, 2, p. 696.

not others who now concentrate exclusively on the medical side be instructed to assist him?[1]

The critical trend of the times was in favour of such requests and in 1859 the school was reconstituted on a bigger scale as the Hakushūdō—the Hall of Extensive Studies—and charged with 'studying in close detail the military and naval systems of Western countries, their histories, the merits and defects of their political systems, and of the character of their peoples and also current affairs, in order that this knowledge shall be of use in defence of the country'.[2] In practice, as the curriculum developed, priority was given to naval and military matters. Sailing techniques, ship-building, surveying, navigation (a schooner was acquired for practice in 1859), naval gunnery, field gunnery, entrenchments, field tactics, ballistics and logistics were the required subjects, history and geography were recommended, and physics, chemical analysis, mathematics and astronomy were optional.[3] Both translations and original texts were used, but all the students studied the Dutch language and about twenty of the more advanced boarded at the school. The school was also a centre of practical research as well as of instruction, and the blast furnace and cannon foundry at Hagi was one of its products.

The medical school was not idle in the meanwhile. About 1859 it too made a request for more funds, particularly for the development of Western studies, pointing out that medicine ranked as one of the four major branches of study in Holland. It requested more official patronage in the way of visits by important personages and daimyo prizes for good students. It suggested that young students should be expected to read original Dutch texts since the translations used hitherto were inadequate. Seating in the school should depend entirely on accomplishment and not at all on rank in order to stimulate a spirit of competition. Students should be allowed into the school from other fiefs. All these requests and suggestions, except the last, were approved, and so was a further suggestion that all druggists should be put under the control of the medical school. (This had been urged in the original request as

---

[1] *NKSS*, 2, pp. 701–2.
[2] *NKSS*, 2, p. 760.
[3] *NKSS*, 2, pp. 760–1.

a useful measure if it should ever be necessary to mobilize medical resources for a military campaign.) A plea for the purchase of more Dutch books and medical instruments was met with the promise favourably to consider requests for specific items. A request to expand the herbal garden was granted, but the fief deferred consideration of two further requests, one for a small hospital—for clinical training—and another for a chemical laboratory for the analysis of drugs. (The request for the latter pointed out that if foreign commerce was stopped there would be an urgent need for home production of imported drugs.)[1] Gradually, thereafter, it seems, Dutch medicine came to dominate the curriculum. In 1863 an order was issued to the effect that all students should start studying Dutch from the beginning of their training instead of, as hitherto, giving a year exclusively to Chinese medicine first.[2]

Despite the manifest success of Dutch medicine it was usually late in the period before it secured official recognition in the fief schools. Professional conservatism was strong, particularly among the higher-ranking samurai doctors who controlled the fief medical schools. Their privileged position meant that status-striving did not reinforce intellectual curiosity as an incentive for inquiring into new ideas, and the fact that their position was usually hereditary meant that reverence for their family traditions of Chinese medical practice was a matter of positive piety, not simply of indolence. In Fukui, Dutch medicine was practised secretly by non-samurai town doctors for some time before they won over a number of lesser samurai doctors and in 1848 eventually got the backing of fief officials and forced Dutch medical studies into a respectable place in the school curriculum—in the teeth of opposition from the school director.[3] At Fukuyama there is no evidence that Dutch medicine was ever taught at the fief medical school despite the fact that general Western studies (chiefly military) were taught in the main school from 1854 on—and originally by a doctor.[4] In Saga too there were several Dutch scholars among the town doctors long before Dutch medicine was taught in the fief

---

[1] *NKSS*, 2, pp. 697–8.
[2] *NKSS*, 2, p. 720.
[3] *NKSS*, 2, p. 43.
[4] *NKSS*, 2, p. 637.

school (some of them pupils of Siebold, the scholarly doctor of the Nagasaki trading mission).[1] The Bakufu had had a medical school in Edo ever since 1765, a large and well-endowed establishment with dormitories for senior students. Dutch studies were never allowed within its doors, however, despite the fact that some of the earliest pioneers of Dutch medicine had been Bakufu doctors. The Bakufu in fact contained a good many people who recognized the value of Dutch medicine, but rather than create dissension by forcing it into the established school, support was given instead to an unofficial school which some eighty doctors had set up, originally as a vaccination centre, in 1858.[2]

The tolerance of the head of the Chōshū school was exceptional, therefore, and this was, in fact, one of the first medical schools to start Dutch studies. The Sakura fief began in the same year, in 1843, with two teachers of Dutch medicine, but here the initiative seems to have been taken personally by the daimyo, Hotta Masayoshi (1810–64), who was later to distinguish himself in the treaty negotiations. He had prepared the way five years before by sending a doctor to Nagasaki expressly to study Dutch medicine.[3] In a good many fiefs it seems that the introduction of vaccination about 1849 was the critical factor in demonstrating the value of Dutch medical practices. A number of what became Dutch medical schools started soon after this as vaccination centres.[4] The Bakufu, which in 1849—such was the influence of the conservative doctors—went to the trouble of issuing a special order forbidding the practice of Dutch medicine (except for surgery and ophthalmic medicine, in which fields, presumably, since the success or failure of treatment was externally apparent, its efficacy could hardly be reasonably disputed) was by 1857 advertising widely in Edo for volunteer doctors to go to vaccinate the Ainu who were, apparently, particularly susceptible to smallpox.[5]

Dutch studies apart, the gradual systematization of medical

---

[1] Kume Kunitake, *Kaikoroku*, 1, pp. 76–8.

[2] Yokoyama, *Kinsei kyōikushi*, p. 551.

[3] *NKSS*, 1, p. 251.

[4] E.g. Usuki (*NKSS*, 3, p. 99); Funai (*NKSS*, 3, p. 108); Saga (*NKSS*, 3, p. 153); Fukui (*NKSS*, 2, p. 63).

[5] Shihōshō, *Tokugawa kinrei-kō*, 6, p. 592.

teaching was a common feature of many schools in the last decades of the period, and so too was the institution of general fief control over doctors, such as Chōshū began around 1850. In the memorandum in which he first proposed such a system the head of the Chōshū school was able to point out that already the fiefs of Kumamoto, Yonezawa and Matsue went as far as to limit practice to doctors who had passed an examination and secured a fief licence.[1] So did the Kōchi fief from 1846 onwards and here a further innovation was the establishment of a primitive free health service in 1841. The order announcing it speaks of the daimyo's distressed concern that so many people are dying for want of the money to buy medicines. Henceforth the indigent sick were to inform the village headman who would visit them and arrange for them to receive treatment from a doctor. The doctor was to give them what medicines they required, and the bills for such medicine were to be presented by the headman twice a year and paid by the fief. All doctors treating subsidized patients were to report to the medical school details of the patient's illness and treatment, and to report again when the patient recovered or died. It was presumably one purpose of the scheme to collect case histories for research purposes.[2]

Western Learning: Military

It was more often the military than the medical value of Dutch studies which secured their recognition and incorporation in fief schools. Most of the schools or departments established in the 1850s and 1860s gave pride of place to navigation and gunnery. In this field, too, the ground was prepared not by official patronage but by the energy of subordinate officials and rōnin such as Takashima Shūhan (1798–1866), an official of the Nagasaki trading office, and Egawa Tarōzaemon (1801–55), the Bakufu intendant in the Izu peninsula.

There were, to be sure, some in the Bakufu and among the daimyos who gave such men support; the Bakufu itself established a translation section in its astronomy office in 1811, but Takahashi Sakuzaemon (1785–1829), its energetic organizer,

---

[1] *NKSS*, 5, p. 585.
[2] *NKSS*, 2, p. 921.

was destined to die in prison eighteen years later for the sin of giving maps to Siebold. He believed that the exchange of scientific information should be free and mutual. But to the Bakufu authorities, as to modern governments, powerful foreign nations were first and foremost potential invaders and only secondarily sources of useful knowledge. The students of Dutch learning had to contend, too, with the envious animosity of some of the traditional Confucian scholars. It was one of these, Torii Yōzō (c. 1800–74), a member of the Hayashi family and later chief adviser of the Regent Mizuno Tadakuni, who was responsible for the wholesale arrests of Dutch scholars in 1839 and later of Takashima, the gunnery expert, as well— arrests which were a severe blow to the development of Dutch studies throughout Japan. The trumped-up charges of involvement in traitorous plots which he used to ensnare Watanabe Kazan (1793–1841) and Takano Chōei (1804–50), the chief victims of the 1839 arrests, were believed by no one, and there was more than a suspicion that he had never forgiven them for their help in a survey of Uraga Bay which demonstrated the utter incompetence of his own survey carried out by traditional methods.[1] But there could be no doubt of their guilt on other charges—that they had shown unseemly temerity in criticizing (in openly circulated memorials) the Bakufu's lack of policy for dealing with the visits of foreign ships and the inadequacies of its coastal defence.

The atmosphere of suspicion which surrounded Dutch studies was certainly not such as to encourage their growth. It is true that there was an element of boyish xenophilia and love of the exotic in the attitude of many 'Dutch scholars' to their studies which might well have appeared offensively un-Japanese to conservative patriots. Even the broad-minded Suzuki Akira (1765–1837) who remarks that the Dutch seem to be of a superior moral disposition to the Chinese (sober and sincere; not given to frivolity, and thorough in their scholarship) and speaks of the development of Dutch studies as bringing great potential benefit and being a sign of the enlightened rule his contemporaries enjoyed, nevertheless inveighs against the way in which many 'Dutch scholars' become infatuated with the West. They allow themselves to be fascinated with

[1] Satō Shōsuke, 'Bansha no kigen' and 'Bansha no goku'.

167

useless toy devices and theories of no practical value; they have a taste for foreign luxuries and they would even flirt with Christianity. In this respect they are no different from the Chinese scholars who are prostrate with admiration of China.[1] And indeed, the New Year parties of Otsuki Gentaku and his doctor friends, eaten at tables on improvised chairs, with knives and forks and makeshift Dutch clothes, were not very different from Sorai's Chinese parties a century before.[2] And the fad for adopting Dutch names was reminiscent of the habit of Sorai and his followers of giving themselves pseudo-Chinese surnames.[3] To add to their offensiveness, the 'Dutch scholars' were apostles of doom, reminding the Bakufu of foreign dangers which most officials preferred to forget and which they were only too prone to dismiss on the grounds that the 'Dutch scholars' disloyally underestimated the strength of Japan and in their blind fascination with things Western exaggerated the strength of her potential enemies. Even the daimyos who were convinced of the value of Western studies did not aid their diffusion, partly because of the suspicion which surrounded them, partly because, as one 'Dutch scholar' said early in the century, 'it is an old parochial tradition to seek exclusive profit for one's own fief and to keep secret any discoveries from others'.[4]

When, with Perry's arrival, the promise of doom seemed about to be fulfilled, there was a change. Egawa was appointed to a responsible position in Edo and allowed to start building a reverberatory furnace in Izu. (Saga had built the first in 1850). Takashima was released from prison and set to propagating his knowledge of Western gunnery. Daimyos with coastal fiefs were ordered to install Western-style gun emplacements, and Western-style military drill was begun on hastily constructed

[1] *Hanareya gakumon*, p. 389.

[2] Yokoyama, *Kinsei kyōikushi*, pp. 727-8. Otsuki (1757-1827) apparently sobered up after receiving an appointment to the Bakufu's translation office and somewhat modified his championship of Dutch medicine, claiming only that it was useful to fill out the weaker spots of Chinese practice—facts which one scholar sees as the 'sell-out' of what was once a radical anti-Bakufu movement as soon as the authorities began to take a semi-benevolent interest and seek to turn Dutch studies into yet one more instrument of oppression (Satō Shōsuke, 'Yōgaku no kenryoku-reizoku-ka').

[3] Tokutomi Iichiro, *Kinsei kokuminshi*, 26, p. 130. A Kyoto fan is supposed once to have called on Doeff, the Dutch Factor to ask for a new Dutch name. He had grown tired of the one an earlier Factor had given him some years before.

[4] Ohara Shōkingo, *Hokuchi kigen* (*Nihon bunko*, 7), p. 17.

training grounds. In 1856 the Bakufu established the first large-scale school of Western studies, the Bansho shirabe-sho, or Office for the Inspection of Foreign Books. It was first conceived as a translation office but it rapidly developed into a flourishing school with, at the end of the first year, nearly two hundred students. A dormitory was installed in 1858 and the number of students swelled with the admission of retainers from other fiefs. It was with reluctance that the Bakufu thus opened its doors to non-Bakufu students, but this was no more than just, for all the teachers had had to be borrowed from other fiefs. Such was the improvidence of the Bakufu that there were none competent for the job among the Bakufu's own retainers. Still, in 1862, thirty-two of the thirty-four teachers of the highest ranks were samurai from other fiefs, and of the two Bakufu retainers one had only belatedly been released from prison in 1859.[1]

At first Dutch was the only language taught in the school, but in 1860 English was added, in 1861 French, and the next year German. By this time metallurgy, mathematics, 'industrial studies', and Western art had supplemented military tactics and navigation in the curriculum. In 1862 the name of the school was changed. The 'foreign books' it was to 'inspect' were now called Yōsho ('Western') rather than Bansho (literally 'Barbarian'), a nice indication of the growing feeling that there was no point in being gratuitously offensive to those who held the whip hand, and of the gradual weakening of the tradition of insular arrogance. Four years later the name was again changed to Kaiseijo, the Place for Fruitful Discovery, a name also used at Kōchi and Satsuma,[2] conveying a rather more positive assertion of the school's function. By this time geography, physics and history had been added to the curriculum.[3]

Most of the other fiefs were slower than the Bakufu in establishing such schools—most were set up in the last four or five years of the regime. The Chōshū school described above was exceptionally early and the Saga fief was likewise ahead of the field—it appears to have set up a department of Dutch studies in the fief school in 1840. The subsequent history of this

[1] *NKSS*, 7, pp. 667, 665.
[2] *NKSS*, 2, p. 926; 3, p. 288.
[3] *NKSS*, 7, p. 663.

department again illustrates the tussle between military and medical interests. At one point the department was transferred to the gunnery school and only in 1861 restored to the fief school for the teaching of Dutch studies in their own right.[1]

Where details of the curriculum of Dutch studies are available it is clear that they were taught very much as Chinese was taught. Blind-reading sodoku was the first step. The Chōshū school used a two-volume Dutch primer and teachers were told: 'For volume one first teach the reading and when students have thoroughly mastered this explain to them the meaning in detail. For the first part of the second book go through once giving the reading and then go straight on to explanation. For the second part you may start straight away with explanation.'[2] As with Chinese studies—and out of even direr necessity given the shortage of teachers—students who were partially trained were set to teach sodoku to their juniors.

Like Christian theological students studying comparative religion, or West Point cadets being introduced to the works of Marx, the good samurai had to be careful to approach Dutch studies in the proper spirit. 'Immature minds', warns a directive of the Chōshū school when Dutch studies were started on a comprehensive basis in 1859,

> are easily fascinated by exotic ideas and strange facts. Those who take a delight in foreign ways end up by losing their native Japanese spirit and become weakly cowards, a shocking eventuality against which you must ever be on your guard.

A supplementary order urges that respectable Japanese translations should always be invented for the technical names of parts of cannon and ships.[3] Both the Bakufu and the Kaga fief had issued much the same order somewhat earlier, and inveighed against those who took a frivolous and un-Japanese delight in rolling barbaric Dutch words off their tongues.[4] The proper attitude was outlined by the daimyo of Satsuma in an order of 1856. Quoting Sun Tzu to the effect that a knowledge of the enemy was essential to victory, he goes on:

[1] *NKSS*, 3, pp. 152–4.
[2] *NKSS*, 3, p. 763.
[3] *NKSS*, 2, pp. 706–7.
[4] *NKSS*, 7, p. 677; 2, p. 120.

At this time when defence against the foreign barbarians is of crucial importance it is the urgent duty of all samurai both high and low to co-operate in learning of conditions in foreign lands so that we may adopt their good points to supplement our deficiencies, reinforce the military might of our nation and keep the barbarian nations under control. Hence, in whatever time you have, study translations of foreign books to gain close acquaintance with foreign customs and mechanical devices so that they may become wings for our endeavour to spread the Imperial influence throughout the world.[1]

The Military Skills

Only a few samurai were ever directly involved in Dutch studies proper, but most of them were affected by the change in military techniques which resulted in the last two decades of the period from the conjunction of a Western military threat and a gradually developing acquaintance with Western military science. The formal individual arts of swordsmanship, archery and the use of the lance were no longer enough to meet the challenge. In the 1770s Hayashi Shihei had written of the need for co-ordinated drill. He complained that none of the fief horses which trod so prettily in riding exhibitions would last five minutes in battle and warned that Hideyoshi's defeat at the hands of the Ming troops—a defeat solely due to the enemy's drilled co-ordination of their efforts—could easily be repeated unless the samurai got some practice in *chōren*—team-work drill.[2] At the time his was a lone and unheeded voice, but in the nineteenth century the realization gradually dawned that military training had to be in earnest.

The process of reform began somewhat before Perry's arrival. Tactical drills were being held in Edo for some time before 1844, and a series of Bakufu orders concerning their regulation gives a nice measure of the growing sense of crisis. Until 1844 this noisy pursuit which involved the use of drums and gongs had been encouraged but, within the precincts of Edo, only at a minimum distance of 30 *chō*—about 2 miles— from the outer moat of the Shogunal palace. (Apart from

---

[1] *NKSS*, 3, p. 285.
[2] *Jōsho* (*NKS*, 12), p. 11.

concern for noise abatement there was also, presumably, thought to be a security risk. A drill could be used as a cover for a conspiratorial attack on the palace.) In that year, in view of the urgency of the situation, a special dispensation permitted daimyos to hold drills at their residences if they were more than 20 *chō* from the outer moat. In 1847 the distance was reduced to 5, in 1850 to 3 *chō*, and finally in 1853 it was ordered that drills could take place anywhere beyond the moat.[1]

The insistence on the importance of co-ordinated drill became more strident in the following years and increasingly it was Western-style drill which was required. Saga had introduced drills as early as 1844[2] and Chōshū by 1850;[3] in the 'fifties most other fiefs followed suit.[4] The Bakufu built a number of training grounds for the purpose in Edo and so far recognized its importance that in 1864 permission was given for samurai to call at the palace on their way home from training still wearing their drill clothes if necessary.[5] Even the niceties of proper etiquette were beginning to give way.

A second associated innovation was a sudden revaluation of the importance of rifle and cannon. Musketry, which had been a despised skill of the inferior foot-soldiers, was allowed into the Kaga fief school for the first time in 1853;[6] by 1863 Enfield rifles were being reproduced in the fief and all samurai were being urged to learn how to use them.[7] Another order three years later refers to the lessons of the Chōshū campaign as demonstrating the superiority of the new rifles and ordered the final abandonment of traditional schools of musketry.[8] A number of other fiefs issued similar orders recommending rifle training for samurai and the replacement of traditional weapons. The Kumamoto fief by 1867 had bought as many as 16,000 rifles of various patterns from England,[9] and the Tosa fief

---

[1] *NKSS*, 7, pp. 674–6.
[2] *NKSS*, 3, p. 185.
[3] *NKSS*, 2, p. 687.
[4] Mentions of *chōren* first appear in the school records of the Kaga school in 1858, the Fukui school in 1854, Fukuyama, 1853 and Kagoshima, 1856 (*NKSS*, 2, p. 124; 2, p. 6; 2, p. 637; 3, p. 280).
[5] *NKSS*, 7, p. 689.
[6] *NKSS* 2, pp. 174–5.
[7] *NKSS*, 2, pp. 129, 130.
[8] *NKSS*, 2, p. 904.
[9] E. M. Satow, *Diplomat in Japan*, p. 279.

finally went as far in 1867 as to organize all its samurai into infantry companies.[1]

The military arts traditionally taught in the schools were also affected. As a number of fief directives emphasized, although the next war was likely to be a war of bullets there might be close in-fighting too.[2] In any case the sword and the lance were to be treated as weapons for use in earnest, no longer as adjuncts of a graceful gymnastic display. Writing in 1843, Fujita Tōko describes the growth of combat training in the Mito fief. The face and body guards which permitted the trainee to use full-weight leather and bamboo mock swords with full force and still inflict nothing much worse than bruises on his oppenent had, in fact, been developed by the Shin-kage-ryū in the eighteenth century, but they were not much used until considerably later. (Apart from the disapproval of duelling, it was thought to be un-samurai-like to protect the body, and more proper, in any case, that fencers should learn to protect each other from harm by self-restraint.) In the first decades of the nineteenth century a few reformers had insisted on the importance of combat training, and by the 1830s it was becoming general in Mito despite considerable opposition.[3] From the late 'forties onwards, various fiefs began to encourage duels as a form of training, and at Fukui the fief issued face and body guards to make this safely possible.[4] The secretive exclusiveness of the various *ryū* was generally recognized to be an abuse and a hindrance to the development of useful skills, and orders urging all the *ryū* to train together and rescinding earlier bans on duels were common.[5] The Tsuyama fief so far rationalized the process as to introduce a scheme whereby new teachers of the sword and lance had to prove their worth by winning at least six out of ten duels with would-be teachers of other *ryū*. Any *ryū* which could not produce a single pupil capable of winning six duels was to become extinct. Established teachers were still

---

[1] *NKSS*, 2, p. 904.
[2] *NKSS*, 2, pp. 5–6; 2, p. 130.
[3] *Hitachi-obi*, p. 493.
[4] *NKSS*, 2, p. 6.
[5] In Fukui in 1850 (*NKSS*, 2, p. 5); in Sakura in 1851 (*NKSS*, 1, p. 251); in Chōshū in 1853 (*NKSS*, 2, p. 688); in Tosa in 1855 (*NKSS*, 2, p. 902); in Kagoshima in 1856 (*NKSS*, 3, p. 280); in Tsuyama in 1858 (*NKSS*, 2, p. 572); and in Tottori in 1861 (*NKSS*, 2, pp. 429 and 342.)

forbidden to duel with each other, however—too much pride was at stake there—and it was still half-apologetically that the system was instituted. 'To duel and go all out to force a victory may seem like fostering a spirit of rivalry with all the troubles which that causes, but this is necessary, for you are training for moments when life and death will hang in the balance.'[1]

Archery suffered a decline in these years. Foot-soldiers in Kaga who were trained in it for supposedly practical purposes were ordered to give up their bows and take to rifles in 1853,[2] and archery was similarly excluded from the Bakufu military schools in 1862,[3] and from the Tosa school in 1867.[4] In Chōshū it was not abolished, but samurai were ordered to give up target-shooting as a garden-party game and go out into the hills to shoot duck.[5] Horsemanship, too, underwent a metamorphosis in Chōshū. In 1863 mounted samurai were told to train for the new cavalry squadrons which a year or so later served the fief so well in its war against the Bakufu. They were to give up their traditional exhibition riding, and further, the order added, they were definitely not to continue the practice of substituting formal indoor exercises with wooden horses on rainy days.[6]

The rather timid and apologetic tone in which many of these orders are couched, and the frequency with which they had to be repeated, are an indication both of the looseness of discipline which had developed in Tokugawa military establishments and of the dead weight of tradition which innovation had to overcome. Change was beginning in the last years of the Tokugawa period, but it was a slow beginning and one which still did not represent a response commensurate with the potential challenge. One reason was that the attempts at innovation were hesitant, selective and half-hearted. The source of the innovations was Western and so suspect. Insular patriotism combined with the traditional suppression of curiosity and fear of individualistic innovation inherent in

[1] *NKSS*, 2, pp. 566–7.
[2] *NKSS*, 2, pp. 174–5.
[3] *NKSS*, 7, p. 686.
[4] *NKSS*, 2, p. 916.
[5] *NKSS*, 2, p. 709. This was in 1859.
[6] *NKSS*, 2, p. 720.

Tokugawa educational practices to hold in check the love of novelty as an end in itself which the Meiji Government was to liberate. The Bakufu, smarting from its defeat at the hands of Chōshū in 1866, issued an order complaining that:

> of recent years military training has lost sight of reality and tended to useless ornament. There are many who try out pet schemes of their own from a sheer delight in novelty, and look on the whole business as little more than a game. Or else, regardless of established rules, they dress themselves up in foreign-style costumes . . .[1]

One of the differences between Japan in the 1860s and Japan in the 1870s was that the Meiji Government gave full rein to the young bloods who wore top hats and ate beef from a sheer delight in novelty and looked on the whole business of 'civilization and enlightenment' as exciting and enjoyable—and it managed at the same time to turn their energies to good use.

[1] *NKSS*, 7, p. 689.

Chapter VI

TALENT, TRAINING AND THE SOCIAL ORDER

IT IS ONE OF THE AWKWARD FACTS of human life that men differ widely, and in ways that admit of no exact prediction by the laws of heredity, in their natural endowments —in the capacity to develop those skills and qualities which are valued by their fellow-men and are necessary to keep their society going. It is awkward because all societies so far have had stratification systems—systems of differential allocation of income, prestige and power—and all societies have had families of a kind which give parents a natural incentive to transmit privileges they themselves enjoy to their children. The fact that there is no very close correspondence between the capacities of children and those of their parents creates a problem, therefore, for any society which seeks to relate its stratification system to the actual performance of certain socially valued functions. How great the problem is depends on three main factors; firstly, the extent to which societies feel they need to ensure that pegs of an infinite variety of shapes are placed in the holes they correspond to—a function partly of the complexity of the economy and the degree of occupational specialization, partly of the size and nature of the problems (of invasion, famine, lagging economic growth, etc.) which the members of the society feel they have to face. The second variable is the set—or rather the various sets—of values and assumptions current in the society concerning status differences; the extent to which an unequal distribution of wealth and power and prestige is accepted as natural and proper, the importance attached to heredity or to achievement as a justification for such inequality, whether the model of inequality accepted is a 'class' one which sees society as divided into broad groups of different 'kinds' of people, a 'pyramid-ladder' one which sees society as an infinitely graded pecking order, or a 'feudal one' which sees society as a network of small groups made up of masters, young masters, senior servants, junior servants and so on. The third variable is the actual distribution of income, power and prestige which, in fact, obtains in the society.

The educational system is a nodal point between these three. The form it takes will greatly influence the actual status system. At the same time the forms it is likely to take are very much circumscribed by the other two factors—the awareness of a need for differentiated talents, and the ideal status system.

When these two are hard to reconcile, or when a change in one upsets the compromise which has been reached between them, the educational system has to bear the brunt of the necessary adjustments. In North America, for instance, the political ideal of equality requires that invidious distinctions between the able and the not so able should be kept to a minimum level consistent with the need to induce students to achieve the necessary competences. Thus all varieties of achievement are equated in value. The course in dancing, social and square, carries its meed of credits along with the course in literature and physics. 'The gifted child' and the 'specially handicapped' are grudgingly admitted to exist as problems to be studied by a special branch of educational theory. The system works well until sputniks raise a scare about the society's competitive performance and the demand arises that the generous pursuit of equality of prestige should give way to the ruthless stimulation of certain special kinds of excellence.

In nineteenth-century England, by contrast, the school system reflected a society which took for granted invidious distinctions of human worth, a society in which the major status division coincided with an occupational division between leaders, officers and managers on the one hand, and the hewers of wood, drawers of water and feeders of cannon on the other, and a society in which substantial hereditary continuity in the composition of the 'two nations' was considered genetically inevitable and morally desirable. Different kinds of schools developed, respectively, qualities of leadership for the one class and the literacy, numeracy and thrifty diligence necessary for the other. At the same time they imparted widely differing cultures which validated these status differences and ensured that when a man's occupational life took him across the status barrier his children, at least, would be properly socialized for accepted membership of the class that he had joined.

In England the situation has been altered by a change in both the relevant factors. Occupational specialization has required the schools to play a far greater part in developing economically useful skills—many of them in a vast new range which can be classed neither as leadership nor as the hewing of wood. Gradually, assessments of the national need for such skills have prompted politicians to find ways of seeking the capacities to develop them among as wide a section of the population as possible. At the same time a growing egalitarianism challenged the legitimacy of a system which both emphasized differences in human worth and accepted their largely hereditary determination. The compromise result was the doctrine of 'equality of opportunity'. A differentiated educational system was preserved and the differentiation continued to imply invidious differences of worth, but with public, grammar, technical and secondary modern schools at one level, and with Oxbridge, Redbrick, institutes and training colleges at the next, the differentiation became more graduated and more clearly related to occupational needs. At the same time access to these different facilities was allocated increasingly on the basis of tested talent rather than of birth. It was a nice compromise. It provided a wide enough range of recruitment for important occupational positions to ensure at least that minimum level of competence necessary to keep the system ticking over, and it marked a concession to the egalitarianism of the left. At the same time the particular kinds of tests chosen to measure innate capacities, together with the facts that there *are* rough correspondences between the capacities of parents and those of their children and that there has been enough ability-selecting mobility over past centuries to produce a higher concentration of superior capacities in the upper status groups, have ensured that the amount of inter-class mobility has not been so very great. Thus there has been enough hereditary continuity of class groups to preserve in large measure the cultural and prestige differences between them. The intellectual and aesthetic standards of English high culture have been preserved, the psychic consolations of snobbery (straight, inverted or defensive) have not been lost, and those members of the upper classes who had to design these concessions to egalitarianism and national efficiency have never had cause to feel that anything they held dear was seriously threatened.

Only recently has the gathering strength of a new kind of egalitarianism, which challenges the desirability of invidious distinctions of worth altogether, begun to upset this compromise and push the educational system in a North American direction. At present the schools and universities are caught between a number of conflicting trends. The new egalitarianism has to contend on the one hand with a growing pressure to use differential rewards—at least of money—to develop certain desirable scarce capacities, especially scientific ones. On the other hand it must contend with the emphasis on preserving cultural standards which derives from the nineteenth-century status system, and with the emphasis on high intellectual standards which derives from the more recent meritocratic age of equality of opportunity.

The way this universal problem was dealt with in Tokugawa Japan is of some interest. We shall examine in this chapter first of all how the school system was shaped by these two factors— the existing degree of appreciated need for differentiated talents and the ideal status system, and secondly the effects of a change in one of these variables—an enhanced appreciation of the need to develop special capacities. It will become obvious that the educational system itself was by no means simply a dependent variable in the equation. Ideas about status changed, too, and this was in part because of the schools and of their inherent tendency to call attention to differences in innate capacities and developed talents.

In one respect the initial compromise was easy to reach. There was no difficulty in preserving the main status division between the samurai and the rest. With few exceptions (to be considered in the next chapter) commoners, and usually the lower-ranking foot-soldiers too, were excluded from the samurai schools. At the other end of the scale, the daimyo's son in Edo, and possibly the children of some of the fief elders of the highest rank, would be protected from invidious comparisons by being educated at home by private tutors. But the problem lay in the sharp divisions of status within the intermediate stratum of samurai, all of whose children went to the same school. It obviously could be embarrassing if the son of a high-ranking samurai turned out to be a dunce while the son of a lower samurai proved a genius. What devices were adopted to prevent this from happening? Or if it did happen, to prevent the fact from becoming too obvious? Or if it happened and was obvious, to mitigate its social ill-consequences?

These were problems for those who organized schools. There were, potentially, other problems for those with political responsibility for the society, problems related to the other variable. Were they conscious of these problems? Was it at all considered necessary to ensure that men of ability occupied positions of authority? If so, to what extent and in what ways was the kind of ability demonstrated in school performance considered to be relevant to desirable administrative ability? And how were the requirements for such ability reconciled with the exigencies of the hereditary status system?

The Problem in the School

As far as the problem of school organization was concerned, its magnitude was considerably lessened by the general emphasis on the moral purposes of education. The purely intellectual accomplishment of learning to read Chinese was merely a means to an ethical end. A dull pupil who had difficulty with his books, but who nevertheless was virtuous in his conduct, respectful to his superiors, loyal to his lord and filial to his parents, had acquired the essentials. And these were the qualities which were held up to praise. Mere cleverness was disparaged. The school rules of the Nishi-ōji fief put the matter well:

> There is no need to become a scholar widely read and with encyclopaedic knowledge. It is enough to get a thorough grasp of the principles of loyalty, respect, filial piety and trust. Wide learning and literary accomplishments are not necessary. Anyone can manage to get hold of the general principles of the Four Books and the Five Classics by the time he is thirty or forty. It

all depends on diligence. Even the dullest of wits can manage it if he applies himself earnestly enough.[1]

Some people, it goes on, can walk to Edo in ten days. It might take others fifteen, but anybody can get there in the end.

The Sunday School approach implied Sunday School criteria of rating. Regularity of attendance was the clearest objective mark of the right moral attitude. Says one Kumamoto scholar (though, be it noted for later reference, in a tone of bitter complaint):

> A student who attends regularly is rewarded even if he is of only average ability, whereas even an outstandingly good pupil, if he does not attend regularly, be he never so admirably behaved and accomplished, will never be given a prize.[2]

Inasmuch as excellence was judged less by intellectual ability, the distribution of which rarely corresponds with a hereditary status scale, than by effort, regular attendance and good conduct which training can instill in almost anyone, the danger to the status system was minimal. The tuition methods employed at the lower levels minimized it still further. The fact that sodoku and private reading were matters of individual instruction meant that the pupil's performance was a private matter between himself and his teacher, not exposed to the public view. The general lectures, with no give and take between pupil and teacher, required only an appearance of intelligent interest, not necessarily intelligent comprehension. In a good many schools the higher-level discussion groups—where differences in ability could be embarrassingly obvious—were not compulsory. In some they were only for specialist dormitory students; in others only day-boys who were sufficiently confident in their abilities attended on a voluntary basis.

In case there should be any mistake, however, some schools went out of their way to emphasize that rank was all-important, and this was the easier in that rei—one of the cardinal virtues which education was supposed to impart—was interpreted to mean the meticulous observance of status distinctions. Some detailed regulations are recorded. At the Kaga fief school, for instance, it was laid down that members from the very highest

---

[1] *NKSS*, 1, p. 449.
[2] Nakayama Shōrei, *Gakusei-kō* (*NKSS*, 5), p. 614.

rank of families should come to the school accompanied by only two retainers, one additional servant to mind the student's sandals during lectures, and one umbrella-holder on rainy days. The next rank could have one retainer, a sandal-minder and an umbrella-holder. The next, one retainer and a sandal-minder, but they should carry their own umbrella. Younger sons, and those of the lowest rank, should come without servants; the school would provide someone to look after their sandals *en masse*.[1] The similar Yonezawa rules governing the precise place at which examination candidates of different ranks were to sit and remove their swords have already been quoted.[2]

Equally there were rules, such as those quoted earlier from Mito,[3] which regulated the *intensity* of education according to rank. Since education was primarily a means of imparting the degree of moral and intellectual training necessary to all samurai by virtue of their general duty to protect and govern society, it followed that such training was most important for the higher ranks whose responsibility in this regard was heaviest. This, said Hirose Tansō, was the only alternative which made sense in a society which had rejected the Chinese alternative of using education as a selective mechanism, to discover administrative talent as well as to train it.[4]

This was what might be called the traditional pattern, the resolution of the ability-status problem which predominated until the end of the eighteenth century. Thereafter, as we shall see, it was subject to some modifications, but even so it remained a dominant pattern until the end of the period.

Ability Rating by the Back Door

It is not, however, the whole story even of educational practices in the early part of the period. In the first place, despite the moral emphasis, the scholars who taught in these schools did, after all, owe their position less to their superior moral qualities than to their superior knowledge. They were intellectual

[1] *NKSS*, 2, p. 87.
[2] See p. 81.
[3] See p. 85.
[4] *Ugen* (*Tansō zenshū*, 2), p. 37.

specialists, and as such could not be entirely indifferent to the value of intellectual accomplishments.

It is significant that there is much more emphasis on the need for humble respect of the teacher in Japanese than in Chinese Confucian writings. Yoshikawa Kōjirō has commented on this as an expression of Japanese 'disciplinarianism'.[1] It may be that. It may also be related to the differences in the positions occupied by the scholar in the two societies. The Chinese literati—or at least the cream of the Chinese scholar class—occupied positions of power, of prestige, and of relative affluence. The Confucian scholar in Tokugawa Japan rarely exercised power and he was usually poor. Deference was all he could claim, and it is not surprising that he was jealous of this, his sole form of privilege. He claimed such deference, however, as Dazai Shuntai made clear in a reported remark quoted earlier,[2] not for himself but for his mastery of the Way of the Sages. In this sense, an insistence on the explicit award of recognition to such mastery was a means of bolstering the Confucian scholar's own uncertain claim to deference from society at large.

Secondly, there were certain practical considerations. Scholarship was in itself a distinct profession of which these teachers were the chief exponents, and it was a profession the need for which was recognized by fief authorities as well as by the scholars themselves. The mediocre level of general moral education for all was not such as to train specialists. More intensive and more intellectually oriented training was necessary if the teachers were to reproduce themselves.

This was one of the principal objects of the widespread practice of selecting a limited number of dormitory students to live in the school for full-time study. The group methods used for teaching at this level were such that differences in ability could not be ignored. To insist on differences of hereditary rank would have been difficult. Moreover, this was something like the teacher's private domain where his natural tendencies to value talent could find expression. It is not surprising, therefore, that other systems of allocating prestige were devised.

It was in the first place impossible for questions of status to be ignored in a general assumption of equality. In a society

---

[1] *Nihon no shinjō*, pp. 148–50.
[2] See p. 54.

in which etiquette was as minutely regulated as it was in Tokugawa Japan two people could not pass through a doorway or sit together in the same room without some implication of 'higher' or 'lower' being attached to the order or position in which they did so. Some criterion of status was essential. Among the dormitory students it was usually not that of hereditary rank, but of relative age. In the Okayama school, for instance, the rule for boarding students was laid down as follows:

> When you are together in the lecture halls, even if there are only two or three of you, never break the principle of seating by age precedence. If you do the younger will feel uncomfortable or arrogantly proud. At the daimyo's court, rank is all-important and the inferior may not vie with the superior. But in learning seniority is important and the essential thing is to respect the proper relations of elder and younger.[1]

Here was a convenient compromise. Very roughly age differences corresponded to differences in academic achievement so that respect for intellectual excellence was, as it were, covertly built into the system, but it was smuggled in under cover of the respectable Confucian principle of respect for seniors—and there were good precedents in Chinese educational practice.[2] It was, too, a principle not too subversive of the hereditary status system. The high-ranking samurai had to defer to his low-ranking senior, but this was less damaging to his *amour propre* in that no judgment of his merit was implied. He, too, would be a senior in his turn.

Some schools used yet another criterion for determining status—that of the order in which pupils entered the school. This was similar to the age criterion in its effect, but was likely to be even more closely correlated to actual achievement. The early rules of the Chōshū fief say, for instance:

> Among the dormitory students, the order of seating shall, irrespective of nobility or baseness of rank, depend on the order of entering the school. In this way, of course, those who are advanced in their studies will provide models for those who are

---

[1] Okayama-ken, kyōiku-iinkai, *Okayama-ken kyōikushi*, 1, p. 56.

[2] Ogyū Sorai, Hosoi Heishū and Hirose Tansō all quote the *Li chi* to the effect that even an Imperial Prince, when he goes to school, should take the place dictated by his age and learning, not by his rank (*Taiheisaku* (*NKS*, 3), p. 539; *Omeikan isō* (Inoue, *Rinri ihen*, 9), p. 49; *Ugen* (*Tansō zenshū*, 2), p. 40.

less advanced, and those who are less advanced will respect
those who are ahead of them.[1]

In a few rare instances—and still within the framework of
traditional educational practices—a few teachers went the
whole way and awarded formal prestige openly on the basis of
performance. An example is the system outlined in the 1770s by
Kamei Nammei which was quoted in an earlier chapter.[2]
Seating in each group discussion was determined by marks
earned on the previous occasion. Kamei was a follower of Ogyū
Sorai and as such more readily inclined to emphasize intellectual
achievement at the expense of moral character.

The drawback of such schemes from the point of view of
a Confucianist of the Sung school was that they introduced an
element of competition. Ambitious striving was subversive of
the social order, moreover it provided an incentive which was
inimical to the proper end of learning. Backed by such an
incentive learning becomes perverted into the pursuit of 'fame
and profit' against which Chu Hsi had warned.[3] Kamei is
aware of the force of such arguments and seeks to meet them.
Confucius did, he admits, say in the *Analects* that 'the superior
man does not competitively strive'. However, he points out,
in the first place there is a Chinese word meaning 'the battle of
the commentators' which shows that even in China scholars
did strive competitively in the difficult task of interpreting the
classics. Secondly, he says:

> Young people hate to lose. Since they hate to lose they will
> strive to win. If they strive to win they will put forward their
> best efforts. As they put forward their best efforts they will be-
> come diligent in their studies. As they become diligent they will
> progress. As they progress they will come to enjoy their work.
> As they come to enjoy it they will stick at it. As they stick at it
> long enough their learning will become a part of them, and
> once it is a part of them this process of self-cultivation will pro-
> ceed of itself and nothing can check it.

As a final argument he adds that even Confucius said: 'Archery
is the competitive pursuit of the superior man. He does not bear

---

[1] *NKSS*, 2, p. 661. (Rules of 1720.)
[2] See p. 142.
[3] See p. 62.

a grudge against the winner, but seeks the cause of his failure in his own lack of righteousness.'[1]

Though Kamei's was a minority view, by applying the milder non-competitive criteria of age or order of entry, it was possible for scholars even within the framework of traditional ideas to organize their own privileged domain in a way which ignored the hereditary ranking system, if only partially, as at Aizu for instance, where the principle of age-seating was applied within three separate groups of higher, middling and lesser samurai, though the groups themselves were kept separate.[2]

Another compromise device suggested by Hirose Tansō (it is not clear if it was ever adopted) was to have all students sit according to age, but with members of the daimyo's family, upper samurai and lower samurai distinguished in three categories by the colour of their clothes.[3] There were other ways, too, of limiting the boundaries of the scholar's privileged domain. Sometimes the age-seating rule applied only to dormitory students, sometimes to all the regular teaching activities of the school but not to the general lectures. Even in the case of boarding students the exact definition of the boundaries of this privileged island was often a ticklish matter which required precise regulation. The rules of the Yonezawa school, for instance, say, *a propos* of the normal duty of politeness which required students to attend the funerals of their fellow-pupils' parents:

> However, although all students are the same within the school, outside the gates there are differences of rank, and hence it is proper for students of higher rank simply to send a servant to the funerals of parents of low-ranking students.[4]

Ability in Administration

So much for the means whereby, within the schools, the bias of teachers towards the explicit recognition of ability was adapted to the exigencies of the status hierarchy. What of the problems of running the society and of the relation of scholastic training to administration?

---

[1] *NKSS*, 3, p. 17.
[2] Ogawa, *Aizu-han kyōiku-kō*, p. 101.
[3] *Ugen* (*NKS*, 32), p. 124.
[4] *NKSS*, 1, p. 758.

Confucius's insistence on the 'rectification of names', on making sure that the prince was princely and the minister ministerial, was open to two interpretations. One was that embodied in the Chinese examination system, to the effect, namely, that those who demonstrate ability should be raised to the status which those abilities warranted. The second was that each person should be properly trained to acquire the abilities requisite to the status to which it had pleased heredity to call him.

It was the second which held sway in Tokugawa Japan. It is not surprising, therefore, that although there are occasional references to the problem of differing natural talents in Tokugawa educational writings, most explicit discussions on the question of the relative importance of nature and nurture come down heavily on the side of nurture. To be sure, teachers everywhere lean towards this view—for who would wish to minimize the importance of his own profession?[1] Tokugawa writers, indeed, use the argument of the superior importance of environment to emphasize the need and the efficacy of earnest study. Another possible implication, though not, as far as I have discovered, one that they explicitly drew, is that there can be no better qualification for occupying the top positions in society than being brought up in top families.

Proof usually takes the form of citation of authorities. One writer quotes Mencius to the effect that 'heredity has a small effect, environment has a long-range effect', the *Shih chi* to the effect that 'water takes the form of the vessel, men are formed by good or evil companions', and a Japanese proverb to the effect that 'it is upbringing, not pedigree that makes the man'.[2] (In proof of the last adage another writer describes a circus trainer whose stunt was to make a cat sit on a dog's back, and then produce a rat which sat on the cat's head and amicably licked its face.)[3] The important thing is to start young enough; a young sapling can be trained into any shape but not a grown tree.[4] 'The heart of a child of three stays with him until he is a

---

[1] Those, perhaps, as Ernest Gellner points out to me, who might need to flatter a limited upper-class clientele.

[2] Komachi Gyokusen, *Jishū-hen* (*NKS*, 19), p. 433. This, and most of the subsequent references, have been collected by Ototake, *Shomin kyōikushi*, 1, pp. 318–19, 517–34.

[3] Yamana Fuminari, *Nōka-kun* (*NKS*, 15), p. 578.

[4] Komachi, *Jishū-hen*, p. 435.

hundred' is a proverbial expression of a good Freudian principle quoted by Hayashi Shihei.[1] He will admit that there may be one congenital idiot for every hundred births, but for the rest 'no one is a fool by nature', though in another context he does speak of 'native' brilliance and dullness, and goes so far as to say that the goodness or badness of a child's character may be only nine-tenths due to upbringing and one-tenth to hereditary disposition.[2] Significantly, two of the three writers quoted here add regretfully that the 'common run of mankind' does not realize this and blindly ascribes individual differences to inborn character.[3]

One question is whether the acceptance of birth as the main criterion for the distribution of prestige and authority, supported as it was by such comforting psychological theories as these, still permitted the society to be operated with reasonable efficiency. By and large it probably did, and for a number of reasons.

Firstly, and most importantly, selection for ability was not entirely ruled out. The central administration of the Bakufu and each fief administration had more samurai retainers available than there were administrative offices to be filled. A system of bureaucratic offices separate from the system of hereditary family ranks, but related to it in that each office could only be filled from a certain limited range of ranks still, therefore, permitted a certain amount of selection for ability while making it rare for a man to be in authority over a status superior. Small fiefs might be saddled with fief-elders who held office as a hereditary right, but there was more room for selection in the bigger fiefs[4] and most of all in the Bakufu, where there was a fairly wide choice even for the highest administrative posts in, say, the Council of Elders.

Secondly, the practice of adopting adolescents or adult youths into families without heirs or with congenitally deficient sons permitted the occasional importation of ability into high-ranking families.

Thirdly, one should not forget that, the regime having been

[1] *Fukei-kun* (Dōbunkan, *Kyōiku-bunko: Kunkai*, 1), p. 675.

[2] *Ibid.*, pp. 677, 674.

[3] Komachi and Hayashi, *loc. cit.*

[4] For an excellent illustration of how the system worked in Okayama, see Taniguchi Sumio, 'Han-kashindan no keisei to kōzō'.

established and the routines worked out, no great administrative skill was required. Those in high positions needed authority rather than intelligence, and authority is more easily acquired by the simple expedient of being born and bred to it. If there were still irreducible personality defects in those born to command, the extreme formalization of respectful behaviour helped to compensate for them.[1]

Fourthly, the device of allowing able inferiors to do the real work of incompetent superiors further mitigated the possible damage of a hereditary system. And fifthly, in order to ensure that there would be able inferiors, it seems that there always was, in practice, and despite the accepted theory, a certain amount of promotion across rank barriers at the lower levels of the hierarchy.

The professional Confucian scholars and their military equivalents, the teachers of swordsmanship and the lance, were obvious examples. They moved with relative freedom from fief to fief, secured appointments on the basis of their demonstrated talents, and were only partially involved in the hereditary status hierarchy. The clerical staff who did the actual book-work of administration were appointed from among the foot-soldiers or even sometimes from the commoner class. In the middle of the seventeenth century Nakae Tōju complained that a good many students studied only 'to get a reading and writing job'.[2] Nishikawa Joken makes the same complaint, specifically about commoner students, in the Genroku period,[3] and Ishida Baigan, a little later, quotes one of his questioners as saying that seven or eight out of every ten merchants or farmers who acquire a little scholarship are careless about their shop or farm and look forward only to getting a sword.[4] (He adds that —a phenomenon familiar to students of social mobility via

---

[1] It is more difficult to withhold deference from those who lack the temperamental weight to command it when the forms of deference required are precisely regulated and deviation becomes therefore obvious and glaring. Moreover, as de Tocqueville remarked, in feudal societies 'the master readily obtains prompt, complete, respectful and easy obedience from his servants because they revere in him not only their master but the whole class of masters. He weighs down their will by the whole weight of the aristocracy' (*Democracy in America* (Vintage edn., 1954), 2, p. 189).

[2] *Okina mondō* (Tsukamoto, *Nakae Tōju bunshū*), p. 178.

[3] *Chōnin-bukuro* (*NKS*, 5), p. 74.

[4] *Tohi mondō* (*NKS*, 8), p. 299.

education in the West—a number of them also despise and are
irritated by their parents and develop grossly unfilial tendencies.)

Given these mitigating factors the hereditary system was not,
then, likely to lead to the total breakdown of society, and in the
seventeenth century it seems to have been little questioned.
Even then, of course, the system was not rigidly fixed, quite
apart from the loopholes in the fields of specialist employment.
There were promotions and demotions; but their character is
important. In the first place, with few exceptions,[1] these were
promotions and demotions in *hereditary* rank and salary.
Secondly, they were generally the result of favouritism rather
than of a desire to employ men of ability. The large number
of Nō actors promoted by Tsunayoshi are unlikely to have
been greatly distinguished for their administrative skills.

The Need for Ability

By the 1720s, however, when the sense of financial and moral
crisis first begins to grip the Bakufu, there is a change. Traceable
in Yoshimune's reforms at that time, in the reforms of Matsudaira Sadanobu at the end of the century, in the more short-lived
reform attempts of Mizuno Tadakuni from 1841 to 1843, and
in the accelerating upheaval of the 1860s is a consistent trend
to modify the system of official appointments in such a way as to
give more scope for men of ability. And this trend in the Bakufu
administration was duplicated—and stimulated—by similar
moves in the reforms of the various fiefs. The increasing
emphasis in educational writings on the function of the schools
to produce *jinzai*—men of talent—which (see pp. 44–5) becomes
universal from the end of the eighteenth century onwards, was
both a consequence and a stimulus of this trend.

In its mildest form the growing emphasis on ability carried
no danger to the status system; 'promoting ability' merely
meant 'honest appointments'. It was said above that the system
of related ranks and offices *permitted* a certain range of selection
for ability. This is not to say that ability was always, or even
usually, the criterion used. Sir James Stephen would have

---

[1] From 1665 to 1682, apparently, there was a limited system of non-hereditary
job salaries for certain guard officials (Kawade Shobō, *Nihon rekishi daijiten*,
article *'tashidaka'*).

found plenty of corroborating evidence in Japan for his comment (on the report recommending competitive entry into the British civil service) that 'in every age and land and calling, a large share of success has hitherto always been awarded to the possessors of interest, of connection, of favour, of what we would call luck'. And many Tokugawa statesmen would have echoed his rhetorical question: 'Can it be that all the world is and always has been wrong about the matter?'[1] Tanuma Okitsugu, during his reign as virtual dictator in the mid-eighteenth century, made no bones of the fact that he judged the sincerity of a man's intentions by the value of the presents he brought him. It was one of the objects of the reformers—and particularly of Matsudaira Sadanobu who followed Tanuma—to reassert the need to consider ability in selecting among those qualified by hereditary rank. In this their motives were as much moral as utilitarian; they were as much concerned to restore integrity to the administration by eliminating bribery as they were to utilize the best talents.

But some of the reforms went further than this. The system of *tashidaka*—of salaries for the job—was deliberately introduced by the Bakufu in 1723 to permit promotions *across* the barriers of hereditary rank. A large range of positions were given standard salaries; those whose hereditary stipend fell below the standard level were given the necessary supplements—but for the duration of their tenure of office only (though incumbents of some of the highest offices could also claim a lesser increase in their hereditary stipend).[2] The object was to open up higher administrative positions, formerly the prerogative of higher ranks, to men of ability in the lower ranks.[3]

At the same time there were increased opportunities for promotion into the lower ranks of professional specialized occupations (more schools, for one thing, meant a demand for more teachers) and simultaneously a growing professionalization of the more technical, financial side of the Bakufu bureaucracy.[4] Appointments in the office of Kanjō-bugyō—

---

[1] Quoted in L. Silberman, *The Analysis of Society*, p. 58.

[2] Kaiho Seiryō, *Shōridan* (*NKS*, 21), p. 203.

[3] The supplements were necessary not simply to lend suitable prestige to the holders of high office, but also because they usually had to recruit a large part of their subordinate staff out of their own resources.

[4] Tsuji Tatsuya, 'Kyōhō kaikaku'.

the Bakufu Treasury—were not easily taken and left. Increasingly officials stayed in this branch for life, and ability was recognized in promotions from the lowest ranks to the top. Towards the end of the eighteenth century an ambitious silk merchant who bought himself foot-soldier status rose through the office to become the Town Magistrate of Edo,[1] and a writer about the turn of the century remarks that most of the district Intendants (for their functions see p. 7) who were responsible for tax collection and thus under the Kanjō-bugyō's jurisdiction) rose from humble origins. 'Although these are hereditary offices, those who are capable at writing and arithmetic and other arts can rise.' Though some, he adds, can still get there more quickly by bribery.[2]

Another aspect of this increased fluidity of appointments for scholarly and technical posts was that it offered some solution for the problem of spare younger sons of the samauri class. Those who could not find a suitable position as adopted sons in established families had to equip themselves with some skill which could reasonably justify permission to establish new retainer families of their own. There are frequent references in the school records to special consideration for younger sons who devote themselves to acquiring higher education for this purpose.[3]

The institutional arrangements designed to give greater scope for ability did not always work in the way their authors intended, but they were gradually improved. As one writer complained in a memorial to Matsudaira Sadanobu, the *tashidaka* system sometimes acted as an obstacle to promotion by merit. Candidates for the post of Osaka guard were usually overlooked if they had a sufficiently large hereditary salary not to require a supplement to bring them up to the standard rate for the job. The appointments went to those of lower hereditary rank, not because they were able but because, having more financially to gain from the appointment, they offered bigger

---

[1] *NKSS*, 7, p. 601. The man was Negishi Shigenori, Edo Machi-bugyō from 1798 to 1815.

[2] Yamagata Hikozaemon, *Meiryō tairoku* (Kondō, *Shiseki shūran*, 11), pp. 93–4 Quoted in Ototake, *Shomin kyōikushi*, 1, pp. 771–3.

[3] See the following examples in the *NKSS*, 1, p. 630 (Nanukaichi); 2, p. 278 (Shibata); 7, p. 101 (the Bakufu); 1, p. 361 (Kasama); 2, p. 662 (Chōshū); 1 p. 234 (Matsuo); 1, p. 557 (Komoro); 3, p. 280 (Kagoshima); 2, p. 637 (Fukuyama)

bribes. In other cases, where the appointing officials did have the interests of the Bakufu at heart, they sometimes avoided appointing low-ranking samurai to posts with high standard salaries in order to save the money which would have to be paid in supplements. As a result of this official's recommendations (at least according to his account) the practice was introduced of starting the supplementary salaries not immediately on appointment, but only after ability had been demonstrated by a period of adequate performance.[1]

By the end of the eighteenth century the principle of awarding official posts on the basis of ability *as well as* of hereditary rank was generally accepted as an ideal, however much, in the back-sliding periods between reforms, it may have been ignored. The extent to which hereditary rank could be overlooked in promoting the able was still limited, but no one's life-chances were entirely determined at birth. Even the ordinary depressed retainer had something to hope for, if it was only entry into a minor guard corps. Sugita Gempaku, complaining that 'seven or eight out of every ten Bakufu retainers look like women and think like merchants', goes on:

> The best of them go in for archery and horsemanship and the lance, practising the military arts as they call it, but this is only to get on in the world and get into the Shogunal guard. They fawn on their teachers and try to make a good show before their superiors, and if they can manage not to miss a fourteen-inch target at the reviews and can keep their seat on their horse (a horse trained to the quietness of a cat) they get their reward. They are in the guard ... And—what they are really after— they get the guard supplementary salary which gives them the chance to restore the family fortunes after generations of reckless extravagance.[2]

Merit Society versus Hereditary Society

If the hereditary system was to give way somewhat in favour of considerations of ability, the question was, just *how* much? Why not go the whole way, abolish hereditary distinctions and

[1] Moriyama Takamori, *Ama no takumo*, pp. 30, 36.
[2] Sugita Gempaku, *Yasō dokugo* (*NKS*, 19), p. 7. Quoted in Yokoyama, *Kinsei kyōikushi*, p. 750.

appoint to official posts solely on the basis of demonstrated competence? It was an idea which was bound to occur to the writers of memoranda on good government, and the relative advantages of the hereditary system and the merit system are a frequent topic of discussion in their writings.

A number of the attacks on existing systems of making appointments go no further than condemning personal favouritism, while implicitly accepting the principle of selecting within hereditarily qualified ranks. Sorai, for instance, points out that daimyo tend to choose as subordinates people who are similar to themselves in temperament and ability with the result that the deficiences in their own character are merely magnified.[1] Kamei Nammei notes that officials appointed for reasons of favouritism are not really trusted by their superiors. The superiors therefore constantly interfere so that the subordinates lose both authority and the incentive to work well.[2]

A good many others, however, go further in attacking the hereditary system itself. Ise Sadatake is sweeping. The result of appointing officials by the accident of birth, he says, is 'like keeping cats to scare burglars and setting dogs to catch mice'.[3] Both Hirose Tansō and Kaiho Seiryō, writing in the nineteenth century from different parts of Kyūshū, point out that in ancient China only retainership was hereditary; rank and stipends were awarded according to personal merit and each generation started out from scratch with a hereditary right to no more than a minimum retainer fee.[4] Another Kyūshū scholar from Kumamoto joins them in praising the ancient Sages who 'established a school for the education of children, and selected their officials according to ability, irrespective of rank'.[5]

Inevitably China provided a model of the opposing ideal and there are a number of references to the Chinese examination system. One or two are approving in general terms,[6] though they admit that it might be difficult to adopt the system in contemporary Japan. Most, however, who consider the matter

---

[1] *Taiheisaku* (*NKS*, 3), p. 551.
[2] *Higo monogatari* (*NKS*, 15), p. 529.
[3] *Anzai zuihitsu*, p. 127.
[4] *Ugen* (*NKS*, 32), p. 104, and *Shōridan* (*NKS*, 26), p. 204.
[5] Nakayama Shōrei, *Gakusei-kō* (*NKSS*, 5), p. 606.
[6] E.g. Tanaka Kyūgū, *Minkan seiyō* (*NKS*, 1), pp. 442-3; Karashima Ken *Gakusei wakumon* (*NKSS*, 8, pp. 2-3).

in more detail, advance arguments against the Chinese system. Nishikawa Joken, at the beginning of the eighteenth century, is content to say that 'all nations in the world have their own system'. China promotes to office by examinations; Japan by hereditary rank; a certain Indian state goes so far as to insist that all except a few hereditary officials remain illiterate and ignorant of anything except the laws they have to obey. The result is that they are excellently governed, and this perhaps is a model Japan should lean towards; for ancient China and ancient Japan were surely very little different from this.[1]

Ogyū Sorai (if he really is the author of *Kenen danyo*) has more considered arguments. He contrasts the feudal hereditary system with the centralized governmental system ruled by merit-appointed officials, and says that it is no accident that good and stable government has only been found in the feudal societies of ancient China and contemporary Japan. In the first place the examination system is such that the small men succeed where the 'superior man' fails. Secondly, officials who move from post to post are not bound by any emotional ties of obligation to their superiors or their inferiors. Consequently, in the absence of any moral control over their conduct, a harsh system of punishments has to be devised as a means of supervising officials. Suspicion and constant rebellion are the inevitable result.[2] Hirose Tansō has a similar argument a century later. Chinese officials have no security; here today, they may be gone tomorrow; their descendants are guaranteed nothing. Hence they are concerned only to enjoy their moment of power without any sense of responsibility to future generations.[3] A lesser-known contemporary, the Wakayama samurai, Endō Yasumichi, is full of praise for the Chinese ideal, but he points out that in practice it has been corrupted since the end of Ming when rich merchants began to employ scholars to prepare examination answers for them, and, having thus passed the examinations, went on to secure appointments by bribery. Japan's problem would not be solved by introducing the Chinese system, partly because there would always be danger of

---

[1] *Hyakushō-bukuro* (*NKS*, 5), pp. 169–70.
[2] *Kenen-danyo* (*Nihon bunko*, 4), p. 17. There is doubt about the authorship, and it is not a manifestly Sorai-like sentiment.
[3] *Ugen* (*NKS*, 32), p. 99.

O

similar corruption, partly because scholars in Japan had been for too long removed from practical affairs. As a result, scholarship had become a matter of literary dilletantism, textual pedantry and routine pedagogy; scholars had thus earned the contempt of men of affairs, and so been even more completely excluded from administration. No examination system would be likely to cure *that* state of affairs.[1] Shōji Kōgi's merchant background comes out clearly in his elaboration of much the same point. Scholars are unaware of the conditions of the lower classes; they have no practical ability in the kind of sharp 'horse-trading' necessary in administrative office; and a good many of them are alcoholics who could not hold the respect of their subordinates. Hence, the system of appointing people to office straight from school on the basis of scholastic ability would never work. Only when a man is older, has succeeded to the headship of his family, married, run his own household, suffered and enjoyed life and been buffeted by fortune can he really absorb the teachings of the classics and apply them to practical affairs. No one should be appointed to an official post until he is forty. The system works in China, he adds, because the candidates for the scholastic examinations come from the lower classes and, hence, are already well acquainted with the conditions of the masses.[2] Shōji, it is apparent, could only conceive of a Chinese-type system being applied within the samurai class; to suggest that Japanese commoners, too, could bring their acquaintance with the masses to bear on higher adminstration would have required too great a psychological leap.

Both Endō and Shōji think of China as providing a possible model, not simply for the principle of personnel selection by some kind of objective test, but also for the means of selection as well. Naturally enough, perhaps, since Japanese scholarship was also the scholarship of the Han-lin academy, they could not conceive of any other objective system of selection but the Chinese one. Nor, earlier, could Amemori Hōshū, whose chief argument against the adoption of the Chinese examination system in Japan is that it would be difficult to find Japanese who could write eight-legged essays in the approved Chinese style.[3]

---

[1] *Shigaku mondō* (*NKS*, 26), pp. 237–8.
[2] *Keizai mondō hiroku* (*NKS*, 22), pp. 103–6.
[3] *Kissō sawa* (*NZZ*, 9), p. 157.

Similarly, the Kumamoto scholar, Nakayama, criticizes the Chinese examination system because of the emphasis placed on prose and poetry since T'ang times,[1] and Yuasa Jōzan, more concerned with its deplorable effects on scholarship than on the quality of officials, complains that study becomes a mere matter of mechanical preparation for examinations and once they are through the barrier the literati make no effort to improve themselves or their style.[2]

It is not, in fact, until the very end of the period that Yasui Sokken, quoting the *Shu ching* for an authoritative statement of the *principle* of ability tests, recommends that examinations of candidates for official posts should consist of a number of questions on practical matters of taxation, judicial administration, land reclamation, welfare policy, and so on, to be answered not in Chinese, but in everyday Japanese.[3]

Whether they referred to Chinese examples or not, however, no Tokugawa scholar was bold enough to recommend the sweeping abolition of the hereditary system. However much it might be deplored, the existing order seemed too firmly established. It could only be accepted. Hosoi Heishū's acceptance is backed with a well-reasoned theory of the relative appropriateness of the two opposing ideals of appointment by merit and appointment by birth:

> There are times of turbulence and times of peace . . . In times of turbulence, irrespective of nobility or baseness of rank, one promotes those who are useful and will help to win tomorrow's battle and strengthen the domain. In times of peace, however, divisions of status and rank are rigidly fixed. If one dislikes the fief to which one belongs one cannot go to another. Unless one accepts the rule of one's hereditary lord, there is no place to lay one's head . . . Those who are plain samurai should be ready to spend their lives as samurai, quietly performing their allotted tasks, their hearts filled with a spirit of loyal duty. This, to the man of learning, is the true source of contentment.[4]

There was, in point of fact, historical justification for Hosoi's thesis. The period of civil wars before 1615 was notoriously the

---

[1] Nakayama Shōrei, *Gakusei-kō* (*NKSS*, 5), p. 610.

[2] *Bunkai zakki* (*NZZ*, 2), p. 562.

[3] *Kyūkyū wakumon* (*NKS*, 32), p. 433. Although none of these scholars seems to have known it, such examinations were, in fact, held in Wakayama after 1803. See p. 206.

[4] *NKSS*, 1, p. 747.

period of *gekokujō*—when inferiors beat down their superiors. There is a vestigial legacy of the ideas and assumptions of this period in the first issue of the Tokugawa Regulations for the Military Houses—the *Buke shohatto*—in 1615. Daimyos are exhorted to select men of ability for their administration. This article is missing from the code when it is next issued in 1629, however. Instead, beginning with the 1635 version, and much elaborated in Tsunayoshi's of 1683, there is an insistence on *rei* —on the proper observance of status distinctions.[1]

'To advance the wise and demote the incompetent is a basic principle of government ... a universal principle of which everyone is aware,' begins Hirose Tansō. However, it is impracticable in contemporary Japan because, 'Japan has a feudal system'. All that could be hoped for was so to modify that feudal system as to allow greater scope for talent to come forward. Hirose proposes that, in the first place, 'since it is difficult to do away with old-established families, there is no alternative but to educate the children of the upper families so that they will lean towards the good, reject evil and be of benefit to their country'. Secondly, there should be consistent observation of the character and scholastic ability of all young samurai, and those who fail to reach certain minimum standards should be refused permission to succeed to their family's headship or to be adopted as heirs. Thirdly, those of high rank and stipend who are not selected for official posts because of youth or lack of ability should have their stipend taxed. The taxes so collected should be used to provide non-hereditary salaries for particular jobs to which low-ranking samurai of ability could be promoted. Fourthly, deliberate use should be made of adoption. (As a good Confucianist he could not but deplore the fact that contemporary Japan had departed from accepted Chinese practices of adopting only agnatic relatives, but since she had, fief authorities should exploit the good in this ill-wind.) If there were rigorous control over succession to family headships, parents would voluntarily modify the rule of succession by primogeniture and set aside an eldest son in favour of a younger brother or an adopted son. And if the approbation of ability were to become general people would be more concerned about the personal merits of the children

[1] Maruyama Masao, 'Kinsei jukyō no hatten ni okeru Soraigaku', p. 38.

they adopt and less about the status and wealth of the family they adopt them from. As a result, low-ranking men of ability would be able to take over high-ranking families.[1]

Hirose—and five decades earlier, Nakai Chikuzan, from whom Hirose may well have got some of his ideas[2]—were realistic enough in their appreciation of the impossibility of doing more than gently to undermine the hereditary system by subtle modifications. Even later in the period, Yasui Sokken, quoted earlier as advocating practical examinations in Japanese for official candidates (he also suggested that official appointments should all be for three-year terms, reconfirmation always to depend on adequate performance) is quite explicit about the practical lengths to which one can go in allowing ability to override heredity. If one goes too far those of high rank will become disheartened and those of low rank will develop ambitious cunning. As a rough guide, he suggests that if a person of low rank has eight parts of ability and a person of much higher rank two, they should be treated as equals. Similarly, if the ranks are closer together, a person with six parts of ability should be considered the equal of a person of four parts just one rank above him.[3]

What Kind of Ability?

Though they differed over the precise degree to which merit could be allowed to override heredity, these writers are generally agreed that to some extent, 'to advance the wise and demote the incompetent is a basic principle of proper government'. Inevitably they had also to consider the question: What constitutes wisdom? What are the qualities which make good officials? And what relevance did the education provided in fief schools bear to these qualities?

There is often conceded to be the possibility of conflict between the dual requirements of moral excellence and intellectual ability. The early-nineteenth-century author of the

---

[1] *Ugen* (*NKS*, 32), pp. 105, 119–22, 130.

[2] *Sōbō kigen* (*NKS*, 16), pp. 320–3. Nakai suggested the idea of cuts in stipends and salary increments—of 10 per cent, 20 per cent or 30 per cent according to the degree of deficiency or merit.

[3] *Kyūkyū wakumon* (*NKS*, 32), pp. 434–5.

Tokugawa jikki has an interesting passage in praise of Ieyasu's flair for appointing able villains to high office. He knew how to utilize their talents and he knew also when to have off with their heads at the exact point at which their potential harm outweighed their usefulness.[1] This, however, was a practice of which only a genius like Ieyasu was capable. It was hardly questioned by this time that moral probity was an essential qualification for office—the more so in that the emphasis of Matsudaira Sadanobu's reforms lay as much in the elimination of bribery as in the utilization of ability. One observer of the Bakufu's system of administration lists the kind of qualities which were looked for in the second decade of the nineteenth century when checking the backgrounds of candidates for office among the *kobushin*—the pool of middle-ranking unemployed Bakufu retainers. Two separate agencies made investigations—afterwards collated—of the candidate's 'management of his household, the behaviour of his retainers, his financial affairs, whether amity prevailed in his family, and what skills he had learned to what degree'.[2]

'Skills' included gakumon—book learning—though, among the military arts it was only one of a number of qualifications which might be required. A century earlier, Muro Kyūsō records an argument he had had with Arai Hakuseki over whether a man needed scholarship to qualify him for office. Arai held that he did. Muro thought the right moral attitudes were enough.[3] By now, with the general expansion of school education, Arai's was the general view, but there is a variety of opinions on the exact nature of the connection between education and suitability for office. The discussion is not always clear since many of the writers who consider the question are concerned chiefly with the promotion of gakumon as an end in itself, and urge the appointment of those who have studied primarily as a bait to encourage others to study, rather than as a means of securing good administration.[4] However, a sharp opposition emerges between those who look on the efficacy of gakumon for officials as itself primarily a matter of morality,

[1] Kuroita, *Kokushi taikei*, 38, p. 301.
[2] Yamagata Hikozaemon, *Meiryō tairoku*, p. 35.
[3] *Kenzan (reitaku) hisaku (NKS,* 2), p. 258.
[4] E.g. Shūdō Gakuzan in *NKSS,* 5, p. 596. Ogyū Sorai, *Seidan (NKT,* 9), pp. 189–93.

and those who see it as either providing necessary information and skills, or, alternatively, acting as a sieve by means of which the possessors of intellectual ability can be identified.

One of the most ponderous of Tokugawa moralists, Hosoi Heishū, is a proponent of the former point of view. The study of the Way of the Sages produces 'good men' and those who are astoundingly good should be promoted—preferably in a dazzling leap from low to high rank which will have the maximum exemplary effect. However, 'those who are filial and loyal are not necessarily intelligent and resourceful, so the daimyo should take care in selecting the exact offices to which they are appointed'.[1] The retired daimyo of Nobeoka, however, is inclined to stress the importance of the intellectual knowledge directly provided by study. The ignorant can only take the trend of the times, the way of the world, as his guide. But administrators must know the *right* way, and these principles only a study of the classics can provide.[2] In a rather rare statement of the sieve principle Shōji Kōgi invokes the metaphor of the maker of the stone counters for the game of *go*. He collects shells and stones, polishes them and grades them and sells them at fifteen *mon* a *koku* for the best, two *mon* a *koku* for the worst quality. As a result of his efforts even the worst quality can fetch its proper price and people are willing to buy his wares because they can clearly see the comparative qualities of the different grades. In the same way, 'to establish a school ... polish natural endowments, divide talents into their respective grades and appoint to office according to those grades' is the mark of good government.[3]

These differences were at the heart of the contentious disputes which arose within the Bakufu at the time of the first Bakufu examinations in the classics held in 1794. The examinations were partly inspired by the Chinese system, and although their major purpose was to encourage study by rewarding the proficient, it was also intended that they should identify talent for later promotion. The question was how well they identified the right talent. Moriyama Takamori, one of Matsudaira Sadanobu's lesser advisers, describes at length how his views

[1] *Omeikan-isō* (Inoue, *Rinri ihen*, 9), pp. 39–40.
[2] *NKSS*, 3, pp. 229–30.
[3] *Keizai mondō hiroku* (*NKS*, 22), p. 69.

clashed with those of the Confucian teachers at the Bakufu school. They insisted on awarding marks strictly on the basis of performance in the examinations. Consequently, a good many 'men of a boisterous disposition and dissolute habits who until yesterday had spent all their time playing on the samisen and practising popular dramatic recitations, decided there was nothing they couldn't set their hands to, went to lectures for a couple of months and offered themselves for examination'. Since they simply repeated their teachers' words verbatim they got good marks while earnest scholars 'who had long been devoted to learning, were well acquainted with books, of a fine character and fit to serve in responsible positions' often came out badly because they thought more deeply about the questions they were asked and sometimes offered their own opinions. He constantly urged, therefore, that prizes, and later appointments, should be awarded on the basis of 'general character and conduct and *devotion to* learning', rather than on mere intellectual performance. As a result of his representations one samurai in particular (he happened to be the nephew of one of the examiners, to complicate matters) was deprived of a prize. Though placed in the top grade for his examination answers, he was known to be of a dissolute nature, and after much argument he was rewarded only with a commendation. (Much to Moriyama's delight, he disgraced himself some days later and had to be relieved of his official post.) As Moriyama says, 'when it further came to decisions concerning appointments' in the light of the examination results, 'there was much argument and nothing could be decided'.[1] Ota Nampo, who abandoned his career as a comic poet and popular litterateur to take the examinations (very possibly one of those at whom Moriyama's comments were directed), received the top prize in the lower samurai division. But it was two and a half years later that he first got promotion—and then only to a very minor office which raised his salary from 70 to 100 bales. His literary talents were later put to virtuous uses, however, when he was set to writing a compilation of tales of filial sons for the edification of the common people.[2]

Although in this way the exact connection between scholastic

[1] *Ama no takumo*, pp. 67–71.
[2] Tamabayashi Gyokusen, *Shokusanjin no kenkyū*, pp. 518–25.

ability and administrative aptitude was vague and disputed, the existence of some connection was increasingly recognized. As regular examinations were instituted in more and more fief schools there appeared a number of policy statements promising that academic ability would be taken into account in making official appointments. Kumamoto was a leader in this regard. According to Kamei Nammei (who may, however, be exaggerating for didactic purposes, much as the writers of the French enlightenment drew a Utopian picture of Chinese society in order to admonish their own), there was already, well before the end of the eighteenth century, a careful system of compiling school dossiers on each young samurai in the fief recording his academic record as well as reports on his moral character. These reports were used by the personnel office for selecting administrative officers.[1] The advantages of such a system were detailed at great length by Hirose Tansō (who lived in a town bordering the Kumamoto fief) several decades later,[2] and it seems also to have been adopted at Saga by the end of the period.[3] Clear statements at least of the intention to take academic accomplishments into account in appointing to office come from Hagi in 1840,[4] from Wakayama in general terms in 1803 and much more explicitly at an unspecified later date,[5] from Tottori in 1858,[6] and doubtless many other examples could be found. At a different level, insisting not so much on the appointment of the specially talented to the most important posts as on the disbarment from any post of those who lacked certain minimum accomplishments, the regulations which a number of fiefs introduced in the last decades of the period have already been quoted in a previous chapter.[7]

How far these regulations and policy statements were consistently applied in practice only detailed studies of fief appointments and school records could show. There can, however, be no doubt that in the last two decades of the period there were numerous examples of the promotion of 'men of

---

[1] *Higo monogatari* (*NKS*, 15), pp. 528–9.
[2] *Ugen* (*NKS*, 32), pp. 121–2.
[3] Kume Kunitake, *Kaikoroku*, 1, p. 22.
[4] *NKSS*, 2, p. 676.
[5] Horiuchi Shin, *Nanki Tokugawa-shi*, 17, pp. 30–6; *NKSS*, 2, p. 816.
[6] *NKSS*, 2, p. 431.
[7] See p. 88–9.

talent' across status lines. When Hashimoto Sanai writes a memorial on talent and school organization to the Fukui daimyo in 1857, he has, unlike most memorialists on the topic, no complaint about the present position. The right men, by and large, have been chosen. (Hashimoto himself had soared up through the hierarchy.) He is concerned chiefly to ensure that the supply of talent is maintained.[1] And there were quite a number of Hashimotos in Japan by 1857. It was recognized that the new crisis situation demanded imaginative innovations. Perhaps Hosoi Heishū's theory of the difference between times of peace—when the hereditary system should prevail—and times of disorder—when all talent should be mobilized—provided a charter for such promotions as the age was increasingly defined as one of incipient disorder. Certainly a further factor for the change was the establishment of new types of learning which demonstrated, in a much more conclusive form than traditional Confucian education, the connection between intellectual training and fitness for positions of leadership.

Practical Education

From the end of the eighteenth century onwards, as the recognition of a *general* connection between scholastic and administrative ability grew, more thought was given to one aspect of this connection—the provision in the school curriculum of information directly useful to administrators. One reason why those who wrote on education and administration were more apt to stress the moral rather than the cognitive benefits of schooling was because the traditional curriculum really did seem to offer very little in the way of *practical* guidance to current problems. One could learn from the classics that one should be just with subordinates, but it was hard to derive hints from them on the efficacy of reminting the coinage. Actual administrative skills were learned on the job, and they consisted in large part of that knowledge of the world, the importance of which prompted Shōji Kōgi to suggest that no one should hold office until he was forty.

Nevertheless, there were people who began to see that certain elements of a good administrator's mental equipment could be

[1] *Gakusei ni kansuru iken tōshi* (Keigaku-kai, *Hashimoto Keigaku zenshū*, 1), p. 254.

systematized and taught. The proposal of the Kumamoto scholar, Nakayama Shōrei (it dates from around 1790) that a compendium of useful knowledge should be compiled concerning the geography and the economy of the fief and its administrative forms and practices has already been quoted. Nakayama was not alone in this. Similar proposals were made by Tanaka Gensai, an elder of the Aizu fief, in 1787. He recommends six special vocational courses for samurai between the ages of twenty-five and thirty who had completed their general training. They were to be in fiscal matters, village administration, ceremonies and protocol, military affairs, criminal detection and law, and public works and utilities. The students should, he says, read widely in Japanese and Chinese sources and also study contemporary affairs.[1]

Neither in Kumamoto nor in Aizu, however, do these ideas seem to have been put into effect. The arguments, however, must have gained sufficient currency for Confucian scholars to take pains to refute them. Thus, for instance, Karashima Ken, writing in 1816:

> It is a great mistake to imagine that there is some special method of study for producing 'men of talent'; such as concentrating on the details of administration, investigating the tax system in the provinces, or examining the methods of central financial administration.

He admits that all these things—the criminal code, military strategy, irrigation, arithmetic and so on—are of value and are a part of gakumon coming under the rubric of *kakubutsu*—'the investigation of things'—a phrase used by the Sung Confucianists to describe an eminently respectable activity.

> But to fail to clarify the important moral basis and to concentrate on such minor matters as these betrays a preoccupation with the politics of intrigue and with practical utility, and is certainly not the way of producing talented men taught by the Sages and their wise interpreters.[2]

Eventually, and to a limited extent, the Karashimas gave

---

[1] Ogawa Wataru, *Aizu-han kyōiku-kō*, pp. 105, 599. Tanaka was known to be influenced by a Kumamoto follower of Ogyū Sorai who was a contemporary and colleague of Nakayama, so that the ideas may have had a common source.

[2] *Gakusei wakumon* (*NKSS*, 8), p. 5.

ground. Wakayama seems to have been the first fief to introduce (in 1803) not teaching but at least examinations in problems of practical administration at the fief school. They were to be answered in Japanese, not in Chinese. Candidates were to make judicious citation of historical examples, but also to use their own imagination.[1] The use of Japanese rather than Chinese was important; it encouraged attention to the content rather than to the display of scholarship. Japanese was the language of practical administration and the language, too, which academic Confucianists used for their memorials on political affairs, their Chinese being reserved for the more lofty discussion of general principles. Hirose Tansō, writing in 1840, recognizes its importance and urges that specific instruction should be given in writing Japanese in fief schools. People need to be trained to express themselves clearly and to make a strong and direct impact on their readers, and this training could be given in the class-room by practice in drafting the judgments of law suits or orders to subordinates.[2]

I have seen no evidence that Hirose's advice was anywhere adopted, and still at the end of the period Yasui Sokken (see p. 197) is writing of the need for examinations in Japanese on the Wakayama model in terms which suggest that it was still something of an innovation. By then, however, the Wakayama fief did have some imitators, notably the Bakufu (from 1852),[3] and also Kurume (from 1865)[4] and Iwamura (from what date it is not clear).[5]

There may well have been, too, if not formal changes in the curriculum, at least a broadening of the range of ideas to which the students of fief schools had access. By now there were in circulation large numbers of treatises and memorials on the conduct of practical affairs written in Japanese by Confucian scholars and others. Some circulated in semi-secrecy in manuscript, for they contained opinions which capricious authorities might find subversive. Others were openly printed. A good many of them probably found their way into school libraries or

[1] *NKSS*, 2, p. 816.
[2] *Ugen* (*NKS*, 32), p. 122.
[3] *NKSS*, 7, p. 87.
[4] *NKSS*, 3, p. 41.
[5] *NKSS*, 1, p. 479.

otherwise got into the hands of young students. They were doubtless read avidly by politically interested youths, especially as the sense of national crisis deepened towards the end of the period. They do not seem to have been formally brought into the curriculum as required reading, largely, presumably, because, being written in Japanese, they did not require exposition by a teacher. Also, perhaps, because the eager discussion of political problems by youthful minds, inclined more to the pursuit of righteousness than to compromise with reality, was looked on by most fief authorities as a source of embarrassment rather than of benefit. (The Bakufu's new rules for dormitory students issued in 1866 included one to the effect that: 'There must be no reckless composition of Chinese prose and poetry satirically treating of contemporary events. It is unbecoming the student who wishes to prepare himself for useful service.')[1]

Which is not to say that there were no attempts to reform the curriculum. The teachers at the Bakufu school began to think hard in 1853, a few months after the order introducing examinations in the vernacular. In a memorial written just a few days before Perry's arrival at Uraga, they confess their failure to produce talented and serviceable students. The composition of Chinese prose and poetry has played too big a part in the curriculum. Students are allowed to feel satisfied if they can understand the classics, have memorized a lot of historical facts and can play around with words. There has been a lack of 'down-to-earth practical wisdom and preparation for administrative service'. Henceforth there will be less emphasis on prose and poetry, and their studies of the classics and of history will be more practically oriented, designed to find in the classics lessons for the treatment of current problems, eschewing lofty abstractions. They acknowledge a need to supplement this with actual teaching of criminal codes, economics, arithmetic and so on, but they lack the resources to do so at the moment.[2]

Three years later, at the beginning of 1856, they have got a little further. They present plans for an expansion of the 'Judicial and Administration Department'. It already has three sections, one dealing with legal codes—studying the T'ang, the Ming and the Ch'ing codes, the early Japanese codes and

[1] *NKSS*, 7, p. 212.
[2] *NKSS*, 7, p. 99.

the Shogunal codes since Kamakura—one on foreign countries whose students read works in Japanese on the customs and forms of government of Western nations; and, curiously, one concerned with prose and poetry. They announce their intention of eventually adding astronomy, geography, calligraphy, arithmetic, economics and the study of ancient ceremonial.[1]

Already, however, they were too late. It was in this same year 1856 that the Bakufu established its new school for the teaching of foreign languages and for the general study of Western science and techniques. It was the new Western learning which finally and conclusively demonstrated the relevance of formal intellectual training to administrative and professional talent. Its students gained new knowledge of military techniques, metallurgy, map-making, medicine and chemistry, the value of which was immediately recognized. They acquired some knowledge, too, of the social, economic and political institutions of foreign countries, enough, at least, to realize that the social institutions of their own country were not a fixed part of the order of nature and that they could, by conscious planning, be changed. We have seen how, in the 1840s the more farsighted daimyos who wished to 'educate human talent' sent promising students to Nagasaki or to one of the private Dutch academies in Edo or Osaka, and in the 1850s and 1860s they began to set up centres of Western studies in their own schools. It was the products of these academies and schools who received the promotions at the end of the period, carried out the reforms in their own fiefs, and eventually brought about the political revolution of the 1860s. Men like Hashimoto Sanai of Fukui, Oshima Takatō of Morioka, Sano Tsunetami of Saga, who helped to reform the administration of their fiefs in the 'fifties and 'sixties had all been at one of the Dutch academies. Of the Restoration leaders, Saigō from Satsuma, Kido, Itō and Inoue from Chōshū, Soejima and Okuma from Saga, Gotō, Sakamoto and Sasaki from Tosa, Yuri from Fukui, Mutsu and Katsu from the Bakufu, had all at some time studied in Nagasaki.[2] It may not have been the knowledge they acquired there which made them capable reformers and leaders. It may have

[1] *NKSS*, 7, pp. 101–5.
[2] Watanabe, 'Yūgaku-seido', pp. 7–8.

been their natural energies and capabilities which drove them to seek new knowledge as it drove them to gain control of their fiefs. But whatever were the real causal connections, the correlation between leadership ability and intellectual training seemed to have been amply demonstrated. There was good reason why one of the five articles of the Meiji Charter Oath of 1868—and that the most explicit—should have spoken of 'seeking knowledge throughout the world in order to strengthen the foundations of the Throne'.

Status and the School

Changing approaches to the problems of running the administration eventually affected the treatment of the status problem in schools. The point was made earlier that, right from the beginning of the period, Confucian educators managed within the schools to modify status distinctions in order to give recognition and reward to achievement in the class-room. It is not surprising that the growing emphasis on the function of the schools to produce talented men should, in the nineteenth century, have encouraged them to go further. More schools introduced the seating-by-seniority principle. Even the conservative Kaga school, whose rules about the appropriate number of retainers were quoted earlier, introduced the principle in 1839, though still within three separated rank groups.[1] A few schools went further and adopted more explicit forms of merit rating. The large and highly organized private school of Hirose Tansō on Bakufu territory in Kyūshū had a system of continuous numerical rating of its (predominantly commoner) students which determined seating positions and promotions, and the private Dutch schools, equally untrammelled by feudal patronage, were relentlessly consistent in this regard. In Ogata's school in Osaka, for instance, seating in the class-room was strictly determined by achievement and so, by monthly reshuffles, was the allocation of spaces on the dormitory floor.[2]

It was more difficult for a fief school so to ignore distinctions of rank, but some of them came fairly close. The Chōshū school

[1] NKSS, 2, p. 176.
[2] NKSSS, 4, p. 233, and E. Kiyooka, ed., The Autobiography of Fukuzawa Yukichi.

at Hagi is a good example. It was one in which, from its start in the early eighteenth century, priority-of-entry seating had been insisted on. It was, too, one of the earliest to declare, in a directive to the school issued probably in 1796, that its business was primarily the 'production of talented men to serve the fief'.[1]

Later the insistence on this theme becomes more strident. In 1840, at the time of Murata Seifū's reforms, a memorandum to the school promises that graduates will be taken into fief service according to the talents they show. It then goes on to urge the school administrators not to keep in the school as dormitory pupils those who fail to show promise in their first three-year term, nor to keep for a third period those whose achievement had fallen off in the second. 'The success or failure of the school', it says, 'depends entirely on its production of talented men, not on the number of students.'[2] As might be expected, such a rigorous insistence on the importance of ability ran up against opposition. Another order three months later complains in strong language that despite all instructions to the contrary members of the school are too concerned about rank and are failing to co-operate with each other, with deplorable results.[3]

These complaints are repeated in succeeding years and eventually, in the 1850s, a system of classes is introduced further to institutionalize the differentiation of students on the grounds of ability. They were divided into five groups: the prize pupils, the daily improvers, the diligent, the idle and the outcasts—there was to be no question of sparing anyone's feelings.[4] Seating order was to depend on the class and the order of promotion into it, and a couple of years later it was ordered that a register should be kept of those who reached the top two classes; students who appeared in the register would have priority in filling official positions.[5] Another order, probably of 1858, again details the deplorable effects of rank consciousness as a hindrance to effective co-operative study and insists:

[1] *NKSS*, 2, p. 665.
[2] *NKSS*, 2, p. 676.
[3] *NKSS*, 2, p. 677.
[4] *NKSS*, 2, p. 748. This system began in 1859 according to Suematsu Kenchō (*Bōchō kaitenshi*, 2, p. 564).
[5] Suematsu, *Bōchō kaitenshi*, 4, p. 535.

Henceforth everything that happens in the school shall be considered as 'outside the system'[1]; differences of rank shall be ignored and in all matters precedence shall depend on the extent of a student's ability and achievement, and on his accomplishments in the various skills.[2]

In the mid-sixties, as will be discussed in the next chapter, the elimination of status barriers was carried further to the point of admitting commoner students to the school—though still not, at first, on equal terms.

The rules and directives which have been used in this chapter give some inkling of the organization of the schools and of the experience of the students in them, but they do not tell the whole story. How far did the institutional changes which took place in the Chōshū school materially alter the school's atmosphere? Did they make for a much greater spirit of competition and a greater individualistic drive for achievement by the student? And were such elements of competitive striving absent in the other schools? The following extract from an autobiographical memoir by a Meiji scientist who was a boarding student at the Akita fief school in the 1850s gives the kind of glimpse into school life of which there are far too few examples. None of the documents from the Akita school suggests that it was one which went far in the process of trying to institutionalize competition, yet its advanced dormitory students, it is clear, provided themselves with competitive stimulants and took them very seriously indeed. The extract is taken from an inspirational magazine for boys published at the beginning of the twentieth century, and describes how he and three of his dormitory friends engaged in a prolonged reading competition:

> We really went all out that month. If one of us got a page ahead the others would turn pale. We hardly took time off to chew our food properly, and we drank as little water as possible in order that the others should not get ahead in the time wasted going to the lavatory—so keen were we to get a line or two ahead of the others.[3]

[1] An almost contemporary edict to the pupils of the Kagoshima school uses this same term 'outside the system' (*seigai*) to indicate what the school is *not*. Learning, it says, is for the good of the fief and those who look on it as *seigai*, like Buddhism, are in grievous error (*NKSS*, 3, p. 284).

[2] *NKSS*, 2, p. 706.

[3] Nemoto Tsūmei, 'Risshi-den'.

Should one read this as an indication that in the last years of the period there was a general nation-wide surge in the drive for self-improvement and the self-assertive desire to shine above one's fellows? Or should one—and this is perhaps nearer the truth—assume that the emphasis on performance which Bellah has seen as a major defining characteristic of Tokugawa *values*[1] was at least strong enough in the samurai ethic and in the childhood training provided by samurai families for it to have always produced, in a certain proportion of the more energetic and more self-confident, the kind of 'need achievement' which drives men not simply to conform to the standards their society imposes, but to seek to outdo and dominate their fellows? We simply do not know how frequently, when samurai children played together, their play naturally tended to challenge and competition—to see who could jump the highest, who could run the fastest. Two things that can be said with certainty are: firstly that the spread of formal school education provided in the child's and adolescent's life a whole new field of activity eminently suited to invidious comparisons of performance and bound, as a consequence, to catalyse such competitive urges as early training had implanted; secondly, that the sensitive pride and the fear of shaming defeat, the strength of which probably led the majority of samurai to avoid competitive situations and certainly prompted most educators and teachers of military skills deliberately to refrain from creating them, also meant that, once competition was declared and the race was on, the self-respecting samurai really did go all out to win.

School and Society

The attempt has been made in this chapter to trace a number of interacting and converging trends. The two major stable variables were, on the one hand the principle of ascription on which the allocation of status and power in the society was based, on the other the natural tendency of teachers (at least of teachers intellectually committed to their subjects) to find ways

[1] See *Tokugawa Religion, passim.* The stress on *values* is deliberate. One should emphasize more than Bellah does the difference between the values embodied in an ideology and the principles of social organization.

of awarding recognition to achievement. The conflict between them produced various institutional devices in the schools by which a compromise was achieved. Towards the end of the period other dynamic factors intervened to shift, and keep shifting, the balance of that compromise. There was, firstly, the growing sense of external and internal crisis leading to a demand for ability in leadership and administration. Secondly, partly as a response to this, partly as a result of the introduction from the West of new branches of learning, there was an increasing incorporation into school curricula of elements of clear vocational relevance to administration. Thirdly, one should not overlook the effects of the cumulative growth in the *quantity* of education. The sheer expansion in the size of schools led naturally to the rationalization of their organization, the division into grades and the establishment of objective tests of fitness to pass from one grade to the next. The combination of these three factors operated to reinforce, and give greater scope to, the tendency to stress achievement inherent in the teacher's role. The principle of ascription was necessarily weakened, both in the school and in the bureaucracies of the fiefs and of the Bakufu—the trend within the school being at once an effect and a stimulus of the trend in the bureaucracies. Gradually the barriers of status began to give way. By the end of the period a man's prestige and his power, if still not his income, increasingly came to depend less on who he was than on what he could do.

Chapter VII

THE COMMONER AND HIS MASTERS

EVERY TOKUGAWA WRITER who discussed education agreed that the samurai needed it. There was no such unanimity concerning the desirability of educating commoners. In part, the differences of view in this respect corresponded with different conceptions of the purpose of education and why the samurai ought to receive it. For those who looked on education as primarily a matter of training in the skills of government it was unnecessary, and even positively undesirable, that the non-samurai should be educated. They might get ideas above their station; they would become intractable, and proper divisions of status would be blurred. For those, on the other hand, who held that gakumon was primarily a matter of moral refinement, education of the commoners had its proper place. The texts did, after all, say that '*man* is the soul of creation' and even the farmers were men. The good ruler should promote morality wherever opportunity offered. Moreover, the morality to be promoted stressed the fulfilment of duty and the proper observance of status distinctions. Morally refined commoners should be more obedient, more loyal, more devoted to their superiors, more efficient and diligent producers, more tractable subjects.

It will be useful, in discussing samurai attitudes towards commoner education, to distinguish three levels of scholastic accomplishment; first, mere literacy, the ability to read and write Japanese; second, instruction in a few elementary Chinese classics of mainly moral import such as the Four Books or the *Classic of Filial Piety* (this will be called 'basic moral Chinese education') and third, broader acquaintance with the more recondite classics, Chinese literary prose and poetry and historical writings (to be referred to as 'full-scale Chinese education').

It is rare to find any definite assertion of the view that commoners should be kept wholly ignorant of even the Japanese script. Ogyū Sorai seemed to be implying this when, at the beginning of the eighteenth century, he said that Japan was easy to govern because the people were illiterate,[1] but even he grudgingly admitted that a little acquaintance with books might be permissible for the lower orders provided they confine themselves to the *Classic of Filial Piety* and a few simple works of moral instruction.[2] Hayashi Shihei uncompromisingly said that the commoners should be forbidden to learn any other arts than those necessary for them to concentrate on their hereditary occupations, but the context does not make it clear whether he included literacy among the forbidden arts.[3] Nishikawa Joken (not himself a samurai) spoke approvingly of an Indian state which kept its people illiterate, but it is clear from other contexts that he did not really mean that Japan should follow its example.[4] Even Aizawa Yasushi, who insisted quite vehemently in a memorandum concerning educational policy that it is no duty of the feudal authorities to educate the common people, did not say that they should be prohibited all learning, and even admitted the possibility that a few commoners of superior ability might be selected for education and service.[5]

If few writers on education actually held (publicly) that the common people were better illiterate, there does seem to have been in some districts a prejudice against farmers—or at least their wives—learning to read and write. The anonymous author of a collection of observations on the contemporary world wrote as late as 1837:

People talk of illiteracy as being a great practical handicap and even more, a shameful thing, but in some districts girls are absolutely forbidden to read and write. In such places even men are not expected to do more than learn to write their names. They are expected to concentrate on their farming. Even more so the women. It is thought that if they can read and write they will become idle, or they will write letters [love letters, perhaps,

---

[1] *Taiheisaku* (Kishigami, *Nihon bunko*, 2), p. 10.
[2] *Ibid.*, p. 43.
[3] *Fukei-kun* (Dōbunkan, *Nihon kyōiku bunko, Kunkai*, 1), p. 685.
[4] *Hyakushō-bukuro* (*NKS*, 5), pp. 169–70.
[5] *Gakusei ryakusetsu* (*NKSS*, 5), p. 461.

or letters to their parents complaining of their mothers-in-law?]
and cause all kinds of undesirable upsets, and this will prevent
them from devoting themselves to their proper duties. Reading,
it is thought, is the business of the village headman.[1]

There may well have been some village headmen who
enforced such prohibitions in order to preserve their privileged
status (though, as we shall see, there is far more evidence of
village headmen who made it their business to teach villagers to
read and write). In any case, it seems to have been rare for such
prohibitions to be enforced by the fief authorities. In the
questionnaire sent in 1883 to prefectural authorities by the
Ministry of Education, from which the *Materials for the Study
of the Educational History of Japan*[2] was compiled, one question
specifically asked whether there was record of any such ban on
study by commoners. For only two fiefs—that of Tsuwano and
that of Yonezawa—is such a prohibition mentioned (and the
Tsuwano case is doubtful).[3] There may well have been other
instances; the prefectural respondents may have been reluctant
to admit to practices which by the values of 1883 reflected ill on
the traditions of their fiefs, and there is often a note of over-
protesting indignation in the replies denying the existence of
any such ban. But it is fairly safe to say that such instances were
very rare.

Equally, there were few fiefs which actually banned basic
moral Chinese study. Two instances only are recorded in the
Materials. In the 1770s some Fukuoka farmers are reported to
have put some money together to buy books only to have them
impounded by the local Intendant on the grounds that it was
detrimental to public morality for farmers to read.[4] In the early
years of the nineteenth century a Tokushima boatman (apparently of something like lower foot-soldier status) was supposed to have been punished for being too fond of books.[5] Both
these are isolated incidents, though the reporter for the Fukuoka

---

[1] *Edo gūzoku tsurezure-banashi* (Yoneyama-dō, *Mikan zuihitsu*, 13), p. 277. Quoted
in Kaigo Tokioma, *et al.*, *Nihon kyōikushi*, p. 199.

[2] The *NKSS*.

[3] *NKSS*, 2, p. 504; 1, p. 732. In the Tsuwano report the odd construction of the
sentence suggests that it may be a miscopying of an original to the effect that there
was *no* ban.

[4] *NKSS*, 3, p. 6.

[5] *NKSS*, 2, p. 853.

fief says that thereafter a 'semi-ban' remained in force for some years.

If actual prohibition was rare, it was, nevertheless, about the appropriateness of teaching commoners to this level—of basic moral Chinese—that many writers had doubts. It is here that the divergence between the proponents of the two approaches to education becomes apparent. Ogyū Sorai, as the exponent *par excellence* of the view that gakumon was primarily a matter of learning the art of government, was scornful of the moralists of the Sung school who suggested that the way to improve the behaviour of the people is by encouraging each individual to study and improve himself. On the contrary, he suggested, the only cure was to devise appropriate political and legal institutions to keep people in good order. The moralists were like a man who tries to hull rice a grain at a time instead of putting it in a mortar and pounding.[1] If the lower classes were encouraged to read anything beyond a few simple moral treatises it would only 'increase their cunning and lead to disaster'.[2] '*The Greater Learning, Mencius,* the *Shu ching* —these are for princes and ministers who govern the country', according to another writer. 'What possible value can there be for the common people to over-reach their proper station in life and study such books?[3]'

The author of an 1817 treatise on gakumon elaborates on the ill-effects of 'overly superior learning' on the common people:

When they acquire a little skill at letters they tend to become arrogant, they look down on their fellow-men, despise their elders and superiors and question the instructions of the author-ities.

They also tend to feast and drink to excess, become dissolute

[1] *Taiheisaku* (Kishigami, *Nihon bunko*, 2), p. 30.

[2] *Ibid.*, p. 43. Sorai would have found himself at home with Hannah More who, while prepared to establish schools at which labourers' children could be taught to read the Catechism and even to teach writing and arithmetic to the sons of farmers, was shocked at a contemporary's 'extravagant plan that there is *nothing* which the poor ought not to be taught . . . Now the absurdity of the thing is most obvious . . . Where would they find time to read [these books] without the neglect of all business and the violation of all duty? And where is all this to terminate? Only cast back your eye upon Athens . . . Was there ever a more ungovernable rabble?' (Letter to the Bishop of Bath, 1801, in J. Aitken, *English Letters of the Nineteenth Century*, p. 58).

[3] Shōji Kōgi, *Keizai mondō hiroku* (*NKS*, 22), p. 78.

braggarts and so damage public morals and exercise a bad influence on honest citizens. In fact, what is called the 'spread of culture' to the villages is nothing but the destruction of the simple honest ways which formerly prevailed.[1]

Even non-samurai writers themselves issued such warnings. A Wakayama farmer, in his collection of precepts for farmers, said that learning, while excellent for children, should not be carried to the point where they lose interest in their proper agricultural pursuits.[2] Nishikawa Joken, in his homily for farmers, agreed that 'even farmers should follow the trend of the times and learn to read and write' but as far as gakumon is concerned the single volume of the *Greater Learning*, or perhaps the *Classic of Filial Piety*, was enough. In his companion volume for townsmen he poured scorn on the idea that they should study in order to 'regulate their homes and cultivate their persons'. Do the unlearned all bring their families to bankruptcy? Do they necessarily steal? If there were not severe laws against theft would not scholars also be tempted?[3]

A *senryū* comic poem expresses succinctly the kind of thing men like Nishikawa had in mind when they spoke of the danger to the family fortunes which came from 'getting culture'. The founder of the family fortune is safe enough, and his own children are not likely to be brought up to bookish luxury. It is the grandchildren who bankrupt the family.

> House for sale,
> He writes in fine Chinese style—
> The third generation.

Among serious writers, however, this stress on the dangers of excessive study for commoners is the emphasis of a minority. Rather more writers were concerned to stress the positive desirability of encouraging gakumon among the people as a means of improving their moral standards.[4] And, in fact, in some form

---

[1] Karashima Ken, *Gakusei wakumon* (*NKSS*, 8), p. 11.

[2] Yamana Fuminari, *Nōka-kun*.

[3] *Chōnin-bukuro* (*NKS*, 5), pp. 97–8. The last three sources are all quoted in Ototake, *Shomin-kyōikushi*, 1, pp. 534–5, 540, 559.

[4] See, for instance, the works of Kaibara Ekken and Kumazawa Banzan quoted earlier; Yamaga Sokō, *Yamaga gorui*, p. 295; Shūdō Yasuzaemon, Memorial to the daimyo of Tokushima in *NKSS*, 5, p. 595; Shōji Kōgi, *Keizai mondō hiroku* (*NKS*, 22), pp. 76–7; and the anonymous author of the *Hyakushō denki* (*NKT*, 31), p. 416.

or other, the Bakufu and a few of the fiefs did do something to this end.

Ignoring for the moment Bakufu territory, what they did can be roughly summarized under the following headings:[1]

1. Fiefs in which commoners were allowed into the fief school 17
2. Fiefs in which commoners may possibly have been admitted to the fief school 75
3. Fiefs in which commoners were allowed to attend special sermon-lectures at the fief school . . 6
4. Fiefs which established special institutions to give sermon-lectures to adult commoners . . . 18
5. Fiefs which sent out travelling lecturers to give sermon-lectures to adult commoners . . . 76
6. Fiefs which distributed morally exhortatory pamphlets for use in commoner schools 4
7. Fiefs which established schools for commoner children 7
8. Fiefs which may have established schools for commoner children 7
9. Fiefs which exerted some licensing control over the establishment of *terakoya* schools for commoners . 21

[1] This summary is based on the details given for 244 fiefs in the first three volumes of *NKSS*, supplemented by Ishikawa's researches into the Shingaku movement (*Sekimon Shingakushi kenkyū*, pp. 1023–48). The figures are necessarily approximate since the information on which they are based is fragmentary and classification in these categories often requires considerable guesswork. It is almost certainly incomplete since the *NKSS* only records the documents and personal reminiscences readily available to prefectural officials in 1883. Many other fiefs may have taken similar measures which went unrecorded. On the other hand many of the actions and policies detailed here were fleeting in duration. The first two categories require explanation. One question in the questionnaire sent out in 1883 asked whether commoners were allowed into the fief school. The answer for a large number of fiefs is that they were. Other authorities have taken these replies at their face value (e.g. Kasai, *Hankō*, p. 197). They should be treated with suspicion, however. In the first place the questionnaire asked about the state of affairs before the establishment of the new school system in 1872, and consequently some of these replies may refer to the sudden opening of the school to commoners after the Meiji Restoration. Secondly, prefectural reporters may have been anxious to represent local traditions as progressive at the expense of the exact truth. It is significant that a number of these replies come in batches, and in the same form of words, from the same prefecture. The seventeen fiefs placed in the first category are, therefore, those for which documents are quoted supporting the assertion that commoners were allowed in the schools before the Restoration. The others are placed in the second, 'may have permitted' category.

Commoners in Fief Schools

Of the seventeen fiefs which seem with reasonable certainty to have admitted commoners to the fief school, the most detailed documentation exists for the Okayama school, which was also the first fief school to be established. Here, provision was made for commoners from the very foundation of the school. When the temporary school was set up in 1666 a number of farmers' children were admitted to study and act as servants and errand boys of the officials and teachers.[1] When the school was rebuilt and reorganized a few years later, they were given a special study-room—the *shosei-beya*—and as *shosei*[2] their status in the school was minutely defined. An order to the official in charge, dated 1671, lays down the disciplinary regulations which were to apply to them. They were to have two hours of fresh instruction and three hours of revision each day. In order that they should fully appreciate that the purpose of learning was to 'discipline the heart and improve behaviour' they should be called together three times a month to reflect on their conduct and mutually to urge each other to better efforts. They were to be tested monthly and the number of characters whose readings they had forgotten noted in a register. Marks for conduct should also be recorded and five black marks warranted a summons to the school office. There follow details of their menial tasks, the cleaning of the lecture rooms and dormitories, beating the clock shell-gongs and so on.

[1] *NKSS*, 2, p. 585.
[2] The word is written with the characters 'various students' rather than the more usual 'book students'. They were also given another title, the reading of which is obscure, possibly *kozamurai-mono*.

Miscellaneous regulations include a prohibition on boys who had not yet reached *gempuku* age (roughly puberty) bathing with those who had, and a warning that in the military training huts they should not play with the equipment in imitation of their betters. They should, it is added, always be respectful to students of the school and to other samurai.[1]

They were clearly second-class citizens and on no occasion did they actually study with the other students. They were, however, allowed to wear swords while at the school.[2] The text of the order which permitted this is perhaps indicative of the ideas behind the system. The measure is justified on the grounds that 'samurai originated from the peasant class and should return to it'. This was, indeed, less than a century after Hideyoshi's sword-hunt, the round-up of weapons that finally institutionalized the separation of the samurai from the peasant class. The samurai were still not far removed from the land and it was the thesis of some contemporary thinkers that they ought to return more intimately to it. (Kumazawa Banzan was the most prominent of these thinkers and he may well have been behind these measures since his brother was in charge of the school and was specifically mentioned as the source of the order to wear swords.) It is significant that only the children of farmers—not of merchants—are mentioned as being eligible for the school. The division between samurai and farmers being less rigid than it was to become in later years, many of the district headmen (*ōjōya*) and village headmen (*shōya*) were allowed swords and surnames and enjoyed a status distinctly superior to that of an ordinary foot-soldier. Many of the early students whose names are given in the Okayama records did, indeed, have surnames and some others who did not are listed as sons of *shōya*.[3]

There was, then, nothing very startlingly radical about this system and it was presumably thought advantageous to the fief to have its village administrators well educated. The system seems not to have lasted long, however. The annual records of the school show that the number of *shosei* rose to a peak of sixty-seven in 1673, but thereafter declined until only eleven are

[1] *NKSS*, 2, pp. 591–2.
[2] *Biyō kokugaku-ki*. Order of 30th, intercalary tenth month, 1669. The *NKSS* says that only outstanding students were allowed swords as a reward (2, p. 597), but the text of the 1669 order seems clearly to include all students.
[3] *Biyō kokugaku-ki*.

recorded in 1680. After this they disappear from the records, though an enigmatic category of *tsugi-no-ko* (messenger children? attendant children?), which may or may not refer to farmers' children, recurs at intervals until 1703,[1] and commoners' children continued to be admitted for basic moral Chinese training to the Shizutani Gakkō, a lesser school operated by the fief in a country district.[2]

The Aizu fief was another in which commoners were allowed to study at the fief school early in the period but not later. In this case no details are available concerning the status they enjoyed, but their admission seems to have been little more than elementary justice since the fief school had formerly been a private school which the fief later (in 1664) adopted, and as a private school its pupils had been predominantly merchants' children. All sense of gratitude to merchant pioneers was soon lost, however. By 1820, not only commoners but also foot-soldiers and even lesser samurai were forbidden to enter the school.[3]

If the practice at Okayama and at Aizu can be seen as a reflection of the still indistinct division between the samurai and the prosperous commoner class, in at least three fiefs the admission of commoners towards the end of the period reflects the gradual breakdown in the Tokugawa class (or better, estate) system and a move towards the freer society of Meiji Japan. In Chōshū the order to admit commoner students came in 1865[4] as the culmination of a series of measures designed to break down the rigidity of the status system within the samurai class in order to promote men of ability (see p. 210) and, perhaps, as a logical conclusion of the formation of new types of army unit, some of which were made up largely of commoners. Here it appears that the commoners studied together with the samurai. They were still, however, second-class pupils, and it seems that the school authorities tried against opposition from their fief superiors to remove the disabilities from which they suffered. In 1865, the year in which they were first admitted, the school complained of the fact that they were

[1] *Biyō kokugaku-ki*, various years. The *NKSS* (2, p. 600) makes no mention of such students except for the period 1669–82.
[2] *NKSS*, 3, pp. 426–8.
[3] Ogawa, *Aizu-han kyōiku-kō*, pp. 63, 79, 44.
[4] *NKSS*, 2, p. 726.

excluded from the *sekiten* ceremonies and the ceremonial examinations—the functions attended by the daimyo or his deputies. This disbarment, it is suggested, might well reduce the efficacy of the daimyo's encouragement to commoners to study.[1] The effect of this complaint is not recorded, but another request two years later presses a similar point. The top class of the lower school is allowed to take part in certain lectures held in the bottom class of the upper school. Commoners in that class, however, are expected to withdraw whenever the daimyo makes a visit. Could they not be allowed to remain, at least when the visit is an occasional, non-ceremonial one? The answer was: No, but the question would be reconsidered should any commoner achieve the distinction of full entry into the upper school.[2]

In the Tosa fief the effect of ending the samurai monopoly of military skills, which may have been a factor in Chōshū, is quite clearly apparent. The only commoners said to have been admitted to the fief school in Kōchi (from 1862) were commoner soldiers (*mimpei*).[3] The Kyūshū fief of Omura also opened its doors to commoners at about the same time (in 1864), but here the order simply specifies 'farmers and merchants' and no military connection is apparent.[4]

What scanty details are available about the other fiefs which admitted commoners from an earlier date suggest at least three different motives for doing so. Firstly, there were fiefs which carried to its logical conclusion the principle that gakumon was for the purpose of moral improvement and hence necessary to all ranks of society. This was at least in theory the case at the Kaga school which was founded, according to the official order of 1792, 'for the instruction and guidance of the four orders of society' (i.e. samurai, farmers, artisans and merchants).[5] In the same year an order concerning the establishment of dormitories specifies that commoners 'of tolerably affluent means' should be admitted along with rear vassals and foot-soldiers. But a special addendum notes that poor commoners who evinced a desire to study but could not afford to do so might be

[1] *NKSS*, 2, p. 726.
[2] *NKSS*, 2, p. 736.
[3] *NKSS*, 2, p. 907.
[4] *NKSS*, 3, p. 182.
[5] *NKSS*, 2, p. 84.

boarded free.[1] There is, however, no evidence among the voluminous documents quoted from the Kaga fief that commoners ever did enter the school for regular study. The time-tables cater only for their admission to the regular sermon-lectures.

In the Tatsuno fief, on the other hand, another school with a strong moral emphasis, it appears that commoners actually were admitted for regular study from the opening of the school in 1834. A special order of that year instructs the school authorities to admit 'those of the town or country districts who wish to study literature' (*bungaku*), and the time-tables indicate that special times were set aside for commoners to receive instruction in elementary reading.[2]

In the second category are those fiefs which restricted the privilege of admission to a limited number of commoners of high status. The Shibamura school, for instance, admitted only the children of commoners who were permitted surnames and swords,[3] rather on the lines of the Okayama school, though by the nineteenth century powerful merchants as well as village headmen were included in the privileged category. The Minaguchi fief admitted commoners who boarded with samurai of the fief.[4]

Thirdly, at the Bakufu school, the Shōheikō, and in some other fiefs, the motive for admitting commoners seems to have been to train professional scholars. Commoners were not being educated to be better commoners; a selected few were being groomed for useful service. This is quite clearly so at the Bakufu school. One of the regulations issued at the time of the reforms of 1793 says specifically, after enumerating a number of categories inadmissible to the school, 'however, merchants, artisans and so on, who are of earnest intent and devoted to learning and *give up their family trade* may be admitted as students of the lowest rank'.[5] In at least four other schools[6] the same kind of motives seem to have prevailed. Commoners were

[1] *NKSS*, 2, p. 203.
[2] *NKSS*, 2, p. 518.
[3] *NKSS*, 1, p. 25.
[4] *NKSS*, 1, p. 436.
[5] *NKSS*, 1, p. 31. It appears that the permission for commoners to enter was later withdrawn, but they were admitted to a second Bakufu school—the Kōjimachi Kyōjusho—established in 1842 (*NKSS*, 1, p. 490).
[6] The two Shikoku fiefs of Takamatsu and Uwajima, Kumamoto and Kakegawa.

not given elementary instruction; they were admitted only after they had attained a reasonable level of scholarship and shown special promise. In one they had formally to pass a fairly advanced examination,[1] and in another they were admitted only to the senior dormitory—that is, at an advanced level—and if they showed particular promise were given a small scholarship stipend.[2]

Similar motives seem to have operated in the six fiefs which, while not admitting commoners to the fief school, provided special rewards or recognition to outstanding commoner scholars. The Kyūshū fief of Kashima, for instance, gave commoners of exceptional scholastic ability appropriate official duties and awarded them a retainer's stipend for their period of office, for life, or in perpetuity,[3] and in the neighbouring fief of Fukue those who completed an examination in the Four Books, two of the Five Classics and the *Classic of Filial Piety* were automatically given samurai status for life.[4]

And even in fiefs where such promotion of commoners was not regularly institutionalized there were examples of individuals receiving such rewards.[5] The commoners involved seem often to have been village headmen or doctors or merchants closely involved in the fief's finances; men, that is to say, who were on the fringes of the samurai bureaucracy, shared samurai values and often, though of non-samurai status, had some regular function in the fief administration. Indeed, Kamei Nammei notes one case in Kumamoto of the son of a village headman who was accepted by the Kumamoto authorities for entrance into the school dormitories as a promising scholar fit to be promoted to samurai rank, only to have the permission withdrawn on the objection of the Intendant administering his district. The latter complained that village administration would suffer if able village headmen were elevated to higher spheres.[6]

---

[1] Kakegawa. They were to be examined in one of two Chinese histories, the *Kuo-shih-lüeh*, or the *Shih-pa-shih-lüeh* (*NKSS*, 1, p. 179).

[2] At Uwajima (*NKSS*, 2, p. 889).

[3] *NKSS*, 3, p. 186.

[4] The other fiefs were those of Takata (*NKSS*, 2, p. 267); Shibata (2, p. 281); Aizu (1, p. 680); and Takahashi (2, p. 610).

[5] See, for example, instances from the Hikone fief (*NKSS*, 1, p. 372).

[6] *Higo monogatari* (*NKS*, 15), p. 499. Kamei quotes this, it is interesting to note in passing, as an example of the admirable rationalization of the administration in Kumamoto. Functions were specifically delegated to the degree that a low-ranking

The Tokugawa system was not by any means as cut and dried as is suggested by the neat formulations of those Tokugawa writers who speak of the four orders—the samurai, the farmers, the craftsmen and the merchants. It was rather a world of infinite gradations in which the dividing line between the samurai proper and the commoner was a blurred and shifting one. The Bakufu itself and many other fiefs employed within the military hierarchy large numbers of foot-soldiers who had no hereditary status and were simply recruited for life at a regular salary—a major source of dispute when formulating the either/or registration categories of *shizoku* (samurai), and *heimin* (commoner) after the Meiji Restoration. In particular the status of the professional scholar was an ambiguous one as has already been pointed out (p. 116), retained as he was for his special 'family skill'; in, but not quite of, the samurai class. Table 4 showed earlier that only a relatively small proportion of scholars, in fact, inherited their position, and since the posts of *jusha* or teacher were not particularly attractive to samurai the only source of new blood was in the commoner class. As Nakai Chikuzan said, the unfortunate consequences of the hereditary system were most marked in the case of doctors and Confucian scholars, so that a daimyo 'who wishes to employ men of ability has no choice but to promote them from the ranks of the common people'—and he has to go on doing it since the sons of those who are thus promoted to a hereditary income often prove worthless in their turn.[1]

Special Commoner Schools

There is, in short, no evidence that any fief admitted commoner students to the main fief school in large numbers or on a footing of equality with samurai students. There is no reason to expect that they should have done, since even foot-soldiers were often excluded. A number of fiefs did, however, for one or more of the three motives just outlined above (moral improvement of

---

[1] *Sōbō kigen* (*NKS*, 16), p. 321.

Intendant could override superior officials at the centre on matters within his own delegated sphere of competence. The elevation of the headman's son was not, to him, a particularly unusual aspect of the story.

the masses, favouring of wealthy commoners, or absorption of commoner talent), establish or aid in establishing special schools for commoners which provided either basic moral Chinese education (presumptive evidence of the first motive) or the more full-scale literary kind (presumptive evidence of the third).

The Bakufu's grant of land to an unemployed samurai (in 1723 when Yoshimune was particularly active in educational matters) to enable him to start a school[1] and similar assistance given to the Nakai school in Osaka soon after are the earliest examples. There is no clear evidence that these were, in fact, primarily designed for commoners, though commoners certainly did study in the Nakai school, and Nakai's grandson, writing at the end of the century, speaks of the Edo school as being the first official provision of a place where 'even commoners' could study.[2]

These early examples were full-scale literary schools and in so far as they were intended for commoners are probably evidence of the desire to train useful professional scholars. But the bulk of the establishments which were clearly intended for commoners were restricted to basic moral Chinese education and date from later in the period. They were all founded after Matsudaira Sadanobu's ban had boosted the prestige of Sung Confucianism and at a time when much more official interest was being shown in the morals of the populace.

The first examples are two founded in the 1790s by Hayakawa Hachirōzaemon, the noted Intendant of Bakufu territory in what is now Okayama prefecture. They were not the result of central Bakufu policy, but of Hayakawa's own initiative. He described their origin in a document addressed to the Bakufu in 1798 requesting tax exemption for the land on which his schools had been built.[3] When he took office in the district some eleven years previously he had been struck by the large area of formerly cultivated land now gone to waste. He discovered that the reason lay in a decline in population due to infanticide.[4] He found, too, that the evil disposition and lack

---

[1] *NKSS*, 7, p. 74.

[2] *Sōbō kigen* (*NKS*, 16), p. 352.

[3] *NKSS*, 7, p. 800.

[4] He was probably misinformed. Even the most alarmist descriptions of infanticide at this time rarely suggest that families failed to replace themselves.

of a sense of responsibility which this indicated was also reflected in a tendency to excessive litigiousness. He accordingly did what he could on his tours of the district to lecture to the people on the evil of their ways, and later he hired two Confucian scholars to give lectures every month at temples near the two administrative centres of his district and to travel periodically to more outlying parts. Later, a group of local farmers got the idea (doubtless at his prompting) of building proper schools (*kyōyusho* is the term used, *kyōyu* being one of the words for—chiefly adult—moral instruction). These were to be both centres for the monthly lectures and places for the scholars to give local children basic Chinese instruction in their spare time. The farmers had provided the land and the building expenses.

Some details of the financing of one of these schools are extant. A part of the considerable sum of money collected was used to purchase land and to erect the school building. The remainder was lent to the Bakufu and the annual interest was used to cover running expenses and the teacher's salary.[1] They should, however, have chosen a better banker. A document of 1850 tells a sad story. In 1842 the Bakufu had ordered that the principal of all Bakufu debts should be reduced by half, and for some time no interest was to be paid on the remaining half. The school was thus deprived of its source of income. The village officials in charge petitioned that it should be allowed to continue nevertheless (though they did not suggest how). The Bakufu was unco-operative, however. It ordered that the school should be abandoned and added, to put them in their place, that henceforth, as in other provinces, the Intendant would take responsibility for the instruction (*kyōyu*) of the people, for improving morals and encouraging agriculture; though, of course, village officials should do their part by reading official regulations to the people and encouraging them in obedience.[2]

Hayakawa later established another school in the Musashi

[1] *NKSS*, 7, pp. 803–4.
[2] *NKSS*, 7, p. 805.

Famine or epidemic is a more likely explanation of the fact that land went out of cultivation. All the same, this was a good politic argument to use with the tax authorities.

district near Edo to which he was transferred, and his example seems to have inspired other local Intendants in Bakufu territory. At least three other schools were started in the same way, in 1824 and 1851 in parts of Kai province,[1] and in 1834 in the Kurashiki district.[2] The fact that the existence of another started in Kyoto in 1806 is known only from the gravestone of the school's teacher[3] suggests that there may well have been many others. They usually seem to have adopted similar methods of financing, and to have resulted from the same kind of co-operative initiative by Bakufu officials and commoners of the rich-farmer-headman class. A few details are available for one of these Kai schools. It is said to have had an average of fifty pupils, some of whom boarded with the teacher. They were taught reading and writing and basic Chinese. A sub-official of the Intendant's office had administrative charge of the school, and full-scale *sekiten* ceremonies were held, with music and all officials in attendance in full regalia, every spring and autumn.[4]

As the story of the origin of Hayakawa's school suggests, as schools these were incidental outgrowths of the officials' concern to provide lecture-sermons for the moral instruction of the people. The teachers combined school-teaching with lecture tours, and from the officials' point of view the latter was their primary function. The schools themselves contributed by sending back to the villages literate children with a smattering of the Confucian moral classics who could be expected to help provide a more receptive ground for the lecturer's teaching. The schools may also have trained a few minor officials of the Intendant's staff.

The same ideas lay behind similar schools in the fiefs. Isezaki and Mito both established a number of such schools in the first two decades of the nineteenth century.[5] Saga established one for merchants in the castle town in 1839,[6] and Tsuyama followed two years later with a school which also had a branch for girls where they were taught sewing and read improving

[1] *NKSS*, 7, pp. 715, 716–17.
[2] *NKSS*, 7, p. 797.
[3] Ototake, *Shomin kyōikushi*, 1, p. 771.
[4] *NKSS*, 7, p. 718.
[5] *NKSS*, 2, p. 281; 3, p. 383.
[6] *NKSS*, 3, p. 119.

works.[1] In the Takahashi school, also built in the castle town, in 1855, foot-soldiers attended in the morning and commoners, taught by commoner teachers, in the afternoon.[2] Shibata established a number of schools in the 1850s[3] and the Tsu school for merchants of the castle town was established in 1858 and taught elementary Japanese literacy as well as basic Chinese.[4] The Sadowara and Takanabe fiefs also established what are described as *kyōgaku* (the generic name for this type of school), but these were probably for samurai stationed in country districts or for the 'farmer-samurai' *gōshi*.[5]

There is every reason to suppose that the teachers of these schools also had the function of giving general sermon-lectures to the people. The fact that the Chinese education they provided for children was strictly limited to the basic moral texts is proved at least for the Shibata schools by a directive issued by the fief in 1858. It regrets that they have lost sight of the fact that their chief duty is to improve morals. There has been a deplorable tendency in some cases to deviate into poetry, literary prose and miscellaneous erudition. In future they should keep to the Four Books, the *Hsiao hsüeh* and the *Classic of Filial Piety*. Collections of T'ang poetry and Chinese histories should be banned from the schools.[6]

Kyōka

The provision of non-scholastic lecture-sermons to the people at large—with which function these schools were intimately linked—was, in fact, the field in which the feudal authorities were most active. This was not a matter of *gakumon* or of *kyōiku* —of the education of children—but of *kyōka*, *kyōdo* or *kyōyu*[7]— of the indoctrination of adults.

Several means were employed to this end. The most elementary was the posting on special notice-boards in the towns and villages of succinct moral precepts exhorting the people to be

[1] *NKSS*, 2, p. 570.
[2] *NKSS*, 2, p. 616.
[3] *NKSS*, 2, pp. 279–81.
[4] *NKSS*, 1, p. 77.
[5] *NKSS*, 3, pp. 254, 271.
[6] *NKSS*, 2, p. 280.
[7] The words become fashionable in roughly that order (Ishikawa, 'Edo-jidai makki no kyōka undō', pp. 2–9).

filial to their parents, to be obedient to their superiors and to treat their servants kindly, to live in harmony with their neighbours, avoid quarrels and gambling and not gather at public executions. These were usually intermixed with practical administrative injunctions concerning the reporting of suspicious travellers or Christians, terms of contract for hired labourers, rates of exchange, prohibitions on monopoly price-fixing and the like;[1] no distinction between public duty and private morality was recognized. These *kōsatsu*[2] were issued by the Bakufu at least as early as 1642.[3] Amended versions appeared from time to time, usually at the beginning of each Shogun's reign.

Another means of instructing the people was first resorted to the Bakufu in 1682, though it had been vigorously employed by Ikeda Mitsumasa during his rule of the Okayama fief.[4] It was an application of the Confucian principle of government that one should judiciously use rewards as well as punishments. Examples of specially filial conduct which came to the notice of the authorities were rewarded with gifts or public recognition.[5] The practice was especially common at the time of the periodic reforms. Matsudaira Sadanobu ordered local officials to search out and report such men of merit, and in 1800 the Bakufu published a *Record of Filial Duty* containing selections from their reports.[6]

Thirdly, there were the prefaces to the *gonin-gumi* registers. These, essentially census registers provided by the authorities

---

[1] See the 1711 version reprinted in Asaoka, *Ishinzen shōgakkō*, p. 52.

[2] Of *takafuda*. Both readings seem to have been used.

[3] Heibonsha, *Rekishi daijiten*, 22, p. 259.

[4] Hall, 'The Confucian teacher', p. 276.

[5] The first Bakufu award of 1682 was to a very rich Shizuoka farmer who had 'exerted himself for the good of the village' as well as being notably filial. He was given tax remission on his large area (some 90 *koku* in yield) of land (Ototake, *Shomin kyōikushi*, 1, p. 629).

[6] *Kōgiroku*. (See Ototake, *Shomin kyōikushi*, 1, p. 702.) Hosoi Heishū once noted sadly that there were generally fewer reports from the villages of exceptionally meritorious persons than of criminals. This did not at all mean that the evil really out-numbered the good. The reporting system was at fault. Village officials were eager to report criminals because criminals were a nuisance to everybody, the officials were afraid of being implicated if they failed to report, and they were sometimes given rewards for handing over criminals. Reporting the noble deeds of a filial son, however, was an unattractive proposition. It involved them in endless paper work and they got nothing out of it themselves. He suggested that there should be rewards for this too (*Omeikan isō* (Inoue, *Rinri ihen*, 9), p. 42).

and kept up to date by village headmen, were given prefaces which somewhat elaborated the text of the village notice-boards and contained the same mixture of moral precepts and administrative regulations.[1] When issued, these were read to the assembled farmers and each had to append his seal or signature in token of his digestion of the contents and of his loyal intentions to obey their purport. Subsequently, village head-men were supposed to reread them at intervals to the assembled villagers. Though edifying, these were doubtless not the most exciting of entertainments for the farmers. Nishikawa Joken in his *Hyakushō-bukuro* warns his imaginary interlocutor, a village headman, that he should not consider this a tedious duty. Do not such sects as the Ikkō-shū read the same texts over and over again as a spur to their devotion?[2] The use of the Imperial Rescript on Education in modern times would seem to derive from a long and honoured tradition.

Later in the Tokugawa period, as the number of writing schools increased, several short books or pamphlets were printed by the Bakufu and by fief authorities to be used both as copy books and, like the register prefaces, for reading periodically to assembled adults. The first of these was the *Rikuyu engi tai-i* prepared by Muro Kyūsō at the request of the Shogun, Yoshimune, and printed in 1722. It was a simplified version of edicts issued for the instruction of the people of China by the first Ch'ing Emperor in 1652. The daimyo of Satsuma had acquired a copy from the Ryūkyū islands and presented it to Yoshimune in response to the latter's request for information about China. When it was ready the Edo Town Magistrate summoned ten of the most prominent teachers at commoner *terakoya* schools in Edo and gave them a copy each with instructions to use it themselves as a copy-book for their children and to pass it on to their confrères for reproduction. The work was reprinted several times for the same purpose and in one recorded instance, in 1809, the Osaka Town Magistrate commissioned an edition and, rather more generously, provided enough copies for every *terakoya* teacher in the town to be given one.[3]

[1] See Nomura, *Gonin-gumi-chō no kenkyū*.

[2] *NKS*, 5, p. 182. Quoted in Ototake, *Shomin kyōikushi*, 1, p. 534.

[3] Ototake, *Shomin kyōikushi*, 1, p. 780. Kondō (*Shina gakugei daijiten*) lists nineteen subsequent printings of Muro's, or similar, versions of the *Rikuyu engi*, five of them as late as Meiji. The Muro version is reprinted in Dōbunkan, *Kyōiku bunko, Kunkai*, 1.

A number of other similar works were written and distributed by fief authorities or by provincial Intendants in Bakufu territories.[1] Generally they tend to rather abstract description of the five relations and the five virtues with the usual exhortations to diligence and warnings against extravagance, but sometimes they come a little closer to daily life and the commonplaces of popular morality. The *Chūkō jōmoku*, for instance, produced in the Takata fief in 1744, includes instructions on such things as being kind to servants, preventing children from singing obscene songs and paying respects to parents' memorial tablets at New Year and on their death anniversaries. (To parents, be it noted, not ancestors; the full version of the theory of 'the Japanese family system' which became widely diffused in the Meiji period[2] had presumably not yet reached the farmers.) There is also a short disquisition on that kingpin concept of popular (but not properly Confucian) morality, *on*— a 'favour' and the corresponding sense of obligation.[3] A great deal of trouble and conflict comes from people forgetting the *on* they have received or, on the other hand, remembering too well the *on* they have given and expecting too much in return.

The morality expounded in these treatises is generally of a distinctly authoritarian kind; a typical passage from the *Kyōyu sanshō* of the early nineteenth century runs:

> Among the many people one must respect, an elder brother is one of the most important, for he is the first-born and his instructions must be obeyed in everything. Even if his manage-

---

[1] The following are mentioned in the *NKSS*, doubtless only a small sample of the total: *Kyōyu sanshō*, used by Yamamoto Daizen, a Bakufu Intendant, in his bailiwick in Kai province (*NKSS*, 7, pp. 713–14). Yamamoto is generally thought to have been the author (see, e.g. Ishikawa, *Shomin kyōikushi*, p. 204), but, according to Hibata ('Tokugawa Ienari to *Kyōyu sanshō*'), it was prepared by the Bakufu central authorities for use in all the Bakufu's East Japan territories and may well have been written by Hayashi Jussai. *Kangaku hikki* by the daimyo of the Shibata fief (*NKSS*, 2, pp. 273–5). *Chūkō jōmoku* used in the Takata fief (*NKSS*, 2, pp. 264–5). *Kuse jōmoku* used by Hayakawa Hachirōzaemon (see p. 227) in his bailiwick, Bakufu territory in Mimasaka (*NKSS*, 7, pp. 807–12). *Fushi-kun*, used in the Hayashida fief (*NKSS*, 2, p. 560). *Gojō shikyō*, written by an Intendant in Izumi province (extracted in *NKSS*, 4, pp. 187–8.)

Ishikawa notes one or two others (*Sekimon Shingaku*, pp. 326–7).

[2] For an account of the Meiji doctrine, see e.g. N. Hozumi, *Ancestor Worship and the Japanese Law*.

[3] For a description of this concept, see R. Benedict, *The Chrysanthemum and the Sword*.

ment of the family affairs is at fault, even if his division of money or provisions is unfair, you must simply bear it.[1]

These tracts are often, too, sternly comminatory in tone, and sometimes downright abusive of the ignorance and folly of the farmers to whom they are addressed. It is noticeable, though, that the Town Magistrate speaks much more softly to the people of Osaka when he recommends the *Rikuyu engi tai-i* to them in 1809. They are not half bad, really, and in particular he commends the generous response to his appeal for flood relief contributions the year before. But he adds that the town still sometimes has occasion to see criminals' heads stuck on the gateposts, and unless the generous promptings of their hearts are informed by an adequate knowledge of the proper duties of man theirs will be nothing more than an empty virtue.[2]

One of these treatises, however, is somewhat exceptional in content if not in tone. It is the *Kuse kyōjō*, written by the rather remarkable Bakufu Intendant, Hayakawa, whose innovating school-building activities were described earlier. He had it printed in 1799 after it had been circulating for some time in manuscript. One of his major concerns is to condemn the practice of infanticide which had so shocked him when he took over the territory, but at one point he also goes to the trouble of actually explaining to the people just why they should be grateful to the government and why they should pay taxes. He points out that the country was in utter disorder until Ieyasu unified it and established the rule of law, thanks alone to which they can now sleep peacefully in their beds and prosperously pursue their legitimate occupations; the Shogun acts as a protective fence for the people and prevents the strong from devouring the weak. They should be grateful for this and express their gratitude by obeying the laws and working hard. As for paying taxes, he points out that they are necessary for the defence of the country and other official expenditures:

The defence of the country means defence against foreign nations, such as putting the Sō family on Tsushima and the Matsumae family in Hokkaido. And so on down to Magistrates and Intendants like myself who all have our own guard forces.

---

[1] *NKSS*, 7, p. 713.
[2] Quoted in Ototake, *Shomin kyōikushi*, 1, p. 780.

Then, also, all the expenditures on river banks, dikes and bridges mount up to a vast sum. By 'other official expenditures' I mean all the expenses of the Imperial Palace at Kyoto, all the gifts made to daimyos and to hatamotos and to shrines and temples, and also the cost of building and repairing temples and shrines.

All these expenses have to be met from the rice tax. In other words 'the wealth of the nation is put to the nation's use'.[1] His is clearly a different theory of government from that embodied in the famous phrase: 'the people should be made to obey, not allowed to know'.

A further development of this policy was to provide lecture-sermons for commoners either in the fief school, in the special commoner schools already mentioned, in other specially built lecture halls in the fief, or by sending out itinerant lecturers.

The Bakufu was probably the first to allow commoners to attend this sort of lecture primarily intended for the samurai class. The first order for their admission came in 1717 and was repeated at intervals down to 1866.[2] Lectures were held daily (though they seem to have dropped off in periods when the Bakufu school fell on hard times) and any commoner except a Buddhist priest or a *yamabushi* exorcist could attend provided only that he dressed properly in *hakama*. There is no record of how many actually did so.

In most of the six other fiefs which allowed commoners to such lectures they were usually segregated from the samurai in some way—in a special roped-off 'inferior' part of the room or left outside on the veranda.[3] In Kaga they were allowed only at special lectures for commoners held on special days.[4]

These lectures held at fief schools were probably the some-what erudite kind of *kōshaku* (see p. 139), with a little textual criticism and citation of commentaries intermixed with the ethical message, making fairly liberal use of technical Confucian terms. The commoners who attended them were doubtless mainly wealthy men who had some direct dealings with the

---

[1] *NKSS*, 7, pp. 807–12. The word he uses for 'nation' is *tenka*—as in the popular nationalist (and anti-authoritarian) slogan of the Bakumatsu period: 'tenka wa tenka no tenka nari'—the nation is the nation's (i.e. the people's) nation.

[2] *NKSS*, 7, pp. 25, 76–7, 80, 82, 3.

[3] *NKSS*, 3, p. 183. (Omura.)

[4] *NKSS*, 2, p. 89.

samurai class and some smattering of gakumon. The lecture-sermons provided exclusively for farmers and townsmen were, however, of a more popular character. Sometimes they were given on lecture tours by the teachers in fief schools, sometimes by lecturers specially invited to the fief, sometimes they were a major function of the teachers of the schools specially set up for commoners, and sometimes special lecture centres were built for this exclusive purpose.

The feudal authorities were lucky in being able to use for these purposes the Shingaku movement—a popular ethical sect which drew on all the currently available stock of religious ideas, but with special emphasis on Confucian concepts of duty.[1] At first the movement developed among the commoner towns-people of western Japan without any institutional religious connections and without encouragement from feudal authori-ties. Indeed, it sometimes met with their suspicion. Teshima Toan had to answer a sharp inquiry into his activities by the Kyoto Town Magistrate around 1766.[2] By the 1780s, however, he already had some adherents among the samurai class and even among daimyos before whom he was on occasion invited to lecture.[3] He, and other Shingaku preachers, were soon being invited to make lecture-sermon tours of various fiefs and Bakufu territories. This was a turbulent period; a series of natural calamities had wrought widespread destruction, the Bakufu administration had reached a nadir of corruption, if not of inefficiency, and a widespread rash of town and country revolts[4] had given feudal authorities good grounds for disquiet. They were understandably concerned about the moral con-dition of the people and ready to use any suitable remedy which came to hand. Motoori was distinctly in a minority when he remarked on the disagreeable way in which the Chinese classics harp on moral exhortation, unlike the Japanese ancient books which naturally assume man's innate goodness. 'People do not become better as a result of exhortation, and by continually

---

[1] For a description of the movement in English, see R. Bellah, *Tokugawa Religion*.

[2] Ishikawa, *Sekimon Shingaku*, p. 246. Simply, it seems, because any large gather-ing of people aroused fears of conspiracy.

[3] *Ibid.*, p. 295.

[4] At least eighty-one are known to have occurred in the years 1783–87 (Hei-bonsha, *Sekai rekishi jiten*, 22, pp. 448–9).

warning people in the most unpleasant way about things which any normal person takes for granted [the preachers] are, without realizing it and contrary to their own intention, only increasing the number of rascals and villains.'[1] Motoori was wasting his time. The verbose didacticism of Tokugawa society was too much for him.

Altogether, Ishikawa has unearthed twenty-six instances of Bakufu officials employing Shingaku scholars or giving them assistance, and he finds evidence of similar support for Shingaku from at least seventy-four fiefs.[2] Usually these are instances of invitations to give a single lecture tour, though some were arrangements of longer duration. The Bakufu had a standing appointment for a Shingaku lecturer to go three times a month to instruct the labourers in the Edo 'coolie camp' established by Matsudaira Sadanobu as a means of clearing Edo of vagrants and unemployed. This lasted from soon after the opening of the camp until the Meiji Restoration and was probably the most permanent of such arrangements.[3] The Shingaku movement was also used and encouraged in other ways. Daimyos and local Intendants sometimes printed extracts from Shingaku tracts for distribution in their territories, issued directives urging people to attend Shingaku lectures, gave financial assistance to Shingaku teachers who wished to set up a centre, provided, in one instance, funds for a lending library of Shingaku texts, or in a few instances actually established Shingaku centres to be run entirely under fief supervision— there was one, for instance, attached to the Kurashiki school mentioned earlier. As one source succinctly put it, 'scholars were taught in the school and non-scholars were preached to in the hall next door'.[4]

Members of the Shingaku movement did not have a monopoly of these activities; none of them seems to have been involved in a number of centres established for monthly sermons in part of what is now Yamanashi prefecture, in the early nineteenth century. The purport of the message was much the same, however, whether the preacher was a follower of Shingaku or not;

1 *Tamakatsuma* (*Zenshū*, 2), p. 13.
2 *Sekimon Shingaku*, pp. 1165–1256.
3 *Ibid.*, pp. 1165–9.
4 Odate Tengai, *Reigaku gorin dōmō-kun* (1836), postscript. Quoted in Ishikawa, *Sekimon Shingaku*, p. 1194.

obedience, diligence, respectful humility, satisfaction with one's lot were the major themes. There was, to be sure, an element of resistance to official ideology in the early teachings of Ishida Baigan (1685–1744), the founder of the Shingaku movement. He was less concerned to stress the differences of status than the differences of function of the four orders of society. He held, heretically, that the merchant was just as worthy of respect as any other man, and he did so, as Ishikawa has shown, in fearful awareness of the possibility of official displeasure.[1] But his successors showed no such subversive tendencies. 'Crows caw, sparrows chirp, willows are green and cherry blossom pink. Everything is the way it is and the way it should be, and to desire nothing more is the true secret of life', said Nakazawa Dōni.[2]

But although these popular preachers taught much the same doctrine as the orthodox Confucianists, they did so not in the abstract terms of the Confucian scholars, but using Japanese traditions and the concepts of popular Japanese morality. There survives a verbatim report of a lecture given by Hosoi Heishū, reportedly to an audience of 2400 people in the city of Nagoya in 1783.[3] It rambles in simple colloquial style from subject to subject with liberal use of anecdotes dramatically presented in the dialogue style of the street story-tellers. There is no pretence of a Confucian text. He begins with the statement that all men are good at heart. This goodness consists in *makoto* (the central ethical concept of revived Japanese Shinto) —the obeying of natural laws. The physical world has its natural laws; the sun, the tides, the seasons obey them. So man has natural laws of proper human relations which some people can obey without instruction just as some people can walk for a time in the dark without falling in a ditch. But a lantern—the kind of guidance he proposes to give—can help. When he begins to elaborate on the proper nature of human relations he gives

[1] *Sekimon Shingaku*, p. 182.

[2] Quoted by Akiyama Kenzō, 'Shingaku kyōka to Meiji ishin', p. 109. Akiyama's article serves as an interesting counterpoise to Ishikawa's book. Writing in 1935 at a time of reviving authoritarianism he is concerned mildly to debunk Shingaku. The decline of the movement in Meiji and Taisho periods in his view reflects the progressive nature of Japanese society at those times, and he urges that the attempts then current to revive the movement should be viewed with suspicion.

[3] Reprinted in Takase, *Heishū zenshū*, pp. 915–49, and Ototake, *Shomin kyōikushi*, 1, pp. 433–69.

pride of place to the relation between husband and wife, and in this he was doubtless closer to popular sentiment than the orthodox Confucianists with their main emphasis on the father-son relation or, in the Japanese emendation, the relation between master and retainer. Marriage, he says, being started by Izanagi and Izanami, the Japanese creator gods, is the foundation of all human relations. He then illustrates with a snatch of dramatic dialogue a picture of marital intimacy—a husband and wife discuss together what kind of gift they should make for a relative's wedding. He remarks that women might be likely to want to economize on such expenditure—not surprisingly since they are ignorant of the outside world and of the need to fulfil one's social obligations punctiliously. This reflection prompts him to a digression on the beauties of thrift and the evils of luxury, condemning the way local women wear three or four decorative combs in their hair where only one was worn before, and adducing as evidence of the daimyo's great concern for economy the fact that he allows him, Hosoi, to appear before him in the very same cotton clothes as he is wearing that night. This brings him to the subject of the daimyo's goodness. True, punishments are harsh, but when the daimyo burns a man alive for arson or has him beheaded for burglary he does it only as a painful necessity, and he hates it as much as the loving parent who turns a wayward son from his door with tears in his eyes lest he infect others of the family.

> It is thanks to the lord's goodness that you live at peace in this province, thanks to his goodness that you can earn each your own living and clothe yourself appropriately for the four seasons, thanks to his goodness that you live out your lives in peace. So make sure that you never go against his wishes, that you obey carefully all his edicts, that parents and children, brothers and sisters, each one of you down to the humblest of the humble, fulfil your proper duties. Live out a blameless life on earth, and afterwards you can be sure of going to Heaven.

Whatever the response may have been, it was probably not cynical. Hosoi himself describes in a letter the reception he got on a lecture tour in Yonezawa in 1776.

> It is difficult to give you a proper account of my preaching activities [kyōka] here in Yonezawa. Not merely the whole

239

retinue of the daimyo, both high and low, but even the common people in both town and country have shown immense respect for my teachings. Some rich farmers from the neighbouring country districts joined in petitioning the fief authorities that I should go for three days at the beginning of February to preach [kōshaku] in a village called Komatsu some dozen miles north-east of Yonezawa ... I stayed at the local camp headquarters there, and day and night the farmers flocked in their hundreds to hear me. They were all choked with tears, and especially the older men were so sad to see me go that when I left for Yone-zawa seven or eight hundred of them prostrated themselves in the snow and wept aloud.

As one of their leaders pointed out, the proper regulation of the house requires that women as well as men be given the chance of instruction. Accordingly, for half a day I went to the house of one Kaneko Jinsaburō who has sword and surname privileges, and there about two hundred of the wives and daughters of leading farmers gathered. I lectured to them on the *Classic of Filial Piety* and the women were all touched with humble gratitude and said that they understood the real intentions of the authorities' benevolent rule. My words cannot properly convey an impression of the scene.[1]

His lectures seem often to have been tearful affairs. On another occasion he lectured to some three hundred leading townsmen of Yonezawa gathered in the presence of the Town Magistrate. At first it was only with difficulty that he could get them to look up at him; they all sat with heads respectfully bowed. As he proceeded, however, the tears came into their eyes and one by one the heads went down again as they sobbed into the *tatami*. Hosoi himself wept, the Town Magistrate wept and when they had all gone the *tatami* looked as if someone had spilled buckets of water over it.[2]

Not everyone had Hosoi's revivalist skill or was able equally to touch that nerve of sentimentality which persists in Japanese moralism to the present day. Some lecturers met with a less than appreciative response. The Intendant of the northern part of what is now Yamanashi prefecture, who established a dozen lecture centres in his district, was in the habit of making occasional visits to see that the rules were obeyed (one of them

---

[1] Takase, *Heishū zenshū*, pp. 349–50.
[2] *Ibid.*, p. 351.

was to the effect that there should be no drinking of *sake* during lectures), and to make sure that the attendance was good. On one occasion he found a very poor audience and was angry. The village officials hastily sent out a note to surrounding areas asking for reinforcements in future and pointing out that the Intendant had expressly said that women could also attend and sit in a separate section of the lecture hall.[1]

A memorandum concerning the operation of a school and lecture centre in the Mito fief also speaks of the difficulty of getting an audience. Here the lectures, held twice monthly, were of a slightly more erudite Confucian kind, though still of moral rather than scholastic purport. The memorialist remarks, however, that the word *kōshaku* suggests to the local farmers something rather highfalutin', concerned with ancient matters and incomprehensible books. In ancient China the Sages instructed the common people, but this did not mean that the common people became scholars. Nowadays, however, a good many farmers' sons take up learning and when they do they tend to develop a high opinion of themselves and neglect their proper occupations. Hence, farmers and merchants think that learning is something to discourage in their children and so they are reluctant to send then to such *kōshaku*.[2]

If there was some prudent resistance of this kind to lecture-sermons and to basic moral Chinese study, there was also, by the nineteenth century, as this same document indicates, a growing number of wealthy commoners of the village headmen class who did aspire to gakumon as part of their general adoption of samurai values and identification with the ruling class. (They were, after all, the non-commissioned officers of the administrative system, and theirs was often the first house to be burned when the peasants rioted.) There is no reason to doubt the genuineness of the wealthy farmers' co-operative intentions when they invited Hosoi Heishū to lecture in their villages or provided funds for Hayakawa's schools. They were genuine admirers of the Sages; their financial interests led them to share the officials' fiscal concern with the villagers' readiness to pay taxes, and they shared their sense of paternal responsibility for the general moral well-being of the people of their

---

[1] *NKSS*, 7, p. 728.
[2] *NKSS*, 3, p. 383. The document is undated, but must be later than 1830.

villages. They could also afford to buy books and they could afford to send their sons to one of the towns to enter the private school of a Confucian teacher. A study of the founding of seven schools and lecture-centres in the Isezaki fief in the first two decades of the nineteenth century leaves no doubt that the initiative of the local village headmen was quite genuine. They were assisted by two officials of the fief who had previously, before they achieved office, run private schools in the castle town. In nearly every case one or more of the villagers involved in the foundation of the schools had been a pupil at one or other of these schools.[1]

Not all the rich farmers shared these interests, of course. The author of the *Seji kemmonroku* leaves no doubt about their adoption of samurai values, but he suggests quite different directions in which they expressed this identification. The 'village officials and rich farmers', according to his observations:

> leave the actual work of cultivation entirely to their hired men and women. They themselves wear fine clothes, hold large-scale parties, follow samurai standards in their marriage and adoption ceremonies and funerals. Some of them support a tame *rōnin* in their household and learn military arts unsuited to their station in life, or they find someone to teach them the writing of Chinese prose or poetry, or they take up calligraphy in Chinese style, or study painting, Chinese or Japanese, or they take into their household a teacher of the tea ceremony, of *waka* or *haiku* verse, or of dancing, and spend their time acquiring these accomplishments.[2]

This is almost certainly not a complete picture either. One suspects that he does not include serious gakumon among the pursuits of these richer farmers because it would too much modify his picture of idle frivolity and forgetfulness of proper station. A good number of these men did use their wealth to pursue sober scholarly interests, and when they did it was hard for samurai officials, in all conscience, to withhold approbation from them. This was a sphere in which they could

[1] Takai, 'Isezaki-ryō kyōgaku'.
[2] Buyō-inshi, *Seji kemmonroku* (Honjō, *Kinsei shakai keizai sōsho*, 1), pp. 48-9. Also extracted in *NKSSS*, 4, p. 292.

out-samurai the samurai and still receive nothing but praise for it.[1]

Literacy

If the Bakufu and the fief authorities did show occasional interest in providing or encouraging basic moral Chinese education for a limited number of commoner children and moral instruction for all commoner adults, their interest in the *terakoya* writing schools which provided the bulk of commoner education was sporadic, and generally confined to the provision or recommendation of texts which would ensure that in acquiring a basic literacy children would also absorb a modicum of moral instruction. For the most part their attitude was that basic Japanese literacy was something which commoners could well be allowed to provide for themselves.

An early exception was, again, the Okayama fief. At the same time as it was leading the field in the establishment of a fief school, an ambitious plan was also devised to build elementary schools throughout the fief. A letter from the official in charge to a provincial Intendant explains the plan.[2] The schools are primarily to provide instruction in writing and arithmetic, though basic moral Chinese may also be taught to a select few. Local teachers—retired village headmen, their unemployed sons or brothers—should take charge of the former; teachers would be sent out on tour from the fief school to provide the latter. Pupils would be the sons of village headmen and village elders and 'even of ordinary farmers who are well enough off,

---

[1] Cf. Matsudaira Sadanobu's approving remarks concerning some of the learned and virtuous merchants of Osaka in *Taikan zakki* (*NZZ*, 14), p. 318. See also Kamei Nammei's story describing how moved he was to discover, in the fastnesses of southern Kumamoto in the middle of the eighteenth century, an inn-keeper who had been fond of reading the Four Books since childhood and who adamantly refused to take anything for his night's lodging beyond a piece of Kamei's calligraphy written out as a souvenir. 'In over thirty years since I have been running this inn, this is the first time a Student of the Way of the Sages has stayed here. You can imagine what a happiness it is for me to have you.' The episode ends with Kamei writhing with shamed mortification as he discovers that he has really hurt the man's feelings by trying persistently to leave the money regardless (*Higo monogatari*, (*NKS*, 15), p. 534.)

[2] *NKSS*, 3, p. 424. This is presumably the only surviving copy of a circular sent to all local Intendants. It bears no date, though Yokoyama puts it—probably several years too early—in 1663 (*Kinsei kyōikushi*, p. 337).

say, to have servants', (though he is none too sanguine about the prospects of getting such farmers to send their children to school). The primary purpose of the schools is the practical one of training capable village officials. (They were made necessary, according to another source,[1] by the decline of the temples where farmers' children could formerly learn to read and count and receive moral instruction.) There was to be an initial fief subsidy, but it was hoped that the schools would be self-supporting after six or seven years. Touring lecturers would also give sermons at the school for adults in the agricultural slack season.

The experiment was short-lived. The order to establish the schools seems to have gone out in 1668[2] and one document of uncertain date lists 123 schools which were supposed actually to have been established—with supporting details of the number of teachers and pupils in each.[3] Yet, in 1673 the official in charge of the school system is reported as giving an address to a group of farmers, the purpose of which was to overcome their reluctance to allow their children near the schools. (The education is free whereas it would normally have to be paid for. The daimyo expects to get nothing out of it. He is motivated solely by his sense of responsibility as lord of the province.)[4] The next year the number of schools was reduced to fourteen—one in each *gun* district—and a year later the whole scheme was abandoned. The fourteen schools were 'combined' into one central school which became the Shizutani Gakkō and which continued until the end of the period to admit some commoner students along with locally stationed samurai, but gave them basic moral Chinese instruction, not elementary training in Japanese literacy.[5]

---

[1] *NKSS*, 3, pp. 425–6. The lecture quoted below.

[2] *NKSS*, 3, p. 422.

[3] *Ibid.* Usually the schools report one teacher and from seven to forty pupils, though one exceptional establishment had sixty-one pupils, a teacher of writing, a teacher of (Chinese) reading and arithmetic and three teachers of reading who were also 'directors of village funeral rites'. Ikeda Mitsumasa, the daimyo, was (see p. 93) one of the few who took their Confucianism seriously enough to follow Chinese burial rites.

[4] *NKSS*, 3, pp. 425–6.

[5] An economy drive by the new daimyo, who by no means shared his retired father's concern with education, seems to have been the reason (Tsukui, *Shizutani Gakkō*, p. 4). But the fairly generous endowment of the Shizutani school meant that

The next generally known record of any official action in regard to popular writing schools concerns a chance encounter between the Shogun Yoshimune and a doctor who taught the local children in a village on the outskirts of Edo. Yoshimune, out on a falconry expedition in 1722, had chosen the doctor's house to rest in and was intrigued to see the desks and paraphernalia of a school. His interest turned to approbation when he discovered that the doctor was using as a copy-book, according to one source, the official rules of the Falconry Grounds, according to another, a general collection of Bakufu ordinances. The next day he sent the worthy doctor a gift of ten pieces of silver and a lavishly bound copy of the *Rikuyu engi tai-i* (see p. 232) which he had just had published.[1] A month later the Edo Town Magistrate issued general instructions to teachers of writing recommending that they use government ordinances as texts,[2] and the next year he reinforced his command by issuing copies of the ordinances which teachers could use.[3]

After this, as far as the Bakufu is concerned, apart from the Osaka Magistrate's distribution of copies of the *Rikuyu engi tai-i* in 1809, there is no record of any official action until the Tempō reforms of Mizuno Tadakuni. In 1843 the Bakufu issued an ordinance to all teachers of reading and writing in Edo. It says, as if enunciating a truism, that the ability to read and write is necessary for everyone 'high and low, men and women', but goes on to urge that the teachers should not stop at this. Bad habits developed in youth can become ingrained, and in this

---

[1] Ototake (*Shomin kyōikushi*, 1, pp. 664–7) quotes the *Tokugawa jikki* and the letters of Muro Kyūsō which are in substantial agreement in their accounts. See also *NKSS*, 7, p. 74.

[2] Takayanagi and Ishii, *Kampō shūsei*, p. 695.

[3] Asaoka, *Ishin-zen shōgakkō*, p. 52.

---

the economy was not very great. The 123 schools had cost a subsidy of 620 *koku* (*NKSS*, 3, p. 422). The Shizutani school was given an endowment of 278 *koku* of land (*ibid.*, p. 430) though this latter figure probably refers to total yield, not actual tax yield. Some rather expensive buildings were provided in addition, however. Doubtless, it was retained in preference to the village schools because its ceremonials and architectural elegance provided a more satisfying consolation for the retired daimyo's old age than the more utilitarian village schools. He had already chosen a near-by site for the (Confucian) reburial of his ancestors. There is also a popular local theory that the school, surrounded as it was (and still is) by very substantial stone walls, provided a covert fortification on an important route into the fief.

matter the teachers have a special responsibility 'to improve conduct, to make a special point of matters of etiquette and to teach loyalty and filial piety'. To this end, the ordinance repeats the earlier recommendation that they should use the texts of Bakufu *kōsatsu* notice-boards (see p. 231) and other ordinances and also lists a number of other texts of generally improving purport. It concludes by urging them to be kind to their children and to make no distinction between children of their own ward and those of others.[1] (An incidental indication of the extent to which the Edo *chō*, or ward, was still a self-contained village-like community.) The next year a total of sixty-two teachers were summoned to the Magistrate's office to be commended for their good work and presented with copies of the *Rikuyu engi tai-i*.[2]

Apart from this episode and the distribution by a Bakufu Intendant in Musashi of *printed* copies of *gonin-gumi* register prefaces (because there had been mistakes in copying) with the incidental recommendation that teachers should use it as a text,[3] there is no further evidence of Bakufu concern for these schools apart, that is, from an ordinance issued in 1848 warning against riotous misbehaviour on school flower-viewing outings, and the extravagance of procuring matching head-scarves and parasols for such occasions.[4]

The fiefs generally displayed as little interest as the Bakufu. A number did at least recognize the existence of these schools in requiring that their establishment should be reported to the authorities, in some cases only if the teachers were samurai,[5] or samurai of other fiefs,[6] or if the school was on such a scale as to

[1] *NKSS*, 7, pp. 11–12. Two versions of this ordinance are given here with only slight verbal differences, the one dated 1711 and the second 1843. Although it was not unknown for the Bakufu to reissue ordinances in this way, Ishikawa Ken seems to prove conclusively that the dating of the first as 1711 is an error and that the ordinance was, in fact, first issued in 1843 (*Shomin kyōikushi*, pp. 310–15).

[2] *NKSS*, 7, p. 85.

[3] Ishikawa, *Shomin kyōikushi*, p. 325.

[4] *NKSS*, 7, p. 86. Asaoka (*Ishinzen shōgakkō*, pp. 50–4) enumerates as other instances of Bakufu assistance: permission given to teachers to live in samurai districts, the granting of surnames to teachers, and the employment of writing teachers as Bakufu clerks. The first, however, was quite probably to facilitate the establishment of schools for lower samurai, and the last can hardly be described as helpful for the development of popular education.

[5] At Yamagami (*NKSS*, 1, p. 459).

[6] At Maebashi (*NKSS*, 1, p. 571).

need a special building distinct from the teacher's house.[1] One fief had a ban on Buddhist priests opening schools,[2] and another on out-of-fief *rōnin*.[3] The Hikone fief is the only one recorded as having created a guild of teachers in the castle town (in 1796). The purpose of the guild is not clear since other teachers, apparently, were also allowed to practice. The fief did, however, evince a continued interest in the schools, issuing directives from time to time urging that teachers should concern themselves with the morals as well as the literacy of their charges, and also urging parents to co-operate with the teachers and make their children respect them.[4]

Some fiefs went a little further and held regular or occasional inspections of *terakoya*, giving rewards to the efficient and reprimanding the bad.[5] In two the encouragement took the form of allowing children at the schools to present periodically to the daimyo the products of their ceremonial 'first-writing of the year', rewards being given for the best specimens of calligraphy.[6] There are also two records of financial assistance. The Annaka fief provided half the cost of repairs to buildings,[7] and the Shibata fief provided the town schools with paper, ink and also candles so that the merchants' children could study at night and not waste precious daylight hours.[8] There is no evidence that any fief actually built schools specifically for this kind of elementary education, though it seems that one or two of the schools, mentioned earlier, which were established for commoner instruction in basic moral Chinese also held classes in Japanese calligraphy.[9]

Some people were disturbed by the lack of active official

---

[1] At Kururi (*NKSS*, 1, p. 236), Takanabe (*NKSS*, 3, p. 254), and Takamatsu (*NKSS*, 2, p. 874.) This was also, apparently, the practice in some Bakufu territories. A request is extant for permission to open a school in Kai province which was accompanied by plans of the buildings to be erected (*NKSS*, 7, p. 718).

[2] At Sanda (*NKSS*, 1, p. 54).

[3] At Ogi (*NKSS*, 3, p. 160).

[4] *NKSS*, 1, p. 374–5.

[5] For example, Shibamura (*NKSS*, 1, p. 25), Sasayama (*NKSS*, 1, p. 36), Tatsuno (*NKSS*, 2, p. 521) and some others.

[6] Matsumoto and Yonezawa (*NKSS*, 1, pp. 511, 732).

[7] *NKSS*, 1, p. 620.

[8] *NKSS*, 2, p. 281. The Obama fief is supposed to have provided buildings for samurai teachers whose homes were too small, but these may well have been schools for samurai children (*NKSS*, 2, p. 1).

[9] This was certainly the case at Tsu and Tsuwano (*NKSS*, 1, p. 77; 2, p. 570).

concern with the reading and writing schools. One of them was the author of the *Gakusei wakumon*, whose account of the evil effects of 'overly superior learning' was quoted at the beginning of this chapter. His prescription is for the fief school to take over direction of all commoner schools of the fief to make sure that they give due attention to the teaching of morals.[1] The same plea for control is made, *a propos* of Edo, by Asakawa Zen'an, whose chief concern, however, is less the teaching than the teachers. Edo is too full of *rōnin*, responsible to no one and forced to scrape a living in any way they can find, many of them shady. They all have an eye to the main chance and switch occupations at will. 'A man who was a day-labourer last year becomes a doctor this year. Yesterday's fishmonger turns up today in the guise of a teacher of reading and writing.' There ought, he thinks, to be proper guilds of teachers and doctors to keep such people under control.[2]

Nakai Chikuzan had also recommended control of popular schools in 1789, some thirty years before these writers, but his main concern is to combat what he considers the deplorable influence of Buddhist priests. It is particularly common to hire them as teachers in the villages; they have no family and so cost less to support; they have no descendants and so there is no problem of unsuitable sons expecting to succeed their father. The main drawback of the arrangement is that these priests are generally near-illiterates. It would be far better to have a properly educated layman even if he does have a family and costs more. He could be hired for life, with no obligation to accept his son. He finally concedes, however, that such matters have in practice to be left to the villages; they are beyond the range of central control. In the towns, however, the authorities should rule with a heavier hand, allowing teachers surnames to improve their prestige as long as, and only as long as, they prove worthy of their tasks.[3]

A number of Confucian writers express a similar concern that Buddhist priests, whom they hold in the lowest regard, should so frequently have charge of children's education and be the only substitute for moral guidance available to the

---

[1] Karashima Ken (*NKSS*, 8, p. 11).
[2] *Saiji shichisaku* (*NKS*, 21), pp. 465–6.
[3] *Sōbō kigen* (*NKS*, 16), pp. 358–61.

villagers.[1] This was what chiefly bothered Shōji Kōgi, a Kyūshū scholar of merchant origins, but his recommendations go somewhat beyond the negative controls of the writers just quoted.

'Priests nowadays only teach people to revere the Buddhas; they say nothing of etiquette and manners, much less of the ethics of human relationships. You won't hear a word from them about taking off your head-scarf when meeting an official on the road, about respect for the aged or avoiding drink or gambling. The priests even drink themselves and so set a bad example to the children.'

He recommends, as a cure, that the authorities should actually establish schools themselves, one in every village and one for every three to five hundred families in the towns. The teacher need not be any great scholar, nor need he be much of a calligrapher. The first condition is that he should not drink. His moral conduct is all-important. No tuition fees should be paid and books should be provided for the children. The school should make a small charge for wear and tear of the *tatami* mats—if it were entirely free people would not bother to (or would not like to—the text is ambiguous) send their children. But the main source of income should be a capital gift of fifty *ryō* of gold to be lent out at 20 per cent. There should also be a lesser samurai official to give overall supervision. Shōji's ideas (his preface is dated 1841) clearly derive in part from European sources. He mentions that in Holland there are three kinds of public institution: hospitals, orphanages and schools. These are supported by charitable gifts. How much better, he says, if Japanese would direct their charity into such useful channels, instead of giving futilely to temples.[2]

A similar, but even more carefully delineated plan was proposed to the Bakufu some two years later by the author of *Yuniwa no ho*.[3] There should be three schools for every 10,000

---

[1] See, for instance, a memorial from a village headman of the Nagoya fief written in 1835 (*NKSS*, 1, pp. 135–6); Otsuka Shōhaku, *Keizai gosaku* (*NKS*, 26), p. 546; and Hoashi Banri, *Tōsempu-ron* (*NKS*, 26), p. 419. Most of these sources are cited in Ototake, *Shomin kyōikushi*, 1, pp. 408–83.

[2] *Keizai mondō hiroku* (*NKS*, 22), pp. 77–82.

[3] *NKS*, 21, pp. 488–92. According to the editor of *NKS* the author was probably Umetsuji Norikiyo, a Kyoto priest later exiled to Hachijōjima.

koku of land, thus making a total of 2400 schools and teachers on Bakufu territory as a whole. In each group of three schools one should be headed by an upper samurai with the right of audience with the Shogun, the other two by lesser samurai. Their term of office should be from five to eight years. He even suggests the proper dimensions of the school house and of the teacher's house, and suggests that a rice granary (of the full-in-fat, empty-in-lean-years variety), a guest house for visiting officials and a prison should be concentrated with it in one official centre. Many advantages are claimed for this scheme; the teachers would become well acquainted with the condition of the people and be excellent candidates for official posts later on; it would provide a good emergency auxiliary force and act as an excellent intelligence system covering both Bakufu territory and that of neighbouring daimyos. The schools should teach *bungaku*—which suggests something a little more than mere literacy—but they should also concentrate on conveying the moral injunctions of the Shogun to the people. It is this prime function, the author suggests, which would make it inappropriate for fees to be taken; people should not be allowed to imagine that they go to school for their own profit, presumably. The teachers may, however, accept occasional gifts of vegetables and local products.

At least two other writers proposed similar schemes before the end of the period—Satō Shinen as part of his general plan for a totalitarian central government in 1857, and Oshima Takatō in a memorial to the Nambu daimyo in 1863. Both were primarily concerned with mobilizing all the talents of the common people in the service of the nation—not quite such an urgent consideration to the other writers of the less critical previous decade. Satō would have a two-tiered system; elementary schools in approximately every village, and one middle school to every twenty villages to give basic moral Chinese instruction to the ablest students selected from the elementary schools. There would also be a university in the capital for the ablest graduates of the middle schools. As in the *Yuniwa no ho* scheme, the local schools would also be centres of ritual, moral instruction and administrative control.[1] Oshima, the metallurg-

[1] *Suitō hiroku* (*NKT*, 18), pp. 659–64. This section is translated in R. Tsunoda, *Sources of the Japanese Tradition*.

ist and student of Western learning, proposed a much more radical scheme avowedly based on foreign models; his elementary schools should provide for all, the fief's children without exception and without distinction between samurai and commoner, and they should teach not only Japanese and Chinese, but also Western languages, arithmetic and geography.[1]

Within ten years Japan did have a government which was ready to promulgate by government decree just such an ambitious plan as Oshima's on a nation-wide scale. It would have been a little too much to expect such action on the part of the feudal authorities to whom these proposals were addressed. They had many pressing problems in the last years of the regime, but the spread of literacy among the people was not one of them. In so far as they (or indeed most of the writers quoted in this chapter) were concerned at all with the reading and writing schools, they were anxious not so much to increase their quantity as to improve—by their standards—the quality of the instruction they gave; to ensure that they should operate to good effect in producing responsible and dutiful subjects. As far as quantity is concerned they might well have reason, as the next chapter will show, to consider that the people were managing well enough by themselves.

[1] See Y. Horie, 'Business pioneers of modern Japan', p. 11.

Chapter VIII

TERAKOYA

SAMURAI EDUCATION was over-burdened with theory. Some of its practitioners leave one with the impression that they must have spent more time writing their prescriptions for an ideal education than actually trying to give one to their pupils. The education of the non-samurai masses, by contrast, was relatively free from the incubus of educational theory. The schools developed, though partly from charity, largely in response to an effective economic demand. And they served practical vocational ends. They provided a training in the basic skills of writing, reading and arithmetic, together with a certain amount of useful information and some of the accumulated practical wisdom needed by the ordinary citizen to get along in a closely regulated feudal world. It was not an idealistic education, and it did not usually cater for those who wished to 'improve themselves'. It was, rather, a delegation, by parents to professional teachers, of the task of preparing their children to succeed them in their hereditary occupation.

The usual name for these schools is *terakoya*,[1] though in the Tokugawa period this was a word chiefly used in western Japan. In Edo they were usually called *tenarai-sho*—writing schools. The word *terakoya* reflects the fact that, in the sixteenth and still for much of the seventeenth centuries, the *tera*—the Buddhist temples—were about the only centres of formal education. So *terako*—literally 'temple children'—came to mean simply 'pupil' and *terakoya* thence came to mean a 'house (or family)

[1] The account in this and the subsequent chapter of general practices in *terakoya* is based on: Ishikawa, *Terakoya* (1960); Asaoka, *Ishinzen shōgakkō* (1892); Ototake, *Shomin kyōikushi* (1929) *NKSSS*, 4, Other fairly detailed accounts, e.g., Tōkyō Maiyū Shimbun, *Ikuei no Nihon*, and Anon., 'Les Terakoya, ou anciens écoles primaires du Japon' derive—as does much of Ishikawa's material—from the second of these works.

which makes a business of taking pupils'. (It is a false popular etymology, making the word mean 'temple hut', which has led many people to suppose that the Buddhist temples continued to be the main sources of popular education throughout the period.)[1]

It is impossible to chart accurately the growth in the number and capacity of these schools; the material is far too fragmentary and unreliable. A letter written in 1722 records, at third hand, that a survey had discovered 'more than eight hundred' professional teachers of writing in Edo,[2] but this is an extremely doubtful figure, if not quite so patently untrue as the statement of the author of Setsuyō kikan that there were 2500 schools with 75,000 pupils in Osaka in 1752.[3] (It is improbable that nearly a quarter of the Osaka population was at school at the same time.) A source of 1810 speaks of 'two or three teachers in every ward' in Edo, but considers this a sign of recent progress—'there used to be hardly any'.[4]

Given the growing volume of references to terakoya education in literature and the known facts concerning the development of book production, there is every reason to believe that the last-quoted author is right in suggesting that a rapid expansion of popular terakoya education began around the end of the eighteenth century. Unfortunately the evidence usually quoted for this—the fact that prefectural replies to the Ministry of Education's 1883 questionnaire reported details of 10,000 schools known to have existed before 1868, of which only 400 date from before 1800[5]—is largely worthless because (the schools often being ephemeral in duration) earlier schools are quite likely to have disappeared without trace.

There is somewhat more solid evidence from which to estimate the number of Edo schools in the nineteenth century in two books published in 1821 and 1830. The first, volume

1 See Komatsu, ' "Terakoya" ni tsuite no ronsō', and Ishikawa, Terakoya, pp. 67–71. The earliest use of the word terako so far discovered dates from 1695, and of terakoya from 1716. The alternative way of writing the word which gave rise to this false etymology (writing the ko of terakoya with the character for 'small' rather than the character for 'child') is apparently a later development.

2 Muro Kyūsō, Kenzan hisaku (NKS, 2), p. 524.

3 Hamamatsu Utakuni, Setsuyō kikan (Funakoshi, Naniwa sōsho, 3), p. 494. Quoted in Tōkyō shisei chōsakai, Kōmin kyōiku, p. 304.

4 Anon., Asukagawa (Kokusho kankōkai, Shin-enseki jisshū, 1), p. 9.

5 Ishikawa, Terakoya, pp. 86–7, calculating from NKSS, 8, 9.

one of a directory of all teachers of writing in Edo (the promised second volume was apparently never published), lists 496 teachers including those who catered for samurai children. The second is a directory exclusively of teachers of the non-samurai classes and lists 230 names, though the title (something like 'Calligraphy Teachers' claims to the Championship') suggests that it does not pretend to be a complete list.[1] The Ministry's 1883 survey elicited reports of 223 schools known to have existed before 1868, but this again, being a survey by not necessarily industrious officials of memories and traditions surviving fifteen years after the event, is likely to be far from complete.[2]

It is therefore difficult to make any quantitative estimate of the diffusion of this type of education at the time of the Restoration. The most informed guess (the reasons for which are argued in an appendix) would seem to be that somewhat more than 40 per cent of all Japanese boys and about 10 per cent of Japanese girls were getting some kind of formal education outside of their homes.

This four to one ratio of boys to girls is an average of a wide range of variation. Merchants were perhaps the most likely to be willing to spend money educating their girls, since shopkeepers' wives needed to read and write in order to help in the shop. Even within farming districts there was considerable variation, however. If one compares the figures reported from two agricultural prefectures in the 1883 survey, there were forty girl pupils for every hundred boys in Okayama, compared with only twelve in Nagano. Ishikawa, making a rough calculation on the basis of the figures of this survey, estimates that there were forty girls for every hundred boys in Edo, thirty in the central region surrounding Osaka and Kyoto, twenty in west Japan and only five in the north-east.[3]

Schools and Teachers: Motives and Costs

The names terakoya and tenarai-sho covered a wide range of different institutions. Schools varied considerably in size, in

---

[1] Respectively the *Hitsudō shika jimmeiroku* and *Hitsudō shika kōmei kurabe*, quoted in Ishikawa, *Terakoya*, pp. 92–3.

[2] Asaoka, *Ishinzen shōgakkō* includes in its list of 107 pre-Meiji schools surviving into the 1890s at least thirty-five not found in the 1883 list.

[3] *Terakoya*, p. 152.

scope of tuition offered, according to whether they were designed primarily for samurai or commoner children, and according to the relative extent to which the desire to earn a living or the desire to do good predominated in their teachers' motives.

The charitably disposed were mostly to be found in the villages; sometimes they were priests or doctors, sometimes well-to-do farmers or village officials. Literacy was essential for village headmen and some of them considered it a part of their paternalistic duty towards their villagers to share their learning, the more so since the copy-books used could be an excellent means of inculcating those virtues of diligence and sobriety which the village officials were as anxious as the feudal authorities to promote. It was, too, a subsidiary means of establishing links of something like retainership with poorer families. In one Yamanashi village where overt patron-client (*oyabun-kobun*) relations vestigially persist today, a number of the clients of one landlord's family are supposed to have been originally *fudeko* (literally 'brush-children')—pupils of the head of the family a century ago. The richer farmers had to teach their own children in any case, and it was no great trouble—and might be more stimulating for their own children, too—to take a few other pupils as well. And no doubt many of these teachers, particularly old men who had retired from the family headship and had time on their hands, simply enjoyed having young children around and sharing their delight in acquiring new skills and accomplishments.

By no means all the village schools were of this kind, however. Sometimes teachers were brought in and set up in the village as a co-operative endeavour, their living being guaranteed out of village funds, or from a special educational fund established for the purpose.[1] Sometimes doctors, priests, *rōnin* or farmers with some physical disability took pupils for the express purpose of supplementing their income or even, if the village was large enough, as a full-time job.

It was the latter type of teacher who predominated in the towns. Most of them made a living by their brush, in part as scribes drawing up official applications and legal documents for a fee (they found plenty of clients among the samurai who

[1] See the example of a school in Kai province described in *NKSS*, 7, pp. 717–21.

had constantly to be presenting applications for permission to do this or that),[1] in part as teachers of children, and some of them also, who had some pretensions to artistry, in part as teachers of calligraphy to adults who wished to improve their style. Some of the teachers were samurai; for the lower ranks it was a means of supplementing a scanty hereditary income, and for the rōnin who had no hereditary position and no hereditary stipend it could be a full-time job, an alternative to teaching swordsmanship or the tea-ceremony, or getting a job as a professional debt-collector or a hatamoto's steward, alternatives between which, as Asakawa Zen'an complained (see p. 248), some of them oscillated with excessive frequency. In Edo such samurai teachers predominated in the samurai districts and taught mostly samurai children. It appears, however, that there was no absolute prohibition on samurai and commoner children going to the same school. According to one report, even the secretaries at the various fief mansions, who taught writing chiefly to children of their samurai colleagues stationed in Edo, sometimes took merchant children, too—provided that they did not too offensively advertise their merchant status by bringing an abacus to their writing classes.[2]

Among the commoner teachers—who catered mostly but not exclusively for commoner children—there were again some part-time teachers (doctors or priests, for instance), and some for whom it was their whole livelihood. The latter became teachers as others became carpenters and the occupation was as likely as not to be hereditary.[3] It was thought to be particularly suitable for those with some physical disability which precluded a more active life, and there were some who taught because they were not fit for anything else. The Terakoya monogatari[4] describes one who:

[1] Moriyama Takamori describes how angry he used to get to see his indigent subordinates forced to spend money they could ill afford to get such documents written, only to have them rejected by his fellow-officers on the grounds that in some footling respect they failed to conform to the standard phraseology, or that the hand-writing was not good enough (Ama no takumo, p. 15).

[2] Asaoka, Ishinzen shōgakkō, p. 4.

[3] Of the 107 schools listed as still in operation in 1892, twenty-five were run by the founder, forty-four by the founder's heir, twenty-two were in their third generation and sixteen had lasted for four or more generations (Asaoka, Ishinzen shōgakkō, appendix).

[4] Extracted in NKSSS, 4, p. 114.

was supposed to be descended from a Kyoto samurai family. A flabby individual and a dullard if there was one, he had no idea of the origin of characters or how to spell in *kana*. His hand went uncertainly down the page like a rudderless boat on the ocean in no distinguishable style. But he had no other accomplishments and he had no capital to start a business. He realized it was brazen of him, but he had to make a living . . .

In a more respectable category of teachers were widows, or women who had spent so long 'in service' at a daimyo's mansion that their age or their excessive refinement had spoiled their marriage chances. In Edo, about a third of the teachers reported in the 1883 survey were women.[1]

Ishikawa has analysed the results of the question in the 1883 survey which asked for details of the teachers' status. His figures are reproduced in Table 6. The categories are of necessity ambiguously broad—commoners, for instance, include a high proportion of village headmen in Aomori, a lesser proportion in Ehime and none at all in Edo; samurai range from the *rōnin* making a livelihood from full-time teaching, and the village-samurai *gōshi* who taught from paternalistic motives, to castle-town foot-soldiers who needed a side occupation. Nevertheless, the figures do provide some useful information. The high proportion of samurai in north-east Japan, Kyūshū and west Japan is probably a sign of the underdevelopment of commoner education in those districts; either because a high proportion of the schools were for samurai pupils, or because the number of commoner pupils being too small to support a professional teacher, they too were often taught by charitably disposed samurai. A study of the development of *terakoya* in Aomori suggests that until about 1800 nearly all their teachers were samurai; commoner teachers appear only when a rapid expansion of the number of schools sets in. The correlation between widespread diffusion and a preponderance of commoner teachers seems to be clearly demonstrated in this case.[2] The high proportion of samurai teachers in Edo reflects both the

---

[1] Ishikawa, *Terakoya*, p. 132.

[2] Maeno, 'Aomori-ken terakoya shishō'. A special factor in Aomori, which does not, however, invalidate the argument, is that the class barrier between samurai and farmer seems to have been weaker than in most districts. Intermarriage between samurai and farmer was permitted, for instance, so that commoners might well go to samurai teachers.

TABLE 6. TEACHERS OF WRITING SCHOOLS (PERCENTAGES)

Area	Total numbers	Samurai	Commoners	Buddhist priests	Shinto priests	Doctors	Others	Not known
Edo	297 (100%)	42	53	3	2	—	—	—
Rest of south-east Japan	943 (100%)	7	40	18	4	3	1	26
North-east Japan	1616 (100%)	36	31	8	8	8	6	3
East-central Japan	3643 (100%)	8	35	20	5	6	1	24
Kyoto-Osaka area	3000 (100%)	10	33	29	5	9	1	14

TERAKOYA

West Japan	3547 (100%)	24	34	13	12	9	1	8
Shikoku	645 (100%)	21	29	4	4	17	1	24
Kyūshū	1794 (100%)	40	36	8	4	5	1	7
All Japan	15,514 (100%)	20	34	16	7	16	1	14
Rural Aomori	272 (100%)	38	36	8	9	9	—	—
Rural Ehime	783 (100%)	17	28	31	14	8	1	—

Sources: Ishikawa, *Terakoya*, pp. 124, 140, 145, and Tōkyō Shisei Chōsakai, *Kōmin kyōiku kenkyū*, 1, p. 304. The first eight rows derive from the lists in *NKSS*, 8 and 9. The last two from the *Aomori-ken kyōikushi* and the *Ehime-ken kyōikushi* respectively.

high proportion of samurai in the Edo population and the fact that it was to Edo that *rōnin* naturally gravitated. Priests are much more commonly found among teachers in the older parts of Japan where, firstly there were more temples, and secondly scholarly traditions of the middle ages still maintained some glimmering of life. There the *terako* more often were quite literally 'temple children'. The contrast between Ehime and Aomori is very marked in this respect.

Size and Income

Professional teachers hardly made a fortune out of their schools. Few of them were large; the average school had about thirty pupils and less than 10 per cent of those listed in the Ministry of Education's survey had over a hundred.[1] Moreover, the fees were modest. According to one estimate a teacher with 200 pupils might expect an income of about 20 *koku*, equivalent to that of the lower ranks of samurai and better than that of the foot-soldier class. With a hundred he could be comfortably provided for, but with less than fifty he would have a hard time making ends meet.[2] Actual incomes are difficult to discover, however, since fixed fees were generally not charged. The relation between pupil and teacher and parent was more than simply an economic one. Learning was too much respected to be treated simply as a commodity, and the tradition of the scholar who simply fulfilled a duty to mankind by passing on his scholarship was still sufficiently strong, and still played a real part in the motives of a high enough proportion of teachers, to prevent those who did rely on teaching for a living from lowering their dignity to the point of setting too explicit a price on their services. Schools did often make fixed charges of mat-money in summer (towards the expense of re-covering the *tatami* of the floor) and of charcoal-money for heating in winter, but for the rest the parent committed his child to the teacher's benevolence, the teacher by the exercise of that benevolence laid a claim to the pupil's affection, reverence and gratitude, and the payments which parents made to the teacher were expressions of that gratitude, determined in amount by

[1] Ishikawa, *Terakoya*, pp. 150–1.
[2] Asaoka, *Ishinzen shōgakkō*, p. 55.

its intensity and their own financial means, and presented—
duly disguised in gift wrappings—on appropriate festive gift-
giving occasions—New Year, the midsummer Bon festival, the
twice-yearly school examinations, the four *sekku* festivals (the
3rd of the 3rd month, the 5th of the 5th and so on), and when
initially entering the school. In country districts the gifts were
mostly in kind; in the big towns mostly in money, though not
exclusively—the *sekku*, for instance, were properly recognized by
presents of appropriate cakes. The teacher's receipts were not all
profit. On certain of these gift-giving occasions he, for his part,
would provide cakes and biscuits for his children as a festival
treat.

But he could, especially in the villages, expect numerous small
attentions and gifts from the parents of his children beyond
the formally expected ones. An illustrated book of 1781[1]
describes the happy state of one teacher adopted by a village in
central Japan:

> When people decide to be kind they don't do things by halves.
> 'Let's help with your rice field', and they work till the sweat
> pours from them. They repaper the partitions, send the sliding
> doors to the artist, have the *tatami* re-covered. 'A kakemono?
> Yes, I'll give you one.' 'A flower-vase? Hey, you have a spare
> one.' And so it goes.

This teacher was in effect a village employee. The other
type of village teacher, the charitably disposed village headman or elder, had no need of such gifts, but he got them just the
same, for no self-respecting parent would accept the favour
of having his child educated without showing some material
recognition. The records of one such teacher in Gifu prefecture show the great variety of gifts—of money, noodles,
pears, turnips, dried fish and the like—which the parents
brought him, varied according to their means. Such was the
nature of these gifts and of village relations in general that they
were usually requited with a return gift of somewhat lesser value
—fans, persimmons, money and writing materials were this
teacher's staple.[2]

---

[1] *Anon., Tōsei shishō katagi* (Hakubunkan, *Teikoku bunko: Katagi zenshū*), p. 1017.
Extracted in *NKSSS*, 4, p. 117.
[2] Hattori, 'Edo-jidai nōson ni okeru terakoya'.

In this way the nakedness of the economic relation-involved was decently clothed, and the rational calculating attitude of the parent who operated on the principle:

> What it comes to is this:
> If it works out cheaply
> He can go and study.
> But if it costs too much
> Then ignorant he stays.

was a fit subject for a *kyōka* comic verse.[1] And the teacher who graded his attentions to his pupils according to the scale of gifts he received from parents was an object of scorn. There were, alas, far too many of them, complained Komachi Gyokusen; 'the relation between teacher and pupil becomes a mere market transaction and the importance of the moral bond is lost'. The children, too, come to grade their respect for their teacher in inverse proportion to the fees they pay him, and he warns parents that they should never let their children know, or evince an interest in, the amount they take to school in their gift envelopes.[2]

By the end of the period, however, education was becoming general in strata of the population which lived too near subsistence level to have too nice a concern with such refinements. The author of a mid-eighteenth-century work remarks on what he describes as a recent change in the economics of terakoya. Until that time the observance of proper ceremony was strictly enforced. A new boy's entry into the school was an expensive affair for his parents, requiring appropriate formal clothes, presents to the teacher and other pupils, cakes and *sake* for the bond-contracting ceremony between teacher and pupil. More recently teachers had become 'vulgarly remiss' about such niceties, and education having become much cheaper 'nowadays an illiterate is a rarity'.[3] By the end of the period there were teachers in the poorer quarters of Edo who taught in shacks 'made from joining two or three tenement rooms to-

---

[1] Anon., *Terakoya monogatari* (Ishikawa, *Orai-mono ochibo-shū*), p. 20. Extracted in *NKSSS*, 4, p. 115.

[2] *Jishū-hen* (*NKS*, 19), pp. 436–7.

[3] Anon. (*Kampō enkyō*) *Kōfu fūzokushi* (Hayakawa, *Kinsei fūzoku kembunshū*), p. 4 Extracted in *NKSSS*, 4, p. 122. Takeda Izumo's play *Sugawara denju tenarai kagam* contains a good picture of the ceremonial inception of a terakoya pupil.

gether . . . open to the rafters, with no walls better than planks and those full of knot-holes, *shōji* sliding doors pasted with used paper—already torn—and dirty shredded *tatami* mats on the floor, the worst holes pasted over with paper. Rain leaked through the roof and made the room uninhabitable in wet weather, and the filth defies description'.[1] These teachers took children for 4 *mon* a day[2] and, like the dame schools in England, one of their prime functions was to get children out of the way of harrassed parents. As another *kyōka* verse had it:

> Four *mon*, Mummy! Four *mon*, Mummy!
> They pester the life out of you
> When they're at home.
> At least it's quiet
> When they're at the teacher's.[3]

Even 4 *mon* a day was no sum to be treated lightly. (A day's allowance of rice usually worked out, in, say, the 1830s, at about 25 *mon* a day.) And in schools which really did leave fee payments to the parents' grateful discretion decency obviously imposed a minimum limit. Nor had the increasingly 'vulgar remissness' mentioned by the eighteenth-century writer really eliminated extra incidental costs. There were gifts to be taken to fellow-pupils when entering the school—a writing brush, perhaps, a small bundle of paper or some sweetmeats. Like the initial gifts to the teacher, they were means of establishing relations and emphasizing the request implied in the standard formula, 'dōzo yoroshiku'—'I commend myself to your good offices' (much as new residents take presents to their neighbours soon after moving in). Then there was the cost of the child's desk (usually second-hand), of paper and writing brushes and ink, and of other incidentals as well. As one of Shikitei Samba's housewives complains to another in his bath-house dialogues, it was hard work keeping up with the Jones's little girl:

> 'Then they always want to have their lunch at school. If you're late taking it they'll come back home to fetch it. Then off they trot to eat it at school.'

---

[1] Asaoka, *Ishinzen shōgakkō*, pp. 14–16.
[2] *Ibid.*, p. 3.
[3] Anon., *Terakoya monogatari*, p. 20. (*NKSSS*, 4, p. 115).

'I know, they're all the same. It's all right letting them take their lunches when it's raining or the wind's blowing. But when they start picking and choosing: I want that Mummy, and I don't want that, Mummy—it gets a bit too much. And then it's a flower to put in their water pot, or some cinnamon to chew, or some cloves to make cloves water. There's no end to it.'

'Ah, it's the same with all of them. They beg for gold-dust paper and patterned paper, and then cut it up and waste it on useless things. Or these flick moving pictures of actors . . .'[1]

Cost was obviously an important factor limiting the diffusion of terakoya education. Whether it was a more or less important limiting factor than indifference it is impossible to say.

Buildings and Organization

Most schools were individual enterprises run by a single teacher possibly helped by his wife and one or two senior pupils; only the biggest schools with a hundred or more pupils had regular hired help. The school was at the same time the teacher's house. In the average school with thirty or forty pupils the partitions would be removed from two or three adjoining rooms in a largish house to become the schoolroom. Three rooms of eight mats each (totalling about fifty square yards in area) could be made to accommodate as many as seventy or eighty pupils.[2] Sometimes two floors were used with a mezzanine landing on which the teacher sat and from which, alternately craning his neck and crouching down, he could observe what was afoot on both floors. In single-floor buildings the teacher sat on a raised dais with shelves behind him and desks on two sides to which the pupils came in turn to receive his instruction. For the rest of the time they returned to their own desks and busied themselves with practising what they had learned. Boys and girls usually sat in the same room, but with boys on one side and girls on the other. Each was allocated his own desk, and it was the task of the day's monitor to stack the desks to one side of the room at night and put them out again the next morning so that the schoolroom could revert

[1] Shikitei Samba, *Ukiyo-buro* (Tsukamoto, *Yūhōdō bunko*), pp. 117–19.
[2] Asaoka, *Ishinzen shōgakkō*, p. 15.

264

overnight to its original function as the teacher's living space.

Other Educational Institutions

Such terakoya did not exhaust the possibilities of formal education for commoner children. Although not many of them got into the fief schools, it was not difficult for the son of a merchant or well-to-do farmer to enter one of the numerous private schools which provided a training in gakumon—in full-scale Chinese education, or more rarely in medicine, in the Japanese classics, or, towards the end of the period, in Dutch or Western learning. Some of these private schools, like Hirose Tansō's in the town of Hita in Kyūshū, provided a highly systematized training in the Chinese classics (on much more rationally organized lines than in most fief schools) to large numbers of students. Most were little more than the private house of a single teacher at which he gave *sodoku* and held group readings and group discussions for anyone who, bearing suitable gifts, wished to become his *deshi*—his disciple. Tokyo had at least eighty such schools at the time of the Meiji Restoration which were still remembered when the Ministry of Education made its survey in 1883, and so did Nagano prefecture and Okayama prefecture. Altogether, 1492 were recorded from the whole country, though this includes a number founded between 1868 and 1873.[1]

The majority of these schools catered primarily, and some of them exclusively, for the samurai class. It was they for whom such an education was considered necessary, and the private schools often offered a geographically more convenient, and for lower samurai a less restrictive, alternative to the fief schools. For the intellectually alive, some of them—the coterie schools of the famous late Tokugawa heretics such as Yoshida Shōin or Yokoi Shōnan—often a much more imaginative and politically conscious education. In provincial castle-towns where the social barriers were stronger, it was probably difficult for non-samurai to enter such schools, but it was easier in the big urban centres, and there were some teachers who had an exclusively commoner clientele. In fact, the Nakai school in Osaka and the Hirose school in Hita—two towns dominated by merchants

[1] *NKSS*, 8 and 9.

with only a very small merchant population—were very much like fief schools for the commoner man.[1] Gakumon was far from universal among the non-samurai, but (see p. 242) it was far from being a rarity either, and among the richer merchants and the headman class of villagers it was a common accomplishment.

Even in circles where a terakoya education—or even a smattering of gakumon—was an accepted and normal part of a child's preparation for adult life, it was still, of course, only a small part. It was at home that the merchant's child learned to talk and to bow, to package and weigh, to discriminate between good money and bad, safe customers and poor credit risks, to appreciate the sanctions against giving short weight or breaking guild agreements. It was at home that the farmer's son learned his botany and his biology, learned the use of a hoe and respect of language, how to treat the village god and the village landlord. For all except the floating fringe of urban wage-labourers—who often lacked a settled family life in any case—the family was an economic enterprise and children were almost from birth apprentices to the family trade. Some enterprise-families fared better than others, and in expanding their scale of operations they absorbed, as indentured apprentices, the younger sons of other families. Hence there soon developed, most clearly in merchant families but in craft and upper-class farmer families too, a regular institutionalization of apprentice-ship, both as a system of employment and as a system of training for adult life.

The term of indenture was usually ten years,[2] starting, possibly after three or four years at a terakoya, from the age of ten or eleven by Japanese reckoning. (Contracts for longer

---

[1] The Register of Disciples printed in Katō, *Tansō zenshū*, 3, gives one some idea of the origins of pupils at Hirose Tansō's Hita school, the Kangien. Of the 129 pupils of his first decade, 1801–10, 98 per cent were from the island of Kūyshū, 73 per cent of them came from villages, 54 per cent of them were Buddhist priests and 43 per cent other commoners. In the school's fourth decade the 541 pupils came from farther afield (his fame had spread) and more from the urban commoner class. Only 76 per cent were from Kyūshū, 43 per cent from villages (40 per cent from towns, 17 per cent unclassified), and 28 per cent were priests compared with 70 per cent other commoners. Samurai pupils never made up more than 3 per cent of the total.

[2] The following account derives from Himata Shūji, 'Totei seido', and from extracts in *NKSSS*, 4, of the *Osaka shōgyō shūkan roku*, (1883).

6. Sodoku instruction at the Iwatsuki fief school. From a nineteenth-century drawing. One child receives instruction while the next waits his turn and the others practise in the next room. A child who has finished his stint for the day goes home.

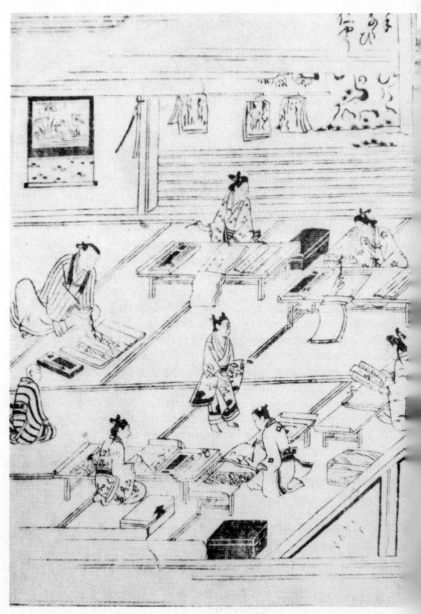

7. A seventeenth-century terakoya. An illustration from the *Otoko chōhōki*. Note the copybooks hanging up to dry before re-use.

periods were forbidden.) For the first few years the apprentice
—*detchi* as he was called in merchant and craft families—
learned chiefly industry and obedience, but possibly also
reading and writing and the use of the abacus if he had not
previously been to school. He lived with his employer, but
apart from his food and gifts of clothes at New Year or in mid-
summer, he received no wages, and his parents would normally
help to keep him in clothes and pocket-money. His was a life
of dusting and sweeping, fetching and carrying. It was expected
to be a hard life and its hardness was considered its educational
virtue. 'You should think of the hard time you have as an
apprentice as sowing the seeds for getting on later in life—for
growing the flowers of success.'[1]

At about the Japanese age of fifteen he would be promoted to
semi-adult status, a promotion symbolized by a change of hair-
style. His tasks were still largely menial, but he might now be
sent on more responsible errands, and be allowed to accompany
senior employees on purchasing or bill-collecting expeditions
for the express purpose of seeing how things were done. Some
three years later he would finally leave his *detchi* status behind
him. As a *tedai* he was now fully adult; at the ceremony marking
his change of status he would be given a set of adult clothes, a
pipe, a tobacco pouch. From this time on he had regular
functions in the business —highly specialized in larger merchant
establishments. At the same time he would be expected to
learn all he could about the business as a whole, and within a
few years he might be allowed to take responsible decisions
himself, partly as an explicit means of training and of testing
his ability and fitness for further promotion. He would usually
in any case stay on after the end of his term of indenture, at
least for five years of 'thank-you service' in recognition of the
training he had received. If he showed promise he might reach
the top rank of *bantō*—manager—and after some years of
running his master's business be rewarded by being set up
independently as a 'branch family' of the house he had served.

The system had a triple function; it provided labour for
businesses which had need of it; gave youths with no family
prospects a vocational training, and it was supposed at the

[1] Quoted from *Chōka shikimoku bungen tama no ishizue* in Himata, 'Totei seido',
p. 255.

same time to make men of them. It was this last function which prompted richer merchants and farmers who themselves employed apprentices to send their own sons—both eldest and younger—into service with other families. Occasionally two friendly families would have a standing arrangement over the generations to take in each other's children.[1] The intention is well caught in another snatch of feminine gossip overheard in Shikitei Samba's bath-house:

> 'Our eldest boy is a real trial. We don't know what to do with him. He's our only boy, for better or for worse, and we rather spoiled him and didn't send him out to service. We're regretting it now, though. It's no good being smart and clever if you don't know how to get out among strangers. He doesn't know a thing about making money. He only knows how to spend it.'
>
> 'Ah, well, they all have to go through that stage and sow their wild oats. We sent our second boy into service with the main family; we told him it would be good for him to live with strangers.'
>
> 'Did you? He must be a good boy to take it so well. You're right, unless they go out and eat somebody else's rice they've no conception of how other people think or feel. When you have people under you, for instance. Until you pinch yourself you don't understand how pinching hurts other people. Children who never go away from home don't know what hurts and itches mean.'[2]

'If you love your child send him on a journey' is the proverbial expression of this particular educational maxim, and similar practices of educational apprenticeship, though they have long since died out in merchant families, persisted until very recently in landlord families in northern Japan.

For girls there were other things to be learned, too, which neither the home nor the terakoya could provide. To a wide range of middling Edo townsmen the height of ambition for their daughters was to get them 'into service' at a daimyo's mansion.[3] There, if they were lucky, they might even bear a

---

[1] See e.g. the entry under Aeba Kōson in Heibonsha, *Dai-jimmei jiten*.

[2] Shikitei Samba, *Ukiyo-buro* (Tsukamoto, *Yūhōdō bunko*), p. 123. Also extracted in *NKSSS*, 4, p. 335.

[3] The chances must have been fairly good. The main Shogunal palace was supposed to have a staff of 250 women (Kawade Shobō, *Nihon rekishi daijiten*, 'O-oku') and the total for all the daimyo and hatamoto establishments in Edo

daimyo's child or marry into the lower reaches of the samurai class. In any case, they would acquire something of samurai feminine culture and improve their marriage chances. But 'service' was something that had to be prepared for. A ten-year-old complains to her friend in another of Shikitei Samba's dialogues:

Mummy is so strict and she scolds me like anything. Listen. I'll tell you. As soon as I crawl out of bed in the morning I go to put out the desks at teacher's. Then I go to the samisen teacher for my morning practice. Then I come home for breakfast, and then after dancing lesson I go to writing school. Then back home for dinner and then, by the time I've been to the bath it's soon time to go to the lute teacher's, and *then* when I come back I've got to start samisen and dance exercises. I just have a teeny bit of play and by that time it's dark and I still have my lute exercises to do. There's no time to play at all. I hate it, I really do! Daddy—he's nice and he likes me and when Mummy keeps on saying: 'Do your exercises now. Do your exercises,' he says, 'What do you make such a fuss about it for? You might just as well let her alone. She'll manage all right somehow if you let her go her own way. It's only to go into service after all,' he tells her, 'a little bit will do'. But Mummy's so strict. 'What do you mean?' she says. 'If she's going to learn these things it's not a bit of good unless she gets them at her finger-tips. Bringing up a girl's a woman's job. You leave her to me. She'll regret it when she grows up. It's because you say things like that she won't take me seriously and won't do what I tell her . . .' She goes on and on. And you see, Mummy has always been initerate or something ever since she was a girl and she can't read at all. Do you know, she was born in a place where there are mountains and sea and . . . and ever so far away, so she doesn't know anything about playing the samisen and all that. 'That's why,' she says, 'I'm going to make certain I give her a good training.' She doesn't half go on, our Mummy.[1]

Going into service, of course, was not the only use to which these talents could be put. Indeed, the author of the *Seji kem-monroku* remarks in 1816, though doubtless with exaggeration

---

[1] Shikitei Samba, *Ukiyo-buro* (Tsukamoto, *Yūhōdō bunko*), p. 216.

must have numbered many thousands—a major symptom of the decadence of the times according to Fujimori Kōan, who pointed out that Ieyasu made do quite well with only seven girls to wait on him (*Shinsei-dan* (*NKS*, 32), p. 206).

for he was admittedly a crotchety old man who thought the world was going to the devil, that by his time it was only the primly respectable or the parents of ill-favoured daughters who sought to put them into service. Serving girls now dressed as well as their mistresses, and since their wages were insufficient to cover their expensive tastes they had to be supported by their parents instead of dutifully supporting them. The parent with foresight nowadays sought to turn his girl into a *geisha* or a restaurant serving maid, the object being to make her the mistress of somebody with real money in order to get a nice fat maternity allowance as soon as she should bear a child.[1] The thousands of teachers of music and dancing, of drumming and story-telling, of 'art' calligraphy and painting, of haiku and waka poetry and so on, did not, of course, cater exclusively for the vocational needs of such professional sirens. They also found pupils among the prospective clients and victims of these girls, for these were participant sports and the well-to-do merchant gentleman was not simply a patron connoisseur. He would be expected to entertain, as well as be entertained by, his mistress. And quite apart from the social advantages which such accomplishments conferred many men and women found in them intrinsic aesthetic satisfaction. To the disgust of the Confucian writers who deplored the tendency of townsmen to neglect their family trade and forget their proper station in unseemly devotion to such pursuits, a good many of them believed that life was meant to be enjoyed; and they had their own standards of what were boorish, and what cultured, ways of doing so.

[1] Buyō Inshi, *Seji kemmonroku* (Honjō, *Kinsei shakai keizai sōsho*, 1), pp. 257–61.

Chapter IX

THE CONTENT OF TERAKOYA EDUCATION

SIMPLE WRITING PRACTICE was the main staple of terakoya education, conducted in much the same way as at the samurai schools. Hours of attendance were irregular—there were no clocks in any case—and the usual practice was for pupils to go to the teacher for their day's brief lesson as soon as they arrived and then settle at their desks to practise what they had learned. They did not necessarily go every day. One Gifu village teacher, for instance, whose records have been examined, held classes on seven or eight days of each month, and most of his pupils attended for only three or four.[1]

In some poorer country districts sand trays or ash trays or lacquered boards were used for writing practice, but the usual material was a note-book of rather coarse paper on which the children wrote and rewrote until the whole book was ebony black, the latest try being distinguished only by the dampness, and hence relative blackness, of the ink. After going once through the book they were entitled to amuse themselves in play while it dried, before starting to practise again. There was, in consequence, much to-ing and fro-ing and little possibility of enforcing iron discipline. As at the samurai schools, after the teacher had finished giving individual lessons to each of the pupils it was common to set up a tablet marked 'Silence', or to light a stick of slow-burning incense and demand silence until it had disappeared. Some schools also had a wooden privy tablet without which pupils could not leave the room—a device for ensuring that they went one at a time and so did not congregate outside for illicit games.

Very often, at the end of the morning, the desks would be cleared away and the pupils would gather in a circle round the

---

[1] Hattori, 'Edo jidai nōson ni okeru terakoya', p. 45.

teacher to recite arithmetic tables or to read their copy-books, or sometimes other special reading-books, in chorus. This was somewhat like hymn-singing since the range of texts used was limited and they soon knew them off by heart. In some schools, particularly in the Kyoto-Osaka area and particularly early in the period, the teachers taught *utai* in this way—the extracts from verse dramas which were recited at weddings and village festivals and which every self-respecting villager was expected to know. In some Wakayama schools the whole afternoon was devoted to *utai* to the exclusion of everything else.[1] Sometimes, too, the teacher would offer at these sessions improving little stories of filial sons and loyal apprentices. Writing practice might continue into the afternoon, or alternatively there might be arithmetic teaching with the abacus instead, or instruction for girls in sewing, flower arrangement or the tea ceremony.

The daily routine was broken by a number of special events. Most schools held monthly examinations at which—on clean pieces of paper this time—pupils were expected to write from memory passages selected at random from the texts they had practised during the month. There would also be a yearly examination at which each pupil would bring to the school all the books he had used during the previous year and be expected to write out from memory a passage from any one of them. Marks were awarded—often posted on the walls of the class-room—and prizes would be given. Some schools had regular grades with promotion depending on performance in these tests. In many Wakayama schools there were five grades, distinguished by the kind of brushes they used—the upper grades having more versatile brushes which required greater skill. Then, three times a year there would be further tests which were half examinations and half festival occasions. These—the *kaki-zome* (the 'first writing') at New Year, and the *sekigaki* ('extempore writing') usually in April and August—had to be dressed up for, the teacher, usually, in wing-shouldered *kami-shimo*. (See Plate 8). Each pupil according to his accomplishments, was given a single phrase to write in large characters on a big sheet of paper—usually a proverb or some uplifting sentiment drawn from the classics. These were marked by the teacher (in Wakayama the most deprecating of the five customary

[1] Horiuchi, *Nanki Tokugawa-shi*, 17, p. 133.

ratings was 'quite excellent really') and hung on the walls of the class-room for the delectation of parents at the subsequent feast.

There were other festive occasions, too; expeditions to view the cherry blossom, the raucous participation of tipsy parents in which aroused the disapproving attention of the Edo Magistrate in the 1840s (see p. 246); the *tanabata* festival in July when poems were written to celebrate the meeting of the seamstress star and the cowherd star across the Milky Way. This, too, was an excuse for at least tea and cakes, after which the poem cards would be taken in procession and floated down a near-by river. There was also a great variety of ceremonies in honour of Tenjin-sama, the deified Sugawara Michizane, a ninth-century scholar of legendary calligraphic skill. Prayers to Tenjin-sama were supposed to be a great help in improving one's style (and doubtless were indeed, if only in reawakening and strengthening the child's will to progress). Many children had small brightly coloured papier-mâché dolls of Tenjin-sama on the god-shelf at home, and there was a great deal of child-lore—finding eight-pointed maple leaves, measuring the height of bonfire flames and so on—concerned with divining the degree of luck which Tenjin-sama was likely to vouchsafe. In temple schools the wise boddhisatva, Monju-bosatsu sometimes replaced Tenjin-sama as an object of worship.

It seems to have been a genial kind of education, predicated on the assumption that children were basically well-disposed creatures who could be easily persuaded to co-operate, whose delinquencies were mostly harmless and who had a right to their occasional fun. They did not necessarily have to be beaten for every sneeze in order to tame the devil in them. There were regular scales of punishment in most schools, but rarely anything worse than detention, standing in the corner or on a desk (sometimes with a cup of water in one hand and a burning stick of incense—to mark the duration of the trial—in the other), or a beating with a fan wrapped in stiff paper—productive of a loud noise but not much pain. One report speaks of some tough schools in Edo where occasionally fights would break out and be fought with such ferocity (with writing-box lids as weapons) that even the teacher hardly dared to intervene, but there seems generally to have been little violence, and even a famous Edo teacher whose strictness earned him the respectful title 'Thunder-teacher' relied on nothing more than a steady accusing eye and a sermonizing tongue for his disciplinary effect.[1]

Even men of lesser authority seem to have had little trouble. Tsubouchi Shōyō describes with contempt the uninspired terakoya education he got from a teacher who was 'a truly dull fellow, without an ounce of dignity in him'. Some thirty boys between the ages of seven and thirteen were crowded into as many square yards of floor space.

> There we were cramped in a confined space like tits in a coconut, and what's more facing each other in lines of double rows, peeling off one wet strip of scrawled copy paper after another. One would think it wouldn't need a malicious child, only someone slightly self-assertive, for eyes soon to start to glare and tempers to fly out of control; but with us—a truly ordinary group of boys to the nth degree of ordinariness we must have been . . .—everything was as calm and quiet as you could imagine. Sometimes there would be a collision of backsides and a boundary dispute with the boy behind, but after two or three minutes of negotiations in that indistinct, plaintive, not-quite-sure-whether-it's-male-or-female tone that went with the Nagoya accent, things would settle down with the plaintiff simply resigned to his fate. Just occasionally somebody would start a quarrel; one would shriek, the other would howl; by-standers would jeer and the whole room would be driven by childish group instinct into one collective yell. But then a mere shout—no, not even a shout; just an oh! so feeble, oh! so un-authoritative word from the teacher and all would soon be quiet again. Such an easily handled bunch of young sparrows were we that although I went to that school from the age of eleven to the age of thirteen for some three years (though to be sure about a third of the year was holiday) I was never once put to standing snotty-nosed on the desk with the tea-cup and the incense stick. Nor do I ever remember seeing anyone else being made to stand and snivel. You can imagine from that just how prosaic, how monotonous, my experience of terakoya education was.[2]

It was partly in disciplinary scoldings, partly in the proverbs and texts written at 'first-writing' parties, partly in the contents

[1] Asaoka, *Ishinzen shōgakkō*, p. 35.
[2] 'Watakushi no terakoya jidai' (*Shōyō senshū*, 12), pp. 11–13.

of copy-books that the schools did more than give a training in writing; they reflected, and they passed on to the next generation, the moral standards and the practical worldly wisdom, the possession of which marked the difference between the respected successful citizen and the failure in Edo commoner society. An appendix translates the disciplinary precepts which were codified at length by one terakoya teacher, apparently one who was a little less genial and more fussily don't-ish than most. They are an interesting mixture. They combine the emphasis on neatness, tidiness, serious-minded diligence and sober good behaviour which is a common characteristic of school-masterishness in any country, with specifically Confucian elements like the insistence on filial piety or reverence for the teacher, with characteristically Japanese elements like the stress on the sanctions of shaming and being disliked, and with specifically commoner-culture elements like the recourse to the sanction of 'not getting on' and the popular Buddhist notions of the natural this-worldly deserts of wrong-doing. As one reads a set of precepts such as this it comes to seem even odder that there should apparently have been so few problems of discipline in these schools given the solemn way children are expected to conform to adult standards of unexuberant sobriety, and the shocked horror with which the teacher speaks of even trivial offences. Perhaps the explanation is that nobody really believed it; that most teachers still preserved a sufficient modicum of childishness to retain an instinctive sympathy with their charges, and that the shocked horror over trivial offences conveyed in these precepts is less the authoritarianism of the domineering punishing adult—*de haut en bas*—and more like the awed admonitions of the ten-year-old as she tells her little brother of the fearful consequences which will follow from his getting a stain on his shirt; a mixture, that is, of relish and anxious sympathy at the thought of the sanctions which external forces— society and the logic of social sanctions—will impose. It is not the teacher who overawes the child, but society and the moral law which overawe them both.

Text-books

A fuller idea of the minds and values of the terakoya teachers can be gained from looking at some of the text-books they used.

Many hundreds of different texts are known to have been printed, and this was probably only a small proportion of the texts actually used, since teachers frequently wrote their own manuscript models for their pupils' use.[1]

It is an indication less of the unchanging nature of Japanese society than of the weight of tradition and of the conservatism of Tokugawa teachers that some of the texts used—including some of the most popular—were several centuries old. The Tokugawa schools took over the practices, and the texts, of the temple schools of the earlier feudal period which themselves followed patterns set by the education of the children of the court aristocracy in Heian times. The earliest known copy-books (beyond simple compilations of the syllabary, the numerals and so on) were collections of letters—actual letters such as might have been written by one aristocrat to another—usually spread over the year so as to permit all the appropriate references to the seasons which good letter-writing required. A later development was deliberately to devote each letter to a particular subject in order to bring in a wider range of vocabulary. Finally, this was carried to the point of inserting long lists of words in thesaurus style, whereby the letters lost their plausibility as real letters but gained in their exhaustiveness as primers.

It was one of these, the *Teikin Orai*, a work of uncertain authorship dating from the Ashikaga period, which was among the two or three most popular copy-books in the Edo period, being reprinted at least 170 times as a single work and probably many more times in combination with others.[2] It preserves the letter form with one letter and a reply to it for each month of the year, beginning with all the appropriate greetings. Four letters are devoted to ceremonies, games and pastimes; four to the menial occupations of the farmer, the craftsman and the merchant; four to building, household equipment, cooking, clothes, etc.; four to Buddhism, priests and temples; two to

[1] Ishikawa has identified 1993 different works belonging to the Tokugawa period (*Terakoya*, p. 214).

[2] Ishikawa, *Teikin ōrai no kenkyū*, p. 15. Of about 3000 people educated in terakoya who answered Ototake's questionnaires, over 500 reported that the *Teikin ōrai* was used as a copy-book in their school. Except for the *Shōbai ōrai* (see below), the only other works which occurred more frequently were the syllabary and lists of personal or place names which varied from school to school (*Shomin kyōikushi*, 3, p. 968).

warfare, weapons and military training; two to local administration; two to justice and court procedure; and two to illness and medicines. The whole is written in stiff Muromachi Sino-Japanese. It is a work of considerable ingenuity in the way in which it incorporates its lists of words and still manages to run a thread of purposeful sense through each letter. It was undoubtedly an excellent primer for the children of landed warriors in the middle ages, and it has some merit as a source of historical knowledge of the society of the time, but it is difficult to know what the Edo fishmonger's son made of it:

> I was just feeling pleased that things had settled down and thinking of a hunting or a fishing expedition when some rebels started trouble and were joined by [exhaustive list of robbers, footpads, etc.] who stole, robbed, raped, ravaged over a wide area. As a result my commander has given orders for military operations (seige, attack ...) against them. Unfortunately I lost a lot of equipment in the last campaign and I would be glad if you would lend me some spears, halberds ...

One can understand why one of the few educational theorists who bothered with the terakoya should have complained that the texts they used were such as to induce in the common people a spirit of litigious cunning[1] when one finds, for example, for the eighth month:

> Your suit ought to get through quickly ... If you give your man the letters I will tell him where to go [list of officials], also how to administer bribes, gain favour, request consideration, [etc., eight similar phrases] to the ... and the ...

It was not simply that the content was hardly appropriate or useful for Tokugawa children, it was not even intelligible. The institutions described in the letters had long since ceased to exist and even the names of common everyday articles had changed. The editor of one of the best annotated editions[2] might well say in his preface that while the book is an excellent primer for children 'it has tended to become incomprehensible with the passage of time', an unfortunate drawback which his copious notes are intended to remedy. Even he, however, does not do very well. Faced with a list of fifty-seven articles of daily use (the writer wished to borrow them because he was

---

[1] Shōji Kōgi, *Keizai mondō hiroku* (*NKS*, 22), p. 78.
[2] Kuroda Seidō (*Kashira-gaki kundoku*) *Teikin ōrai seichū-shō* (Pref. 1844).

having important guests) he leaves thirty unannotated either because they were still intelligible or because he could not explain them. For four he gives contemporary equivalents. For thirteen he provides explanations since there were no contemporary equivalents (for four of them two explanations are offered as 'conflicting theories'). For the remaining ten he gives explanations which he admits are only tentative guesses. He certainly does the best he can. In addition to notes on individual words there are general explanatory disquisitions on the life of the time, a full 'interpretation' showing how the original Sino-Japanese is to be 'read off', and a separate translation into contemporary Japanese. If the intention were historical instruction he could not do better, but there is no indication in the preface or anywhere else that this is the explicit intention. Rather, it seems, no one questioned the appropriateness of the *Teikin ōrai* because it always had been used. Editors simply gave what help they could, and found considerable satisfaction of their own historical curiosity in doing so. The obvious Western parallel in terms of remoteness from the child's experience and the growth of commentaries on a text the content of which is of secondary importance, is the use of Caesar's *Gallic Wars* to teach children the elements of Latin prose—with the difference that the *Teikin ōrai* was supposed to teach children the elements of writing their *own* language.

There were other ways of mitigating the austerities of the original text. One was to fill the top margin—about a quarter or a fifth of the page—with useful notes and tips of a kind which will be discussed later. Another was to add illustrations, sometimes of a strictly practical kind, depicting the objects mentioned in the text, but sometimes simply to delight the eye and relieve the tedium. One edition which has no explanatory notes has instead illustrations by Hokusai. He was allowed to spread himself over half of each page. His sketches are typically full of life and humour, though they bear only occasional relevance to the text. When they do, they show scenes of contemporary Edo life as often as of the Muromachi society to which the text refers.[1]

[1] *Ehon teikin ōrai.* (The British Museum edition is undated, but according to Ishikawa the work was first published in two parts in 1819 and 1848 (*Teikin ōrai no kenkyū*, p. 154).)

Other popular Tokugawa copy-books had equally archaic origins. A similar one was the *Imagawa-jō*, the testament of the cultivated fourteenth-century warrior Imagawa Ryōshun, containing his Lord Chesterfield-like advice to his son on how to move in society and govern his territory. Another, less used towards the end of the period, was the *Jōei shikimoku*, the fourteenth-century legal code with its complex regulation of the family and property relations of the Hōjō warrior.

Two works of a different type, but even greater antiquity, were the *Jitsugo-kyō* and the *Dōji-kyō*, popularly supposed to have been written by Kōbō-daishi and Po Chu-i respectively and, though these attributions are most improbable, certainly surviving from the Heian period.[1] They are written in pure Chinese—or at least an approximation to it—in sets of parallel five-character phrases, and are concerned, unlike the texts just described, not with practical information, but with moral instruction. They were widely used (nearly a half of Ototake's sample remembered reading the *Jitsugo-kyō*); they were rather more intelligible than the *Teikin ōrai*, and since teachers often did, it seems, take trouble to explain at least what the easier passages meant, they ranked among the most important influences on the ethical ideas, or at least the ethical vocabulary, of generations of Tokugawa commoners. Their contents became folk knowledge and many of their phrases passed into the language.[2] Most of the proverbial metaphors used in the precepts of the terakoya teacher which are translated in the appendix—about axle-pins carrying chariots for a thousand miles and mugworts growing straight among reeds—are derived from these texts, being in turn derived from phrases in the Chinese classics.

The morality is basically Confucian. There are the usual exhortations to filial piety and respect for teachers, including the rather extreme formulation of the *Jitsugo-kyō*: 'Your father

---

[1] Both have been translated by B. H. Chamberlain; the *Dōji-kyō* in *Transactions of the Asiatic Society of Japan*, 9, No. 3, 1881, and the *Jitsugo-kyō* in the *Cornhill Magazine*, August 15th, 1876.

[2] At least one phrase—*sekizen*, meaning to 'pile good deed on good'—became a not uncommon boys' given name, so that the sentence in the *Dōji-kyō* 'there shall be happiness in the house which piles good deed on good' became 'there shall be happiness in Sekizen's house,' to further which pious hope parents doubtless expected that their son would be guided by his name into paths of righteousness.

and your mother are like heaven and earth; your teacher and your lord are like the sun and the moon. All other relations may be likened to useless stones.' The *Dōji-kyō* has some of the stories of the twenty-four paragons of filial piety who found happiness in serving their (usually crabbedly querulous) parents. (There was, for instance, the man who decided to kill his son in order to leave more food for his aged mother on the principle that children can be reproduced for the asking whereas parents are irreplaceable. While digging the pit in which to bury the boy alive he came across hidden treasure which obviated the necessity for such drastic action.) There are the usual exhortations to study—'if a gem be not polished it lacks lustre, if man does not study he lacks wisdom' was the opening phrase of the *Jitsugo-kyō*, another of those which became proverbial—and the *Dōji-kyō* tells the stories of some of the Chinese heroes of scholarship under difficult conditions—the man who put a rope round his neck and tied it to the ceiling to prevent himself from dropping off to sleep, the man who used a cage-full of fireflies to study at night, and so on.

However, these works were written by Buddhist priests and it is a distinctly Buddhist-digested Confucianism which they contain. The *Dōji-kyō*, for instance, adds weight to its exhortations to filial piety by pointing out that fathers earn themselves aeons of hell by killing living creatures to feed their children, and even the exaggerated insistence on respect for the teacher is more in the tradition of Buddhist perversions of Confucianism than of Confucianism itself. Yoshikawa Kōjirō points out, for instance, that the phrase from the *Dōji-kyō* (quoted in the terakoya teacher's precepts translated in the appendix): 'Keep seven feet behind your teacher and never tread on his shadow', though thought in modern Japan to be one of the most typical expressions of Confucianism, in fact derives from an obscure Chinese Buddhist work and is not only unknown in China but contrary to the general spirit of Chinese teacher-pupil relations.[1]

There is much in these works, too, which is purely Buddhist, with no pretensions to Confucian derivation. There are promises not only of Heaven and Hell, but also of immediate this-worldly rewards; for goodness in happiness and wealth; for

[1] *Nihon no shinjō*, pp. 137–54.

badness in misfortune and poverty. There are references to the eight correctnesses, the ten iniquities, the eight tribulations and other of the numerical categories so beloved of pedantic Buddhist theologians. There is the typical Buddhist emphasis on the ephemerality of life and the vanity of the ways of the world—'direct your thoughts then, only to Nirvana' says the *Doji-kyō*. There is also that particular Buddhist contribution to practical everyday morality which served to modify the narrow particularism of the Confucian ethic, the insistence on the need for charity towards one's fellow men.

That Japan continued to be a Buddhist country into the Meiji period, not simply in the sense that funerals were conducted according to Buddhist rites, but in the sense that elements of Buddhist theology and ethics remained alive in popular attitudes to life, was probably as much due to the efforts of terakoya teachers with their *Jitsugo-kyō* and *Dōji-kyō* (not all of them priests by any means) as it was to the priests themselves and their none too frequent sermons. The agnostic rigour of pure Confucianism was too austere for the average sensual peasant or townsman; it became more acceptable when watered down and spiced with the supernaturalism and the eschatology of popular Buddhism. Some of the Confucianists deplored this (see p. 248), but others accepted it. It was in the terms of this popular folk morality that Hosoi Heishū spoke in his lectures to villagers and merchants (see p. 239).

The texts mentioned so far were the staple texts for the reading sessions with which a morning's writing practice often closed (though they were also, of course, designed for writing practice too).[1] This was the poor man's gakumon; the texts, being all written in a kind of Chinese syntax, were the equivalent of the samurai's Four Books. Since they were sodoku texts, it did not matter if they were in large part unintelligible since the purpose of sodoku was to learn to 'read off'—with occasional explanations of easy phrases within the child's understanding— rather than to reach a full understanding of the contents. Some schools aimed rather higher and used the Four Books themselves or other Chinese classics, but this already made the school

---

[1] In Ototake's survey, for instance, 1341 people reported using the *Jitsugo-kyō* for reading and only 132 for copying. The *Teikin ōrai* was read by 981 and copied by 513 (*Shomin kyōikushi*, 3, pp. 968, 991.)

into an academy for gakumon and it was rare for it to be combined with writing practice, the defining characteristic of the terakoya proper. Texts in Japanese were rarely used in the reading sessions except for girls;[1] it was generally thought that the ability to read Japanese was acquired naturally in the process of learning to write it.

When these Sino-Japanese texts were used as copy-books it was usually at a relatively advanced stage. Children commonly started by learning to write the syllabary, lists of numbers, poems written in the phonetic script, lists of place names or of characters commonly used for personal names, or Japanese imitations of the Chinese *Thousand Character Classic*. There were also large numbers of other texts, many of them printed, which were practically designed to meet the particular needs of particular kinds of pupils. Some of the earlier ones preserved the letter form of the *Teikin ōrai*, but this was finally abandoned in favour of simple vocabulary lists useful for particular occupations or particular districts, though the titles of most of them still contained the word *ōrai*—exchange (of letters)—as a mark of their lineage. One version of the most common of these, the *Shōbai ōrai* or 'Merchant's *ōrai*', simply starts with the phrase: 'Generally speaking the words which a merchant has to use are . . . ' and launches straight away into lists of grains, clothes, weapons, precious stones, furniture, the technical terms for bills of exchange, receipts and invoices. There were similar compilations for farmers, craftsmen, warehouse dealers, carpenters, seamen, booksellers, clothiers and so on. Some manage to preserve something like a sentence form so that examples can be given of the use of verbs amid the lists of names, and often useful tips as well. (In the *Wholesaler's ōrai*, for example: 'Some smart rogues try to pass false money, counterfeit, bad coins, underweight coins, clipped coins, so be sure you examine, scrutinize, inspect . . .')[2] Other texts take a geographical rather than a professional theme, describing a journey, say, made along the Tōkaidō from Edo to Osaka or to a famous shrine or temple, giving the names of the places on the way, their local products, descriptions of natural features and legends or historical

---

[1] In Ototake's survey the only reading texts in Japanese used in more than a hundred schools were girls' texts (*Shomin kyōikushi*, 3, p. 991).

[2] Katō Zuiō (calligrapher) (*Kashira-gaki e-iri*) *Tonya ōrai*.

8. A *sekigaki* festival day at an Edo terakoya in the late Tokugawa period. Both teacher and pupils are dressed in their holiday best and a mother has come along to help. The teacher watches as a pupil writes an aphorism on special paper. Other compositions are already up and on display, and in the background one group has already started the feast. From Asaoka, *Ishinzen*.

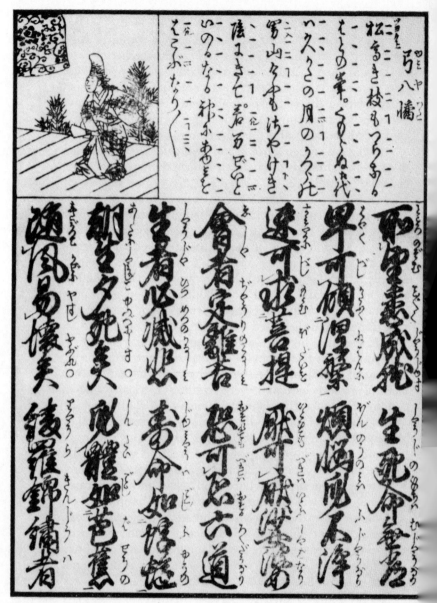

9. A sample page from the *Terako chie kagami*. The bottom two-thirds of the page contain a part of the *Dōjikyō*, the Chinese characters in a cursive script, the diacritical marks indicating the order in which they are to be read on the left of each line and phonetic indications of the Japanese reading on the right. At the top is a passage from a famous Nō play, with chanting notation, and a drawing of a Nō dancer.

incidents associated with them. Somewhat similarly the *Edo ōrai*,[1] written for children in western Japan who had never seen the capital, describes the sights of Edo and at one point digresses into an account of the New Year ceremonies at the Shogun's palace with a list of the presents made to the Shogun which provides an opportunity to give the names of a variety of provincial products and the places from which they originate.

As a logical consequence of the divorce of the thesaurus type of copy-book from its original letter form there were also special epistolary handbooks—*Shōsoku ōrai* is a common name—which gave lists of polite phrases and seasonal greetings, sample letters and instructions on the subtleties of addressing, folding, sealing and so on. Shikitei Samba once compiled a rather elaborate version of one of these, intended to be used for adult reference as well as for children's instruction. It includes sample letters for all occasions—inviting friends to view plum blossom, congratulating a neighbour's wife on assuming the pregnancy belt, informing one's friends of one's escape from a fire, disowning a dismissed employee, or admonishing a friend who is spending his substance on women of ill-repute.[2]

A number of these copy-books contrive also to bring in the occasional moral precept. One version of the *Shōbai ōrai*, for example, inserts here and there warnings against giving short-weight or adulterating food, and ends with a little peroration urging the importance of diligent study for merchant children, the avoidance of luxury or addiction to frivolous pastimes, the necessity of keeping a tidy shop, of treating your neighbours kindly and of not seeking immoderate profits. The merchant who works honestly and hard and seeks only moderate and legitimate gain will be assured of wealth and happiness.[3]

A *Farmer's ōrai* used in a village in Aichi prefecture[4] contains an even higher quotient of didacticism and may well be typical of the texts used by the village headman type of teacher who taught as a social service rather than to make money. It paints a dreadful picture of those who:

---

[1] Fushimiya, *Edo ōrai.*
[2] *Taizen ippitsu keijō* (*The Complete Dear Sir*).
[3] See the version printed in Anon., *Terako chie kagami.*
[4] *Nōjin ōrai* (MS. preserved in the village records of Shimo-tsugu-mura, Kita-shidara-gun, Aichi prefecture).

. . . practise swordsmanship or learn military strategy unbecoming their station, or take to drink and carnal pleasure, are addicted to gambling and games of chance, sleep late in the morning and waste the night in pleasure. Such people who neglect their family occupation pile up debts they cannot pay and bring themselves to poverty, destitution, bankruptcy. Or else they become criminally greedy and heedless of the judgment of Heaven, seize land that is not theirs, secretly shift boundary stones, steal wood from the mountains and the thickets, and crops from their neighbours' fields. They may for a time profit from their greed, but eventually the punishment of the Gods and Buddhas will reach them, they will be seized and put in handcuffs and chains, suffer torture and imprisonment, their family will become extinct and they will be shamefully expelled, banished . . .

If, on the other hand, they are honest and diligent, spend their days in the fields and their nights making rope and sandals and bales, if they obey all the feudal regulations and the instructions of their village headmen, then they will be free from bad harvests and enjoy prosperity and happiness.

Similar exhortations to obey the feudal laws are common. There is no doubt of the loyal support the authors of these texts gave to the *status quo*. The *Edo ōrai*, for instance, digresses from its description of the sights of Edo into a sycophantic eulogy of the Shogun's benevolence in designing the Tamagawa canal to bring drinking-water to the people of Edo, and in building the Ryōgoku bridge where formerly so many lives had been lost on the ferry. These references seem to have been gratuitous expressions of the authors' loyalty, rather than the result of the promptings of feudal officials. The Bakufu's rare pronouncements on school texts were confined (see p. 246) to encouraging the use of *gonin-gumi* register prefaces or village notice-board edicts, but they seem, in fact, to have been rarely used. Few of Ototake's respondents mention them,[1] and Takigawa has found only a half-dozen printed versions of such material whereas the totally irrelevant Hōjō code, the *Jōei shikimoku*, was reprinted at least 132 times between 1600 and 1872.[2]

Mention was made in an earlier chapter of copy-books provided by feudal authorities (mostly Bakufu Intendants)

[1] *Shomin kyōikushi*, 3, pp. 970-2.
[2] Takigawa Masajirō, 'Terakoya ni okeru hōgaku kyōiku'.

which were almost entirely concerned with moral instruction. There were many others of similar content which were produced not by officials but by public-spirited townsmen and village headmen on their own initiative. One of the more interesting of them is the *Nōmin kyōkunjō*[1] apparently written in the early nineteenth century. The main purpose of its specious, but hard and purse-appealing, arguments is to wean farmers away from their improper fascination with the city lights. It is a eulogy of the country life which expresses amazement that so many farmers should be lured away to the brash, ignoble and difficult life of the city simply because they are bedazzled by the way in which city-dwellers dress and eat in a manner unbecoming their proper station in life. The author's arguments to prove the folly of such conduct are, firstly, that the townsman has to work all the year round, while the farmer has natural periods of rest in the agricultural slack season. Secondly, the farmer is self-sufficient except for salt and agricultural implements whereas the townsman has to buy everything, even drinking-water. Thirdly, the townsman has to pay enormous taxes—1 *momme* per mat as a basic tax with numerous additions which would work out at approximately 300 *koku* per *tan*, whereas the farmer has to pay less than 2 *koku* of tax per *tan* of rice land, *and* there are generous reductions in years of bad harvest. The townsman is always subject to the risks of fire and robbery; he is always losing money on the exchanges, and he is always having to borrow money. His interest payments grow while he is asleep. While the farmer sleeps it is his crops which grow. Rather more realistic than the writers who promise a large automatic cash reward for goodness, the author goes on to say that hard work will not bring a great fortune but it will bring a comfortable competence. It is this which should be aimed at, not the dizzy heights of affluence which are only reached by luck. He concludes with some practical advice on the advisability of growing sweet potatoes as an insurance against a failure of the rice crop, on the profitability of sericulture, on the advantages of growing fruit and flowers around the house (particularly to give old men in the family something to do), on the

[1] Bound together with an edition of the *Hyakushō ōrai* published by Ryūshōdō Kansai in Kyoto in 1829, and also reprinted in Ishikawa, *Orai-mono ochibo-shū*, p. 126–9.

virtues of organic fertilizer, and finally on the importance of paying taxes promptly and honestly, and obeying the feudal laws.

Some of these printed copy-books did more than simply offer lists of characters or ethical precepts. They also provided little snippets of historical or scientific information, practical hints and did-you-know-that type of quiz-contest facts and figures. Generally these play a subordinate role; one finds them mixed with proverbs and thoughts-for-the-day running along the top margin of a copy text. They play a bigger part in works published later in the period, however, and there were some large compendia of which they form the major part. One such, the *Terako chie kagami* (*The Terakoya pupil's book of knowledge*) will serve as an illustration.

The book contains a number of complete texts of popular copy-books—the *Jitsugo-kyō*, the *Dōji-kyō* and the *Shōbai ōrai* among others. It has much else besides. There is first a picture of a shrine to Tenjin-sama, the God of Calligraphers, with details of his earthly life as Sugawara Michizane. Then comes an explanation of the five relations and the appropriate five virtues illustrated in turn (filial piety, for instance, by a picture of a happy family with a child climbing over its father and the mother leaning forward in an attitude of delighted interest). 'The Four Orders' is a set of pictures of the samurai, the farmer, the craftsman and the merchant with a short description of the function of each in society (the samurai's, rather interestingly and shrewdly, is to preserve a proper balance between the conflicting claims of his daimyo on his loyalty and of the peasants on his benevolence). A literature section contains descriptions of Chinese poems and Japanese *waka*, *renga* and *haiku* (e.g. '*Waka* have existed since the Age of the Gods. They consist in saying in thirty-one syllables your thoughts on anything seen or heard. It is thanks to the *waka* that the noble traditions of our country have been handed down. You should study the details of spelling and the use of particles from a teacher.') Similar short pieces follow on the origin of the tea ceremony, incense smelling, the Nō drama and flower arrangement. A section is devoted to illustrations of samurai armour and weapons with all the parts named, then of the equipment used for Nō dancing, of the brushes and ink stones used for calligraphy, and of the three Shinto treasures. For no particular reason there are two pictures of a scholar giving a lecture and of men poling a raft down a stream. Then comes a list of the provinces of Japan followed by a picture of a hairy Ainu. There is a small collection of a dozen popular songs (*kouta*); a few hints on etiquette (when carrying a tray hold it with your left thumb over the edge of the tray and your right hand resting against the other side and walk with your eyes fixed on the ground about three feet ahead of the tray); a list of auspicious phrases and proverbs which can be used for a ceremonial 'first writing'; samples of how to draw up a list of ceremonial presents, and diagrams showing how to wrap and label the presents themselves for such occasions as a marriage, an adoption or an engagement; a list of the common elements of Chinese characters with their conventional names and illustrations of the way they appear in various styles of calligraphy; a list of practical charms for such things as snake bites (turn over the nearest stone) hiccups (write the character for 'persimmon' on the palm of your hand and lick it), dust in the eye (lick your left cheek for the right eye and vice versa) and stopping a member of the family from grinding his teeth (go to a shrine that has a stable attached, pick up a bean from the stable floor, grind it and put it secretly in his food). Then come various forms of the syllabary, examples of *kakihan* personal seals; a guide to the major constellations of stars; the multiplication table with rules for division and for estimating the number of bales that can be piled pyramid-fashion given the number in the bottom row; a list of characters used in personal names indicating with which of the five elements each has affinity (the combination of husband's and wife's element being important in arranging a match); a picture of the proper ceremonial form for drinking *sake* to seal a bond of retainership or discipleship; a list of Chinese and Japanese variants for the names of the months; instructions on how to make useful redink annotations for reading off a Chinese text (see p. 137) and on how to tell the time by the way the Great Bear is lying (rather confused, this); sample forms of the written declarations to be made by the original and the adoptive father in cases of adoption; a list of the lucky and unlucky days for disposing of after-births; a chart which purports to forecast the day of one's death from the date of one's birth; a general astrological chart; pictures of the twelve signs of the zodiac and the ten celestial stations; and finally a list of the fourteen sects of Buddhism.

Other similar works range less widely but contain more information. The much earlier *Otoko chōhōki*,[1] for instance, includes in its section on Nō detailed instructions on breathing, on preventing hoarseness, distinguishing between the times when the drummer and the times when the singer should set the pace and so on. It also has a highly ingenious, but highly inaccurate, set of rules for guessing the contemporary Chinese pronunciation of characters from the Japanese reading. Others contain such items as a table showing the relation of the tides to the phases of the moon,[2] and how to tell the time by looking at a cat's eyes or observing your breath (it goes up the right nostril at the even hours and up the left at the odd).[3] One includes such esoteric elements of calligrapher's lore as the various appropriate ways to rub ink on an ink stone (slantwise in front of a superior, circularly clockwise in normal circumstances, but circularly anti-clockwise when sitting in front of a criminal).[4] It is doubtful if many Tokugawa children were destined to have frequent occasion to make ink while sitting in front of criminals, but it was doubtless the kind of titbit of information which delighted a childish heart.

These compendia were designed primarily for boys, but there were also some for girls and women, notably the *Onna chōhōki* which went through several editions in the Tokugawa period.[5] It contains a somewhat higher proportion of moral instruction, but then it was the general opinion that women needed more. They probably did, if not for the generally adduced reason— that women were essentially baser creatures—at least because their ideal role in Tokugawa society was more restrictively

---

[1] Kusata Sankeishi (??), *Otoko chōhōki*, 1693.

[2] In Anon., *Terako setsuyō-shū*, and Kimura Akinori, *Shin dōji tenarai kagami*.

[3] Kimura, *op. cit.*

[4] Anon., *Teikin ōrai e-shōkai*.

[5] Anon. (*Shimpan zōho*) *Onna chōhōki*. The earlier editions in the British Museum bear no date, but the 1693 preface to the *Otoko chōhōki* speaks of this companion volume for women as already selling well, so it presumably dates from about this time. Takai Ranzan who did a later edition in 1829 speaks in his preface of the original as having been published 'sixty or seventy years ago', but the name-period system does not encourage an accurate time-sense. (See *E-iri nichiyō onna chōhōki*, reprint 1847).

defined. The author of the *Onna chōhōki*, who was probably a woman,[1] asserts, however, that women were not always such despicable creatures. Amaterasu, the founder of the Japanese race, was a woman, and in olden times women were innocent and pure. But the Golden Age never lasts and all societies decline. She shudders to think of what the women in contemporary China and India must be like if even in antiquity they were as wicked as they are portrayed in the Confucian and Buddhist classics. The same cycle of decline is to be observed, she notes, in individual women who are often obedient and gentle and straightforward creatures before marriage but become spiteful harridans afterwards. Women must do what they can, by taking thought, to counteract such natural tendencies and an exhaustive list of the things to avoid is given.

A good deal of the practical advice is medical—how to detect the symptoms of tuberculosis, how to diagnose a pregnancy, foods to avoid during pregnancy (crabs, or the child will come out sideways, etc.), lucky directions in which a pregnant woman should contrive to face on various days of the zodiac, charms to secure an easy delivery, herbs to improve the flow of milk, hints on the care of infants, remedies for warts and bed-wetting and other kinds of Spockery. There is also an explanation of the commonly observed fact that daimyo families were often childless while the lower classes multiplied like rabbits. Daimyo society is the Heaven of this world and daimyos are the this-worldly Buddhas. The world having declined to its present state, current deaths do not provide enough soul-seed of sufficiently Buddha-like quality to supply all daimyo families, while there is an abundance of the inferior sort fit to be reincarnated in the lower classes. While perhaps a less plausible explanation than the alternative theory that too many daimyos had syphilis, it has its poetic merits and the author uses it to draw the moral that women should pray to the Gods and Buddhas with special urgency during pregnancy.

There are also a good many hints on etiquette and personal deportment, and on the correct forms for various ceremonies, especially weddings. Cosmetic advice includes tips on how to clean and set the hair without washing it, the various types of coiffure, the application of powder and tooth-blacking, and so

---

[1] The preface ends with the feminine salutation, *kashiko*.

on. (A woman should always wear powder; otherwise she will not be able to leave it off when she goes into mourning.) There is a certain amount about clothes and furniture (mostly lists of names for copy-book use) with the odd hint on, say, the removal of stains. As the inexplicable Japanese disregard of the pleasures of the palate would lead one to expect, there is nothing about food except how to arrange it for weddings.

The acquisition of feminine 'parts' is adequately covered, however, with sections on writing poetry, musical instruments, and indoor games with incense and poem cards. Women should, of course, in all things cultivate a proper femininity; there are lists of women's words with the male equivalents which should not be used; snakes and ladders is permitted for women, *go* is mannish; women should never imitate masculine styles of hand-writing. The Kyoto prostitutes can provide an excellent model, but a model, be it noted, only of calligraphic style; the language of their letters is often unbecomingly flamboyant. (Similarly, it is not necessary for ordinary women to learn to play the samisen, the favourite instrument of these women, though in order not to be thought too much of a prude the author gives, in passing, the names of the parts of the samisen complete with diagrams.) Once or twice the means-to-an-end aspect of these accomplishments is mentioned—they add to a woman's power to attract and influence men. More often they are presented as essential to feminine self-respect. There is hardly a suggestion that they provide any enjoyment in themselves.

Certainly the early eighteenth-century editions of these compendia were written for the more wealthy only of the townsman class. By the nineteenth century they probably reached a wider audience, but they were still expensive, and probably not many children owned them. Their contents, however, with their mixture of half-believed superstitions, calendrical lore, empirical medicine, folk traditions and hints on etiquette and airs and graces, are probably a good sample of the type of information teachers passed on orally to their children, along with the basic skills of reading, writing and arithmetic—and, of course, a goodly share of moral advice.

Chapter X

THE LEGACY

ONE THING SHOULD BY NOW BE CLEAR. If the
Tokugawa period was a time of stagnation in many social and
technical fields and of cyclical fluctuation in its repeated phases
of administrative reform and decline, in the field of education at
least there were steady and consistent trends—a trend of growth
in the sheer amount of schooling provided and, though much
more hesitantly and painfully, an evolution in its content and
purposes. Did these developments in any sense condition the
changes which took place in Japan in the last quarter of the
nineteenth century? Are they germane to an explanation of
why Japan, alone among Asian countries, was able to keep her
independence and carry through the process of politically
directed change which has made her a highly industrialized
nation?

Literacy and Its Advantages

However approximate our calculations of the diffusion of
popular education must necessarily be, there can be no doubt
that the literacy rate in Japan in 1870 was considerably higher
than in most of the underdeveloped countries today. It probably compared favourably even then with some contemporary
European countries. As late as 1837 a British Select Committee
found that in the major industrial towns only one child in four
or five was ever getting to school,[1] and it may have been more
than a desire to jolt his fellow-countrymen which prompted a
Frenchman to write in 1877 that 'primary education in Japan
has reached a level which should make us blush'.[2]

---

[1] B. Simon, *Studies in the History of Education*, p. 170.
[2] G. Bousquet, *Le Japon de nos jours*, 1, p. 337.

But what does widespread literacy do for a developing country? At the very least it constitutes a training in being trained. The man who has in childhood submitted to some process of disciplined and conscious learning is more likely to respond to further training, be it in a conscript army, in a factory, or at lectures arranged by his village agricultural association. And such training can be more precise and efficient, and more nationally standardized, if the written word can be used to supplement the spoken.

Secondly, the wide diffusion of basic education—and education which was not forced on an unwilling populace but supported by parents' voluntary choice and sacrifice—argues that Japan had already got over the first hurdle in a process of purposeful development, the diffusion of a simple notion of the possibility of 'improvement'. It was no longer the kind of 'traditional society', where things are as they are and the individual does not see himself as offered the choice between doing or not doing anything to alter his society or his position in it. By taking thought one could add an inch to one's child's stature, not only enhance his prestige and his self-respect, but also improve his life-chances in a material sense. It is this latter feature which marks the difference in significance between the high literacy rate in Japan in 1870 and the high literacy rate in Burma in, say, 1930, for popular education in Japan was secular and it was practical. To be sure, it contained a good many elements of traditional formalism, but it nevertheless provided —and this was the main reason why parents were willing to buy it for their children—the kind of knowledge which made men better able to fulfil their economic functions in society. For a few, 'self-improvement' meant moving out of one's hereditary position, perhaps 'getting a reading and writing job'; for most it meant being a more efficient carpenter, a more respected or a more affluent merchant, than one otherwise would have been. The important thing is that the desire for self-improvement was already awakened, so that when the Meiji period offered new knowledge to be acquired and new levels of self-improvement to be reached, there was no want of candidates for such endeavours. And where the notion of individual self-improvement was widely diffused, the notion of *national* improvement could be more readily understood and accepted.

Note, too, that for some among the commoners, self-improvement did mean 'bettering oneself', in the sense of moving out of one's parental occupation to a higher point in the social scale. The growth of schools helped to stimulate such aspirations since they offered a chance of realizing them (the principle that the presence of a bottle on the shelf helps to stimulate a thirst). Education was one of the major means of social ascent in Tokugawa society. Some rich men were able to buy their way into the samurai class, by direct purchase or by making themselves indispensable to a daimyo's financial solvency. But equally a good many poor men were able to get themselves a surname and two swords in a daimyo's service simply by virtue of their mastery of some kind of gakumon—of Chinese, or of Western, learning. This had two consequences. The fact that mobility aspirations were already at a high level meant that when political and technological change created new opportunities in a more fluid Meiji society they were eagerly taken up. It was easier to create a go-getting competitive society because enough people were already psychologically prepared to offer themselves as competitors. Secondly, education continued to be an important mechanism of social ascent. It was by acquiring new knowledge and new skills—not just by entrepreneurial boldness or a keen eye to the main chance—that one moved ahead in Meiji Japan. Education seems to have become the major mechanism of social selection at an earlier stage of industrialization in Japan than in Western countries. Learning was the royal road not only to the professions and to government, but also to business success as well—as the very high proportion of university graduates among Japanese business-men suggests.[1] Undoubtedly one explanation of this fact is that Japan was a late developer, catching up by learning, and hence having more practical use for already systematized knowledge.[2] But the Tokugawa tradition of climbing by one's brush, by the glib solemnity of one's interpretation of the Four Books, or by one's enthusiastic claim to understand a Dutch treatise on saltpetre, was surely also a factor.

The wide diffusion of a basic literacy also meant that Japan had a better chance, when the process of industrialization and

[1] J. Abegglen and H. Mannari, 'Leaders of Modern Japan'.
[2] See Smith, 'Landlords' sons in the business elite'.

political change began, of putting the nation's best intellectual resources to good use. Fewer potential Noguchis or Hoshi Tōrus remained mute and inglorious than would have been the case if a large proportion of the population had not had the chance early in life to get over the first hurdle towards mental training and demonstrate to themselves—and to teachers who might provide access to helpful patronage—such talents as they might have.

Finally, there are the political implications of literacy. Already, in the Tokugawa period, the public notice board was an accepted means of communication between the rulers and the people. Administration by written directive could, in the Japan of 1870, reach down to the lowest level. It may well be, too, that the teachers of the existing popular schools helped to provide channels of communication; they were already there in the village and country towns to act as the carriers of new ideas and of a new national consciousness to the people. The implementation of new decrees, the new land registration system and the new civil registration system, were only possible because basic literacy was sufficiently widespread. The chances of rumour growing wildly out of fearful suspicion and leading to obstruction and revolt were much reduced when a majority even of the peasants could actually read the documents they were required to set their seals to. The early Meiji uprisings could have been much more serious than they were.

In sum, it was important that the Japanese populace was not just a sack of potatoes. The creation of modern Japan was not simply a matter of top-level changes. It was also a cumulation of a mass of small initiatives by large numbers of people who could appreciate new possibilities, make new choices, or at the very least allow themselves to be persuaded to do for the first time something they had never done before. The new educational system which the Restoration Government exerted itself to establish in the 1870s was, of course, much more effective in all these ways than the mixture of mechanical repetition and gentle moralizing purveyed by the terakoya teachers, but this is not to underestimate the legacy of the terakoya system. It ensured that the generation which had passed childhood in 1870 did not have to be written off as hopeless. And without the traditions, the teachers, the buildings and the established attitudes of the Tokugawa period the development of the new system could never have been accomplished as fast as it was—and almost without central government subsidy.[1]

The Nation

One should be careful not to overstate the case. Not every Japanese in 1870 was simmering with intellectual curiosity and social ambition. There were regions where the mass of the people lived lives of boorish drudgery enlivened only by occasional festival fun. In 1880 an official of the Ministry of Education could still urge that it was too soon to allow straight election of education committees because 'there are districts where the people still do not appreciate the advantages of education; where they will be only too willing to spend a thousand pieces of gold on a dramatic troupe or a festival, but begrudge ten for a school; where they will lay out the red carpet for actors and wrestlers but show little respect for a teacher'.[2] It was, indeed, in the field of popular education—in estimates of school attendance, especially by girls—that the clearest evidence of regional disparities has been given in this book. In education, as in general economic development, south-eastern, central and western-central Japan led the way, while the north-east and large parts of Kyūshū lagged behind. Though the pattern was by no means identical, and statistical indicators are not available, it is nevertheless clear that there were also wide differences in samurai education between the progressive and the stagnant fiefs.

This raises another interesting problem. The Meiji Restoration transformed Japan from a collection of separatist fiefs at varying levels of development, each with its own traditions

---

[1] After the first fine flourish of the 1872 programme with its bold intentions of creating over 54,000 new primary schools *de novo*, the central government was finally forced to accommodate itself to the cloth from which its coat had to be cut. The revised ordinances of 1879 and 1880 permitted private schools (i.e. the existing terakoya) to function as substitutes for public schools if certified as efficient, and in the Ministry's explanation to the Senate of the 1880 order it is admitted that even in the public schools nine-tenths of the teachers had received no training from the new training colleges, and that most of them were 'priests, monks (*shūgen*) or teachers of calligraphy'—i.e. former terakoya teachers (Mombushō, *Kaisei kyōikurei seitei riyū*, pp. 399, 307).

[2] *Ibid.*, p. 401.

and each jealous of its feudal autonomy, into a centralized nation-state. How far had educational developments prepared the way for this change?

They were obviously not the only factor, for people travelled on pilgrimages and on business, but they must have contributed a great deal. Even in the popular schools there was enough in the content of education to give children a sense that they were not just townsmen of the Shogun's capital or peasants of the lord of Okayama, but also members of the Japanese nation. They learned the names of places and products in distant parts of the country; even the *Teikin ōrai* may have had a 'nationalizing' effect, suggesting the contingent arbitrariness of contemporary regional and social divisions by giving children a glimpse of a period when frontiers between fiefs ran very differently, when their ancestors were not so rigidly differentiated into commoners and samurai, and when the Emperor counted for somewhat more than he did in their day. Literacy that is used is almost bound to improve the capacity for 'empathy', a precondition of that fellow-feeling which makes compatriots of people who are never likely to meet. Citizens of Edo could read novels written in Osaka; they might even occasionally receive letters from distant cousins in far-off rural areas.

The Confucian education of the samurai was even more effective in making a nation out of a collection of fiefs. Firstly, it formed a very large part of the intellectual culture which was shared by the members of all fiefs, a bond of common interests, common assumptions and common proverbial aphorisms which was much stronger, because of much more substantial content, than a shared interest in the tea ceremony and fencing, or a shared acceptance of the vague and diverse tenets of contemporary Buddhism could alone have provided. Secondly, in most fiefs the samurai's education had come by the end of the period to include, as a matter of course, some study of Japan's own history. However this was taught it would be bound in some measure to enhance the student's sense of his own Japaneseness, and in some fiefs, of course, it was taught in an intensely nationalistic spirit; Mito, for instance, producing precisely that combination of the Confucian ethic and Shinto-supported racism which was to form the explicit ideology of official Japanese nationalism until 1945. Thirdly, the growth of Confucian scholarship and the teaching profession provided new national channels of communication which ignored fief boundaries. The professional scholars and the intellectually active amateurs read one another's books, exchanged letters, edited one another's poems. They knew one another as individual persons. Hirose Tansō, who never travelled more than fifty miles from his home in Kyūshū, could still write gossip about contemporary scholars he had never met and write it as of colleagues.[1] There is little doubt that he had a sense of membership in a national community of scholars which was stronger than any regional loyalty. In point of fact the stay-at-home Hirose was an exception. Confucian scholars could change their fief of employment with relative ease, and even if they did not, they frequently travelled the length and breadth of the country relying in part on the right a common bond of scholarship gave them to expect the hospitality of their colleagues.[2]

The development of a national consciousness had to overcome not only regional divisiveness but also the barriers of class. Perhaps the single most important factor which transformed Japan in the space of half a century from a society of hereditary 'estates' with clearly institutionalized boundaries to a society in which few people knew or cared to what estate his neighbours' ancestors had belonged, was the decision embodied in the decree of 1872 to establish a universal compulsory system of elementary education for all. How was it that the new and still almost exclusively samurai government could so easily abandon the earliest Meiji plans, which assumed as a matter of course the continuation of a dual system of high schools for the samurai and literacy schools for commoners, and decree instead the creation of a unified and universal school system for samurai and commoner alike?

Nowadays it is axiomatic that a literate populace, with some knowledge of geography and history as well as the three R's, is an essential ingredient of a modern civilized state, but in the 1870s this was not so. In Russia, an intellectual concerned with the conditions of economic progress could still say, in the 1890s,

---

[1] *Jurin-hyō* (*Zenshū*, 2).

[2] Hirose Tansō forbade his students to travel on the expectation of hospitality in other students' homes. It had reached the point that many parents were reluctant to allow their children to take up scholarship seriously for fear of the stream of unwelcome visitors it might lead to (*Kangien kiyaku kokuyu*, p. 9).

that 'a good farm and a good factory constitute the best and the only possible school for the people'.[1] Indeed, the utilitarian arguments for a universal education system embodied in the 1872 decree had only in 1870 achieved victory in England after a long struggle against the fears of 'nearly the whole body of those who are rich [who] dread the consequences of teaching the people more than they dread the effects of their ignorance'[2]— and then only after the growing organization of the working class had won its partial right to the suffrage.

How was it that ideas which had only painfully fought their way to respectability in England in the teeth of class interest and class antagonism aroused no such opposition in Japan? Surely the social cleavage between the samurai and the rest was no less than the gulf which divided the English working class from its betters. To be sure, the distinctions were crumbling; there were mobile men; commoners were being recruited into military formations and tentatively admitted to fief schools even before the period ended, and egalitarianism was strong enough after the Restoration for the principle of equality before the law to be established in most respects. But not in all; and socially the distinctions remained strong. The very growth of education which led to the egalitarian stress on achievement at the same time widened the cultural gap between the samurai who usually had the opportunity to receive that education and the commoners who had not. The cartoons of the Meiji period which show the humble commoner forehead-to-ground before arrogant samurai officials argue that there was a social distance between the classes far greater than even England could match.

Part of the answer lies in the difference of class structure. Social distance between the classes is one thing; class antagonism is another. Japan may have been as much 'two nations' as was England, but in England the two nations were at war. Peterloo, the trade unions, the Chartist movement, represented a growing threat to the traditional ruling class and to the new middle class. The samurai, in a pre-industrial Japan, faced no such threat; peasant revolts were the sporadic tantrums of

[1] Alexander Gerschenkron, 'Economic development in Russian intellectual history', p. 30. (Quoting D. I. Pisarev.)

[2] Francis Place, writing in 1830. Quoted in B. Simon, *Studies in the History of Education*, p. 169.

irresponsible children, not symptoms of a growing, systematic disaffection. The lower orders in Japan still knew and accepted their place. There was nothing in the situation which prompted the Restoration leaders to think of a universal education system primarily in terms of its effect on the distribution of political power within the country.

The educational history of the Tokugawa period was in part responsible for this state of affairs. Schools tended always and everywhere to encourage submissive acceptance of the existing order (whereas in England it was often the working-men's study groups and improvement societies which were the centres of disaffection). The only partially educational movement which ever showed the smallest germ of class sentiment—the Shingaku movement with its early appeal to the merchant's battered sense of self-respect—was soon transformed by feudal patronage into yet one more means of social control—encouraging the common man to derive his self-respect from the respect his superiors would show him were he only a loyal and obedient subordinate. It was a circular process. Because, in the Confucian definition, the purposes of education were primarily moral, and because the morality taught concerned chiefly the correct observance of social relations in a hierarchically ordered society, there were small grounds for discouraging the populace from acquiring it. And because popular education proceeded with official approval, and occasionally even encouragement, it was less likely to deviate into subversive ways. The ideological unity of the samurai class was important, too. Education began to seep down into the lower classes of England at a time when the literate middle and upper classes were already ideologically divided, when there were middle-class radicals, free-thinkers and jacobins whose notion of a proper training for the poor did not begin and end with the Catechism and selected portions of the Bible. In Japan popular education began at a time when the ruling class was still intellectually united by a monolithic orthodoxy which held no dangers to the social system and whose diffusion to the people was no threat, but even an advantage.

Given this background there was no reason to suppose in 1872 that universal education would create subversive disaffection. It might rather have been expected to promote loyal obedience.

And so, in effect, it did, thanks largely to the ethics courses, in conception and content the element of most direct continuity between the Tokugawa and the modern educational systems. Universal education certainly created the labour movement and the tenants' movement in the 1920s. But the efficacy of the ethics course and related features of primary education was such that these beginnings of class antagonism were easily swamped in a flood-tide of national loyalty in the 'thirties.

It was not, however, until the late 1880s and in particular after the Imperial Rescript on Education of 1890 that this use of popular education to create a loyal and obedient citizenry became a predominant motive in educational policy. The men who drafted the 1872 ordinance and its revisions in 1879 and 1880 seem to have had other ends chiefly in view—as indeed had their forerunners, those few men who were already arguing for universal compulsory education in the preceding two or three decades.

In the first place they were concerned to mobilize all available talent in the pursuit of national goals. This was a reflection of their overriding nationalism of which we have already spoken.

Secondly, they did have a paternal sense of responsibility towards the mass of the people. In part, doubtless, this too was a consequence as much as a precondition of their nationalism. (The impact of the national danger coming from the Western powers and of the sense of national separateness arising from sudden contacts with Westerners after centuries of seclusion undoubtedly enhanced the samurai's awareness of the common Japaneseness which he shared with the meanest farmer.) But there is more to it than that. For all that the common and popular forms of the Confucian ethic current in Tokugawa Japan did lay almost exclusive stress on the duties of subordinates to superiors, for those who read more widely in the classics, for those, even, who pondered on the *Analects*, there was plenty to remind them of the superior's duty of benevolence to his subordinates. The samurai had come a long way since the bloody suppression of the Shimabara rebellion in 1638. In 'pacifying' the samurai class Confucian education also modified its arrogance and contemptuous lack of concern for the welfare of the lower classes, and did do something to breed a sense of paternal responsibility. Smith has well described the 'deep sense of the public interest' which to the conscientious samurai was an essential part of 'merit' in public officials:

> This was the cultivated sense which alone disciplined the natural self and 'interest' (*ri*), usually thought of as self-interest. It was, for example, what prompted an official to speak out to his superiors fearlessly, yet moderately and tactfully, without an edge of self-regard; to recognize, without envy, ability in others; to listen to unpleasant advice from subordinates without flush of pique or prejudice. In short, it was the ability to think always of the welfare of the people and the state.[1]

Certainly these qualities were not bred in every samurai. What one reads about extortionate tax levies, about peasant revolts and about examples of cruel arbitrariness in the administration of criminal justice is undoubtedly true. One hears less of the local samurai officials who organized famine relief and flood relief measures, of Oshio, the retired Osaka official whose indignation at popular suffering led him into armed revolt against his superiors, of the Bakufu mission to vaccinate the Ainu or of the Kōchi public health service. It was the commoner author of a child's text-book who defined the function of the samurai as being to balance his loyalty to his lord (who requires him to squeeze out the last ounce in taxation) against the claims of the common people on his benevolence[2]—and he was not repeating standard phrases, it seems, but speaking from his observations of the lesser officials with whom he came into contact. Benevolence may still have been a fairly scarce commodity among the samurai, but there would have been much less of it, less chance of a national education system in 1872 and less chance of creating a viable national community, without the development of Confucian education among the samurai in the Tokugawa period.

The Samurai's Intellectual Equipment

How far had the samurai been intellectually prepared by the Tokugawa schools for a useful role as a member of an innovating *élite* in a Japan bent on 'catching up'? He, too, of course, had

---

[1] ' "Merit" in Tokugawa bureaucracy.'
[2] See p. 286.

been thoroughly imbued with the idea that knowledge and education was a 'good thing', and hence was well disposed in principle to the idea of acquiring new kinds of it. He, too, had had in ample measure a training in being trained. The extraordinary thing is that curiosity and the eagerness to learn also survived the education the samurai were given, for it would be difficult to think of a form of education better calculated to kill curiosity than the early stages of Chinese study. Perhaps the truth is that it was only in a fairly small percentage of the most active minds that it did survive. They were able to get through the dulling initial stages quickly enough to be still alert and eager when the later, more potentially stimulating, stages of Chinese study were reached, and they survived to become the indefatigable note-takers on foreign missions, the students who pumped the Clarks and the Janes and the other hired foreign teachers dry of every piece of information they had to give, the government officials and technicians who embarked late in life on the study of foreign languages or sought the instruction of foreign advisers.

And for the other three-quarters, or perhaps nine-tenths, of the samurai class, the traditional education may have prepared them for a useful role in another way. The authoritarian teacher-pupil relations of the fief schools required humility on the part of the pupil. Knowledge was imparted by the teacher to be accepted, not to be improved upon. And this attitude, given the initial decision to learn from the West, produced a humble attentiveness and an assiduous thoroughness. Every detail went down into the notebook; every utterance of the foreign teacher was accorded solemn respect. Had the Tokugawa schools been mainly concerned to 'teach people to think', had they encouraged the free play of ideas between teacher and pupil on a footing of near equality, there might have been many more steamships ruined by men who thought they could run them by the light of pure reason before they learned how to keep their boilers full of water.

There is another aspect of the efficacy of a Confucian education which is also more or less independent of the values or knowledge consciously imparted. It 'trained the mind'. In the words of Tōhata Seiichi, discussing how it was that the samurai were successful industrial pioneers, their education had given them a high 'general intellectual level ... not simply the ability to understand a single concrete body of knowledge, but an ability which could be applied to the understanding of other bodies of knowledge without falling to a lower level'.[1] It is a difficult concept to express in these latter days of cultural relativism, when societies may be decently rated in terms of *per capita* income or rates of economic growth but never, in the manner of our Victorian ancestors, by their 'level of civilization'. Nevertheless, there are real differences of intellectual sophistication for which one might suggest a variety of criteria. One might be the degree of secularization of the intellectual culture; the extent to which the world is seen to be at the mercy of arbitrary supernatural forces, or alternatively governed by regular ascertainable laws. Quite obviously Confucian education had carried the best samurai minds a long way from the superstitions of popular Buddhism and popular Shinto. They might speak of a moral law of just retribution, externally administered by a supernatural agency, but it was often more in a symbolic than in a literal sense that they did so. Even for the terakoya teacher whose precepts are translated in the appendix, the Punishment of Heaven really amounted to the operation of social sanctions.

Another criterion of 'intellectual sophistication' might be the richness of the vocabulary available for the discriminating expression of abstract ideas. The new chemists of Meiji had to develop a whole set of new words to express new ways of classifying matter, but the students of politics, law or philosophy found that most of the conceptual distinctions found in their European models were already familiar and could be easily expressed in their own vocabulary. The need of the translators to coin a new word for a 'right' is well known. Perhaps the important thing is that so few such neologisms were needed and that the indigenous vocabulary which could be mobilized for the new translations was not the esoteric language of a small intellectual coterie, but the common property of a relatively large section of the nation.[2] The particular character of the Chinese script

[1] Arisawa *et al.*, *Keizai shutaisei kōza*, 3, p. 17.

[2] If one takes, as an example, a random page from an official memorandum justifying the imposition of compulsory education by arguments clearly derived from Western sources, a few of the new words stand out: 'the *rights* of minors', 'the

is also relevant. New words could be easily created in forms which left their etymological components clearly apparent and often made further explanation unnecessary. The reader of Mill in translation might conceivably read and take the sense of the word '*kenri*' without realizing that this was a 'new' word to translate the foreign concept of 'right'.[1]

The sophistication of the political vocabulary which the samurai acquired in Tokugawa schools was perhaps the most important of all. The development of Japan's commercial vocabulary in 1870 reflected simply the contemporary development of Japan's commercial institutions. But the political vocabulary which the samurai had at his disposal enabled him not merely to understand and describe the workings of his own society, but also to conceive of alternative forms of organization. Thanks to their readings in Japanese and Chinese history and legal codes, the samurai had had some training in comparing and contrasting different principles of political organization. This may not have been a particularly refined or subtle knowledge, but, for instance, the mere fact that the contrast between a 'feudal system' and a 'system of centralized government' was part of the stock-in-trade of the better-educated samurai mind in 1870[2] may explain a lot about the rapidity of political change in early Meiji.

---

[1] When Fukuzawa translated *Chambers' Political Economy* in 1866 a Bakufu official objected strongly to its praise of *kyōsō*—the word Fukuzawa had invented to translate 'competition'. He had no difficulty in understanding the meaning of the word, only in accepting the notion that anything involving 'conflict' (the basic meaning of one of the characters used) could be considered praiseworthy (Carmen Blacker, *Fukuzawa Yukichi*, p. 28). Another linguistic feature helped in the popular diffusion of new words as well as of erudite old ones. In popular decrees it was common to write beside difficult words written in Chinese characters an approximate synonym from common speech written in the phonetic script. It is as if in, say, 'anyone creating a disturbance', the word 'disturbance' had the gloss 'noise' written beside it.

[2] The distinction is found even in Yamamoto's mediocre little compendium of Chinese grammar, written not for samurai but for commoners. In a series of short general-knowledge sections at the end, the main point made under the heading of history is that there were two systems of government, *hōken-seido* and *gunken-seido*, and that China started with the first and went on to the second, while Japan reversed the process (Yamamoto Shōitsu, *Dōjitsū*).

---

government, i.e. the *collective force of society*', in the '*eye of the law*'. But these are a small proportion of the indigenous abstract vocabulary: 'to state a reason', 'fixed interpretation', 'impose a responsibility', 'evasion', 'essential criterion', 'minimum period', etc. (Mombushō, *Kaisei kyōikurei seitei riyū*, pp. 402—3).

The Samurai's Political Attitudes

We have seen how, from the end of the eighteenth century onwards, there is increasing emphasis on the function of the
schools to train efficient and honest administrators. Government needed knowledge. Likewise, the purpose of knowledge
was government. The Confucian schools generally rejected any
attempt to teach useful facts or skills for administrators—this
was a field left to be preempted by Western learning. Rather,
'useful' education for men of talent in the departments of
Chinese learning was primarily concerned with ends rather than
with means, with the study of history as a road to knowledge of
guiding precedents in government, concerned, in other words,
with politics.

This overriding preoccupation with politics was perhaps
fortified by the samurai's training in swordsmanship which
brought him face to face with the elemental power situation in
which the strong and skilful holds, but must exercise with discretion, the power of life and death over the weak and inept.
It was certainly strengthened by the decentralized feudal
system of administration. In the bureaucracies of the fiefs very
large numbers of men held, or could reasonably seek to hold,
positions which offered scope for political initiative—a scope
which was progressively widened in the fluid Bakumatsu
period as traditional restraints gave way and routine administrative responses became inadequate to cope with new situations.

In this sense, it has been suggested, the feudal system provided
an admirable training ground for political and administrative
talent which stood the Meiji regime in good stead.[1] The fief
bureaucracies were, to pervert de Tocqueville's phrase, 'the
grade schools of oligarchy'. One might add that they were the
grade schools of opposition and revolt as well. The rebellions
of the first decade, the Popular Rights Movement, the early
development of party politics, the popular nationalism of the
early twentieth century, the plots and assassinations of the
terrorist *shishi* tradition right up to the present day, spring from
much the same roots. Japan did not have to wait for the development of a middle-class chafing under governmental restriction

[1] Matsuda Michio, 'Nihon no chishikijin', p. 13.

of its economic activity before a large section of the nation began to hold political opinions and seek to express them in action. The samurai, thanks in large part to the high political content of nineteenth-century Confucian education, began the period of industrialization with their political consciousness well developed. Yamaji Aizan was not untypical when he declared:

> Politics is my mistress. I love politics, I adore politics, I live and breathe politics. My fate is bound up with the fate of the Japanese nation. 'The governance of the state, the bringing of peace to the world' has been my study since youth.[1]

The phrase he quoted is taken from the *Greater Learning*.

A slightly closer look at the nature of these political pre-occupations is necessary to explain why, among the opposition movements of post-Restoration Japan, one should see the Popular Rights movement and the young officers' *coup d'état* as especially rooted in this Tokugawa tradition, but not, say, the activities of the Seiyukai or the suffrage movement. Excluding for the moment motives of personal pecuniary gain, a passionate concern with national politics might partake (the division is a rough and ready one) in varying proportions of three elements: (*a*) a desire to further the interests of sectional groups within the nation, (*b*) a predilection for political activity as a vocation, the activity in itself, and the exercise of power if that activity is successful, providing intrinsic satisfaction, and (*c*) a desire to promote policies which are conceived to be necessary for the welfare of the nation as a whole.

As for the first of these, there can be no doubt that a good many samurai worked to promote the interests of their own fief, to preserve the privileges of the samurai as a class, to further the sectional interests of business-men or of officials when they became such. But this, in the Confucian scheme of things, was so little a respectable motive for action that they rarely did so openly and avowedly. And those who were most obviously activated by sectional interests rarely achieved positions of much power or prestige.

Nor, to be sure, did the second motive find explicit sanction

---

[1] Quoted (from *Aru hito ni kotooru sho*) in Uchida and Shioda, 'Chishiki seinen no shoruikei', p. 249.

in Confucian teachings. The exercise of political leadership was not, for the samurai, supposed to be an acknowledged source of personal gratification, but a fulfilment of duty. So much for the explicit moral teachings; but the effect of studying history on youthful members of a military class could only too easily produce a different orientation. In large measure the history they read was the history of military adventure in which government and warfare, the responsibilities of power and the glories of military victory, were inextricably intertwined. Government might be a duty in the Tokugawa Confucian ethic, but military adventure, in the less codified samurai tradition nurtured by family legends of the exploits of sixteenth-century ancestors and by Rai Sanyō's descriptions of the heroes of Japanese history, was exciting and pleasurable. Jansen has described the zestful enjoyment with which Sakamoto Ryōma pursued his youthful career as a political activist in the last years of the Tokugawa period,[1] and it was still in a spirit of military adventure that the heirs of the post-Perry *shishi* approached politics in the 1880s—and in 1936. Tokutomi Sohō complained in 1886 that too many of his friends in the Popular Rights movement looked 'on politics as a kind of sport, a form of amusement like letting off fireworks', and their bombastic rhetoric was always shooting off into flights of fantasy in which they pictured themselves riding bravely along the banks of the Yalu, banners streaming in the wind. Better for Japanese youth, he said sadly, if they had chosen as their heroes Adam Smith and John Watt instead of Napoleon and Bismarck, the idols of his day.[2] One might well argue that it is because a passionate concern with politics was in its origins allied in this way with the spirit of military adventure that the pattern of private enterprise violence has persisted in Japanese politics to a more advanced level of industrial and constitutional development than in most other countries.

It was above all the third kind of passionate concern with politics, the desire to promote policies considered to be necessary for the nation as a whole, which was most specifically nurtured by the education samurai received. In the Confucian tradition politics was not the art of the possible, the choice of lesser evils,

[1] M. B. Jansen, *Sakamoto Ryōma and the Meiji Restoration*, esp. pp. 153, 156, 171.
[2] *Shōrai no Nihon*, pp. 204, 95.

the achievement of the best compromise between conflicting interests. A good policy was one which would benefit *everyone*. It was the political philosophy of an uncomplex society in which the chief potential conflict of interest lay between the producing ruled and the consuming rulers. Enlightened government consisted in the kind of benevolence which would enable the ruled to produce more in contentment to the benefit of all. When sectional conflict did rear its head among the ruled, as between peasant and merchant, it was resolved by a simple scale of priorities; the peasantry was of the greater importance to the welfare of the whole; hence its interests should be paramount. It is hardly surprising that men who received training in this kind of political philosophy—and received it at a time when the Japanese nation as a whole did have, in defence against foreign attack, one overriding common concern overshadowing all other political issues—should have developed a concern with politics of this nationally oriented, rather than sectionally oriented, kind. They were *yūkoku no shi*—men anxious for the fate of the *nation*.

There is another aspect of Confucian political training which is directly relevant to the opposition movements of post-Restoration Japan. It was, at least implicitly, a training in *principles*. As such it opened the possibility for every man to become his own arbiter of the correct application of principle to particular situations. True, one of the major principles inculcated was *loyalty*—to the head of one's household or to the head of one's fief—and it is true that in a dominant version of this ethic loyalty meant blind obedience. But Maruyama has shown the persistence in the Tokugawa period of a different tradition which required the loyal servant to be his own judge of what was really in his lord's interest, even his own judge of what constituted benevolent rule in his lord (which he should support) and what constituted wickedness (against which he should remonstrate).[1] Such judgments required criteria over and above the simple principle of loyalty, and these criteria history could offer, for history was chiefly concerned to record and judge the deeds of rulers at the pinnacle of loyalties, for whom loyalty in this sense of blind obedience could provide no guide. We have seen how Rai Sanyō showed the late Tokugawa

[1] 'Chūsei to hangyaku' pp. 393–7.

samurai an example of how Confucian criteria (devotion to the 'public' as opposed to 'private' interests, for instance) could be applied by a Japanese to Japanese history. And if they could be applied to past, they could equally be applied to present, rulers. With a knowledge of the correct principles, the loyal servant could be his *own* judge of what constituted loyalty in a retainer and what constituted good government—true devotion to the public interest of the people as a whole—in a ruler.

The last years of the Tokugawa period provided ample scope for this tradition to grow, the more so because, as Smith has argued, the majority of daimyos had long since forfeited the respect of their subordinates as persons.[1] Craig has described[2] how the loyalists of Chōshū could defy their lord on strictly moral grounds within the Confucian tradition, claiming to be urging on him policies which were in the best interests of the House of Mōri as *they* interpreted them according to *their* principles. The Restoration immeasurably widened the scope for this tradition to develop. The new state had to adopt innovating policies, and innovation, involving a choice between alternatives, requires principles of selection in a way in which the mere routine administration of a system of power may not. There was no lack in the Meiji period of vociferous ex-samurai voices offering to tell the government what those principles should be, and what were the just and proper policies which should follow from them. The point to be made here—a point made by Maruyama in the article just cited—is that one can already find in Tokugawa traditions the source of: (*a*) the hubris which permitted subordinates to offer advice to their superiors, (*b*) the notion that such advice could be offered by any independent thinker who knew the right principles of judgment, and (*c*) some of the content of the principles assumed by government critics in the Meiji period—a notion of the public interest (variously interpreted to mean national glory or popular welfare) and of according with the 'trend of the times' (the meaning of *jisei* becoming modified under the influence of Western doctrines of progress).[3] The tradition which produced these attitudes and

[1] ' "Merit" in Tokugawa bureaucracy.'

[2] A. Craig, *Chōshū in the Meiji Restoration*, pp. 160–1, 224, 352.

[3] See Carmen Blacker, *Fukuzawa Yukichi*, pp. 127–36, for a comparison of Fukuzawa's concept of *jisei* as a 'general state of public opinion' limiting the actions of great men, with that of Rai Sanyō. See also Tokutomi Sohō's *Shōrai no Nihon*

ideas was one of long standing but it was nurtured by study, particularly historical study, in the schools of the Tokugawa period. Fukuzawa's 'spirit of independence', Uchimura's conscience, were not simply grown from foreign roots.

It is an interesting question just how, in those who became the leaders of Meiji society, the three kinds of motive listed earlier combined in their political lives. The fact that the only respectable motive was patriotic devotion to the national good obviously generated a good deal of hypocrisy. The landlords demanding lower land taxes, the importers demanding sugar subsidies, the manufacturers demanding protective tariffs, had to claim that these measures were in *Japan's* interest, not rely on arguments about justice and an equitable satisfaction of their own sectional interests. In fact, as the emphasis of governmental activity shifted from foreign to domestic affairs, the pursuit of sectional interests and the reconciliation of their conflicts actually became an increasingly predominant element of the subject matter of politics. But because it was not respectable it tended to become furtive. 'Pressure group' may be a dirty word in other societies besides Japan, but it is not often that, as in Japan even today, the pressure group which is open and above board in its activities and blatantly unsecretive about its pursuit of private interests does not thereby mitigate its offence but compounds it.[1]

Equally there can be no doubt that the idealistic patriotism of the politician devoted to the national interest was rarely unalloyed with the personal pursuit and enjoyment of prestige and power. But as long as the overt ideology stressed collective goals, prestige, and in the long run power, too, depended on some real performance in the service of the nation, so that these two motives could work in harness rather than in conflict. It was otherwise when the pursuit of 'private' interests took a material form. The business-man, perhaps, could still combine patriotism and the profit motive as long as what was good for

[1] For excellent elaborations of this point see the remarks of Kyōgoku Junichi in Oka, *Gendai Nihon no seiji katei*, p. 475, and M. Maruyama, *Thought and behaviour in modern Japanese Politics*, pp. 6–7.

(esp. pp. 193, 210) for a related but more Spencerian concept of *hitsuzen no ikioi*, a kind of dynamic force impelling society along a road of inevitable progression from the military to the productive form of society.

Mitsubishi could be thought to be good for the nation. But the politician could only enrich himself at the expense of the public purse. 'The road to private aggrandisement was often the road of public service', Bellah has remarked of the Tokugawa period,[1] and Fukuzawa was once explicit and sweeping in his condemnation of samurai hypocrisy. They were, he said,

> to all outward appearances model retainers, given to large talk of loyalty and service to the fief—'Poverty is the rule of the samurai'. 'He who is nourished as a retainer should die in his master's service.'—One would think they were about to seek their death in battle at any moment.

And yet these men who posed as *chun-tzu*, as Confucius's 'superior men',

> were nothing but gilded pseudo-*chun-tzu* . . . Commissioners of Works would take kickbacks from carpenters, Exchequer officials would take bribes from merchants, and such behaviour was almost standard practice in the households of the three hundred daimyos.[2]

Meiji Japan was by no means free of such officials. Not even the leaders of the government were notably abstemious in their enjoyment of the good things of life. Official salary scales were generous, so were expense accounts, and statesmen were not above corruption, not only from patriotic motives (buying the votes of despised politicians in the national interest) but also for personal ends. Tani Kanjō, in an excoriating memorandum written after he resigned from government service in 1887, denounces the corruption of his colleagues and predicts that Japan, too, might well follow in the path of Egypt whose drive for national regeneration under Mahomet Ali foundered in its leaders' self-indulgence.[3]

He was, however, proved wrong. The official ethic may have been unable entirely to eliminate personal cupidity, but it did serve to keep it within bounds. Corruption remained, for the most part, a matter of misusing official position to give favours to friends and allies; it rarely, if ever, reached the more overt level of the contractual sale of favours to the highest bidder.

---

[1] *Tokugawa religion*, p. 37.
[2] Quoted (from *Gakumon no susume*) in Maruyama, 'Chūsei to hangyaku', p. 391.
[3] *Ikensho*, in Yoshino, *Meiji bunka zenshū*, 13, p. 469.

And personal enrichment was held within limits by the ideal. Even if there was a large element of hypocrisy in the statesmen's professedly selfless patriotism, the virtue to which vice thus paid tribute had its restraining effects. Policy was always the result of a dialectic between the ideal and private interest, never solely guided by the latter.

Merit and Competition

Chapter VI attempted to show how the development of samurai education accelerated the trend in fief administrations to give more explicit recognition to 'merit' in the appointment of administrators. Smith has justly argued that the merit ideal spread much faster than its application in practice. Among the liveliest and most public-spirited lower samurai, therefore, there was a growing sense of frustration at the gap between their ideal of justice and the real world they had to live in, a sense of frustration which eventually destroyed their loyalty to their fief superiors and made them enthusiasts for a regime which would destroy the feudal system.[1]

One might further generalize from the growing emphasis on the need for the merit system in administration and argue that this development prepared the way for the creation of a society which should in all spheres award prestige and power and income predominantly on the basis of performance. When Fukuzawa Yukichi urged that it was not hereditary status but contribution to society which made a man worthy of respect and began his preface to the *Encouragement of Learning* with his most famous phrase: 'Heaven did not create men above men, nor set men below men'[2] he was not simply introducing a startling new Western idea; he was succinctly summarizing a current of thought long since developing in Tokugawa society.

Tokugawa Confucianism, despite the particularism of the obligations its ethic enjoined, was in principle universalistic in two senses. It was the Way of Man, and as such Confucian scholarship was not to be forbidden even to the commoner classes. Secondly, its standards of excellence were objective.

[1] ' "Merit" in Tokugawa bureaucracy.'

[2] *Gakumon no susume*, pref. These words are now inscribed at the base of his statue in his home town of Nakatsu, and on the bars of chocolate sold in the booths beside it.

Although it had its schools and coteries they never became as exclusive as they did in the military arts, the dramatic arts or traditional religion; there were no licences of proficiency granted by teachers whose award might be motivated by favouritism rather than the honest assessment of merit. A scholar's knowledge of the classics, the quality of his Chinese poems, were in principle exposed to the judgment of strangers as well as of teachers and friends, and there were objective standards by which to judge them. Even for the ordinary samurai, the introduction of school education meant that a large part of a boy's life was now occupied by a new activity which required him to meet objectively measured standards of performance. These standards were probably more rigorous than those of the only pre-existing comparable activity—his military training. Even if they were not, the mere addition of a new field doubled the proportion of his youthful time spent in such tasks and must thereby have increased his general 'achievement-orientation'.

It also provided a new field in which differences of ability— of natural endowment, of application and of achievement— could become apparent. We have seen how wary teachers were of making use of this fact to stimulate a spirit of competition for fear of the impurity of the motives which would be awakened. Yet competitiveness did develop. It is a remarkable fact that for all the emphasis on collective goals in the ideology there was little in the actual experience of the young samurai to develop a 'team spirit' and everything to encourage individualistic self-assertion. Military training was a matter of individual skill at individual combat. Similarly in the schools, with the possible exception of the licensed gangs for younger pupils at Aizu, there was no organization of 'houses' or of any other kind of groups whose collective performance could be pitted one against the other. The playing fields of Eton, or at least of Dr Arnold's Rugby, would have been much more suitably congruent with the collectivism of the Tokugawa ideology than either the classrooms or the military sheds of the fief schools.

This odd mixture was probably an important ingredient of Japan's recipe for development. The combination of an individualistic will to succeed in the individual personality together with an emphasis on collective goals in the ideology was one which helped to accelerate the rate of economic and social change and at the same time to keep individual efforts within a framework of national objectives. It drove statesmen and business-men to work with zealous energy in order to distinguish themselves, to achieve success. But that success could only be sanctified and could only bring them real honour if it was, or could be represented as, service to the nation.

The Balance Sheet

Every man likes to think well of his subject, but a cautious writer ought perhaps to have stopped before this and asked himself whether he has not exaggerated the beneficent influences of Tokugawa education on Japan's subsequent history. Let us therefore qualify. While it is true that the economic growth of Japan since 1870 is widely regarded as a success story, there are equally, in the social and political sphere, a good many phases of Japan's modern development which most people would agree are much less worthy of admiration. And the Tokugawa schools probably contributed about equally to each side of the balance sheet.

The terrorism of modern ultra-nationalist activists and the furtiveness and hypocrisy attaching to interest group politics were already mentioned in passing in this chapter. One might add that the tradition of benevolent paternalism, too, though really productive of a good deal of enlightened social reform, was also productive of a good deal of self-righteous hypocrisy and oppression—one has only to think of the conciliation societies and the improvement societies which were hastily started in the 'twenties to mollify and emasculate the protest movements of the workers, the tenants and the *eta* outcasts. Again, the use of schools to propagate among the mass of the people a morality of docile submissiveness was an aspect of Tokugawa education which remained unchanged in the modern period (or more particularly between 1900 and 1945) except that it was carried out with immensely improved efficiency. That very combination of a debased form of the Confucian ethic with beliefs in Japanese racial uniqueness and Imperial divinity—the Japanism which hung like a pall of sanctimonious smog, not only over the schools but over the whole of Japanese intellectual and political life until 1945—was first effectively formulated at Mito, in one of the fief schools of the Tokugawa period. Equally the emphasis on collective goals in the ideology inherited from the Tokugawa period led to militarism and disaster as well as to economic advance. The scorn of the public-spirited man for the sordid trivialities of internal politics and his exclusive concentration on foreign affairs (in which it was clearly the interests and glory of *Japan* that were at stake) worked together with the traditions kept alive in the military half of the Tokugawa schools to produce irresistible pressure for the pursuit of military glory and territorial expansion. In 1905 this did not so much matter, perhaps. Japan got away with it against Russia and she did so with honour, for her actions accorded with the morality of the times. But so strong were these pressures and so great the sense of self-righteousness which Japanese nationalism drew from its distant Confucian sources that Japan remained unchanged—or rather moved backwards—when the rest of the world, or most of it, had moved on. As a result she was led into the same kind of venture thirty years later at a time when she could neither gain honour nor, as it turned out, any longer get away with it.

Altogether it is a significant and undeniable fact that it was in the 1930s that pilgrimages to the Mito school became popular, that educational historians began writing fulsome books of praise about their Tokugawa forerunners, that the Shingaku movement was revived, that Tokugawa-style swordsmanship was brought back into the schools and that the selected writings of certain Tokugawa Confucianists became most popular in high school curricula. The decade when Japanese society was being reduced at the hands of fanatics to its most stifling condition of oppressive irrationalism was the decade in which the ideals of the Japanese educational world were closer to those of its Tokugawa past than at any time since 1870.

In some respects the 'good' and the 'bad' sides of the balance sheet are inextricably intermixed; the same features of the legacy bequeathed to modern Japan by Tokugawa educators probably helped to promote both economic growth and militaristic expansionism, and it is doubtful if Japan could have had the one without the other. The very slogan which summed up early government policy as 'enriching the country and strengthening the army' underlines the connection. But in other respects there *are* two sides; some among the descendants of the Tokugawa samurai *were* concerned with popular welfare, whereas others were concerned only with popular loyalties; some used the self-righteous rhetoric of idealism to cover the protection of their own private interests, whereas others helped the weak and downtrodden to organize to protect themselves; some were interested in objective truth, others only in spiritual and ideological unity; some genuinely tried to create a society which would provide equal opportunities for all its citizens, others were more concerned to see that each man knew and kept his proper place. And always the men who were most hypocritical, most jealous of privilege, most concerned with spiritual unity, harmony and proper hierarchy, were the ones who were at the same time most anxious to preserve, or revive, the forms of Tokugawa education in the modern period. Perhaps the best that can be said of the legacy which Tokugawa educators bequeathed to the modern period is that in some of their ideals—in the rationalism, the stress on selflessness and benevolence and the need to put knowledge to the service of others which they taught in theory but failed very often to exhibit in practice—there was still a sufficient glimmer of inspiration to make rebels of the best of their pupils, and to ensure that when the time and opportunity came the latter would seek to destroy the educational traditions which had formed them.

Appendix I

SCHOOL ATTENDANCE AT THE END OF THE TOKUGAWA PERIOD

THE BEST MATERIAL for a numerical estimate of the proportion of the population receiving some kind of schooling at the end of the period is contained in the two volumes of the *Materials for the History of Japanese Education*[1] which reprint the replies of prefectural authorities to the questionnaire sent out by the Ministry in 1883. They were asked to give the names of all writing schools known to have existed before 1872, the date of their foundation and the date when they ceased business, their location, the profession or status of their teachers, and how many pupils and teachers they had of each sex when the school 'flourished'.

There is better information for the early Meiji period. For 1875, for instance, the various parts of the Ministry of Education's[2] year-book include:

(*a*) A list of all primary schools by name and location, together with numbers of pupils.

(*b*) Prefectural and national figures for the number of pupils registered as attending primary school, and the number of children who are of school age, i.e. between six and thirteen inclusive. The national ratios of school attendance according to these figures were, in 1875, 54 per cent for boys and 19 per cent for girls of school age.

Let us start by asking the question whether the impact of the 1872 educational decrees was likely to have been such as to have had much effect on the propensity of parents to send their children to school by 1875. There are good reasons for thinking that it was not. The number of newly trained teachers was still small and a good proportion of the new schools must have been the old ones in disguise. (A sample check through the 1875 report suggests that in that year only a little over 20 per cent of the primary schools were in new 'purpose-built' buildings. Many of the others could still, of course, have been new institutions which took over old houses or temples.) The new primary schools were designed to be bigger than

---

[1] *NKSS*, 8 and 9.   [2] Mombushō, *Dai-san nempō*.

the old terakoya, however, and there were probably fewer of them—two or three districts which formerly each had one or two reading and writing teachers might combine to build a new primary school. The propensity to send children to school is unlikely to have been increased, therefore, by the appearance of new facilities, conveniently located. If school attendance increased at all it is more likely to have been due either to the effect of official exhortation or to ideological change—the diffusion of the idea that a new age of opportunity for all was dawning.

It is possible to believe what one likes about the force of these two factors. Since, to be honest about the purpose of the present exercise, I am trying to prove that the late Tokugawa populace was better educated than people imagine, let us take off from the hypothesis most favourable to that contention, namely, that these factors had no effect and that therefore the 54 per cent for boys and 19 per cent for girls of 1875 might also represent the school attendance ratios for 1868. The question can then be put in the terms: Are the available statistical facts consistent with this hypothesis?

Between 1875 and 1883 (the date of the survey of the pre-1872 situation) prefectural boundaries were considerably changed. It is probable, however, that there was much less change in the boundaries of the next smallest administrative unit—the *gun* or district. A sample was constructed, therefore, of one *gun* chosen at random from each of the forty prefectures which reported in the 1883 survey. Kagoshima had to be dropped because it did not appear in the 1875 tables, and four others because information concerning the date of foundation and demise of the pre-1872 schools was incomplete in too many instances. From the remaining thirty-five the following figures were obtained:[1]

	Boys		*Girls*	
(a) Number of pupils registered in 1875 in primary schools in those *gun*	124,227	(100)	50,943	(100)
(b) For all the schools listed from those *gun* in the 1883 survey as having opened before 1868 and closed during or after that year, the total number of pupils 'when the school flourished'	56,318	(45)	15,465	(30)
Being composed of terakoya pupils	48,284		14,338	
And shijuku pupils	8,034		1,127	

[1] I am indebted to Mr N. Kaihara for his help in these calculations.

(Since shijuku-level schools—which taught something more than just reading and writing, see p. 265—were, like the fief schools, mostly down-graded to primary school level after 1872, the relevant figure for comparison is the total one.)

On the face of it these figures would suggest that the hypothesis is at fault, that there *had* been a considerable increase in school attendance between the two dates—of about 120 per cent for boys and 230 per cent for girls, and that, therefore, the school attendance rates for 1868 should be estimated at about 25 per cent and 6 per cent for boys and girls respectively.

However, there are many reasons why one should not take these figures at their face value.

1. The officials who filled in the 1883 questionnaire had no records to rely on. They must have sent sub-questionnaires to all village offices asking for information on the basis of local memories. We have no idea how complete were these returns, on the basis of which the prefectures made up their reports. One never ceases to marvel at the fact that this survey was made at all and carried through with such loving care that the whole rich store of materials on which this book is based should now be available in print. One marvels even more when one reads, by comparison, of the problems of administration in underdeveloped countries today. Nevertheless, unless one assumes a superlative diligence on the part of village officials, a good many prefectural replies must have been based on an incomplete set of local returns, and a good many local returns must have been based on incomplete inquiries into local memories of what schools had existed fifteen years before. Hence there must be a good deal of under-reporting of schools.

There is not much likelihood of casual think-of-a-number form-filling returns inflating the number of schools, since they had each to be reported individually by name and address.

There is one factor which compensates for this under-reporting. The number of pupils asked for was the number 'when the school flourished'. Our total sums those numbers for all schools in the sample districts operating in 1868. They did not all necessarily have their 'flourished' number of pupils simultaneously at that date, however. Hence, for the schools reported on, the number of pupils is likely to be over-reported.

That under-reporting is likely to be a more important factor, however, may be deduced from the fact that the ratios between the 1868 and 1875 figures for individual *gun* districts vary widely. To take the figures for boys alone; whereas the overall ratio of the 1868 to the 1875 figure is 45 to 100 (see above), for four prefectures it is over 90 to 100 and for another four there were, in fact, more pupils in 1868 than later. At the other end of the scale, for four prefectures the ratio is less than 10 to 100 and for another seven it is less than 30 to 100. The reason for these wide differences is more likely to be found in the differential conscientiousness of officials than in differential rates of change in the parental propensity-to-send-to-school.

2. There was some increase in the total number of children of school age between 1868 and 1875.

3. The 1868 figures doubtless include a good many samurai children, but probably not all. A fairly substantial proportion probably got their basic literacy training at home or in fief schools. In 1875 most of the samurai children would be in primary schools.

4. Fifty-four per cent for boys and 19 per cent for girls represents, officially, the proportion of children of school age at school. School age for this purpose is the eight-year span six to thirteen.

However, it is a fairly safe assertion—confirmed by the more realistic revamping of the school system in 1879—that few of the primary schools in 1875 were equipped to keep the normal child fed with new material for more than about four years. If the average period of actual attendance was indeed four years, and if children were registered as at school only for those four years, the school-age span being eight years, a 50 per cent attendance ratio would mean that every child went to school. Obviously this was not the case. Children were presumably kept on the books longer. Let us assume that every child was kept on the books for the whole eight years, so that 54 per cent represents the total of each age-group of boys getting any kind of schooling at 1875 attendance rates.

The average period of attendance in terakoya seems to have been three to four years. If one assumes a school life of three and a half years, then the fact that the number of boy pupils in 1868 and 1875 stood in a ratio of three and a half to eight (which is roughly, in fact, the ratio in which they do stand) means that there was *no change* in the proportion of boys getting to school; it would be 54 per cent in 1868 as in 1875. (By this reasoning the figure for girls for 1868 would be about 13 per cent.)

If one modifies the eight-years-on-the-books assumption, this means that the proportion-getting-to-school was greater than 54 per cent in 1875. But the change does not affect the estimate of 54 per cent for 1868.

There is a flaw in this argument. The figures of 54 per cent and 19 per cent for the proportion of each age-group attending school in 1875 are based on the Ministry of Education's estimate of the school-age population. How this was compiled one does not know, but the total figure for 1875 is 5.17 million. Between 1920 and 1940 the proportion of the total Japanese population which was aged six to thirteen fluctuated between 18.0 per cent and 18.8 per cent. It is unlikely to have been a smaller proportion of the total in 1875.[1] In numbers, then, in the 1875 population of 35.3 million it is unlikely to have been less than 6.4 million. This 20 per cent underestimate of the total school-age population means a 25 per cent overestimate of the proportion of children attending school; that is to say, 54 per cent and 19 per cent should be 43 per cent and 15 per cent respectively.

If the reader is still with me at this point he will probably be willing to agree to anything. Let us only ask him to grant that the evidence is *not inconsistent* with the hypothesis that the propensity-to-send-to-school did not increase for boys between 1868 and 1875, but increased somewhat for girls. The difference between the two sexes is reasonable if one assumes that the dramatic declaration of sex equality might have brought a number of girls out of homes to which they had been confined more by prejudice than by poverty.

For those who cannot abide uncertainty, let us cut through these arguments with some straightforward assumptions and arrive at speciously precise figures.

Ignoring the samurai question and the increase in school-age children from 1868 to 1875.

Assuming that under-reporting and over-reporting for 1868 cancel each other out and that the figures quoted earlier represent the numbers actually in school in 1868 in the sample *gun*.

And assuming that they went to school for an average of three and a half years.

And assuming that the sample accurately reflects the situation in the whole of Japan.

And assuming that the 1875 figures were based on the principle of keeping all school-attenders on the books for eight years, so that the national attendance ratios equal ever-got-to-school ratios.

Except that the school-age population should be 25 per cent greater than the Ministry reported:

Then, the proportion of each age-group who would ever have got some kind of schooling at 1868 rates of attendance becomes 43 per cent for boys and 10 per cent for girls.

There are two other pieces of evidence which suggest that these

[1] According to figures in the *U.N. Demographic Yearbook 1948* relating to censuses in various countries between 1930 and 1947, the proportion of the total population represented by this age group lay between 11.5 per cent and 16.5 per cent for all of a group of 15 European and North American countries except Greece (18.1 per cent) and between 18.5 per cent and 24.5 per cent for all but one of 24 Asian, African and Latin American countries (the exception being Malaya with 16.9 per cent).

are, at least, roughly the right orders of magnitude. Ototake, collating the results of a questionnaire answered in the 1920s by over 1300 old men and women who were asked to say whether all, most, the majority, less than half or hardly any of the children in their district went to school at the end of the Tokugawa period, concluded that 'somewhat under half' would be a reasonable estimate for the whole country, with the districts close to Edo, Osaka and Kyoto having the highest rate of attendance, and the north and Kyushu falling badly behind.[1] Secondly, the early annual reports of the Meiji Ministry of Education record for two prefectures the results of an inquiry into the proportion of the population 'who could not write their names'. That proportion in Shiga in 1877 was said to be 36 per cent; in Kagoshima in 1884, 81 per cent.[2] (These fall respectively into Ototake's categories of advanced and backward areas.) A similar survey reported from Okayama that in 1890, of all men and women over the age of thirty, the proportion which could 'neither read nor write' was 48 per cent.[3]

[1] Ototake, *Shomin kyōikushi*, 3, pp. 926–8.
[2] Japan, Minister of State for Education, *Fourteenth Annual Report*, p. 48.
[3] *Idem, Eighteenth Annual Report*, p. 49.

Appendix II

A SET OF TERAKOYA PRECEPTS[1]

TO BE BORN HUMAN and not be able to write is to be less than human. Illiteracy is a form of blindness. It brings shame on your teacher, shame on your parents and shame on yourself. The heart of a child of three stays with him till he is a hundred as the proverb says. Determine to succeed, study with all your might, never forgetting the shame of failure.

Goodness and badness depend on the company you keep. Co-operate with each other to behave yourselves as you should, check in yourselves any tendencies to be attracted to evil ways, and put all your heart into your brush-work.

At your desks let there by no useless idle talk, or yawning or stretching, or dozing or picking your nose, or chewing paper, or biting the end of your brush. To imitate the idle is the road to evil habits. Just concentrate wholeheartedly on your writing, giving each character the care it deserves.

Never write too fast. There never yet was a hot-head who earned fame and success. Write your characters firmly, deliberately and quietly.

Don't lean on your desk, or rest your elbow, or write just with the tips of your fingers, or easily and automatically without concentration. You will never develop a good hand if you do. Put all your effort into every character, making sure you hold your brush properly and giving proper attention to each stroke.

One who treats his brushes or his paper without due respect will never progress. The boy who uses carefully even the oldest, most worn-out brush is the one who will succeed. Treat your brushes carefully.

Don't litter the floor around you with scraps of paper. Keep your desks and your drawer neat and tidy and don't spill ink.

Torn and dirty clothes look bad. Even more they are a sign of a

[1] Sasayama Baian, *Sasayama Baian terako seikai no shikimoku* in *NKSSS*, 4, pp. 145–52, and Ishikawa, *Orai-mono ochibo-shū*, pp. 49–54.

torn and dirty spirit. Always behave with proper decorum so that your clothes do not get torn.

Mischievous pranks benefit no one. One thing leads to another and fighting results. You should always be ready to admit your own faults and learn to control yourself. Sumō wrestling, arm wrestling, leg wrestling, tugs of war and such games of strength are unbecoming to young children and are forbidden.

Don't run about on the banks of ditches or rivers, near walls, on verandas, stone steps or platforms. To do so is unfilial conduct for it is the beginning of filial piety to take care and preserve yourself from injury. Behave with proper gravity and avoid roughness.

Ill-natured pupils can never learn to write a good hand. Honour your parents, revere your teacher, respect your elders and be kind to your juniors, for this is the heart and origin of the Way of Man. Follow the rules of correct etiquette and use polite language even among friends.

Purity of heart is of the first importance. Those who come to school to learn the Way of Man with mud on their boots and ink on their hands and faces smudged like used practice paper show great disrespect. Grubbiness in others should be a warning to yourself and a stimulus to take proper care.

A pupil who keeps his hair properly in place, his kimono properly folded across the front, his belt properly tied and his teeth properly white is a model for all and a testimony to the training of his teacher and his parents. You should always remember this and avoid untidiness of dress.

A friend is to friend as brother to brother, as fish is to water. Be nice to your friends and always put their interests first at the expense of your own.

A child who is over-clever and tells untruths will end up a criminal. Never tell untruths and never hide the truth, even in fun.

Luxurious habits begin with the palate. Eat what you are given without fads and complaints. Any child who buys food in secret is guilty of unworthy conduct and can expect to be expelled.

You will never write a good hand unless you learn to practise and go on practising, even when you are cold and hungry. Don't overeat. Meanness of spirit starts with the indulgence of appetite. Eat only what you are given.

The lazy are always eager to eat, like a starved monkey gobbling nuts, as the old proverb says. It is the mark of the idle child to be always wanting to go for tea and water even when he is neither hungry nor thirsty, to be always going to the lavatory even when he has no need to go, but only as a pretext for play. This is mean and unworthy conduct you should be thoroughly ashamed of.

Nobody likes a child who smokes or who drinks *sake* or is always sipping tea. And those who are disliked by their fellow-men in the end incur the wrath of Heaven. Those who are liked by their fellows the gods also afford protection. This is clear as day. In this as in all other things, carefully avoid getting yourself disliked.

When you need something say so clearly and precisely. Never under any circumstances take things from other people without telling them, even a single sheet of paper. It is also strictly forbidden for pupils to buy and sell things from each other, and you should refrain from taking things from younger pupils.

A three-inch axle pin takes a cart a thousand miles. A three-inch tongue can be the ruin of a body five foot tall. No one hates the crow because he is black, only because he is obstreperous. Take heed from this. Useless gossip, rude language, shouting, are the marks of beggars and outcasts. There must be no uncalled-for remarks, telling tales, butting in, provocative questioning, nasty innuendo, talking behind people's backs. Accusations and whispering which embarrass others are signs of a wicked nature.

It is an idle child who speaks ill of his home at school, and when he goes home talks disparagingly of his school—all to cover his own wrong-doing. Be on your guard against this.

Be careful where you tread and what you touch. When walking about the room, opening doors or lining up desks, move quietly and carefully.

Be careful not to put on other people's sandals and clogs. It is the height of rudeness. If you should happen to do so by mistake, always apologize properly.

Avoid rough or quarrelsome companions. In your dealings with them speak politely and without provocation. Fences and fights never have one side, as the saying goes. If there are bickerings and altercations leading to quarrels, both parties shall be held to blame.

There shall be no scrawlings on the walls of temples or public buildings or in school. Likewise, breaking the paper of partitions, carving on pillars or dirtying the *tatami* shall be considered grave offences.

All games of chance, lotteries, penny in the pool and so on are strictly forbidden for they lead to meanness of spirit. Within limits, however, a certain amount may be permitted at New Year up to January 15th.

Children who waste their time on their way to and from school, watching sideshows and pedlars and street cheapjacks, bring their parents and their teacher into disrespect and are guilty of great thoughtlessness.

Those who, thinking no one will hear them, sing songs or hymns or snatches of *jōruri* in a loud voice at night, in open spaces or in the streets, show a lack of respect for their neighbours and betray a vulgar nature. It is a disgusting habit. In places where you cannot be seen or heard you should be all the more careful of how you behave.

Boys who speak roughly to, or pick quarrels with girls or younger children do not deserve to be considered pupils of this school. They are merely lower animals disguised in human form.

Whatever happens, however unusual, there is no need to clamour and shout. And when going to the privy go one at a time.

Make appropriate greetings to your parents when you leave home and when you return. At school enter and leave according to your teacher's instructions. Truancy is a very grave offence.

Men deserve the name of men only when they behave like men. Show due respect for your fellows, and in particular be kind to your juniors and do all you can to help them along.

Take off your hat to walk under a young tree. Training is more important than lineage. So the sayings go. You should not hate or despise your friends even if they are naughty. It only makes matters worse. 'When I am good how can others be bad?' runs the poem. Reprove your bad companions and shame them into goodness, for even the mugwort will grow straight among reeds.

However much better than others your handwriting may be, never lose a proper modesty, never be proud or boastful. The small seeds of pride in a young heart will grow later into a great obstacle to success in life.

Keep seven feet behind your teacher and never tread on his shadow, as the saying goes. Every letter you know you owe to him. Never answer back to your parents or your teacher, observe carefully their admonitions and seek their instruction that you may walk ever more firmly in the Way of Man.

Those who do good shall gain happiness. Those who do ill shall be visited by misfortune. He who is born a man but lacks a spirit of filial piety is no more than a beast. He who does not believe in the Way is little better than a stick or stone. He who thinks these precepts foolish and fails to obey them shall bring shame on himself, lose his good name, and soon live to repent his ruination. This is what is meant by the Punishment of Heaven.

SOURCES CITED

A. COLLECTIONS

NKS   Takimoto Seiichi, ed., *Nihon keizai sōsho*, 36 vols., 1914–17.
NKSS   Mombushō, ed., *Nihon kyōikushi shiryō*, 9 vols. 1890–92.
NKSSS Kokumin seishin bunka kenkyūjo, ed., *Nihon kyōikushi shiryō-sho*, 5 vols., 1937.
NKT   Takimoto Seiichi, ed., *Nihon keizai taiten*, 54 vols., 1928–30.
NZZ   Kokumin tosho kabushiki kaisha, ed., *Nihon zuihitsu zenshū*, 20 vols., 1927–30.
Dōbunkan henshūkyoku, ed., *Nihon kyōiku bunko*, 9 vols., 1910–11.
Fukushima Kashizō, ed., *Kinsei Nihon no jugaku*, 1939.
Funakoshi Masaichirō, ed., *Naniwa sōsho*, 16 vols., 1925–30.
Hakubunkan, ed., *Teikoku bunko*, 100 vols., 1893–1930.
Hayakawa Junzaburō, ed., *Bujutsu sōsho*, 1925.
Honjō Eijirō, ed., *Kinsei shakai keizai sōsho*, 12 vols., 1926–27.
Imaizumi Teisuke, ed., *(Zōtei) Kojitsu sōsho*, 41 vols., 1929–33.
Inoue Tetsujirō, ed., *Bushidō sōsho*, 3 vols., 1905–08.
Inoue Tetsujirō, ed., *Nihon rinri ihen*, 10 vols., 1901–03.
Ishikawa Ken, ed., *Ōrai-mono ochibo-shū*, 1927.
Ito Sei, *et al.*, eds., *Kindai Nihon shisōshi kōza*, 9 vols., 1959–61.
Katō Hatsuo, ed., *Tansō zenshū*, 3 vols., 1926.
Keigakukai, ed., *Hashimoto Keigaku zenshū*, 2 vols., 1943.
Kishigami Misao, ed., *Nihon bunko*, 12 vols., 1891–92.
—— ed., *Onchi sōsho*, 12 vols., 1891–1910.
Kokumin tosho kabushiki kaisha, ed., *Kinsei Nihon bungaku taikei*, 23 vols., 1926.
Kokusho kankō-kai, ed., *Hyakka zuihitsu*, 1918.
—— ed., *Kinsei fūzoku kembunshū*, 4 vols., 1912–13.
—— ed., *Shin-enseki jisshū*, 5 vols., 1912–13.
Kondō Heijō, ed., *(Kaitei) Shiseki shūran*, 33 vols., 1900–03.
Kuroita Katsumi, ed., *(Shintei zōho) Kokushi taikei*, 60 vols., 1929–58.
Kyōiku shichō kenkyūkai, ed., *Nihon kyōikushi kenkyū*, 1944.
Kyōikushi gakkai, ed., *Nihon no kyōikushi-gaku (Kyōikushi gakkai kiyō*, 1), 1958.
Masamune Atsuo, ed., *Banzan zenshū*, 6 vols., 1940–43.
Mozumi Takami, ed., *(Shinchū) Kōgaku sōsho*, 12 vols., 1927–31.
—— ed., *Kōbunko*, 20 vols., 1916.
Muraoka Tsunetsugu, ed., *Motoori Norinaga zenshū*, 26 vols., 1926–44.
Nihon zuihitsu taisei henshūbu, ed., *Nihon zuihitsu taisei*, 9 vols., 1927.
Saeki Ariyoshi, ed., *Bushidō zensho*, 13 vols., 1942–44.

Takase Daijirō, ed., *Heishū zenshū*, 1921.

Tsubouchi Yūzō, ed., *Shōyō senshū*, 12 vols., 1926–27.

Tsukamoto Tetsuzō, ed., *Yūhōdō bunko*, 121 vols., 1913–28, separately titled and including the following:

> *Ekken jikkun*, 2 vols.
> *Meika zuihitsu zenshū*, 2 vols.
> *Nakae Tōju bunshū*
> *Saikaku bunshū*
> *Shingaku dōwa-shū*
> *Yamaga Sokō bunshū*

Uemura Katsuya, ed., *Dai-Nihon shisō zenshū*, 18 vols., 1931–34.

Waseda Daigaku henshūbu, ed., *(Sentetsu ichō) Kanseki kokujikai zensho*, 45 vols., 1909–17.

Yōneyama-dō, ed., *Mikan zuihitsu hyakushu*, 23 vols., 1927–29.

Yosano Kan, ed., *Nihon koten zenshū*, 245 vols., 1925–43.

Yoshino Sakuzō, ed., *Meiji bunka zenshū*, 24 vols., 1928–30.

Yūhōdō, ed., *Kambun sōsho*, 31 vols., 1920–25.

BOOKS AND ARTICLES

Note: Details of collections appearing above are abbreviated.

Before dates *w.* means 'date written'; *pref.* means 'date of a preface'; *ps.* means 'date of a postscript'. Other dates are of first publication or of edition used.

Figures in square brackets indicate pages where the work is cited.

Abegglen, J. C. and Mannari, H., 'Leaders of modern Japan: social origins and mobility', *Economic Development and Cultural Change*, 9, i, pt. 2, Oct. 1960. [293]

Adamson, J. W., *A short history of English education*, Cambridge, 1919. [66]

Aitken, J., ed., *English Letters of the XIX Century*, Harmondsworth, 1946. [217]

Aizawa Yasushi (1782–1863), *Gakusei ryakusetsu*, n.d. (*NKSS* 5, pp. 458–71). [47, 49, 215]

Akiyama Kenzō, 'Shingaku kyōka to Meiji ishin', *Kyōiku*, 3, x, Oct. 1935. [238]

Amemori Hōshū (1621–1708), *Kissō sawa*, 1786 (*NZZ*, 9). [60, 138, 196]

Anon., *Asukagawa*, 1810 (Kokusho kankōkai, *Shin-enseki jisshū*, 1). [253]

—— *Edo gūzoku tsurezure-banashi*, 1837 (Yoneyama-dō, *Mikan zuihitsu*, 13). [216]

—— *Hyakushō denki*, w. c. 1688–1704 (*NKT*, 31). [218]

—— *Gojō sekyō*, 1806 (*NKSSS*, 4.) [233]

—— *(Kampō enkyō) Kōfu fūzoku kembunshū*, n.d. (Kokusho kankōkai, *Kinsei fūzoku*). [262]

—— *Nōjin ōrai*, n.d. Manuscript preserved in village records of

Shimo-tsugu-mura, Kita-shidara-gun, Aichi prefecture. [283]
—— Nōmin kyōkunjō, n.d. (Ishikawa, Ōrai-mono). [284]
—— (Shimpan zōho) Onna chōhōki, 1702. [288]
—— Teikin ōrai e-shōkai, 1811. [288]
—— Terako chie kagami, n.d. [283]
—— Terako setsuyō-shū, 1820. [288]
—— Terakoya monogatari, n.d. (Ishikawa, Ōrai-mono). [262, 263]
—— Tōsei shishō katagi, 1781 (Hakubunkan, Teikoku bunko, Katagi zenshū). [261]
—— (Umetsuji Norikiyo, 1768–1861?), Yuniwa no ho, w. 1843 (NKS, 21). [249]
Asaka Konsai (1791–1860), Konsai kanwa, 1834 (NZZ, 15). [56]
Asakawa Zen'an (1781–1849), Saiji shichisaku, w. c. 1820 (NKS, 21). [248]
Asaoka Yūnosuke, Ishin-zen Tōkyō shiritsu shōgakkō kyōiku-hō oyobi iji-hō torishirabe-sho, 1892. [231, 246, 252, 256, 260, 263, 264, 274]
Barker, E., National Character, 1949. [60]
Beasley, W. G., Select Documents on Japanese Foreign Policy, 1853–1868, London, 1955. [3]
Benedict, R., The Chrysanthemum and the Sword, New York, 1946. [233]
Bellah, R., Tokugawa Religion, Glencoe, Ill., 1957. [3, 212, 236, 310]
Blacker, C., Fukuzawa Yukichi, Ph.D. thesis, University of London, 1957. [304, 309]
—— 'Japanese historical writing in the Tokugawa period', in W. G. Beasley and E. G. Pulleyblank, eds., Historians of China and Japan, London, 1961. [157]
Bousquet, G., Le Japon de nos jours, 2 vols., 1877. [291]
Boxer, C. R., Jan Compagnie in Japan: 1600–1850, 2nd rev. ed., The Hague, 1950. [160]
Buyō-inshi, Seji kemmonroku, pref. 1806 (Honjō, Kinsei shakai keizai sōsho, 1). [242, 270]
Chamberlain, B. H., Things Japanese, 1890 [65]
Chiba Tanehide (?–?), Sampō shinsho, 6 vols., 1830. [147]
Chu Hsi (1130–1200), Chin-ssu lu (Yūhōdō, Kambun sōsho). [34]
Chuang Tzu (?–?), Chuang Tzu (Yūhōdō, Kambun sōsho). [37]
Couvreur, S., Li Ki; ou mémoires sur les bienséances et les cérémonies, 2nd ed., 2 vols., Ho Kien Fou, 1913. [48, 93]
Craig, A., Chōshū in the Meiji Restoration, Harvard, 1961. [3, 309]
Crasset, P., The History of the Church of Japan (tr. into English by N. N.), London, 1705. [52]
Crawcour, E. S., 'Changes in Japanese commerce in the Tokugawa period', Journal of Asian Studies, 22, iv, Aug. 1963. [3]
de Tocqueville, A., Democracy in America (Vintage edn., 1954), 2 vols. [189]
Emura Hokkai (1713–1788), Jugyō-hen, pref. 1783 (Kishigami, Nihon bunko, 3). [51, 130, 138]

Endō Yasumichi (1789–1851), *Shigaku mondō*, n.d. (*NKS*, 26). [196]

Endō Yoshiki, ed., *Osaka shōgyō kanshūroku*, 1883 (*NKSSS*, 4). [266]

Feng, Yu-Lan, *A History of Chinese philosophy* (tr. by Derk Bodde), London, 1937. [35]

Fujimori Kōan (?–?), *Shin-seidan*, 1855 (*NKS*, 32). [269]

Fujita Tōko (1806–55), *Hitachi-obi*, 1845 (Mozumi, *Kōgaku sōsho*, 12). [95, 96, 115, 151, 173]

Fukuzawa, *see* Kiyooka.

Fushimi-ya, *Edo-ōrai*, 2nd ed., 1837. [283]

Gerschenkron, A., 'The problem of economic development in Russian intellectual history of the Nineteenth Century', in E. J. Simmons, ed., *Continuity and Change in Russian and Soviet Thought*, Cambridge, Mass., 1955. [298]

Griffis, W. E., *The Mikado's Empire*, 11th ed., 1906. [2]

Hall, J. W., 'The Confucian teacher in Tokugawa Japan', in D. S. Nivison and A. F. Wright, *Confucianism in Action*, 1959. [91, 92, 231]

—— *Tanuma Okitsugu (1719–1788): Forerunner of Modern Japan* (Harvard-Yenching Monograph Series, 14), Cambridge, Mass., 1955. [3]

Hamamatsu Utakuni (1776–1827), *Setsuyō kikan*, w. c. 1825? (Funakoshi, *Naniwa sōsho*). [253]

Hanejima Terukiyo (?–?), ed., *Bujutsu ryūsoroku*, 1843 (Hayakawa, *Bujutsu sōsho*). [149]

Hara Zen (1774–1820), *Sentetsu sōdan*, 1817 (Yūhōdō, *Kambun sōsho*). [22, 23, 54, 55]

Hashimoto Sanai (1835–1859), *Gakusei ni kansuru iken tōshi*, w. 1857 (Keigaku-kai, *Zenshū*, 1). [204]

Hattori Kiyomichi, 'Edo-jidai nōson ni okeru terakoya no ichi-ruikei, *Nihon Rekishi*, No. 122, Aug. 1958. [261, 271]

Hayakawa Masanori (Hachirōzaemon) (1739–1808), *Kuse jōmoku*, n.d., (*NKSS*, 7). [233]

Hayashi Jussai (1761–1841) *et. al.*, eds. *Tokugawa jikki*, w. 1809–49, (Kuroita, *Kokushi taikei*, 38–52). [16, 18, 21, 22, 200, 233]

Hayashi Shihei (1738–93), *Fukei-kun*, *pref.* 1786 (Dōbunkan, *Kyōiku bunko, Kunkai*). [64, 188, 215]

—— *Jōsho*, w. c. 1775 (*NKS*, 12). [107, 108, 140, 171]

—— *Jōsho*, w. 1781 (*NKS*, 15). [44, 70]

Hayashida-han, *Fushi-kun*, n.d. (*NKSS*, 2, p. 560). [233]

Hiraga Gennai (1729–79), *Fūryū Shidōken-den*, 1764 (Uemura, *Shisō zenshū*, 5). [46]

Hirata Atsutane (1776–1843), *Kodō tai-i*, 1811 (Tsukamoto, *Yūhōdō bunko*). [39]

Heibonsha, *Sekai rekishi daijiten*, vol. 22, 1955. [71, 108, 231, 236]

Hibata Unko, 'Tokugawa Ienari no kyōyu sanshō to bunsei no Kantō torishimari', *Shirin*, 13, iii. [233]

Himata Shūji, 'Edo-jidai no totei-seido ni tsuite', in Kyōiku-shichō Kenkyūkai, *Nihon kyōikushi kenkyū*. [266, 267]

Hirose Tansō (1782–1856), *Jurin-hyō*, n.d. (Katō, *Zenshū*, 2). [62]
—— *Yakugen wakumon*, w. 1831 (Katō, *Zenshū*, 2). [138]
—— *Kangien kiyaku kokuyu*, w. 1843 (Katō, *Zenshū*, 2). [297]
—— *Ugen*, w. 1840 (*NKS*, 32). [114, 138, 182, 184, 186, 194, 195, 199, 203, 206]
Hoashi Banri (1778–1852), *Nyūgaku shinron*, n.d. (Inoue, *Rinri ihen*, 16). [56]
—— *Tōsempu-ron*, w. 1844 (*NKS*, 26). [249]
Hōjō Ujinaga (1609–70), *Shikan yōhō*, w. 1646 (Saeki, *Bushidō zensho*, 2). [148]
Honda Tadakazu (1739–1812), *Kyōsei-ron*, w. c. 1795 (Inoue, *Bushidō sōsho*, 2). [63, 149]
Horie, Yasuzō, 'Business pioneers of Modern Japan: Ishikawa Masatatsu and Ōshima Takatō', *Kyoto University Economic Review*, 30, ii, Oct. 1960. [251]
Horiuchi Shin, ed., *Nanki Tokugawa-shi*, 17 vols., 1930–33. [158, 203, 272]
Hosoi Heishū (1728–1801), *Ōmei kan isō*, *pref.* 1835 (Inoue, *Rinri ihen*, 9). [69, 184, 201, 231]
Hozumi, Nobushige, *Ancestor Worship and the Japanese Law*, 4th rev. ed., Tokyo, 1948. [233]
Ibara Saikaku (1642–93), *Nagori no tomo*, 1699, (Hakubunkan, *Teikoku bunko* 31, *Chimpon zenshū*). [20]
—— *Oridome*, *pref.* 1794 (Tsukamoto, *Saikaku bunshū*). [20]
Imagawa Ryōshun (1320–1420), *Imagawa-jō*, n.d. (in, e.g. Anon., *Terako chie kagami*). [279]
Ise Sadatake (1715–84), *Anzai zuihitsu*, n.d. (Imaizumi, *Kojitsu sōsho*, 1). [194]
—— *Yōgaku mondō*, 1781 (Kishigami, *Nihon bunko*, 4). [58, 61]
Ishida Baigan (1685–1744), *Tohi mondō*, 1739 (*NKS*, 8). [189]
Ishikawa Ken, 'Edo-jidai makki no kyōka undō', *Kyōiku*, 3, xi, Nov. 1935. [33, 230]
—— *Gakkō no hattatsu*, 1951. [29, 85, 86, 143, 144, 145]
—— *Kinsei Nihon shakai kyōiku-shi no kenkyū*, 1938. [33]
—— *Nihon gakkō-shi no kenkyū*, 1960. [73]
—— *Nihon shomin kyōiku-shi*, 1929. [233]
—— *Sekimon shingaku-shi no kenkyū*, 1938. [219, 233, 236, 237, 238]
—— (*Waga kuni ni okeru*) *Jidō-kan no hattatsu*, 1949. [106]
—— *Teikin ōrai no kenkyū*, 1950. [276, 278]
—— *Terakoya*, 1960. [252, 253, 254, 257, 259, 260, 276]
Isomura Yoshinori (?–?), *Zōho sampō ketsugishō*, 1804. [147]
Itō Jinsai (1627–1705), *Dōjimon*, *ps.* 1792 (Inoue, *Rinri ihen*, 5). [55]
Itō Tōgai (1670–1736), *Kimmō yōji-kaku*, *ps.* 1734. [131]
Jansen, M. B., *Sakamoto Ryōma and the Meiji Restoration*, Princeton, 1961. [3, 307]
Kaibara Ekken (1630–1714). *Bumbu-kun*, 1717 (Tsukamoto,

331

Ekken jikkun, 2). [40, 49, 54, 56]
—— *Kakun*, n.d. (Tsukamoto, *Ekken jikkun*, 1). [40, 43]
—— *Raku-kun*, 1710, (Tsukamoto, *Ekken jikkun*, 2). [54]
—— *Wazoku dōjikun*, n.d. (Tsukamoto, *Ekken jikkun* 1). [128, 130]
—— *Yamato zokukun, pref.* 1708 (Tsukamoto, *Ekken jikkun*, 1). [35, 37, 53, 62]
Kaigo Tokiomi, ed., *Nihon kyōikushi*, 1943. [20, 216]
Kaiho Seiryō (1755–1817), *Shōridan, w.* c. 1813 (*NKS*, 26). [191, 194]
Kamei Nammei (1743–1814), *Higo monogatari, w.* 1781 (*NKS*, 15). [117, 118, 119, 194, 203, 243]
Kaneko Masayoshi (?–?), *Tōsei kaisanki*, 1847. [147]
Kan Sazan (1748–1827), *Sazan fude no susabi, w.* c. 1807 (*NZZ*, 17). [57]
Karashima Ken (1754–1839), *Gakusei wakumon, w.* 1816 (*NKSS*, 8). [28, 194, 205, 218, 248]
Kasai Sukeji, *Kinsei hankō no sōgōteki kenkyū*, 1960. [22, 42, 71, 86, 91, 94, 95, 97, 98, 99, 107, 108, 219]
Katō Zuiō (?–?) (*Kashira-gaki e-iri*) *Tonya ōrai*, 1815. [282]
Katsushika Hokusai (1760–1849) (illustrator), *Ehon Teikin ōrai*, 1819–48. [278]
Kawade Shobō, *Nihon rekishi daijiten*, 22 vols., 1956–60. [190, 268]
Kawase Kazuma, *Kokatsujiban no kenkyū*, 1937. [17]
Keizai zasshi-sha, *Nihon shakai ji-i*, 3rd ed., 1907. [70]
Kimura Akinori (?–?), *Shin dōji tenarai kagami*, 1825. [288]
Kinoshita Makoto (?–?), *Kokoro no yukue*, 1836. [40]
Kiyooka, E., tr. and ed., *The Autobiography of Fukuzawa Yukichi (1853–1901)*, 3rd rev. ed., Tokyo, 1947. [209]
Komachi Gyokusen (?–1838), *Jishū-hen, pref.* 1828 (*NKS*, 19). [52, 128, 187, 188, 262]
Komatsu Naoyuki, 'Terakoya ni tsuite no ronsō' (Kyōiku shichō kenkyūkai, *Nihon kyōikushi kenkyū*). [253]
Kondō Moku, *Shina gakugei daijiten*, 1936. [232]
Kumazawa Banzan (1619–91), *Daigaku wakumon, w.* c. 1656 (Masamune, *Banzan zenshū*, 3). [128]
—— *Shūgi washo*, 1672 (Tsukamoto, *Yūhōdō bunko*). [41, 43, 48, 49, 55, 56, 60, 63]
Kume Kunitake, *Kume-hakase kyūjūnen kaikoroku*, 2 vols., 1934. [29, 89, 100, 113, 161, 165, 203]
Kuroda Seidō (?–?) (*Kashira-gaki kundoku*) *Teikin ōrai seichūshō*, 1844. [277]
Kusata Sankeishi (?–?), *Otoko chōhōki*, 1693. [126, 134, 288]
Legge, J., *The Four Books*, n.d. [35, 36, 37, 41, 59, 62]
Maekawa Saburō, 'Tokugawa jidai no kambungaku' (Fukushima, *Kinsei Nihon no jugaku*). [56]
Maeno Kiyoji, 'Aomori-ken ni okeru terakoya shishō no tōkeiteki kenkyū', (Hirosaki daigaku) *Jimbun shakai*, 11, 1957. [257]
Maruyama Masao, 'Chūsei to hangyaku' (Itō, *Kindai Nihon shisōshi kōza*, 6). [157, 308, 311]

Maruyama, (*Cont.*), 'Kinsei jukyō no hatten ni okeru Soraigaku no tokushitsu narabi ni sono kokugaku to no kankei', *Kokka gakkai zasshi*, 54, ii–v. Feb.–May, 1940. [198]
—— *Nihon seijishisōshi kenkyū*, 1952. [24]
Maruyama, Masao, *Thought and Behaviour in Modern Japanese Politics*, London, 1963. [310]
Matsudaira Sadanobu (1758–1829), *Naniwa-e, w*, 1779 (Dōbunkan, *Kyōiku bunko, Jokun*). [66]
—— *Taikan zakki, w.* 1793–1800 (*NZZ*, 14). [27, 40, 46, 51, 60, 63, 94, 138, 144, 160, 243]
Matsuda Michio, 'Nihon no chishikijin', (Itō, *Kindai Nihon shisōshi Kōza*, 4). [305]
Matsuura Seizan (1770–1841), *Kasshi yawa, w.* 1821–41 (Kokusho kankōkai, *Kankōsho*, Set 2). [24]
McEwan, J. R., *The Political Writings of Ogyū Sorai*, Cambridge, 1962. [23, 44]
Minamoto Takashi (?– ?), *Jirin chōka, pref.* 1710. [131, 138]
Minamoto Tokushū (?– ?), *Gekiken sōsho*, 1843 (Hayakawa, *Bujutsu sōsho*). [149]
Miura Baien (1723–89), *Baien sōsho, pref.* 1781 (Tsukamoto, *Meika zuihitsu* 2). [38, 55]
Miyazaki Ichisada, *Kakyo*, 1946. [145]
Mombushō, *Kaisei kyōikurei seitei riyū*, 1880 (Yoshino Sakuzō, ed., *Meiji bunka zenshū*, 10). [295, 304]
—— Dai—nempō, 1874– . [317]
—— (Japan, Minister of State for Education), *Fourteenth (etc.) Annual Report*, 1887– . [322]
Montanus, Arnoldus, *Atlas Japannensis* (tr. by John Ogilby), London, 1670. [52]
Moriyama Takamori (1765–1815), *Ama no taku mo, w.* 1798 (Kishigami, *Onchi sōsho*, 11). [117, 131, 193, 202, 256]
Morohashi Tetsuji, 'Kansei igaku no kin', (Fukushima, *Kinsei Nihon no jugaku*). [26, 28, 29]
Motoori Norinage (1703–1801), *Tama-katsuma*, 1794–99, (Muraoka, *Zenshū* 1–2). [140, 237]
—— *Uiyama-bumi*, 1798 (Muraoka, *Zenshū*, 9). [39, 138]
Muro Kyūsō (1658–1734), *Kenzan (reitaku) hisaku, w.* 1711–31, (*NKS*, 2), [70, 139, 200, 253]
—— *Rikuyu engi tai-i*, 1722, (Dōbunkan, *Kyōiku bunko, Kunkai-hen*, 1). [232]
—— *Sundai zatsuwa, pref.* 1732 (*NZZ*, 3). [138]
Naganuma Muneyoshi (1634–1690), *Hei yōroku*, n.d. (Saeki, *Bushidō zensho*, 4). [148]
Nakae Tōju (1608–48), *Okina mondō*, 1650 (Tsukamoto, *Nakae Tōju bunshū*). [37, 59, 60, 189]
—— *Tōju-sensei seigon*, n.d. (Tsukamoto, ibid.). [37]
Nakai Chikuzan (1730–1804), *Sōbō kigen, w.* 1789 (*NKS*, 16). [64, 199, 226, 227, 248]

Nakamura Tekisai (1629–1702) ed., *Kimmō zui*, 21 vols., 1666. [51, 131]

Nakamura Sachihiko, 'Yomihon no dokusha', *Bungaku*, 26, v, 1958. [32]

Nakayama Kushirō, *Yamaga Sokō*, 1937. [17, 19]

Nakayama Shōrei (1763–1816), *Gakusei-kō*, n.d. (*NKSS*, 5). [45, 47, 91, 93, 104, 181, 194, 197]

Nemoto Tsūmei (1822–1909), 'Risshi-den', *Seikō*, 1, i, pp. 7–9, 1902. [211]

Nishijima Junzō (1760–1823), *Gakkan ryakusetsu*, w. 1814 (*NKSS*, 5). [47, 48, 52, 103, 128]

Nishida Naojirō, *Nihon bunka-shi josetsu*, 1932. [65]

Nishikawa Joken (1648–1724), *Chōnin-bukuro*, 1719 (*NKS*, 5). [189, 218]

—— *Hyakushō-bukuro*, pref. 1721 (*NKS*, 5). [195, 215]

Nomura Kanetarō, *Gonin-gumi-chō no kenkyū*, 1943. [232]

Norman, E. H., *Japan's Emergence as a Modern State*, New York, 1940. [3]

Ōe Gempo (1728–1794), *Ma-ni-awase haya-gakumon*, pref. 1766 (Kishigami, *Nihon bunko*, 4). [40]

Ogawa Kandō, *Kangakusha denki oyobi chojutsu shūran*, 1935. [116]

Ogawa Wataru, *Aizu-han kyōiku-kō*, 1941. [85, 87, 117, 142, 153, 186, 205, 222]

Ogyū Sorai (1666–1728), *Kenen danyo*, n.d. (Kishigami, *Nihon bunko*, 4). [195]

—— *Seidan*, w. c. 1715–25 (*NKS*, 3). [20, 21, 23, 57, 63, 109, 140, 200]

—— *Taiheisaku*, w. c. 1715–20 (Kishigami, *Nihon bunko*, 2). [23, 42, 44, 61, 97, 184, 194, 215, 217]

—— *Yaku(bun) sen(tei) shohen*, 1715. [130, 131, 134, 140]

Ōhara Shōkingo, *Hokuchi kigen*, w. 1797 (Kishigami, *Nihon bunko*, 7). [168]

Oka Yoshitake, ed., *Gendai Nihon no seiji katei*, 1958. [310]

Okano Takao, *Nihon shuppan bunka-shi*, 1959. [17]

Okayama-han, *Biyō kokugaku kiroku*, n.d. (Manuscript Photocopy at Center for Japanese Studies, University of Michigan). [221, 222]

Okayama-ken kyōiku iinkai, *Okayama-ken kyōikushi*, 2 vols. 1937–41. [94, 103, 184]

Okuma, Shigenobu, *Fifty Years New Japan*, 2 vols., London, 1910. [66]

Ōno Kōjō (?–?), *Taihei nempyō*, 4 vols., 1841. [21]

Ono Takanao (1720–99), *Kasan kanwa*, pref. 1741 (*NZZ*, 13). [137]

Ōta Kinjō (1765–1825), *Gosō mampitsu*, 1823–40 (*NZZ*, 17). [24, 65]

Ōta Nampo (1749–1823), *Ichiwa ichigon*, w. 1779–1820, (Nihon zuihitsu taisei henshūbu, *Taisei, bekkan*). [130]

Ototake Iwazō, *Nihon shomin kyōikushi*, 3 vols., 1929. [51, 52, 53, 64, 69, 70, 127, 128, 130, 187, 192, 218, 229, 231, 232, 234, 238, 246, 249, 252, 276, 281, 282, 284, 322]

Ōtsuka Shōhaku (?–?), *Keizai gosaku*, w. 1842. (*NKS*, 26). [249]
Rai Sanyō (1780–1832), *Nihon gaishi*, w. 1807. [144, 156, 309]
Saitō Setsudō (1797–1865), *Shidō yōron*, 1837 (Inoue, *Bushidō sōsho*, 2). [17, 43]
Saitō Tōtaro, *Nijū-roku taihan no hangaku to shifū*, 1944. [74, 84]
Sansom, G. B., *Japan: A Short Cultural History*, 2nd rev. ed., New York, 1952. [3]
—— *The Western World and Japan*, New York, 1950. [160]
Sasayama Baian (?–?), *Sasayama Baian terako seikai no shikimoku*, n.d. (Ishikawa, *Ōrai-mono*). [323]
Satō Shin'en (1769–1850), *Suitō hiroku, ps.* 1857 (*NKT*, 18). [250]
Satō Shōsuke, ' "Bansha" no kigen to sono jittai', *Nihon rekishi*, 69, Feb. 1954. [167]
—— 'Bansha no goku no shinsō', *Nihon rekishi*, 92, Feb. 1956. [167]
—— 'Yōgaku no kenryoku-reizoku-ka ni kansuru ichikōsatsu, *Nihon rekishi*, 105–6, March–April 1957. [168]
Satow, E. M. *A Diplomat in Japan*, London, 1921. [172]
Seki Giichirō, Seki Yoshinari, eds., *Kinsei kangakusha chojutsu mokuroku taisei*, 1943. [116]
Shibata-han, *Kangaku hikki*, w. 1779 (*NKSS*, 2, pp. 273–5). [233]
Shibata Kyūō (1783–1839), *Kyūō dōwa, pref.* 1834 (Tsukamoto, *Shingaku dōwashū*). [39]
Shihōshō, *Tokugawa kinrei-kō*, 7 vols., 1878–90. [165]
Shikitei Samba (1776–1822), *Ukiyo-buro*, 1809 (Tsukamoto, *Yūhōdō bunko*). [264, 268, 269]
—— *Taizen ippitsu keijō* ?th ed., 1858. [283]
Shimokōbe Shūsui (?–?), *Onna kuku no koe*, 1787. [66, 67]
Shinomaru Hikozaemon, *Sakura-hangaku-shi*, 1961. [114]
Shionoya On, 'Rai Sanyō no shihitsu' (Fukushima, *Kinsei Nihon no Jugaku*). [57]
Shōji Kōgi (1793–1857), *Keizai mondō hiroku*, w. 1833 (*NKS*, 22–3). [44, 48, 72, 84, 111, 128, 129, 133, 196, 201, 217, 218, 249, 277]
Shūdō Yasuzaemon (1700–1784), *Kengisho*, n.d., (*NKSS*, 5, p. 596). [63, 65, 114, 118, 142, 200, 218]
Silberman, L., *The Analysis of Society*, 1951. [191]
Simon, B., *Studies in the History of Education, 1780–1870*, 1959. [291, 298]
Smith, T. C., 'Landlords' sons in the business elite', *Economic development and cultural change*, 9, 1, pt. 2, Oct. 1960. [293]
—— ' "Merit" in Tokugawa Japan', unpub. paper to be printed in R. P. Dore, ed. *Social change in modern Japan*, Princeton. [301, 309, 312]
—— *The Agrarian Origins of Modern Japan*, Stanford, 1959. [3]
Spae, J., *Itō Jinsai*, Pekin, 1948. [35, 38]
Suematsu Kenchō, *Bōchō kaitenshi*, 12 vols., 2nd ed., 1921. [210]
Sugaita Gempaku (1733–1817), *Rangaku kotohajime*, 1814–15. [193]
—— *Yasō dokugo*, w. 1807 (Kishigami, *Onchi sōsho*, 4). [193]

335

Suzuki Akira (1765–1837), *Hanareya gakukun*, pref. 1828 (Dōbunkan, *Kyōiku bunko, gakkun-hen*). [125, 168]

Takahashi Shunjō, *Nihon kyōikushi*, 1934. [68]

Takai Ranzan (1762–1838), (*E-iri nichiyō*) *Onna chōhōki*, 5 vols., 1847. [288]

Takai Shiroshi, 'Isezaki-ryō kyōgaku no setsuei keika, soshiki keitai to kyōiku katsudō' (Kyōikushi gakkai, *Nihon no kyōikushi-gaku*). [242]

Takata-han, *Chūkō jōmoku*, n.d. (*NKSS*, 2, pp. 264–5). [233]

Takayanagi Shinzō and Ishii Ryōsuke, *On-furegaki Tempō shūsei*, 1937. [85]

Takeda Izumo (1691–1756), *Sugawara denju tenarai kagami*, w. 1746, (Kokumin tosho, *Kinsei bungaku taikei*, 7). [262]

Takigawa Masajirō, 'Terakoya ni okeru hōgaku kyōiku', *Kyōiku*, 3, i, Jan. 1935. [284]

Tamabayashi Haruo, *Shokusanjin no kenkyū*, 1944. [90, 202]

Tamiya Nakayoshi (?–?), *Tōyōshi*, pref. 1801 (*NZZ*, 1). [127]

Tanaka Kyūgū (?–1729), *Minkan seiyō*, w. 1727–28 (*NKS*, 1). [194]

Tani Kanjō, *Ikensho*, w. 1887 (Yoshino Sakuzō, ed., *Meiji bunka zenshū*, 3, pp. 457–70.) [311]

Taniguchi Sumio, 'Han-kashindan no keisei to kōzō', *Shigaku zasshi*, 66, vi, 1956. [188]

Tokutomi Sohō, *Kinsei Nihon kokumin-shi*:
    Vol. 21, *Yoshimune jidai*, 1926. [70]
    Vol. 26, *Yūhan-hen*, 1927. [168]
—— *Shōrai no Nihon*, 2nd ed., 1888. [307, 309]

Tokyo Maiyū Shimbun, *Ikuei no Nihon*, 1931. [252]

Tōkyō Shisei Chōsakai, *Kōmin kyōiku kenkyū*, 1928. [253, 259]

Tsubouchi Shōyō, 'Watakushi no terakoya jidai' (Tsubouchi, *Shōyō senshū*, 12). [274]

Tsuda Sōkichi, 'Jōdai Shina ni okeru Ten oyobi Jōtei no kannen', *Tōyō gakuhō*, 12, iii, 1922. [35]

Tsuji Tatsuya, 'Kyōho-kaikaku ni okeru shutai-seiryoku ni tsuite', *Shigaku zasshi*, 63, ii. 1953. [191]

Tsukui Taisuke, *Shizutani gakkō*, Okayama, 1951. [244]

Tsunoda, R. *et. al.*, *Sources of the Japanese Tradition*, New York, 1958. [250]

Tsurumine Shigenobu (1786–1859), *Kaisai manroku*, n.d. (Kokusho kankōkai, *Kankōsho, Kōka zuihitsu*, 3). [133]

Uchida Yoshihiko, Shioda Shōhei, 'Chishiki-seinen no shoruikei' (Itō, *Kindai Nihon shisōshi kōza*, 4). [306]

Uesato Shunsei, *Edo shoseki-shō-shi*, 1930. [20]

Uno Tetsundo, Ototake Iwazō, *Hangaku-shi-dan*, 1943. [70, 74, 94]

Wajima Yoshio, 'Edo-bakufu no Shushi-gaku saiyō-setsu ni tsuite', *Kōbe Jogakuin Daigaku Ronshū*, 1, iii, 1954. [15]

—— 'Kansei igaku no kin no kaishaku', *Kōbe Jogakuin Daigaku ronshū*, 3, iii, Feb. 1957. [26, 29]

Watanabe Minoru, 'Kinsei shohan ni okeru yūgaku-seido', *Nihon rekishi*, 54, Nov. 1952. [111, 112, 208]

Yamaga Sokō (1622–85), *Bukyō shōgaku*, pref. 1656 (Tsukamoto, *Yamaga Sokō bunshū*). [55, 66]
—— *Haisho zampitsu*, w. 1675 (Tsukamoto, ibid.). [134]
—— *Seikyō yōroku*, w. 1665, (Tsukamoto, ibid.). [38]
—— *Shidō* (extr. from *Yamaga Goruri*, 1663–65), (Tsukamoto, ibid.). [49, 65]
—— *Yamaga gorui*, w. 1663–65 (Inoue, *Rinri ihen*, 12). [218]
Yamagata Toyonori (?–?), *Meiryō tairoku*, w. 1814 (Kondō, *Shiseki shūran*, 11). [192, 200]
Yamaguchi Satsujō, 'Ieyasu to jugaku' (Fukushima, *Kinsei Nihon no jugaku*). [16]
Yamamoto Taizen (?–?) *Kyōyu sanshō*, n.d. (*NKSS*, 7, pp. 113–14). [233]
Yamamoto Shōitsu (?–?), *Dōjitsu*, pref. 1839, (Waseda, *Kanseki kokujikai*, 7). [124, 129, 135, 137, 304]
Yamana Fuminari (?–?), *Nōka-kun*, w. 1784 (*NKS*, 15). [187, 218]
Yasui Sokken (1799–1836), *Kyūkyū wakumon*, n.d. (*NKS*, 32). [197, 199]
Yokoyama Tatsuzō, *Nihon kinsei kyōikushi*, 1904. [18, 20, 21, 24, 46, 50, 53, 66, 109, 139, 148, 156, 165, 168, 193, 243]
Yoshida Mitsuyoshi (1598–1672), *Jinkōki*, 1627. (Yosano, *Koten zenshū, Kodai sūgaku shū*). [147]
Yoshikawa Kōjirō, *Nihon no shinjō*, 1960. [53, 183, 280]
Yuasa Jōzan (1708–81), *Bunkai zakki*, n.d. (*NZZ*, 2). [24, 51, 58, 62, 131, 197]
—— *Jōzan-rō-hitsu*, pref. 1744 (*NZZ*, 5). [138]

INDEX AND GLOSSARY